ESSENTIALS OF
COMPARATIVE
POLITICS SECOND EDITION

ESSENTIALS OF COMPARATIVE POLITICS SECOND EDITION

PATRICK H. O'NEIL

University of Puget Sound

W. W. NORTON & COMPANY

New York • London

W. W. Norton & Company has been independent since its founding in 1923, when William Warder Norton and Mary D. Herter Norton first published lectures delivered at the People's Institute, the adult education division of New York City's Cooper Union. The Nortons soon expanded their program beyond the Institute, publishing books by celebrated academics from America and abroad. By mid-century, the two major pillars of Norton's publishing program—trade books and college texts—were firmly established. In the 1950s, the Norton family transferred control of the company to its employees, and today—with a staff of four hundred and a comparable number of trade, college, and professional titles published each year—W. W. Norton & Company stands as the largest and oldest publishing house owned wholly by its employees.

Fig. 3.4: © 2003 The Economist Newspaper, Ltd. All rights reserved. Reprinted with permission. Further reproduction prohibited. www.economist.com; Figs. 8.1, 10.5: © Pew Research Center; Figs. 10.1, 10.4: © Foreign Policy Magazine

Editor: Ann Shin
Copy Editor: Janet Greenblatt
Project Editor: Sarah Mann
Editorial Assistant: Robert Haber
Book Design: Chris Welch
Production Manager: Diane O'Connor
Composition by Matrix Publishing Services, Inc.
Manufacturing by Courier Companies

Library of Congress Cataloging-in-Publication Data
O'Neil, Patrick H., 1966–
    Essentials of comparative politics / Patrick H. O'Neil—2nd ed.
        p. cm.
    Includes bibliographical references and index.
    Contents: States — Nations and society — Political economy — Authoritarianism — Democracy — Advanced democracies — Communism and postcommunism — Less-developed and newly industrializing countries — Globalization.

    ISBN-13: 978-0-393-92876-1 (pbk.)
    ISBN-10: 0-393-92876-4 (pbk.)

    1. Comparative government. 2. State, The. 3. Capitalism. 4. Democracy. 5. Post-communism. I. Title.

JF51.O54 2006
    320.3—dc22   2006046354

W. W. Norton & Company, Inc., 500 Fifth Avenue, New York, N.Y. 10110
www.wwnorton.com

W. W. Norton & Company Ltd., Castle House, 75/76 Wells Street, London W1T 3QT

1 2 3 4 5 6 7 8 9 0

CONTENTS

9 LESS-DEVELOPED AND NEWLY
INDUSTRIALIZING COUNTRIES   219

10 GLOBALIZATION   250

LIST OF MAPS

ABOUT THE AUTHOR

Patrick H. O'Neil is Associate Professor of Politics and Government at the University of Puget Sound in Tacoma, Washington. Professor O'Neil's teaching and research interests are in the areas of democratization, conflict and political violence, and the politics of risk and technology. His publications include the books *Revolution from Within: The Hungarian Socialist Worker's Party "Reform Circles" and the Collapse of Communism* and *Communicating Democracy: The Media and Political Transitions* (editor). He is coeditor with Ron Rogowski of *Essential Readings in Comparative Politics*, Second Edition, and coauthor with Karl Fields and Don Share of *Cases for Comparative Politics*, both published by W. W. Norton & Company.

PREFACE

The past twenty years have seen a dramatic transformation of comparative politics: the end of the Cold War and the collapse of the Soviet Union, the spread of democracy around the world, the rise of new economic powers in Asia, and globalization. For a time, many regarded these changes as unmitigated progress that would bring about a decline in global conflict and produce widespread prosperity. Recently, however, there has been growing doubt, as the uncertainties of the future seem to portend more risk than reward, more conflict than peace. It is increasingly difficult to sustain the notion that any nation can function without a good understanding of the billions of people who live outside its borders. We ignore the world at our peril.

This textbook is meant to contribute to our understanding of comparative politics—the study of domestic politics around the world—by investigating the central ideas and questions that make up this field. It begins with the most basic struggle in politics—the battle between freedom and equality and the grave task of reconciling or balancing these ideals. How this struggle has unfolded across place and time represents the core of comparative politics. The text continues by emphasizing the importance of institutions. Human action is fundamentally guided by the institutions that people construct, such as culture, constitutions, and property rights. Once established, these institutions are influential and persistent—not easily overcome, changed, or removed. How these institutions emerge and how they affect politics are central to this work.

With these ideas in place, the book tackles the basic institutions of power: states, markets, societies, democracy, and authoritarianism. What are states, how do they emerge, and how can we measure their capacity, autonomy, and efficacy? How do markets function, and what kinds of relationships exist between states and markets? How do societal components such as nationalism, ethnicity, and ideology shape political values? What are the main differences between democracy and authoritarianism, and what explains why one or the other predominates in various parts of the world?

Once these concepts and questions have been explored, subsequent chapters will apply them directly to various political systems: the advanced democracies, communist and postcommunist countries, and newly industrializing and less-developed countries. In each of these the basic institutions of the state, markets, society, and democracy or authoritarianism shape the relationship between freedom and equality. What basic characteristics lead us to group these countries together? How do they compare with one another, and what are their prospects for economic, social, and democratic development? From here we will consider globalization and how the institutions of politics and the battle over freedom and equality may be transformed by a globalized world. Finally, we shall conclude with a discussion of political violence, looking at terrorism and revolution in particular—their sources, dynamics, and implications.

The format of this text is different from those of most textbooks in this field. Traditionally, comparative politics textbooks have been built around a set of country studies, with introductory chapters for the advanced, Communist/postcommunist, and less-developed worlds. Although such textbooks can provide a great deal of information about a wide range of cases, the trade-off is often a less thorough consideration of the basic grammar of comparative politics. We might know who the prime minister of Japan is but have less of an understanding of, say, political culture, mercantilism, or state autonomy—all ideas that can help us make sense of politics across time and place. This text strives to fill this gap, and can be used alongside traditional case studies to help draw out broader questions and issues. By grasping these concepts, arguments, and questions, students will better understand the political dynamics of the wider world.

This thematic approach to the essential tools and ideas of comparative politics is supported by a strong pedagogy that clarifies and reinforces the most important concepts. "In Focus" boxes throughout every chapter highlight important material that students will want to review. Numerous figures and tables illustrate important concepts and provide real-world data related to the topic at hand. Timelines and thematic maps show important political developments over time and around the globe. The importance of institutions is emphasized by new "Institutions in Action" boxes.

Essentials of Comparative Politics is designed to offer instructors flexibility in creating the course that they want to teach. In addition to the core textbook, a corresponding casebook and a reader are also available. *Cases in Comparative Politics*, coauthored by Karl Fields, Donald Share, and myself, applies the concepts from *Essentials of Comparative Politics* to twelve country studies. In *Essential Readings in Comparative Politics*, my coeditor Ronal Rogowski and I have selected key readings to accompany each chapter in the textbook.

W.W. Norton will also be offering the textbook and casebook in eBook format. Support materials for instructors, including a test bank and PowerPoint lecture outlines, are also available.

Many people have contributed to this work. The text itself is inspired by Karen Mingst's *Essentials of International Relations*. When W. W. Norton first published this work, I was struck by its concision and came to the conclusion that comparative politics would benefit from a similar kind of text. At Norton, Roby Harrington asked me to develop the initial chapters, championed its publication, and provided important feedback at many stages. As editor, Ann Shin held me to a high standard of writing and argumentation on the first edition, which was at times frustrating and demanding—precisely what I needed. On this second edition, Peter Lesser took over editorial duties, helping to further improve the work in content and style. Peter's role as editor was particularly appropriate, since it was he who first suggested that I write this book some years ago. I am thus doubly indebted to him. My thanks, too, to Jessica Box for her research assistance, to John McAusland for helping to develop the artwork, to Birgit Larsson for her manuscript preparation, to Sarah Mann for her project management, and to Janet Greenblatt for her meticulous copy-editing.

In addition to the people at Norton, many fellow academics have helped improve this work. Most important have been my own colleagues at the University of Puget Sound, in particular Don Share and Karl Fields. Don, Karl, and I have regularly team taught introductory comparative politics, and working with these two outstanding teachers and scholars helped generate many of the ideas contained in this book. Don and Karl were also kind enough to use draft chapters of this text in their courses and provided a great deal of feedback and numerous suggestions. I am fortunate to have such valuable colleagues. Important input also came from the reviewers who advised me on various drafts of the first edition: Douglas Durasoff (Seattle Pacific University), Cynthia Enloe (Clark University), Damian J. Fernandez (Florida International University), Michael Fleet (Marquette University), David Leheny (University of Wisconsin), Andrew Milton, Karen Mingst (University of Kentucky), Vincent Wei-Cheng Wang (University of Richmond), and Bruce Wilson (University of Central Florida). I also received valuable advice on the second edition from Kathleen Bruhn (University of California, Santa Barbara), Claudio Holzner (University of Utah), Charles King (Georgetown), Jose Antonio Lucero (Temple University), Csaba Nikolenyi (Concordia University), Kristen Parris (Western Washington University), John Sutcliffe (University of Windsor), and Daniel Unger (Northern Illinois University). I thank them for their words of encouragement as well as their sharp critiques.

Finally, I would like to thank the students of the University of Puget Sound for their questions and insights; the administration of the university for their support of this project; and my wife, Jayne, and son, Thomas, for their patience with me during this long task.

PATRICK H. O'NEIL
Tacoma, Washington
September 2005

Africa, 2006

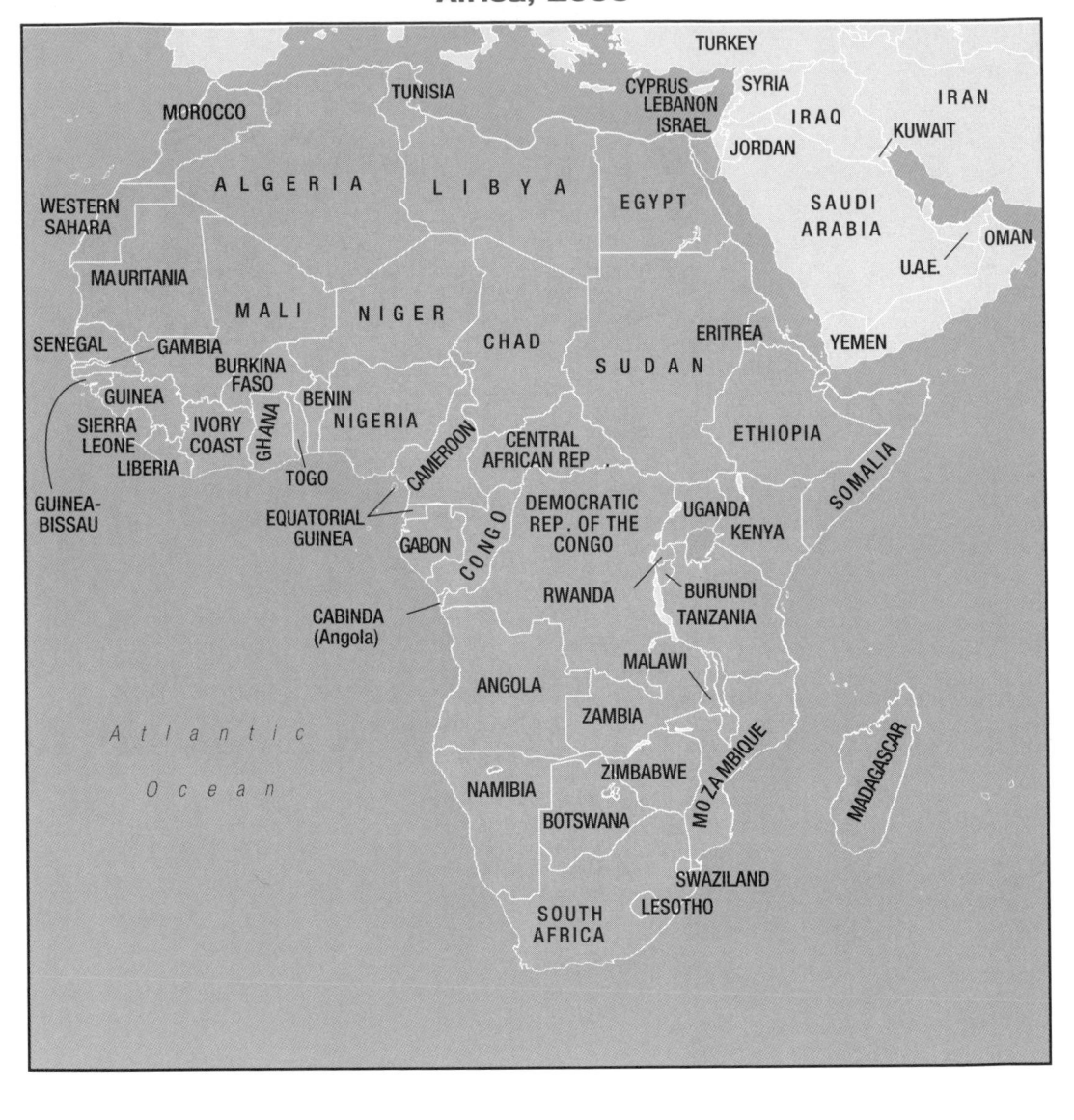

Asia, 2006

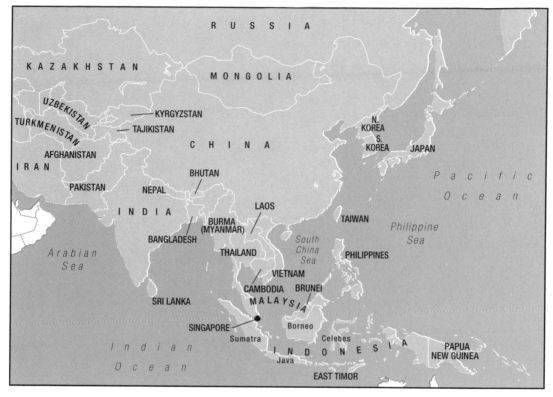

Europe, 2006

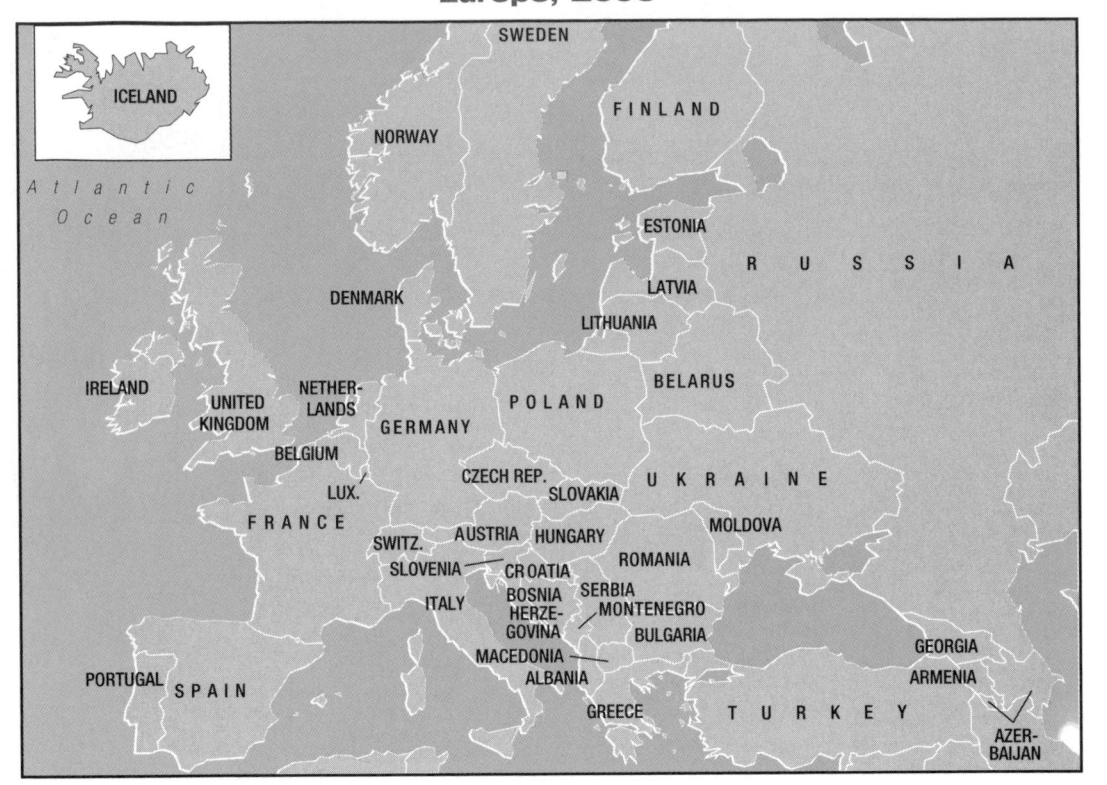

Latin America, 2006

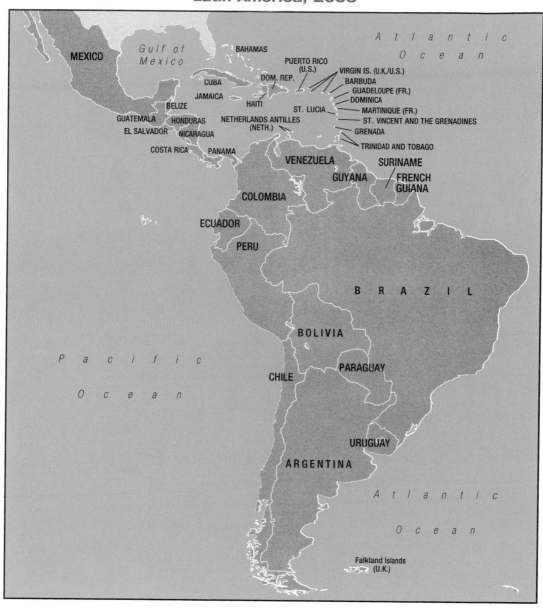

MEXICO

Gulf of Mexico

BAHAMAS

PUERTO RICO (U.S.)

VIRGIN IS. (U.K./U.S.)
BARBUDA
GUADELOUPE (FR.)
DOMINICA
MARTINIQUE (FR.)
ST. VINCENT AND THE GRENADINES
GRENADA
TRINIDAD AND TOBAGO

CUBA
JAMAICA
DOM. REP.
HAITI
ST. LUCIA

BELIZE
GUATEMALA   HONDURAS
EL SALVADOR   NICARAGUA
COSTA RICA   PANAMA

NETHERLANDS ANTILLES (NETH.)

VENEZUELA

SURINAME

GUYANA

FRENCH GUIANA

COLOMBIA

ECUADOR

PERU

B R A Z I L

BOLIVIA

PARAGUAY

CHILE

Atlantic Ocean

Pacific Ocean

URUGUAY

ARGENTINA

Atlantic Ocean

Falkland Islands (U.K.)

ESSENTIALS OF COMPARATIVE POLITICS SECOND EDITION

1 INTRODUCTION

During the past two decades, the world has seen an astonishing number of changes: the rise of new economic powers in Asia; the collapse of communist systems in Eastern Europe and the Soviet Union; the spread of democracy to new parts of the globe; the creation of new technologies, such as the Internet and the World Wide Web; the deepening of international connections, commonly referred to as "globalization"; and the emergence of a new global terrorist threat. As a result of these profound changes, many of the traditional assumptions and concepts used to understand politics have been challenged. New economic forces are shifting wealth around the world, enriching some countries or regions while bypassing others. Technology is rapidly transforming societies everywhere, a change that is attractive to some but threatening to others. People appear to be interconnected as never before, although it is unclear whether this connection brings with it greater understanding and community or inequality and conflict. The terrorist attacks of September 11, 2001, made us all too aware that the very innovations that make up our modern world—skyscrapers and airplanes, e-mail and satellite television—can be turned against us. Politics seems torn by the acceleration of social and economic developments, calling into question the very notion of **sovereignty**—the ability of states to carry out actions or policies within a territory independently from external actors or internal rivals.

These changes are simultaneously fascinating, hopeful, confusing, and terrifying. For some, they represent the onset of a dramatic change in domestic and international politics that will bring an end to ideology, nationalism, and narrow, parochial identities. These observers point to such developments as the European Union, a political and economic integration of twenty-five democratic countries that had waged two horrific wars against one another within the past century, killing tens of millions. Yet these countries are now so highly integrated that the majority of them have relinquished their own national currencies, replacing them with a single currency, the euro. The idea that European countries would ever again go to war against each other seems hard to accept. In one form or another, a global network of connections will bind societies together in prosperity and peace.

Others are less enthusiastic about such developments. They see these changes as leading not to harmonization, but to increasing discord. As the speed of change increases and governments' ability to control these changes declines, these observers predict, a backlash will take form against the "homogenization" of the world. Conflict will intensify, not decline, as people seek to assert what is unique about themselves and to combat ideas they do not accept but cannot avoid. This conflict may take the form of ethnic conflict, as it has already across parts of the former Soviet Union; of domestic and international terrorism, as it has with Al Qaeda; or of public protests against globalization, such as the demonstrations in the United States and Europe against the World Trade Organization and the European Union.

Although it is unclear in which direction politics is heading—greater cooperation or greater conflict or even both at the same time—we need to master the basic language of politics to make sense of these contradictory forces. Only then can we draw our own conclusions about these momentous changes and their implications for politics in our own country and around the world.

This chapter will lay out some of the most basic vocabulary of comparative politics. We will begin with the most basic questions: What is politics? How does one compare different political systems around the world? We will spend some time considering the methods of comparative politics and how scholars have approached the study of politics over time. As we shall see, over the past half century, political scientists have struggled not just with the challenges of analyzing politics, but also with the issue of whether this study can actually be considered a science. Exploring these issues will give us a better sense of the limitations and possibilities in the study of comparative politics. From here we will consider comparative politics through the study of **institutions**—organizations or activities that are self-perpetuating and valued for their own sake. Institutions play an important role in defining and shaping what is possible and probable in political life by laying out the rules, norms, and structures through which we operate. In addition to looking at institutions, we will take up the theme of freedom and equality. If institutions shape how the game of politics is played, then the objective of the game itself is the optimal mix of freedom and equality. Must one come at the expense of the

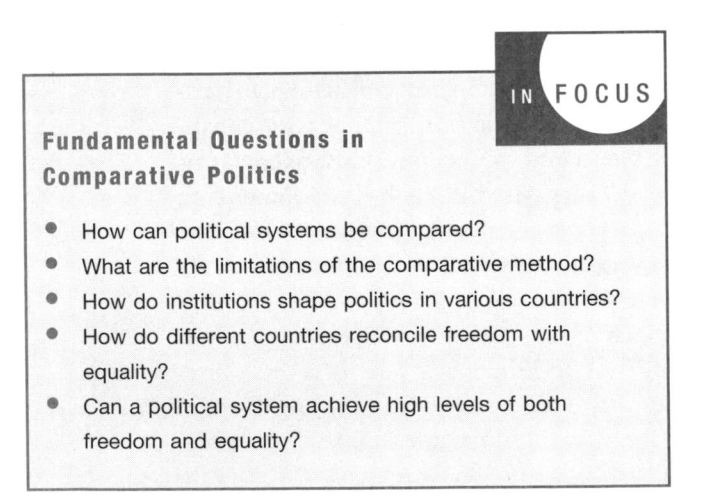

IN FOCUS

Fundamental Questions in Comparative Politics

- How can political systems be compared?
- What are the limitations of the comparative method?
- How do institutions shape politics in various countries?
- How do different countries reconcile freedom with equality?
- Can a political system achieve high levels of both freedom and equality?

other? If so, which is more important? Can both full freedom and full equality be achieved? Or, more provocatively, is neither desirable? With the knowledge gained by exploring these questions, we will be ready to take on the complexity of politics around the world.

What Is Comparative Politics?

Before we go any further, we must identify what comparative politics is. **Politics** is often defined as the struggle in any group for power that will give one or more persons the ability to make decisions for the larger group. This group may range from a small organization up to an entire country or even the entire global population. Politics can be found everywhere; for example, we may speak of "office politics" when we are talking about relations within a business. Political scientists, however, concentrate on the struggle for leadership and power for the community. Politics is essentially the struggle for the authority to make decisions that will affect the public as a whole. It is therefore hard to separate the idea of politics from the idea of power, which is often defined as the ability to influence or impose one's will on others.

Within political science, **comparative politics** is a subfield that compares this struggle across countries. By studying a wide variety of countries, comparativists hope to shed light on the countries under study as well as on their own political system. For example, one important question we will return to frequently is why some countries are democratic while others are not. Why have politics in some countries resulted in power being more dispersed among the people, while in other societies power has been concentrated in the hands of a few? Are these results a function of cultural values or economic development? Is one system superior to the other? These are not simply academic questions: democratic countries actively support the spread of like-minded regimes around the world, whether through diplomacy, aid, or war, but if it is unclear how or why democracy comes about, it becomes difficult to promote or transplant. The comparative study of politics in a number of different circumstances can help us draw conclusions that no single case alone would provide. Moreover, the study of politics beyond our own borders helps place our own system in perspective by highlighting alternatives to our own political order and, as a result, challenging our common assumption that there is one right way to organize political life.

The Comparative Method

It is not enough, however, to simply broaden our horizons by studying politics around the world. *How* we make comparisons between cases is equally important. If there is no criterion or guide by which we gather information or draw conclusions, then our studies become little more than a collection of random details. Comparativists must therefore rely on a **comparative method**—a way to make comparisons across cases and draw conclusions. By comparing two or more countries, we seek to make some generalizations about politics that could be valid in other cases.

For example, if we are interested in why democracy has failed to develop in some countries, we can compare a number of nondemocratic countries and look for patterns or similarities among them, such as a low level of economic development or certain cultural values. By carrying out such studies, we may find a *correlation*, or apparent association, between certain factors or variables. Suppose that, upon investigation, we find that countries with a high rate of poverty are less likely to be democracies than countries where poverty is low. Iran might be one example that would support this hypothesis; 40 percent of Iran's population live below the national poverty line, and political freedoms there are highly restricted. If we look at only this one case, then, poverty and authoritarianism appear to be correlated. But that correlation is not proof of anything. Correlation is not the same thing as causation, in which a change in one variable causes change in another. We do not know, in our simple case study of Iran, whether poverty has led to authoritarianism or whether authoritarianism has led to poverty. Is it the prevalence of poverty that has allowed authoritarian leaders to gain and maintain control, or is the long tenure of authoritarian leaders the source of the country's poverty? Or might there be a third factor, such as certain historical legacies or international influences, that causes both authoritarianism and poverty?

Finding the cause is rarely easy. First, political scientists are unable to control the variables in the cases they study. In other words, in our search for cause-and-effect relationships, we are unable to make true comparisons because each of our cases is quite different. By way of comparison, suppose a researcher wants to determine if increased exercise by college students leads to higher grades. In studying the students who are her subjects, the researcher can control for a number of variables that might also affect grades, such as the students' diet, the amount of sleep they get, or any other factor other than exercise that might influence the results. By controlling for these differences, by making certain that all these variables are the same across the subjects with the exception of exercise, the researcher can carry out her study with greater confidence regarding causation.

But political science offers very few opportunities to control the variables, because the variables are a function of real-world politics. Countries are amazingly diverse in terms of economics, culture, geography, resources, and political structures, and it is difficult to control for these differences. At best, we might seek to categorize countries on the basis of specific factors, controlling as much as possible for variables that might otherwise distort our conclusions. If, for example, we want to understand why gun possession laws are so much less restrictive in the United States than in most other industrialized countries, we would be well served to compare the United States with other countries that have similar historical, economic, political, and social experiences, such as Canada and Australia. This allows us to more effectively control our variables.

This observation leads us to a second problem, however: political scientists are often hampered by a limited number of cases. In the natural sciences, research is often conducted with a huge number of cases—hundreds of stars or thousands of individuals, for example. This breadth allows researchers to select their cases in such a way as to control their variables, and the large number of cases also prevents any single unusual case from distorting the findings. But in comparative politics, we are limited by the number of countries in the world—fewer than 200 at present. If we attempt to control for differences by trying to find a number of cases that are similar (for example, industrialized democracies), our total body of cases may be relatively small. Cases are also limited by time. For example, one debate in international relations focuses on whether democratic countries tend not to go to war against other democracies. But because the history of modern democracy is so short (most democracies have been around only for the past fifty years), critics contend that we simply do not have enough data (or a long enough time frame) to draw such a conclusion.

A third problem in comparative politics concerns how we access the cases that we do have. Even with the limited number of countries available to study, research is further hindered by the barriers that make countries unique. The information that political scientists seek is often not easy to acquire, necessitating work "in the field," conducting interviews or studying government archives in other countries. International travel requires time and money, and researchers may spend months or even years in the field. Interviewees may be unwilling to speak on sensitive issues or may distort information to serve their own interests. Libraries and archives may be incomplete, or access to them may be restricted. As you might imagine, doing such research in more than one country is extremely challenging. A researcher may be able to read Russian and travel to Russia frequently, but if she wants to compare communism between the Soviet Union and China, she would also need to be able to read Chinese and conduct research in China as well. Few comparativists have the language skills, time, or resources to conduct field research in a number of countries. As a result, they often master knowledge of a single country, which limits the kinds of comparisons they can make.

Quantitative versus Qualitative Research

In part because of these limitations, some scholars have attempted to use a **quantitative method** in comparative politics—one that relies on statistical data (such as taxation rates or voter turnout) from a range of countries to construct hypotheses about politics. In the quantitative method, variables that are under investigation are expressed in the form of numbers. Thus, mastery of a language or years of field research aren't as necessary. Data are generated by almost every country around the world, often using similar standards to determine things like inflation, population growth, or electoral outcomes. Unlike those who study only one or two countries, quantitative researchers are able to draw from a large number of cases and control their variables more easily. However, such researchers are limited by those variables that can be expressed in quantitative terms and that exist across a number of cases. Those who use the quantitative approach argue that their work adheres most closely to a true comparative method, unlike those who may study only one or a few countries. Many quantitative researchers believe that their approach represents the future of the field, where questions about politics will be truly answered and puzzles solved.

Other comparativists reject such approaches, embracing instead a **qualitative method**, which stresses that one cannot truly understand a country or region unless one is steeped in its history and culture. Limiting one's research to numerical variables raises the problem that such data may itself be skewed or incomparable: just because something is expressed in numbers does not mean that it is objective or accurate. Furthermore, the quantitative approach restricts the kinds of questions that can be asked, thereby precluding the more complex (but nevertheless important) aspects of politics. As political scientist Philip Converse put it, "What is important to study cannot be measured and what can be measured is not important to study."[1] The qualitative approach tends to focus much more on the unique aspects of countries, such as history and culture, and its adherents are generally more skeptical that a comparative method like that seen in the natural sciences can be achieved. Proponents of quantitative methods often retort that qualitative studies are little more than description and storytelling. Naturally, some seek greater integration of these methods by applying both quantitative and qualitative approaches.

Whatever the method, political scientists are limited as to the comparisons they can make and the conclusions they can draw. They struggle with both explanation and prediction. They wish to determine why events happen: Why is there terrorism? Why does democracy emerge? But even if we know *why* something happens, that doesn't mean we can know *when* it will happen. Few comparativists would claim that they can predict an event except in the most general terms. This difficulty is not all that unusual: just because I understand how the stock market works does not mean I know when it will go up or down.

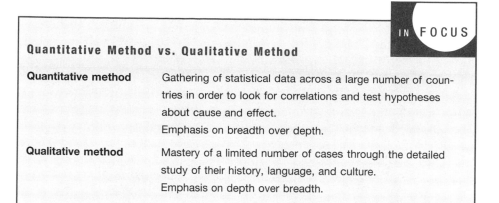

Quantitative Method vs. Qualitative Method

Quantitative method	Gathering of statistical data across a large number of countries in order to look for correlations and test hypotheses about cause and effect. Emphasis on breadth over depth.
Qualitative method	Mastery of a limited number of cases through the detailed study of their history, language, and culture. Emphasis on depth over breadth.

Given all these disagreements and limitations, is it worth our time to study comparative politics at all? Yes, absolutely. Qualitative methods create an indepth knowledge of one or more countries, and quantitative methods can provide a broader analysis across regions and time. Both are valuable for at least two reasons. First, we ignore the outside world at our peril. One could argue that Americans (and many other nationalities) failed to grasp the threat of terrorism before 2001 because they failed to understand the internal political dynamics of the Middle East, which played a major role in motivating the attacks of September 11. A similar argument has been made of the difficult U.S. occupation of Iraq, which some critics say was predicated on a limited understanding of Iraqi and regional politics. By mastering the internal complexities of other countries and investigating broader patterns of politics around the world, we can better ascertain those countries' internal dynamics and how they may affect us. Second, by understanding politics in a comparative setting, we arm ourselves with the knowledge necessary to make informed political choices about our own lives. How is our political system similar or dissimilar to others? What are the advantages and disadvantages of various systems? What would we prefer, and why? Political choices are based not only on abstract ideals, but on very real examples and alternatives. Thus, comparative politics has very practical and important applications.

Debates in Comparative Politics

We have already noted that comparative politics is not a unified field, divided as it is by debates over methodology. Such debates are hardly new, but rather a normal part of intellectual progress that can be traced back at least 2,000 years to Athenian Greece. Then, as now, political thought revolved around notions of the public interest, of how to construct rules and goals to serve society's broader needs and desires. Most relevant for comparativists is the work of the philosopher Aristotle (384–322 B.C.E.). Aristotle departed from his political philosopher predecessors, such as Plato (428–348 B.C.E.), who concentrated on abstract questions such as what would constitute the ideal political system. Instead, Aristotle conducted comparative research on existing political systems, eventually gathering and analyzing the constitutions of 158 Greek city-states. Aristotle's objective was less to determine the ideal political system than to understand the different forms of politics that actually existed and their relative strengths and weaknesses. With this approach, Aristotle conceived of an empirical (that is, observable and verifiable) science of politics with a practical purpose: **statecraft**, or how to govern. Aristotle was the first to separate the study of politics from that of philosophy.[2]

Unfortunately, Aristotle's early approach did not immediately lead to any real science of politics. For the next 1,800 years, discussions of politics remained embedded in the realm of philosophy, with the emphasis placed on how politics should be rather than on how politics was actually conducted. Ideals, rather than conclusions drawn from evidence, were the norm. Only with the works of the Italian Niccolò Machiavelli (1469–1527) did a comparative approach to politics truly emerge. Like Aristotle, he sought to analyze different political systems—those that existed around him as well as those that had preceded him in history, such as the Roman Empire—and even tried to predict their relative success and failure as a result. These findings, he believed, could then be applied by statesmen to avoid their predecessors' mistakes. Machiavelli's work reflects this pragmatism, dealing with the mechanics of government, diplomacy, military strategy, and, above all, power.[3] Most notable is Machiavelli's conclusion that ideals have no place in politics, since the quest for power will inevitably conflict with moral values. It is this emphasis that leads us to use the contemporary (if misleading) term *Machiavellian* to refer to someone cunning and devious, operating without normal moral standards.

Because of his emphasis on statecraft and empirical knowledge, Machiavelli is often cited as the first modern political scientist, paving the way for other scholars. His writings came at a time when the medieval order was giving way to the Renaissance, with its emphasis on science, rationalism, secularism, and real-world knowledge over abstract ideals. The resulting work over the next four centuries reinforced the idea that politics, like any other area of knowledge, could be developed as a logical, rigorous, and predictable science.

During those centuries, a number of major thinkers took up the comparative approach to the study of politics, which increasingly retreated from moral, philosophical, or religious foundations. In the late sixteenth and early seventeenth centuries, authors such as Thomas Hobbes and John Locke followed in Machiavelli's footsteps, advocating particular political systems on the basis of empirical observation and analysis. They were followed in the eighteenth century by such scholars as Jean-Jacques Rousseau and Baron de Montesquieu, whose studies of the separation of power and civil liberties would directly influence the writing of the American Constitution and others to follow. The work of Karl Marx and Max Weber in the nineteenth and early twentieth centuries would further add to political science with analyses of the nature of political and economic organization and power. All these developments reflected widespread changes in scholarly inquiry.

By the early twentieth century, the study of politics had changed dramatically into a discipline not unlike that which we know today. However, in spite of great strides, the field remained limited and ethnocentric, focused on one's own society or culture. In comparative politics, scholars and students focused their attention on a few modern political structures, primarily those in Europe. Moreover, comparativists tended to concentrate on static description over explanation or prediction—on how politics worked in these countries rather than why. But this approach to comparative politics was eventually shaken by international events: the rise of fascism and communism, World War II, and the Cold War. Each of these events raised important questions that political scientists could not easily answer: Why had Germany fallen prey to fascism, and Russia to communism? Could democracy be installed in countries like Germany and Japan? How could Soviet power be kept in check?

Consequently, after World War II, comparative politics was embraced by a new generation of scholars who believed that the field must become a true science. Their conviction was in part shaped by a new wave of technological change and enthusiasm about progress. Nuclear power, space travel, computers, and television generated a common view that economics, society, and politics were being transformed dramatically—and for the better—through scientific advancement. Science would lead politics (technocracy, or rule by technical expertise), and not vice versa. In addition, comparative politics was influenced by international relations. With the emergence of the United States and the Soviet Union as superpowers after World War II, the onset of the Cold War, and the withdrawal of imperial control over Asia and Africa, many political scientists in the West (especially in the United States) saw their role in part as helping to strengthen the position of the capitalist democracies. They believed that by making sense of political development around the world, they could guide foreign policy in ways that would foster the development of economic and political systems similar to those in the West.

Comparative politics was thus not simply a quest for knowledge, but part of the battle between the new superpowers. In this sense, then, comparative politics was a largely conservative discipline, taking capitalism and

Major Thinkers in Comparative Politics	
Aristotle (384–322 B.C.E.)	First separated the study of politics from that of philosophy; used comparative method to study Greek city-states; in *The Politics*, conceived of an empirical study of politics with a practical purpose.
Niccolò Machiavelli (1469–1527)	Often cited as first modern political scientist because of his emphasis on statecraft and empirical knowledge; analyzed different political systems, believing the findings could be applied by statesmen; discussed his theories in *The Prince*.
Thomas Hobbes (1588–1679)	Developed the notion of a "social contract," whereby people surrender certain liberties in favor of order; advocated a powerful state in *Leviathan*.
John Locke (1632–1704)	Argued that private property is essential to individual freedom and prosperity; advocated a weak state in his *Two Treatises of Government*.
Charles Louis de Secondat, Baron de Montesquieu (1689–1755)	Studied government systems; advocated the separation of powers within government in *The Spirit of Laws*.
Jean-Jacques Rousseau (1712–1778)	Argued that citizens' rights are inalienable and cannot be taken away by the state; influenced the development of civil rights; discussed these ideas in *The Social Contract*.
Karl Marx (1818–1883)	Elaborated a theory of economic development and inequality in his book *Das Kapital*; predicted the eventual collapse of capitalism and democracy.
Max Weber (1864–1920)	Wrote widely on such topics as bureaucracy, forms of authority, and the impact of culture on economic and political development; developed many of these themes in *Economy and Society*.

democracy as the ideal. These views were codified in what was known as **modernization theory**, which held that as societies developed, they would become capitalist democracies, converging around a shared set of values and characteristics. The United States and other Western countries were furthest ahead on this path, and the theory assumed that all countries would eventually catch up—unless "diverted" by alternative systems such as communism (as fascism had done in past).

During the 1950s and 1960s, comparativists influenced by modernization theory expanded their research to include a wider number of cases. Field research, supported by government and private grants, became the normal means by which political scientists gathered data. New computer technologies combined with statistical methods were also applied to this expanding wealth of data. Finally, the subject of investigation shifted away from political institutions (such as legislatures and constitutions) and toward individual political behavior. This trend came to be known as the behavioral revolution. **Behavioralism** hoped to generate theories and generalizations that could help explain and even predict political activity. Ideally, this work would eventually lead to a "grand theory" of political behavior and modernization that would be valid across countries. Behavioralism and modernization theory were two different things—modernization theory a set of hypotheses about how countries develop, and behavioralism a way to approach politics. However, the two were clearly linked by a sense of approaching politics in a more scientific manner to achieve certain policy outcomes.[4]

By the late 1960s, however, the great hopes of comparative politics began to fade. New theories and sophisticated methods of analysis increased scholars' knowledge about politics around the world, but this knowledge in itself did not lead to the expected breakthroughs. Those theories that had been developed, such as modernization theory, increasingly failed to match politics on the ground; rather than becoming more capitalist and more democratic, many newly independent countries collapsed in the face of violent

---

IN FOCUS

Trends in Comparative Politics

Traditional approach	Emphasis on describing political systems and their various institutions.
Behavioral revolution	The shift from a descriptive study of politics to one that emphasizes causality, explanation, and prediction; places greater emphasis on the political behavior of individuals as opposed to larger political structures and on quantitative over qualitative methodology; modernization theory predominant.
Postbehavioralism	Rejection of a grand theory of politics; criticism of modernization theory as biased and inaccurate; diversity of methods and political approaches, emphasizing such issues as gender, culture, environment, and globalization.

conflict and revolution, to be replaced by nondemocratic systems that in no way reflected Western expectations or ideals. What had gone wrong?

Some critics charged that the behavioral revolution's obsession with appearing scientific had led the discipline astray by emphasizing methodology over knowledge and technical jargon over clarity. Others criticized the field for its ideological bias, arguing that comparativists were interested not in understanding the world but in prescribing the Western model of modernization. At worst, their work could be viewed as simply serving the foreign policy of the developed world.

In the 1970s and 1980s, comparative politics was divided by ideological and methodological debates. Scholars of different ideological persuasions accused each other of bias and distortion, while advocates of quantitative and qualitative methods argued over how to structure and use research. Yet even as these debates raged among scholars, new global developments were taking shape that would shake the foundations of comparative politics.

The first major development was rapid industrialization in Asia. During the mid-1980s, the region attracted attention as countries such as Taiwan, South Korea, Singapore, and China produced increasingly sophisticated products for export, generating tremendous economic growth in the process. While Latin American, African, and even European and North American economies stagnated or declined, some Asian countries more than tripled the standard of living for millions of people within just a few decades. What explained this sudden growth? Was it due to particularly "Asian" cultural values, specific trade strategies, or perhaps the presence of nondemocratic governments that could withstand the harsh sacrifices necessary for development?[5]

A second major event was the collapse of communism in the Soviet Union and Eastern Europe. In the 1980s, the new leader of the Soviet Union, Mikhail Gorbachev, embarked on a series of dramatic reforms intended to revitalize and liberalize communism. These changes also raised the possibility that with more democratic practices in the Soviet Union, the Cold War might finally come to an end, although many feared that a revamped form of communism would in fact be more dangerous than before. The Cold War did draw to a close, but not in the manner expected. In 1989, the Soviet-controlled countries of Eastern Europe threw off communist rule, and by 1991, Gorbachev's reforms, rather than revitalizing the Soviet Union, led to the country's breakup. Soviet communism had been unable to reform itself, and with its demise, observers now wondered if capitalism and democracy would take root in these postcommunist countries. In addition, many scholars were left trying to explain why, after decades of studying Soviet rule, few had any sense that this system was ready to collapse. Some charged the discipline with an ideological bias that tended to overlook the inherent problems of Soviet rule in favor of its claims about equality, while others argued that it was behavioralism that had blinded scholars to what was unique (and uniquely flawed) about communist systems.[6]

A third and related development was what has come to be known as the "third wave" of democracy.[7] During the 1970s and 1980s, a large number of countries around the world, particularly in Asia, Latin America, and Europe, shook off authoritarian rule. What was the source of this relatively rapid and unexpected democratization across such a diverse set of countries? And would these fragile democracies survive or again succumb to nondemocratic rule?

All three of these events challenged scholars of comparative politics, regardless of their methodological or ideological preferences. The collapse of communism pointed out the limitations of both the qualitative and quantitative approaches, since neither had foreseen the impact of reforms in the region, even when they were under way. Similarly, the rise of new economic powers in Asia challenged those views that poorer countries could not progress because of their domination by advanced economic powers. Finally, the dramatic spread of democracy forced all comparativists to rethink the very future of politics and the role of their field.

This is where we find comparative politics now. In light of the dramatic political changes of the past several decades, scholars such as Francis Fukuyama have gone so far as to say that we are now at the "end of history," meaning that the dramatic struggles between right and left, capitalism and communism, and authoritarianism and democracy are coming to an end.[8] All countries, these scholars argue, will sooner or later become capitalist democracies, and the old ideological divides that separate domestic and international politics are drawing to an end. In other words, the modernization theory was right after all, if somewhat premature. But critics such as political scientist Samuel Huntington counter that the triumph of capitalism and democracy is far from certain. These systems are the product of the unique historical experiences of the West and will not easily transfer around the world, Huntington says. Indeed, in the absence of major ideological distinctions between countries, he believes that political divisions will fall primarily along cultural, ethnic, and religious lines.[9] Still other critics, such as political theorist Benjamin Barber, may accept the spread of Western institutions, but questions their value, pointing to inequalities, the destruction of local cultures, and a growing backlash against globalization.[10] These debates have only intensified since September 11. Some see in the terrorist attacks and the U.S. response a cultural conflict; others see an inevitable result of globalization; still others identify a last, futile gasp against capitalism and democracy. Each explanation asks us to see the world in a different way and draws different conclusions about the nature of political cooperation and conflict.

A Guiding Approach: Political Institutions

A goal of this textbook is to provide a way to compare and analyze politics around the world in the aftermath of these tremendous changes and uncertainties. Given the long-standing debates within comparative politics and the current confusion over the nature of the post–September 11 world, how can we organize our ideas and information? One way is through a guiding approach, a way of looking at the world that highlights some important features while de-emphasizing others. There is certainly no one right way of doing this; any guide, like a lens, will sharpen some features while distorting others. With that said, the guiding approach of this textbook is based on *institutions*, which were defined at the beginning of this chapter as organizations or patterns of activity that are self-perpetuating and valued for their own sake. In other words, an institution is something so embedded in people's lives as a norm or value that it is not easily dislodged or changed. People see an institution as central to their lives, and as a result, the institution commands a great deal of legitimacy. Institutions serve as the rules, norms, and values that give meaning to human activity.

Consider an example from outside of politics. We often hear in the United States that baseball is an American institution. What exactly does this mean? In short, baseball is viewed by Americans not simply as a game, but as something valued for its own sake, a game that helps define American society. Yet no American would say that soccer is a national institution. The reason is probably clear: soccer lacks the kind of public perception of its indispensability that baseball has. Whereas soccer is simply a game, baseball is part of what defines America and Americans. Even Americans who don't like baseball would probably say that America wouldn't be the same without it. Of course, just the opposite is true in Europe and much of the world, where soccer reigns as a premier social institution. Indeed, some go so far as to use soccer (and its weakness in America) as a way to understand comparative politics.[11] As a result of this legitimacy and seeming indispensability, institutions command authority and can influence human behavior; we accept and conform to institutions and tend not to challenge them.

Another example is more directly connected to politics. In many countries, democracy is an institution: it is not merely a means to compete over political power but a vital element in people's lives, bound up in the very way in which they define themselves. Democracy is part and parcel of collective identity, and some democratic countries and their people would not be the same without it. Even if cynical about democracy in practice, its citizens will defend the institution when it is under threat and even die for it. In many other countries, this is not the case: democracy is absent and unknown or weakly institutionalized and unstable. People in such countries do not define themselves by democracy's presence or absence, and so democracy's future there is insecure. However, these same people might owe a similar allegiance to a different set of institutions, such as their ethnic group or religion. Clearly, there is no single, uniform set of institutions that holds power over people all around the world, and understanding the differences is central to the study of comparative politics.

What about a physical object or place? Can that, too, be an institution? Many would argue that the World Trade Center was an American institution— not just a set of office buildings, but structures representing American values. The same thing can be said about the Pentagon. When terrorists attacked these buildings on September 11, 2001, they did so not simply to cause a great loss of life, but also to clearly indicate that their hostility was directed against America itself—its institutions as they shape and represent the American way of life and the U.S. relationship to the outside world.

In general, however, institutions are not physical structures and are not so easily destroyed. Because they are embedded in each of us, in how we see the world and what we think is valuable and important, it is difficult to change or eliminate institutions. When institutions are threatened, people will rush to their defense and even re-create them when they are shattered. This bond is the glue of society. However, one problem that institutions pose is this very "stickiness," in that people may come to resist even necessary change because they have difficulty accepting the idea that certain institutions have outlived their value. Thus, while institutions certainly can and do change, their very nature is one of greater perseverance.

Politics is full of institutions. The basic political structures of any country are composed of institutions: the army, the police, the legislature, and the courts, to name a few. We obey them not only because we think it is in our self-interest to do so, but because we see them as legitimate ways to conduct politics. Taxation is a good example. In many Western democracies, income taxes are an institution; we may not like them, but we pay them nonetheless. Is this because we are afraid of going to jail if we fail to do so? Perhaps. But research indicates that a major source of tax compliance is people's belief that taxation is a legitimate way to fund the programs that society needs. We pay, in other words, when we believe that it is the right thing to do, a norm. In contrast, in societies where taxes are not institutionalized, tax evasion tends to be rampant; people view taxes as illegitimate and those who pay as suckers.

Institutions are a useful way to approach the study of politics because they set the stage for political behavior. Because institutions generate norms and values, they favor and allow certain kinds of political activity and not others. As a result, political institutions are critical because they influence politics, and how political institutions are constructed will have a profound effect on how politics is conducted.

IN **FOCUS**

Institutions . . .

- Are any organization or pattern of activity that is self-perpetuating and valued for its own sake.
- Embody norms or values considered central to people's lives and thus are not easily dislodged or changed.
- Set the stage for political behavior by influencing how politics is conducted.
- Vary from country to country.
- Exemplified by the army, taxation, elections, and the state.

In many ways, our institutional approach takes us back to the study of comparative politics as it existed before the 1950s. Prior to the behavioral revolution, political scientists spent much of their time documenting the institutions of politics, often without asking how those institutions actually shaped politics. The behavioral revolution that followed emphasized cause and effect but turned its attention toward political actors and their calculations, resources, or strategies, borrowing from economic theory. The actual institutions were seen as largely unimportant. The recent return to the study of institutions in many ways combines these two traditions. From behavioralism, institutional approaches take their emphasis on cause-and-effect relationships, something that will be prevalent throughout this book. However, institutions are not simply the product of individual political behavior; they can and do have a powerful effect on how politics functions. In other words, institutions are not merely the *result* of politics; they can also be an important *cause*.

As recent events have shown us, there is still a tremendous amount of institutional variation around the world that needs to be recognized and understood. This textbook will map some of the basic institutional differences between countries, acknowledging their diversity while pointing to some basic features that allow us to compare and evaluate them. By studying political institutions, we can hope to gain a better sense of the political landscape across the globe.

A Guiding Idea: Reconciling Freedom and Equality

At the start of this chapter, politics was defined as the struggle for power in order to make decisions for society. The institutional approach provides us with a way to organize our study by investigating the different ways in which that struggle can be shaped. Yet this begs an important question: People may struggle for political power, but what are they fighting for? What is it they seek to achieve once they have gained power?

At its core, the substance of politics is bound up in the struggle between individual freedom and collective equality, an idea that goes back as far as

Athens. These are terms that mean very different things to different people, and so it is important to define each of them. **Freedom** is the ability of an individual to act independently, without fear of restriction or punishment by the state or other individuals or groups in society. It encompasses such concepts as free speech, free assembly, freedom of religion, and other civil liberties. **Equality** refers to a shared material standard of individuals within a community, society, or country. The relationship between equality and freedom is typically viewed in terms of justice or injustice.

Freedom and equality are thus interconnected, and the relationship between the two shapes politics, power, and debates over justice. What is unclear, however, is whether one must come at the expense of the other. Greater personal freedom, for example, may imply a smaller role for the state and limits on its powers to do such things as redistribute income through welfare and taxes. As a result, inequality may increase as individual freedom trumps the desire for greater collective equality. This growing inequality can in turn undermine democracy if too many people feel as though the political system no longer cares about their material needs. Even if this discontent is not a danger, there remains the question of whether society as a whole has an obligation to help the poor—an issue of justice. The United States, as we shall see, has one of the highest degrees of both personal freedom and economic inequality in the world. Should this be a cause of concern?

At the other end, a primary focus on economic equality may erode personal freedom. Demands for greater material equality may lead a government to take greater control of private property and personal wealth, all in the name of redistribution for the "greater good." Yet when economic and political powers are concentrated in one place, individual freedom may be threatened, since people control fewer private resources of their own. In the Soviet Union under communism, for example, all economic power was held by the state, giving it the ability to control people's lives—where they lived, the education they received, the jobs they held, the money they earned.

Are freedom and equality by nature zero-sum, where the gain of one represents the loss of the other? Not necessarily. Some would assert that freedom and equality can also serve to reinforce each other, with material security helping to secure certain political rights, and vice versa. In addition, while a high degree of state power may weaken individual freedom, the state may also act as the very guarantor of these rights. All of these issues are subject to debate. For some, managing freedom and/or equality necessitates some, or perhaps a great deal, of centralized political power. Others instead view such power as the very impediment to freedom and/or equality. We will consider these debates to a greater extent when we consider political ideologies in the next chapter.

In short, politics must constantly seek to reconcile individual freedom and collective equality. This inevitably leads to questions of power—influencing others or imposing one's will—and the role of the people in political life. Who should be empowered to make decisions about freedom and equality? Should power be centralized or decentralized, public or private? When does power become a danger to others, and how can this be prevented? Each political system must address these questions and in so doing determine where political power shall reside, and how much. And each political system creates a unique set of institutions to structure political power, shape the role that the people play in politics, and form a consensus about justice.

In Sum: Looking Ahead

Politics is the struggle for power in any organization, and comparative politics is the study of this struggle around the world. Over the past centuries, the study of politics has evolved from philosophy to a field that emphasizes empirical research and the quest to explain and even predict politics. This approach has limitations: in spite of the earlier desire to emulate the natural sciences, comparative politics, like political science as a whole, has not been able to generate any "grand theory" of political behavior. Yet the need to study politics remains as important as ever; dramatic changes over the past twenty years have called on comparativists to provide insight on these developments.

Political institutions can help us organize this task. Institutions generate norms and values, and different configurations of institutions lead to different forms of political activity. Institutions can help us map the landscape of politics. If institutions serve as a map to political activity, then the goal of that activity is to reconcile the competing values of individual freedom and collective equality. All countries must strike a balance between these two forces, determining where power should reside and in whose hands. In the chapters to come, we will return to this question of freedom and equality and to the way in which these values influence, and are influenced by, institutions. Armed with this knowledge, by the end of this course you will be able to draw your own conclusions about what combination of these values can or should be sought to construct a better political order.

NOTES

1. Philip E. Converse, "The Nature of Belief Systems in Mass Publics," in David E. Apter, ed., *Ideology and Discontent* (New York: Free Press, 1964), 206.
2. Aristotle, *The Politics*, trans. T. A. Sinclair (New York: Viking, 1992).
3. Niccolò Machiavelli, *The Prince*, trans. W. K. Marriott (New York: Knopf, 1992).

4. For more on the behavioral revolution, see Robert A. Dahl, "The Behavioral Approach in Political Science: Epitaph for a Monument to a Successful Protest," *American Political Science Review* 55, no. 4 (December 1961): 763–772.

5. For an analysis of Asian development, see Stephan Haggard, *Pathways from the Periphery: The Politics of Growth in the Newly Industrializing Countries* (Ithaca: Cornell University Press, 1990).

6. Valerie Bunce, "Comparing East and South," *Journal of Democracy* 6, no. 3 (1995): 87–100.

7. Samuel P. Huntington, *The Third Wave: Democratization in the Late Twentieth Century* (Norman: University of Oklahoma Press, 1993).

8. Francis Fukuyama, *The End of History and the Last Man* (New York: Free Press, 1992).

9. Samuel P. Huntington, *The Clash of Civilization and the Remaking of World Order* (New York: Simon and Schuster, 1996).

10. Benjamin Barber, *Jihad versus McWorld: How Globalism and Tribalism Are Reshaping the World* (New York: Random House, 1995).

11. Franklin Foer, *How Soccer Explains the World: An Unlikely Theory of Globalization* (New York: HarperCollins, 2004).

2 STATES

We begin our study of the basic institutions of politics by turning our attention to the state. This discussion is often difficult for Americans, who are not used to thinking about politics in terms of centralized political power. Indeed, when Americans think of the word *state*, they typically conjure up the idea of local, not centralized, politics.[1] But for most people around the world, "the state" refers to centralized authority, the locus of power. In this chapter, we will break down the basic components of states and discuss how states help reconcile freedom and equality and distribute power toward that end. The chapter will define what states are and what they comprise, distinguishing a state from a government or a regime. We will also consider the origins of states themselves. For most of human history, politics was built on organizations other than states, and myriad forms of authority existed around the world. Yet now only states remain. Why?

Once we have discussed the nature and origins of the state, we will look at some different ways in which states can be compared. This discussion will include an analysis of different forms of legitimacy that give a state power and the actual levels of power itself. Can states be weak or strong? And if so, how would we measure their strength or weakness? To answer this question, we will make a distinction between state capacity and state autonomy and look at different cases in which the combination of the two differs. With these ideas more clearly in hand, we will return to our theme of individual freedom and collective equality and consider the future of the state itself.

Defining the State

What exactly do we mean by the term *state*? Political scientists, drawing on the work of the German scholar Max Weber, typically define **state** in its most basic terms as the organization that maintains a monopoly of violence over a territory.[2] At first glance, this may seem to be a rather severe definition of what a state is or does, but a bit of explanation should help flesh out this concept. One of the most important elements of a state is what we call **sovereignty**, or the ability to carry out actions or policies within a territory independently from external actors or internal rivals. In other words, a state needs to be able to act as the primary authority over its territory and the people who live there, setting forth laws, resolving disputes between people, and generating security.

To achieve this, a state needs power, typically (but not only) physical power. If a state cannot defend its territory from outside actors such as other states, then it runs the risk that other states will interfere, even to the point of taking its territory or destroying it outright. Similarly, if the state faces powerful opponents within its own territory, such as organized crime or rebel movements, it runs the risk that its rules and policies will be undermined. Thus, to secure control, a state must be armed. To protect against international rivals, states need armies. And in response to domestic rivals, states need a police force. In fact, the very word *police* comes from the old French word meaning "to govern."

A state is thus an institution that seeks to wield the majority of force within a territory, establishing order and deterring challengers from inside and out. In so doing, it provides security for its subjects by limiting the danger of external attack and internal crime and disorder—both of which are seen as threats to the state and its citizens. In some ways, a state (especially a nondemocratic one) is a kind of protection racket—demanding money in return for security and order, staking out turf, defending its clients from rivals, settling internal disputes, and punishing those who do not pay.[3]

But the state is not simply an armed body. Unlike criminal rackets, the state is made up of a large number of institutions that are engaged in the process of turning political ideas into policy. Laws and regulations, health care, unemployment insurance, environmental protection, transportation infrastructure, and public parks are but a few things that typically fall under the responsibility of the state. Moreover, the state is a set of institutions (ministries, departments, offices, army, police) that society deems necessary to achieve basic goals regarding freedom and equality. When there is a lack of agreement on these goals, the state must attempt to reconcile different views and seek consensus. And unlike a criminal racket, which people obey out of fear or pure self-interest, the state is typically valued for its own sake. The public views the state as legitimate, vital, and appropriate: Who can imagine politics without it? States are thus strongly institutionalized and not easily changed. Leaders may come and go, but the state remains, even in the face of crisis, turmoil, or revolution. Although destruction through war or civil conflict can eliminate states altogether, even this outcome is unusual. Thus, the state is defined as a monopoly of force over a given territory, but it is also the set of political institutions that transform ideas and conflicts regarding freedom and equality into concrete action. It is, if you will, the machinery of politics, establishing order and turning politics into policy.

IN FOCUS

The State Is . . .

- The monopoly of force over a given territory.
- A set of political institutions to generate and carry out policy.
- Typically highly institutionalized.
- Sovereign.
- Characterized by such institutions as an army, police, taxation, a judiciary, and a social welfare system.

A few other terms that are often used with regard to political organization need to be defined here. Although often used interchangeably with the concept of the state, they are in fact separate institutions that help define and direct the state. First, we should make a distinction between the state and a **regime**, which is defined as the fundamental rules and norms of politics. More specifically, a regime embodies long-term goals regarding individual freedom and collective equality, where power should reside and how it should be used. At the most basic level, we can speak of a democratic regime or an authoritarian one. In a democratic regime, the rules and norms of politics emphasize a large role for the public in governance, as well as certain individual rights or liberties. Power in such regimes tends to be decentralized, and long-term goals tend to center around reconciling individual freedom and collective equality. An authoritarian regime, in contrast, emphasizes a limited role for the public in politics. Power is centralized in the hands of those in power, and long-term goals may vary. Individual freedom may be restricted in favor of greater collective equality, or both freedom and equality may be limited. Power may be centralized for its own sake.

Even among democratic or authoritarian regimes, the basic rules and norms of politics may differ. The democratic regime of the United States is not the same as that of Canada; the authoritarian regime of China is not the same as that of Cuba or Syria. Some of these differences can be found in basic documents such as constitutions, but often the rules and norms that distinguish one regime from another are unwritten and implicit, requiring careful study.

Like the state, regimes are often institutions. Regimes do not easily or quickly change, although they can be transformed or altered, usually by dramatic social events such as a revolution or a national crisis. Most revolutions, in fact, can be seen as revolts not against the state, but against the current regime—to overthrow the old rules and norms and replace them with new ones. For example, France refers to its current regime as the Fifth Republic. Ever since the French Revolution overthrew the monarchy in 1789, each French republic has been characterized by a separate regime, embodied in the constitution and the broader political rules that shape politics. In another example, South Africa's transition to democracy in the 1990s involved a change of regime as the white-dominated system of apartheid gave way to one that provides democratic rights to all South Africans.

In some authoritarian countries where politics is dominated by a single individual, observers may use the term *regime* to refer to that leader, emphasizing the view that all decisions flow from that one person. Or as King Louis XIV of France famously put it, *"L'Etat, c'est moi"* (I am the state). Before the invasion of Iraq, President Bush spoke of his desire for "regime change." He may have been using the term in the individual sense, that the Iraqi regime was little more than the personal authority of Saddam Hussein. However, even our broader definition may apply here, because President Bush's objective was not simply to eliminate Hussein, but to replace the broader rules and norms of Iraqi politics with a democratic system. Whether such a regime change is possible is now one of the most hotly contested debates in political science and policy circles. To some, the war in Iraq will allow a full-scale transformation of the Iraqi regime to democracy. To others, dislodging Hussein was the easy part; building a democratic regime will prove difficult if not impossible, especially in the face of such a weak Iraqi state.

To recap, if the state is a monopoly of force and a set of political institutions to generate policy, then the regime is defined as the norms and rules regarding the proper balance of freedom and equality and the use of power toward that end. To use an analogy, if the state is the machinery of politics, like a personal computer, then one can think of a regime as its software, the programming that defines its capabilities. Each computer runs differently, depending on the software installed.

This brings us to a third term to add to our understanding of state and regime: government. **Government** can be defined as the leadership or elite in charge of running the state. If the state is the machinery of politics, and the regime its programming, then the government acts as its operator. The government may consist of democratically elected legislators, presidents, and prime ministers, or it may be made up of dictators who gained offices through force or other nondemocratic means. Whatever their path to power, governments all hold particular ideas regarding freedom and equality and attempt to use

---

IN FOCUS

A Regime Is . . .

- Norms and rules regarding individual freedom and collective equality, the locus of power, and the use of that power.
- Institutionalized, but can be changed by dramatic social events such as a revolution.
- Categorized at the most basic level as either democratic or authoritarian.
- Often embodied in a constitution.

Government Is . . .

- The leadership or elite in charge of running the state.
- Weakly institutionalized.
- Often characterized by elected officials, such as a president or prime minister, or unelected officials, such as in authoritarianism.
- Limited by the existing regime.

the state to realize those ideas. But few governments are able to act with complete freedom in this regard. Democratic and even authoritarian governments must confront the existing regime, the norms and values of politics that have built up over time. Push too hard against an existing regime, and resistance or even outright rebellion may occur. For example, Mikhail Gorbachev's attempt to fundamentally transform the regime of the Soviet Union in the 1980s contributed to that country's breakup.

In part because of the power of regimes, governments tend to be weakly institutionalized; that is, those in power are not viewed by the public as irreplaceable, such that the country would collapse without them (Figure 2.1). In democratic regimes, governments are replaced fairly frequently, and even in

Figure 2.1 **STATE, REGIME, AND GOVERNMENT**

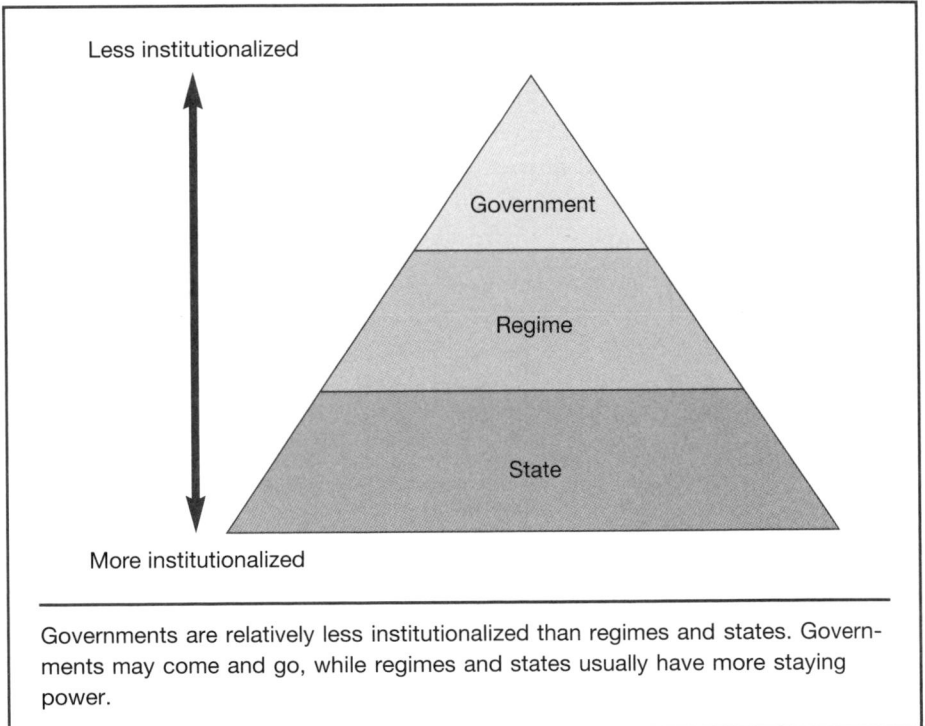

Governments are relatively less institutionalized than regimes and states. Governments may come and go, while regimes and states usually have more staying power.

authoritarian settings, those who rule are continuously threatened by rivals and their own mortality. Governments come and go, whereas regimes and states may live on for decades or even centuries.

Finally, we have the term **country**, which can be seen as shorthand for all the concepts so far discussed—state, government, regime—as well as the people who live within that political system. We will often speak about various countries in this textbook, and when we do, we are referring to the entire political entity and its citizens.

The Origins of Political Organization

So far we have noted that modern politics is defined by states, which monopolize force and execute policies. This political machinery is given direction by a particular regime and by the government in power. Governments generate short-term goals regarding freedom and equality, which are in part based on an existing regime that provides an institutionalized set of norms and values about politics. This combination of institutions, linking state, regime, and government, is relatively new. This is not to say that there is no history of political organization. On the contrary, for tens of thousands of years, human beings have formed collective groups, ranging from relatively simple and fluid gatherings to highly complex systems that incorporated hundreds of thousands or even millions of individuals and lasted for centuries. Tribes, bands, cities, and empires took root anywhere that people settled, serving as fundamental forms of human organization. But as we look over the face of the earth in this millennium, we see that these various forms of political organization have for the most part disappeared. The globe is now clearly demarcated by only one type of political organization—the state—that over the past few hundred years has displaced virtually all other political structures. Almost no inhabitable territory or people on the face of the earth is not claimed by some state.

But where did states come from, and why have they displaced all other forms of political organization? Why are there no longer parts of the world controlled by city-states, tribes, or empires? To answer this puzzle, we first need to go back into human history and discuss the origins of political organization. How human beings have come together and how they have organized their lives will also be a central issue later on as we look at the role of democracy and nondemocratic rule in the modern world. It would appear that states have been able to dispatch all other forms of political organization, in spite of the long history of these other forms. By understanding the origins and power of states, we can better grasp their functions in the modern world and understand that just as human beings once existed without states, states might themselves be replaced in the future by one or more other forms of political organization.

Archeology and history tell us that human beings have always organized into political units, although our findings do not explain why humans organized in the first place beyond that of a small group. For political scientists interested in current affairs, this original motivation may be of little concern, but for anthropologists and others focused on human history and social evolution, the question is important. There are a number of competing explanations as to why humans organize beyond family or tribe. One important factor is probably environment and agriculture. Where people were able to domesticate plants and animals (a much more difficult process than one might imagine), they moved from a nomadic hunter-gatherer existence to one of sedentary living. Concepts that would have previously been meaningless, such as territory, crops, and homes, suddenly became life-or-death issues.

In addition, the rise of agriculture and domestication allowed for the creation of food surpluses, again a great change from the hunter-gatherer days. Food surpluses allowed for greater human specialization: some people could forgo farming and pursue other activities, such as making useful goods that could be exchanged for food and other items. But while agriculture and a sedentary existence created property and specialization, it also created, or at least increased, human inequality. In a system of greater specialization that relies on a wide array of talents, some individuals will clearly benefit more than others; wealth and power inevitably become unequally distributed.

This time period is when political organization most likely had its beginning. In small bands or larger tribes, there tends to be relative equality and communal decision making; but as societies grow larger, more specialized, and more unequal, they require new mechanisms to handle disputes. Those with economic surpluses seek to protect their riches from theft. Those without surpluses seek a greater share of the group's resources. And both fear attack by outside groups or internal competitors that might covet their lands, crops, and homes. Because of such human innovations as agriculture, the very concepts of individualism versus the collective, of freedom versus equality, probably first arose. Who gets what? Who has the right to do what? And how should these decisions be made and enforced? Having to confront and reconcile freedom and equality in turn raised questions about where power should reside and toward what end. Political organizations formed to reconcile these competing demands and concerns. And thus emerged politics.

Organizations could settle or prevent disputes between individuals, generating early notions of law and justice. Political organizations could also punish those found guilty of breaking rules and raise a military force capable of resisting invaders. These roles of punishing and defending paved the way for a monopoly of force. To carry out these activities, though, political organizations required revenue, creating the need for taxation. Clearly, then, many of the elements of modern politics emerged in the distant past, over and over again around the world.

One thing that remains unclear, however, is whether these political organizations emerged through consensus or through force. In other words, did political systems develop because some people managed to impose their will on others, installing themselves as chiefs or kings and using violence to impose their will? Or did people willingly form political systems as a way to overcome the anarchy that would otherwise result in a world that lacked central authority? In the absence of evidence, philosophers have long debated this issue. The philosopher Thomas Hobbes believed that human beings voluntarily enter into a "social contract" or agreement among themselves to create a single political authority to overcome anarchy. In return for giving up many of their rights, people were ensured security and a foundation on which to build a civilization. Jean-Jacques Rousseau, while also accepting the idea of the social contract, emphasized that this contract exists not between people but between ruler and ruled. Those in power are charged with providing security and liberty, and if they fail to do so, the people have the right to dissolve the social contract. Rousseau argued that political systems do not live up to their intention to serve society as a whole, since once established, they inevitably generate inequality between the ruling elite and the masses. Karl Marx went even further, rejecting the very notion of a social contract. Instead, he viewed political organization solely as a tool of exploitation, a system by which those who gain economic power can maintain their spoils by oppressing those they have taken it from. In his view, if human beings were allowed to create a truly equal society, there would be no need for political organization or even politics.

As we shall see in later chapters, those who believe in the institutions of modern democracy reflect the view of politics as a consensus, with people willingly surrendering some of their power in order to gain greater security and prosperity. However, they also assert that politics must serve the wishes of the public; when it does not, the public has the right to replace those in power. In contrast, others emphasize the coercive nature of politics and doubt that the domineering state and the unequal relations it creates can be wholly or truly democratic. All politics reflects this tension between coercion and consensus. Each state balances the two differently, reflecting the tension between freedom and equality.

Through a mixture of coercion and consensus, complex organizations began to emerge over 8,000 years ago in the Middle East, bearing the political hallmarks of politics that exist to this day, such as taxation, bureaucracy, laws, military force, and leadership. Some of these political units were relatively small, such as the city-states that emerged in ancient Greece some 2,700

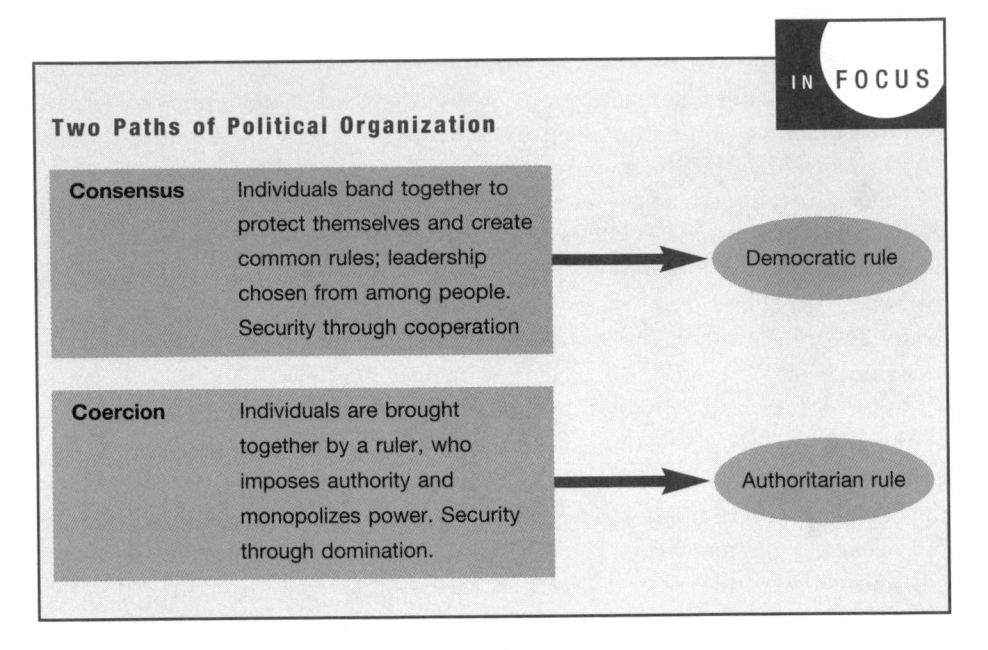

IN FOCUS

Two Paths of Political Organization

| Consensus | Individuals band together to protect themselves and create common rules; leadership chosen from among people. Security through cooperation | → | Democratic rule |

| Coercion | Individuals are brought together by a ruler, who imposes authority and monopolizes power. Security through domination. | → | Authoritarian rule |

years ago. In other cases, large and highly sophisticated empires emerged, as in China, South America, the Middle East, and Africa. Across these political systems, economic relations were based on agricultural production, with more specialized goods and trade as secondary activities. And unlike in modern countries, the borders of these early political systems were often undefined or unclear. Beyond their authority, large portions of the inhabited world possessed no form of complex political organization that would resemble a modern state.[4]

The Rise of the Modern State

This diversity of political systems would eventually give way to the modern state, which would first arrive in Europe. Why the modern state first emerged in Europe and came to dominate the world is uncertain, but it may in part be due to historical chance and the curious advantage of backwardness. Two thousand years ago, Europe, like other parts of the world, was dominated by a single large empire—in this case, the Roman Empire. Spanning thousands of miles across western Europe to North Africa and Egypt, the Roman Empire developed a highly complex political system that tied together millions of people and generated an advanced infrastructure of cities, laws, trade, knowledge, and roads. After a thousand years, however, the Roman Empire eventually declined, succumbing to the pressures of overexpansion and increased attacks by rival forces. By the fifth century C.E., Rome itself was sacked by invaders.

As the Roman Empire collapsed, the complex political institutions and the other benefits that had extended across its territory largely disappeared, particularly in western Europe (Figure 2.2). The security generated by imperial control evaporated, replaced by roving bands of marauders. Roads and the other basic forms of infrastructure that people depended on eroded. Rules and regulations fragmented and lost their power. The knowledge and technology accumulated under the empire was lost or forgotten, and the advanced system of trade and travel between communities came to an end. Much of western Europe reverted to anarchy, entering the period commonly known as the Dark Ages, from about 500 C.E. to about 1000 C.E. Europe's rise to power was thus not preordained; as China, the Middle East, and South America each experienced a period of growth and innovation, Europe experienced decline and decay.

Yet paradoxically, this period of dramatic decline and anarchy appears to have set the stage for the creation of the modern state. As the sociologist Charles

Figure 2.2 EUROPE IN THE TWELFTH CENTURY

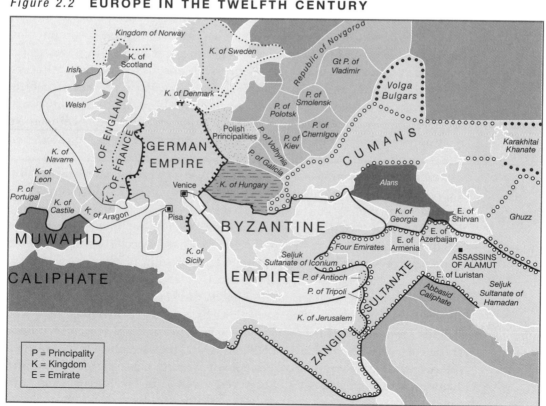

Tilly has noted, in Europe's highly fragmented, unstable, and violent environment, new political organizations began to develop, in constant competition with their rivals.[5] In some cases, these were simply marauders who realized that they could earn a better living by controlling and taxing one group of people rather than by constantly pillaging from place to place. Warlords staked out relatively small areas of land that they could easily defend and consolidated control over these regions, fighting off rival groups. In other cases, the people appear to have banded together themselves to fight off bandit groups. As Tilly and others have concluded, the modern state emerged from or in reaction to what was essentially organized crime, with armed groups staking out turf, offering protection, and demanding payment in return.

The constant warfare among these numerous rivals seems to have generated a kind of rapid organizational evolution. Groups that could quickly adapt survived, while less successful groups were conquered and disappeared. Rapid development was thus encouraged by a highly competitive and fluid environment.

Not only history but also geography has played a role in the rise of the modern state. Physiologist Jared Diamond has argued that Europe's close proximity to Asia and the Middle East provided benefits in the form of new plants, animals, and technical innovations that were unavailable to peoples in the Americas or Africa. At the same time, Europe's diverse geography hindered political centralization under a single language or culture.[6] Even at the height of the Roman Empire, much of central, northern, and eastern Europe had lain beyond the Romans' reach. Contrast this with China, where political power was centralized and institutionalized already by the third century C.E. Because China was more politically stable and lacked the kind of competitive environment seen in Europe, over time its institutions grew inflexible and resistant to political, economic, or technological change.

Out of the constant warfare of the Dark Ages emerged a new form of political organization—the state—that possessed three important advantages over alternate forms. First, states encouraged economic development. Before and during the Dark Ages, most Europeans lived under an economic system based on subsistence agriculture. Property such as land tended to be monopolized by those in power rather than by those who worked it. Warlords could tie the people to the land (serfdom) and extract their labor and levy heavy taxes on those who produced nonagricultural goods. However, such economic conditions were counterproductive for society as a whole: individuals had little incentive to produce if the fruits of their labor were simply taken by others. Those rulers who created laws, regulations, and infrastructure that permitted and respected private property and individual profit, however, found that production grew, giving the ruler more resources to tax or borrow (and with which to make war).[7]

A second advantage emerged when some rulers similarly encouraged technological innovation as a means of increasing their own economic and military
power. As with private commerce and trade, rulers realized that new technologies would also stimulate economic development by providing new goods
and services. When technological innovation was harnessed to commerce, economic development expanded dramatically. Technological change was thus
viewed by some rulers not as a threat to their power but as a means to expand
it. Many of the advantages that made Europe powerful as it set off to conquer the world—gunpowder, advanced mathematics, modern mapmaking,
paper, astronomy—had actually originated in other parts of the world. But
the Europeans absorbed these innovations and put them to new use. What
mattered most was not who had discovered these things, but rather how these
discoveries were encouraged or used by the state and society. Whether this
application of innovation was primarily a function of intense European competition or certain unique cultural values among Europeans is still a source
of intense and bitter debate (see Chapter 3).[8] Whatever the reason, technological innovation, combined with the state's willingness to tolerate or encourage private enterprise, set the stage for modern capitalism—a system of private
property, free markets, and investment in the pursuit of wealth.

A third advantage came about through the creation of domestic stability,
increased trade and commerce, and the development of infrastructure,
whereby the state assisted in the homogenization of peoples who were originally quite different from one another. The fact that people could travel more
freely within the territory of their state encouraged interaction and the development of a shared culture. The state, through printed documents, education,
and legal codes, also contributed to the standardization of language. People
in Europe began to see themselves as belonging to a common ethnic identity
that comprised shared cultural values. Instead of identifying primarily with
their trade, clan, religion, or town, people began to see themselves as English
or French or German. Ethnicity would prove to be a powerful asset to the
state, for it in turn fostered nationalism—a shared political identity. (We will
discuss these concepts in detail in Chapter 3.)

Although the modern state offered all these advantages, by around 1500,
states covered only 20 percent of the globe. But this was soon to change. Well
organized and armed with technological advances, national identity, and economic resources, the states of Europe began to rapidly accrue power. As economic power grew, so did the ability of the state to manage ever greater
numbers of people and ever more territory. Increased finances and state organization also allowed for the development of major militaries. Possessing the
ability to conquer and control larger pieces of land, states began to defeat and
absorb their European rivals. Spiritual rivals also fell by the wayside. The
Thirty Years' War (1618–1648), in part a struggle between Roman Catholi-

cism and Protestantism, culminated in the Treaty of Westphalia in 1648. Under this treaty, the authority of the pope over Europe's people was radically curtailed. Without this rival spiritual authority, states were free to direct religion within their own territory, subordinating the spiritual to the political. State sovereignty as we understand it today is often dated from the Treaty of Westphalia.

At this same time, European states began to expand their economic, technical, and military powers beyond their own shores. During the seventeenth and eighteenth centuries, Spain and Portugal took control of large parts of

TIME LINE / POLITICAL ORGANIZATION IN EUROPE	
10th–9th centuries B.C.E.	Greek dark ages
8th–7th centuries B.C.E.	Beginning of Greek city-states; centralization of political power in Europe
6th–5th centuries B.C.E.	Establishment of Roman republic; first development of democracy in Athens
2nd–1st centuries B.C.E.	Roman conquest of Greece
1st–2nd centuries C.E.	Roman Empire expands across Europe and into the Middle East; zenith of centralized imperial power in Europe
3rd–4th centuries C.E.	Internal decline of Roman Empire; beginning of European Dark Ages; development stagnates
5th–6th centuries C.E.	Rome sacked by the Visigoths; widespread strife among competing European warlords
7th–8th centuries C.E.	Muslim armies enter Spain; Islamic world grows in power during a period of innovation and expansion
9th–10th centuries C.E.	Viking raids across Europe
11th–12th centuries C.E.	European crusades into Middle East; warfare begins to consolidate Europe into distinct political units
12th–13th centuries C.E.	Period of rapid innovation and development: mechanical clock invented; paper, compass adopted from Asia and the Middle East
14th–15th centuries C.E.	Voyages of exploration and early imperialism; early European states centralize; Islamic world stagnates
16th–17th centuries C.E.	Scientific revolution; modern states develop; modern identities of nationalism and patriotism develop

the Americas, while the Dutch, French, and British expanded state power into Asia. By the nineteenth century, nearly all of Africa had similarly been divided up among European states and incorporated into their respective empires.

The organizational structure of the state was thus imposed around the world by force. Yet as European control receded in the twentieth century, the structure of the state remained—indeed, states grew in number as these lands and peoples gained sovereignty. Although peoples all around the world resisted and eventually threw off European domination, they viewed the state as a superior—or at least inevitable—form of political evolution, and they adopted it for their own purposes. The world thus became a world of states. States set forth international boundaries and established international rules and were the primary actors in domestic and international politics around the world. Countries like India or Nigeria might throw off colonial rule, but they retained and expanded the state structures originally imposed by imperialism.

The rapid spread of states may be viewed as the triumph of a form of organization that was able to destroy other political rivals, no matter how sophisticated. But this has not come without a cost. Whereas Europe took several hundred years to create the modern state, much of the world has been forced to take up this form of organization more quickly, adopting an alien institution out of necessity or force. Yet the historical paths of Africa, Asia, and South America were radically different from those of Europe. Many of these new states have lacked the resources and organization that much older states developed over centuries and have faced the challenge of establishing sovereignty over a territory where a multitude of peoples, languages, religions, and cultures may coexist—problems that most European states solved only over the course of centuries and at the cost of many wars, revolutions, and lives. For better or worse, although Europe no longer directly rules over much of the earth, it has left us with the legacy of the state itself.

Comparing State Power

It is clear from the preceding discussion that political evolution has been a lengthy and somewhat arbitrary process. Where conditions allowed for human beings to settle permanently, complex forms of political organization quickly formed, with features that reflect basic aspects of modern politics: freedom, equality, and the allocation of power. But only over the past few centuries has the modern state taken shape, forging new political, economic, and social institutions that have made it so powerful. States quickly eradicated all other forms of political organization and laid claim to all corners of the earth.

Still, not all states are the same. As we already alluded to, some states are powerful, effective, prosperous, and stable; others are weak, disorganized, and largely incapable of effective action. Moreover, a single state can have a commanding presence in one area but appear ineffectual in another. What explains this range of state authority and power? To answer this question and make effective comparisons, we need a few more conceptual tools with which to work.

Legitimacy

The first concept to address is that of **legitimacy**, which can be defined as a value whereby something or someone is recognized and accepted as right and proper. In other words, a legitimate institution or person is widely accepted and recognized by the public. Legitimacy confers authority and power. In the case of states, we know that they wield a great deal of coercive force. But is that the only reason that people recognize their authority? In fact, many people obey the law even when the threat of punishment is slight. Why? They view such behavior as "the right thing" to do. We pay our taxes, stand at the crosswalk, or serve in the military not simply because of fear of punishment or a personal benefit, but because we assume that the state has the authority to ask these things of us. Legitimacy thus creates power that relies not on coercion, but on consent. Without legitimacy, a state would have to use the continuous threat of force to maintain order—a difficult task.

How does a state become legitimate? Let us turn again to Max Weber, who argued that political legitimacy comes in three basic forms: traditional, charismatic, and rational-legal.[9] **Traditional legitimacy** rests on the idea that someone or something is valid because "it has always been that way." In other words, this legitimacy is built on the idea that certain aspects of politics are to be accepted because they have been accepted over a long period of time. In some way, they are seen as inseparable from the identity of the people themselves. Traditional legitimacy often embodies historical myths and legends, as well as the continuity between past and present. Rituals and ceremonies all help to reinforce traditional legitimacy by providing actions and symbols that are ancient, unique, and dramatic. One good example is the legitimacy accorded to a monarchy. What makes a monarch a monarch? Typically, a king or queen is not voted into office, but instead is a member of the monarchy by virtue of his or her birth. The kings of both Jordan and Morocco are considered direct descendants of the prophet Muhammad, who established Islam in the seventh century C.E. They therefore enjoy a legitimacy that stems not just from political continuity, but from religion as well.

In short, traditional legitimacy is a system built on history and continuity. The longer a traditional political system has been in place, the more institutionalized it becomes, as it has the weight of history on its side. Change becomes difficult to imagine if an institution has existed "since time immemorial."

Charismatic legitimacy is in many ways the very opposite of traditional legitimacy. When we use the word *charisma* in everyday conversation, we usually are describing someone who is good-looking or perhaps a witty conversationalist. But in politics, charisma means much more. Rather than relying on the weight of history and the continuity of certain roles or values, charismatic legitimacy is based on the power of ideas, or what is sometimes called "the gift of grace." Charisma is typically embodied by one individual, who can move the public through these ideas and the manner in which she or he presents them. Some individuals possess a certain magnetism that binds who they are to what they say. Jesus and Muhammad are perfect examples of charismatic figures who could gather huge followings through the power of their ideas. In a more modern and more sinister example, Adolf Hitler can also be viewed as a charismatic figure. If we look at pictures of Hitler today, we might think it strange that this unattractive man could so dominate a country and plunge Europe into genocide and war. Yet it is not physical appearance, but rather the force of ideas and power with language, that makes charisma possible.

As you can imagine, charismatic legitimacy is not institutionalized and thus is fairly tenuous, since it commonly dies with the individual who possesses it. But charismatic legitimacy often gets transformed into traditional legitimacy with the creation of rituals and values that are meant to capture the spirit and intent of the charismatic leader's power. Religions and monarchies are good examples of this process. Weber called this kind of institutionalization "the routinization of charisma."

In contrast to the first two forms of legitimacy, **rational-legal legitimacy** is based not on history or rituals (as in the case of traditional legitimacy) or on the force of ideas (as in charismatic legitimacy), but rather on a system of laws and procedures that are highly institutionalized. Leaders or political officials can be legitimate by virtue of the rules by which they came to office. Moreover, people abide by the decisions of these actors because they believe that the rules the leaders enforce serve the public's interest. In this case, it is not the person who is important or even that individual's particular values or ideas, but the title and office that he or she holds. The office is legitimate, rather than the person in it. Once that person leaves office, he or she loses authority.

As you have probably already guessed, the world of modern states is built on a rational-legal foundation. States rely on bureaucracies, paperwork, and thousands of individuals to make daily decisions on a wide range of issues. Ideally, the public accepts these decisions as the proper way to get things done, and they presume that these decisions are reasonably fair and predictable. For example, if there are elections, they accept the outcome even if their preferred candidate loses, and they obey those who won. The 2000 pres-

IN **FOCUS**

Three Types of Legitimacy

Type	Characteristics	Example
Traditional legitimacy	Built by habit and custom over time, stressing history; strongly institutionalized	Monarch (Queen Elizabeth)
Charismatic legitimacy	Built on the force of ideas and the presence of the leader; weakly institutionalized	Revolutionary hero (Vladimir Lenin)
Rational-legal legitimacy	Built on rules and procedures and the offices that create and enforce those rules; strongly institutionalized	Elected executive (George Bush)

idential election in the United States is a perfect example of rational-legal legitimacy. After weeks of bitter disputes over who had actually won the election, the Supreme Court's intervention effectively ended the battle, and the Democratic candidate, Al Gore, agreed to abide by the outcome. In spite of denunciations by some that the election was illegitimate, the majority of Americans accepted George W. Bush as their president, even if they had not voted for him (and the majority of voters had not). What's more, legitimacy is not confined to political actors within the state; our own individual legitimacy comes from a rational-legal foundation: our driver's license, identification numbers, passports, or voter registration cards all confer a certain form of authority and power.

Note, however, that just because the rise of modern states was built on a rational-legal legitimacy, that doesn't mean that traditional or charismatic legitimacy has disappeared. In almost any country, all three forms of legitimacy can be found to varying degrees. Political leaders in many countries throughout modern history have wielded a great deal of charismatic power and become the centers of large "cults of personality," which we will explore further in Chapter 5. These cults portray the leader as the father (or, occasionally, the mother) of the nation and imbue him or her with almost superhuman powers. Charismatic leadership, and the power that it places in the hands of one individual, can corrupt, but some charismatic figures have dramatically changed the course of politics for the better—Mohandas K. Gandhi, in India, or Nelson Mandela, in South Africa, for instance.

Traditional power can similarly be found in a wide variety of circumstances. The United Kingdom, Japan, Sweden, and more than thirty other countries still have monarchs. Although the powers of most of these monarchs are now quite limited, they remain important symbols and attract national and sometimes even international attention. (Think of the international obsession with the British royal family). Even rules and regulations can eventually take on a kind of traditional legitimacy if they function for so long that people can't imagine doing things any other way. The U.S. Constitution, for example, is not only a set of rules for conducting politics; it is also considered a sacred symbol of what makes the United States unique and powerful. Is the difficulty in modifying the U.S. Constitution due to the procedures involved, or has there developed over time a resistance to tinkering with this "sacred" document? If the latter is true, then it is not simply rational-legal legitimacy but also traditional legitimacy that binds American politics together.

To summarize, all states seek authority and power through some form of legitimacy. Traditional legitimacy stresses ritual and continuity; charismatic legitimacy, the force of ideas as embodied in a leader; rational-legal legitimacy, laws and rules. Whatever the form or mixture, legitimacy makes it possible for the state to carry out its basic functions. Without it, a state will find carrying out these tasks very difficult. The public, having little faith in the state, will frequently ignore political responsibilities, such as paying taxes, abiding by regulations, or serving in the armed forces. Under these conditions, the state has really only one tool left to maintain order: the threat of force. Paradoxically, then, states that use the most coercion against their citizens are often the most weakly institutionalized states, for without violence, they cannot get the public to willingly comply with the rules and duties set forth.

Centralization or Decentralization

In addition to varying in the kind and level of political legitimacy they enjoy, states also vary in their distribution of power. As we noted in Chapter 1, Individual freedom is typically associated with the decentralization of power, whereas collective equality is typically associated with a greater centralization of power.

State power can be centralized or decentralized in a couple of different ways, the first of which is the dispersal of power within the state itself. Under **federalism**, significant powers, such as taxation, lawmaking, and security, are devolved to regional bodies (such as states in the United States, *Länder* in Germany, or provinces in Canada) that control specific territory within the country. These powers are defined within the national constitution and therefore are not easily constricted or eliminated by any government. Here the argument is that federalism helps represent local interests as well as check the growth of central power (which is viewed as a threat to democracy). In contrast, **unitary states** invest most political power at the national level, with limited local authority. The central government is responsible for most areas of policy. Territorial divisions within unitary states (such as Japan or France) are less important in terms of political power. The perceived advantage of a unitary state is predicated on the belief that local interests can be represented without recourse to regional bodies and that federalism tends to weaken state efficiency by dispersing power among many local authorities.

Another way in which power may be dispersed is between the state and nonstate actors, such as the public or organized rivals. In this regard, political scientists often make a distinction between **strong states** and **weak states**. Strong states are those that are able to fulfill basic tasks: defending their territory, making and enforcing rules, collecting taxes, and managing the economy, to name some of the more important responsibilities. In contrast, weak states cannot execute such tasks very well. Rules are haphazardly applied, if at all; tax evasion and other forms of public noncompliance are widespread; armed rivals to the state, such as rebel movements or organized crime, may control large chunks of territory or of the economy. State officials themselves, having little faith in their office or responsibilities, may use their jobs simply to fill their own pockets through corruption and theft. In turn, economic development is certain to be much lower as a result of this unstable political environment. In general, a weak state is not well institutionalized and lacks authority and legitimacy. At an extreme, the very structures of the state may become so weak that they collapse, resulting in a complete loss of power; anarchy and violence erupt as order breaks down. This situation has been seen a number of times in the last decade; such states are commonly referred to as **failed states**.[10] Afghanistan prior to 2001 was commonly viewed as a failed state, with no real sovereign authority, even in the hands of the Taliban; and Nigeria, with its economic stagnation and regional rebellions, runs the risk of a similar collapse.

However, speaking of states as merely weak or strong fails to capture the complexity of state power, which can often be strong in one area and weak in another. As a result, comparative politics further builds on the categories of weak and strong states through the use of two other terms: capacity and autonomy. **Capacity** is the ability of the state to wield power in order to carry out the basic tasks of providing security and reconciling freedom and equality. A state with high capacity is able to formulate and enact fundamental policies and ensure stability and security for both itself and its citizens. A state with low capacity is unable to do these things very effectively. High capacity requires not just money, but also organization, legitimacy, and effective leadership. Roads get paved, schools get built, regulations are created and followed, and those who break the law are punished.

In contrast, **autonomy** is the ability of the state to wield its power independently of the public. In other words, if an autonomous state wishes to carry out a policy or action, it can do so without having to consult the public or worry about strong public opposition that might force it to reverse its decision. A state with a high degree of autonomy may act on behalf of the public, pursuing what it believes are the best interests of the country, irrespective of public opinion. A state with a low degree of autonomy will act largely at the behest of private individuals or groups and will be less able to disobey the public will or the demands of well-organized groups.

Each of these concepts helps us to evaluate different states in terms of power. Strong states with a high degree of capacity and autonomy may be able to execute major policies relatively easily. China's current construction of the Three Gorges Dam, the world's largest such project, despite the technical challenges, enormous cost, and widespread international criticism for its possible environmental impact, is a case in point. But too much power centralized within the state can come at the expense of democracy, as has certainly been the case in China, where little dissent is tolerated. States with a high degree of capacity but low autonomy may have similar powers, but they are subject to greater public control. The United States is a good example of such a system, which is further reinforced by its federal structure. Individual freedom in the United States may be high, but it can sometimes fetter the state and hinder change as policy becomes captive to special interests. States with high autonomy but low capacity may lack the ability to execute policy. North Korea is a tragic example in this regard, an authoritarian communist country that over the past decade has become incapable of feeding its own people. Finally, states may lack both autonomy and capacity. This is true of many less-developed countries, such as in Africa, where states have been "captured" by dominant elites or groups and are largely unable to fulfill some of the most important national tasks, such as encouraging economic development or ensuring public education. At an extreme, too little capacity and too little autonomy can bring down the state entirely, as occurred in Afghanistan, paving the way for groups like Al Qaeda to function with impunity.

In short, speaking of state power in terms of autonomy and capacity can help us better understand what states are and are not able to do, and why. However, even when we speak of autonomy and capacity, we should note that

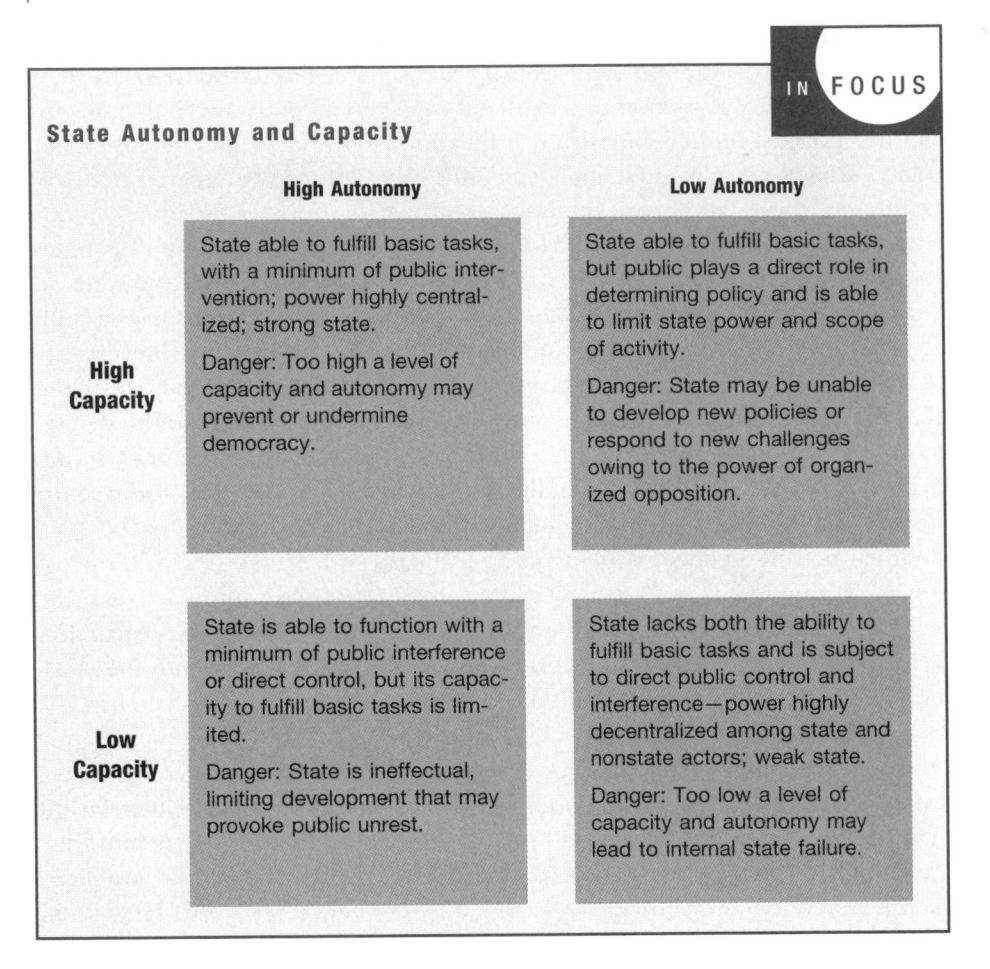

State Autonomy and Capacity

	High Autonomy	**Low Autonomy**
High Capacity	State able to fulfill basic tasks, with a minimum of public intervention; power highly centralized; strong state. Danger: Too high a level of capacity and autonomy may prevent or undermine democracy.	State able to fulfill basic tasks, but public plays a direct role in determining policy and is able to limit state power and scope of activity. Danger: State may be unable to develop new policies or respond to new challenges owing to the power of organized opposition.
Low Capacity	State is able to function with a minimum of public interference or direct control, but its capacity to fulfill basic tasks is limited. Danger: State is ineffectual, limiting development that may provoke public unrest.	State lacks both the ability to fulfill basic tasks and is subject to direct public control and interference—power highly decentralized among state and nonstate actors; weak state. Danger: Too low a level of capacity and autonomy may lead to internal state failure.

even here states may vary widely, depending on the issue or area at hand. One observer of China may conclude from their rapid economic development or ability to censor the Internet that this state enjoys high autonomy and capacity. However, China's high degree of corruption, proliferation of new (and often banned) religions, and widespread disregard of central regulations at the local level are not indicators of a strong state. North Korea, too, may have trouble feeding its people, but it can construct nuclear weapons and thus shape international relations—no small feat. Autonomy and capacity are useful concepts for comparing states, but there are many issues where these definitions do not fit perfectly. State strength is not uniform, but depends in part on the task or challenge at hand.

In Sum: Studying States

This chapter began by defining the state as a monopoly of force, but also as the institution charged with transforming freedom and equality from ideas into concrete action. The kinds of decisions made toward this end, however, are shaped by regimes and governments. Regimes are the fundamental rules and norms of politics, providing long-term goals regarding individual freedom and collective equality and the location and use of power toward those goals. Governments, in contrast, are those political elites in charge of running the state. Influenced and constrained by the existing regime, they attempt to formulate policy regarding freedom and equality that may then be executed by the state. These represent the most basic facets of states everywhere—and indeed, states are everywhere. Although similar political organizations have existed for thousands of years, only within the past few centuries did states arise in Europe and quickly come to dominate the globe. States are the main political players in the world today.

INSTITUTIONS IN ACTION

AUTONOMY, CAPACITY, AND THE CASE OF ARGENTINA

Why do some countries have higher degrees of autonomy and/or capacity than others? What leads to a strong versus a weak or even a failed state? There are no hard and fast rules, but answers lie in the way political institutions are constructed over time. A look at the case of Argentina is instructive in this regard. Argentina is an interesting puzzle for political scientists. At the beginning of the twentieth century, it was one of the wealthier countries in the world. However, over the subsequent decades, the country both declined economically and became politically unstable, eventually succumbing to authoritarian rule. In spite of a recent return to democracy, the country remains plagued by political conflict and economic difficulties. Why? A century ago, Argentinean political elites clashed over the degree of political centralization the state should enjoy. Regional political bosses or strongmen, known as *caudillos,* favored a highly decentralized system to preserve their local power and privileges. National elites favored a greater centralization under a unitary state. The resulting compromise led to a federal system with a great deal of power in the hands of the caudillos to limit state autonomy and capacity in favor of local caudillos. This arrangement contributed to a political system with weak national political parties, state inefficiency and corruption, and eventually authoritarian rule. Though democracy has returned to Argentina, the state's ability to carry out the fundamental tasks expected of it remains limited.

The universal presence of states compels comparativists to find some way to study and evaluate them. One way is by assessing their legitimacy; different kinds of legitimacy—traditional, charismatic, and rational-legal—all create their own kinds of authority and power. The other is by assessing the actual dispersal of power itself; states may be weaker or stronger, with more or less capacity and autonomy, depending on how power is distributed within the state and between the state and the public. Too much power in the hands of the state risks tyranny; too little power risks anarchy. Finding the right mix is not simply a technical question, but one shaped by a people's views regarding freedom and equality. This debate over freedom and equality, then, ranges far beyond the boundaries of the state itself. As we shall see in the chapters that follow, it is influenced by society, through ethnic and national identity, culture, and ideology; by economic institutions and the interaction between states and markets; and by democratic practices and authoritarian ones.

Since the dawn of human civilization, people have relied on some form of political organization to construct a relationship between individual freedom and collective equality. In fact, this is the very hallmark of civilization itself. For the past few centuries, modern states have been that form of organization. Do states now represent an end point in human intellectual evolution, or at some point in the future will new forms of political organization displace states, just as states displaced empires, city-states, and other institutions? Will civilization at some point reconcile or transcend current notions of freedom and equality, such that political organization—at least as we understand it now—will cease to exist? These questions may seem unanswerable, more amenable to fortune-telling than to research. But as we shall see, they lie at the heart of ideas and conflicts that have transformed the world in the past and will continue to confront us in the future.

NOTES

1. In the United States, the word *state* refers to the federal structure of regional government. As a result, for Americans, the word *state* conjures up the idea of local government, whereas for political scientists (and most people around the world), the word *state* refers to national, not local, organization. This confusion stems from U.S. history. During the period of revolutionary struggle and the creation of a federal system, the former British colonies in America viewed themselves as independent political units—in other words, as states. With the creation of a federal system of government, however, their individual powers were subordinated to central authority. The United States of America, in other words, eventually became a system of national government, with the term *state* left as a remnant of that brief period when they acted as largely independent entities.

2. Max Weber, "Politics as a Vocation," *Gesammelte Politische Schriften* (Muenchen, 1921):396–450.

3. This idea has been developed by Charles Tilly, "War Making and State Making as Organized Crime," in Peter Evans, Dietrich Rueschemeyer, and T. Skopol, eds., *Bringing the State Back In* (New York: Cambridge University Press, 1985), 169–191.

4. S. E. Finer, *The History of Government from the Earliest Times, vol. 1, Ancient Monarchies and Empires* (New York: Oxford University Press, 1999).

5. Charles Tilly, *Coercion, Capital, and European States: 990–1990* (Oxford, UK: Blackwell, 1990).

6. Jared Diamond, *Guns, Germs, and Steel: The Fates of Human Societies* (New York: Norton, 1997).

7. Mancur Olson, "Democracy, Dictatorship, and Development," *American Political Science Review* 87, no. 3 (September 1993): 567–576.

8. For the cultural explanation, see David Landes, *The Wealth and Poverty of Nations: Why Some Are So Rich and Some So Poor* (New York: Norton, 1999).

9. Max Weber, "Politics as a Vocation," in H. H. Gerth and C. Wright Mills, trans. and eds., *From Max Weber: Essays in Sociology* (New York: Oxford University Press, 1958), 77–128.

10. Robert I. Rotberg, ed. *When States Fail: Causes and Consequences* (Princeton, NJ: Princeton University Press, 2003).

3 NATIONS AND SOCIETY

Society is a broad term that refers to complex human organization, a collection of people bound by shared institutions that define how human relations should be conducted. From country to country and place to place, societies differ in how individuals define themselves and their relationship to one another as well as their relationship to government and the state. These relationships are unique; for all the surface similarities that may exist between societies, each country views itself and the wider world around it in a distinct way. These differences make comparative politics a rich field of study, but also a frustrating one, as social scientists seek to find similarities that are often few and far between.

In this chapter, we will look at the ways in which people identify themselves and are identified, both as individuals and as groups, and how these identifications relate to politics and the state. Human beings are often defined by such basic identities as "left" or "right," "us" or "them." These identities shape politics and influence the debate over freedom and equality by generating diversity, cooperation, and conflict. How these identities differ from place to place has profound implications for comparative politics.

We will start with the concepts of ethnic and national identity, two of the most basic ways in which individuals and groups define themselves politically. What does it mean to be part of an ethnic group? How is such a group defined? What is the difference between an ethnic group and a nation? We will also make a distinction between ethnicity, nationality, and citizenship. What does it mean, for example, to say that someone is a "Chinese citizen" as opposed to saying that the person is "ethnically Chinese" or just "Chinese"? A related question arises in the distinction between nationalism and patriotism: What is the difference between being patriotic and being nationalistic? We will answer these questions by looking at some examples of each and tracing their historical origins. Throughout recent history, the world has witnessed violent domestic and international conflicts connected to national and ethnic identities. Why do such conflicts occur? Are they a natural and inevitable part of human organization, or are such conflicts manufactured by political leaders to serve their own purposes? In this chapter, we will also look at some of the effects of these different identities when they conflict with one another.

From there we will move on to a discussion of political attitudes and ideologies. Whereas ethnicity, nationality, and citizenship are group identities, political attitudes and ideologies are the values and positions that individuals take with regard to freedom and equality. To what extent can each of these "goods" be achieved through politics? What compromises must be made? And how fast should change be enacted to achieve the proper balance? Ideologies attempt to answer these vital questions. One thing we will see is that although basic political attitudes and ideologies can be compared around the world, their relative strength or influence differs dramatically from country to country. What is considered conservative in one place may be radical in another. One possible explanation for this difference may be cultural. Politics may be more than a free-wheeling contest between different values; it may be fundamentally shaped by how each society views and defines itself. We should note that these identities are not a fixed part of our nature. Most social scientists agree that these identities are all "socially constructed," generated in the minds of women and men, not biological or genetic constructs. This does not make them any less powerful, however.

Ethnic Identity

People identify themselves in many ways. One way that we identify individuals in society is by their ethnicity, as when we speak of people as German or Irish, Kurdish or Zulu, Latino or Ukrainian Canadian. When we use the term *ethnic identity* or *ethnicity*, we emphasize a person's relationship to other members of society. **Ethnicity** refers to specific attributes and societal institutions that make one group of people culturally different from others. These attributes can include language, religion, geographical location, customs, and history, among other things. As these distinct attributes are institutionalized, they provide a people with a particular identity that is passed down over time from generation to generation. This process is called "ascription"—the assigning of a particular quality at birth. People do not choose their ethnicities; they are born into them, and their ethnic identity remains largely fixed throughout life.

These differences are not mere curiosities, but vital components of how people view themselves and their relationship to the wider world. Each ethnic group is characterized by its own set of institutions that embody norms and standards of behavior, and a single society can be broken up into numerous ethnic groups. For example, Singaporean society is made up of ethnic

Chinese, Malays, and Indians. In the United States, there are also numerous ethnic groups, such as African Americans, Japanese Americans, and Native Americans, who further classify themselves as Hopi or Makah, for instance. In both Singapore and the United States, there exists a broader society, made up of many different ethnic groups. In fact, the majority of countries in the world are not ethnically homogeneous; in this world of immigration and globalization, rarely are society and ethnicity one and the same. Societies are made up of various ethnic groups, in some cases only a few, in other cases tens or even hundreds, each with its own particular identity. It is important to note that ethnicity is at its core a social, not a political, identity; people may identify themselves with an ethnic group without drawing any particular conclusions about politics on that basis. Ethnicity in itself is not inherently political, though it can become so.

Although we have listed a number of common attributes that often define ethnic differences, it is important to stress that there is no "master list" of differences that automatically defines one group as ethnically different from another. In Bosnia, for example, the main ethnic groups—Croats, Serbs, and Muslims—speak the same language and are similar in numerous other ways. What divides Bosnians is primarily religion: Croats are mostly Roman Catholic, Serbs are Eastern Orthodox, and Muslims practice Islam. Yet we speak of Germans as a single ethnic group, even though some are Catholic and some are Protestant. Why are ethnic groups in Bosnia divided by religion, while in Germany such divisions don't produce different ethnic groups? In an even more confusing case, that of Rwanda (where some of the most horrific ethnic killing since World War II took place in 1994), the Hutu and Tutsi ethnic groups cannot be easily distinguished by any of the factors we have listed. Both speak the same language, practice the same religions, live in the same geographical regions, and share the same customs. For most outside observers, there is no real ethnic difference between the two, and even Hutus and Tutsis cannot easily distinguish between one another; they rely on such vague distinctions as height, facial features, and diet, and often these are wrong or misleading.

Ethnicity, then, is a good example of what we referred to earlier as a social construction, built not out of a uniform or fixed set of factors but in each case a unique combination of attributes. Ethnicity exists where people acknowledge and are

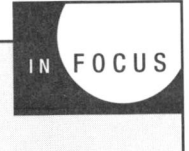

Ethnic Identity Is . . .

- Specific attributes and societal institutions that make one group of people culturally different from others.
- Often based on customs, language, religion, or other factors.
- Ascriptive, generally assigned at birth.
- Not inherently political.

acknowledged by outsiders as belonging to a distinct group. Even though such distinctions may be difficult to observe, these ascriptive identities exist.

National Identity

In contrast to ethnicity, which may be constructed in a unique manner from group to group and is not an inherently political concept, the idea of a nation or national identity is much more consistent across various cases. It is also a much more inherently political concept. Rather than being connected through social institutions, **national identity** can be defined as an institution that binds people together through a common set of political aspirations, among which the most important is self-government. National identity is a sense of belonging to a **nation**. Returning again to the concepts of freedom and equality, national identity often implies a demand for greater freedom through sovereignty, as in a colony's revolt against its colonial master. National identity may also involve issues of equality. For example, it may stem from the belief that one's own group is subject to unequal treatment at the hands of others and that this situation can be solved by creating or gaining control over political institutions to better serve one's own group. Pakistan's secession from India in 1947 for the creation of an independent Muslim state can be seen in this light.

As you might suspect, national identity often—but not always—develops from ethnic identity. For example, an ethnic group may chafe against the political system under which it lives; its members may feel that they lack certain rights or freedoms. Often this dissatisfaction arises because the ethnic group represents a minority within the current political system. As a result, some leaders may argue that the ethnic group should have greater political control and that the group's own interests would be better served if it controlled its own political destiny. Self-government can transform a minority into a majority in a new country and give a group the control it desires.

The interaction between ethnicity and national identity can be seen in recent developments in Canada. There, the French-speaking population of the province of Québec constitutes its own ethnic group, quite distinct from the English-speaking citizens of the rest of Canada (as well as from their own French ancestors). By the 1960s, this ethnicity began to develop into a sense of national identity, as some in Québec argued for separation from Canada, where they saw themselves as a minority whose unique concerns were not taken into consideration. Such arguments actually led to national referenda on the issue of secession in 1980 and 1995. In the latter case, the proposal that Québec secede failed by little more than 1 percent of the vote. Thus, ethnic identity has also fostered a national identity among many—although

IN FOCUS

National Identity Is . . .

- Based on the concept of a *nation*: a group of people bound together by a common set of political aspirations, especially self-government and sovereignty.
- Often (but not always) derived from ethnic identity.
- Inherently political.
- The basis for *nationalism*: pride in one's people and belief that they have a unique political destiny.

not all—Québecois. A similar process can be seen at work among Palestinians, most of whom seek the creation of an independent Palestinian state out of those territories controlled by Israel.

National identity can thus create **nationalism**, a pride in one's people and the belief that they have their own sovereign political destiny that is separate from those of others. In Québec, for example, we find a people uncertain of whether they are just an ethnic group or also a nation—a group that desires self-government through an independent state. This lack of clarity between ethnicity and national identity is also evident in other groups, such as the Scots in the United Kingdom. Some, but not all, members of the ethnic group support the nationalist cause of independence. In other words, although ethnic identity often leads to a political identity built on nationalism, this is not always the case. A minority ethnic group may feel itself to be part of a larger nation, especially where such minorities have been given a great deal of local autonomy. Thus, while in Nigeria ethnic divisions and local identities are powerful, the over 70 percent of those surveyed say that they are very proud to be Nigerian. And what of Native Americans in the United States? If reservations were given the opportunity to secede and become independent states, would many choose to do so?

In short, ethnicity can lead to nationalism if a distinct group develops political aspirations as a way to assert or defend its own uniqueness. But ethnicity does not always lead to national identity. Groups may have a distinct ethnic identity without translating it into a national consciousness and demand for independence. This leads us to a new question: If we can have ethnicity without it leading to national identity, can we have national identity without ethnicity? In other words, must ethnicity always be the source of nationalism? This is hard to answer, and political scientists have not reached any consensus on this question. At first glance, it would seem logical that without ethnicity, there is no foundation for national identity; people would lack a common identity and set of institutions on which to build national pride and a desire for independence. But like ethnicity, nationality lacks a "master list" to define it. In the case of the United States, it is easy to conclude that there is no single American ethnic group. But is there an American nation? Some might say no, because nationalism is often assumed to require an ethnicity on which political aspirations can be built. Yet Americans are bound by certain common historical symbols, such as the flag, the Declaration of Independence, and the Statue of Liberty. One could thus argue that even in the face of great ethnic diversity, the United States is indeed a nation, bound together by a sense of pride in certain democratic and individualistic ideals and by belief in a unique political destiny. This is just as true of other countries of diverse ethnic origin, such as Canada and Australia. Just as some in Spain may consider themselves ethnically Basque and nationally Spanish, or some in the United Kingdom ethnically Scottish but nationally British, so, too, do many see themselves as black or Korean or Hispanic or Indian but also as American or Canadian. Thus, national identity can be constructed even when a common or dominant ethnic identity is absent.[1] Finally, we should emphasize that nationalism is not inherently bad, as is sometimes implied. Nationalism does not necessarily mean hatred of others, and national identity can serve as a powerful force for binding communities together and achieving major goals.

Citizenship and Patriotism

Our final form of identification is citizenship. So far, we have noted that ethnicity is not inherently political, although it may develop a political aspect through nationalism. At the other end of this spectrum, citizenship is a purely political identity, developed not out of some unique set of circumstances or ascripted by birth but rather developed explicitly by states and accepted or rejected by individuals. **Citizenship** can be defined as an individual's or a group's relationship to the state; those who are citizens swear allegiance to that state, and that state in return is obligated to provide rights to those individuals or the members of that group. In a democracy, citizenship includes the right to vote and other civil liberties, whereas in authoritarian systems, one's rights may include little more than the ability to reside in that country. Citizenship can also convey certain obligations, such as the duty to serve in the armed forces or pay taxes. Citizens are therefore defined by their particular relationship to one state rather than to one another. Although citizenship is often gained at birth, citizenship has qualities quite separate from those of ethnic or national identity. Birth is no guarantee of citizenship (a state may not necessarily grant citizenship to all those born on its territory), and individuals may in theory change their citizenship from one state to another, hold citizenship of more than one country, or even lose citizenship altogether—thus becoming what we call "stateless" persons.

Citizenship is thus a potentially more inclusive concept than is national identity or ethnicity, and its boundaries are rather clear—you are either a cit-

IN FOCUS

Citizenship Is . . .

- An individual's relationship to the state; the individual swears allegiance to the state, and the state in turn provides certain benefits or rights.
- Purely political and thus more easily changed than ethnic identity or national identity.
- The basis for *patriotism*: pride in one's state and citizenship.

izen or you are not. Some people change their citizenship when they move from one country to another, while others maintain the citizenship of their home country even if they spend decades living in another part of the world. But even with citizenship, ethnicity and nationality can play an important, often limiting role. In many countries, these three identities of ethnicity, nationality, and citizenship are strongly interconnected. As a result, citizenship is more restricted. In an extreme example, in the 1950s, South Africa's apartheid regime created internal "homelands" for blacks as a means of stripping them of their South African citizenship. Yet because citizenship is a purely political identity, it is much more open to redefinition and change than is ethnicity or national identity. A state may choose suddenly to grant citizenship to immigrants or to extend to all citizens rights that had formerly been restricted to a particular ethnic group.

Citizenship, in turn, can give rise to **patriotism**, or pride in one's state. People are patriotic when they have pride in their political system and seek to defend and promote it. When we think of patriotism, some of the things that may come to mind are our flag, important historical events, wars, anthems—all images that people associate with politics and the state. States that are weak or illegitimate often have difficulty instilling patriotism among their citizens, which makes tasks like defending the state in times of war very difficult. Being a citizen does not automatically make you patriotic. Again, as with nationalism, we should be careful about loading our terms with values, assuming, for example, that while nationalism is a bad form of community, patriotism is somehow good. Both values can bind people together for good or ill.

To sum up, ethnicity, nationality, and citizenship are identities that define groups in different ways and that carry different political implications. Ethnic identity is built on unique social attributes among people, such as language or culture, with no inherent political meaning, whereas national identity implies political aspirations, specifically the desire for self-government. Although an ethnic identity often leads to a national identity and nationalism, it does not always do so, nor does the absence of a single dominant ethnicity prevent nationalism from developing. Finally, citizenship is a purely political identity built on a relationship to the state. As should be clear, none of these identities is exclusive; all of us possess different combinations of ethnicity, national identity, and citizenship, with each contributing to how we see the world and our role within it.

Ethnic Identity, National Identity, and Citizenship: Origins and Persistence

Now that we have distinguished between these three identities, it is worth considering the origins of each: Where did they come from and why do they exist? Contrary to most people's assumptions, ethnic and national identities are relatively recent concepts that emerged in Europe toward the end of the eighteenth century. For example, in the Roman Empire, its people did not think of themselves as "Romans" in the way we might imagine today. Nor did those living in the Chinese Empire imagine themselves to be "Chinese." Citizenship, too, has relatively recent origins: although the concept can be traced back to ancient Athens and to the Roman Empire, this disappeared with the fall of Rome, only to resurface centuries later.

The emergence (or reemergence, in the case of citizenship) of these identities had much to do with the formation of the modern state.[2] As states took form in Europe in the fifteenth and sixteenth centuries, asserting sovereign control over people and territory, their subjects experienced increased interaction. People could travel greater distances within their own country's borders, enjoying the security provided by the state. This mobility in turn increased commerce, which was often centered around the city where the state leadership was based. These fortified capitals served as centers for trade, information, and new social relationships. Such interaction in turn fostered increased homogeneity. The variety of different languages and dialects that existed within countries began to merge into a common tongue; language was further standardized by the state through written laws and other documents. Varied customs were shared and adapted into common norms or activities recognized across villages and regions. Common religious practices also developed, often created or supported by the state (as during the Protestant Reformation). In other words, new social institutions began to take shape that were meaningful to a majority of a country's population. People could now identify themselves not by village or profession, but by the institutions they shared with many thousands of other people they had never met. These institutions formed the foundation for ethnic identity. States built laws, standards, and rules that helped codify the norms, habits, and values of people within their territory. These people in turn slowly began to identify with each other primarily on this basis—as German or French or English. Again, this was a relatively recent process.

Growing ethnic identity was thus in some ways the unintended consequence of state development. As states became more powerful in Europe, they facilitated the development of social institutions that laid the foundation for ethnic identity. However, state leaders also came to recognize this development as something that could serve their own interests. By encouraging the formation of a single ethnic identity, the state could in turn claim that it existed to defend and promote the unique interests and values of its people. The state came to be portrayed as the embodiment of the people. Within this logic we can see the seeds of the next major step, the concept of national identity, which became a potent force by the eighteenth century. National identity, when added to ethnic identity, creates a powerful political force by asserting that the state is legitimate because it maintains national values and that the people and the state are united in the quest to chart an independent political future. This change occurred in Europe as part of a transformation of political authority. In contrast to earlier political systems founded on tradition or charismatic authority, the modern state claims authority on the basis of its rational pursuit of the national interest.

The development and fusion of ethnic and national identities radically transformed states. On the basis of the idea that the people and their state were bound together, states could mobilize the public in ways never before possible. Most importantly, countries with a strong sense of nationalism could raise mass armies, people fighting not for spoils or pay, but for the glory and destiny of their nation. The very thought that individuals would fight and die for some abstract political concept was a radical change in human history. In Europe, Napoleonic France became the first country able to use such nationalist sentiment to its own advantage; Napoleon created a huge volunteer army that would conquer much of Europe. Both threatened and inspired by such nationalist fervor, other European peoples and states in turn forged their own national identities. Across Europe, different peoples began to view themselves as nations with unique political identities and destinies and in turn sought national independence and self-government. This transformation gave rise to the **nation-state**, a sovereign state encompassing one dominant nation that it claims to embody and represent. Within a hundred years, most of the multiethnic empires that dominated Europe would be destroyed, replaced by nation-states that were dominated by distinct ethnic groups and political identities.

Finally, the development of ethnic and national identities paved the way for the reemergence of the concept of citizenship in the eighteenth and nineteenth centuries. As societies viewed themselves first in ethnic and then in national terms, their relationship to the state began to change. If the state was the instrument of national will, some extended this logic to conclude that not only were the people subjects of the state, but the reverse was true as well.

State and people were bound by a set of mutual responsibilities and obligations in the form of a social contract, as we discussed in Chapter 2. How far this citizenship should be extended and what rights it should entail have come to be central concerns for all societies, democratic or otherwise.

The concepts of ethnic and national identity that developed in Europe during the past 500 years spread around the world with the rise of European power, and they transformed the way in which peoples everywhere defined themselves in relation to one another and the state. Yet over the past half century, many political scientists and other scholars began to argue that national and ethnic identities were things of the past. As people became more economically developed, more literate, and more exposed to the world around them, these scholars asserted, they would lose interest in such narrow, "local" identities. Ethnicity would fade away as new ideas and values transformed societies everywhere, and nationalism would be rejected as an outdated and narrow view of the world. Citizenship, too, would be eroded by new global ties and connections, these scholars asserted. Most observers looked on these changes with optimism, for exclusionary forms of membership were presumed to be hostile to progress.

Many scholars have retreated from these earlier arguments, however, primarily because such identities have been much more resilient than expected. In the aftermath of the Cold War, ethnic and national identities have intensified in many countries. In fact, it would appear that in many cases, these identities have resurfaced in response to such factors as development and globalization. As the world grows ever closer together, as borders become more transparent, people may feel themselves increasingly lost in a chaotic global environment. Local identities provide some sense of stability in this period of rapid change. Terrorism, too, has regenerated a sense of ethnic, national, and patriotic values across a number of countries, serving to unify and divide peoples. Paradoxically, then, the closer people come in contact, the more they may come to rely on these identities to define themselves. We'll speak more of this in Chapter 10.

Sources of Ethnic and National Conflict

Political scientists are particularly interested in how national identity and ethnicity can lead to cooperation or conflict between people. Why are some countries able to build on differences between people, whereas in other countries such differences lead to seemingly irreconcilable conflict? Why do some very different identities peacefully coexist for decades and then suddenly flare into violence? Political scientists have different and often contending explanations for such forms of conflict.[3]

At its most basic level, the very process of defining oneself in terms of nation and ethnicity excludes others. Moreover, emphasizing the unique qualities and goals of one's own group can lead to the conclusion that difference equals superiority, that one's own group is somehow better than others. The quest for freedom or equality can involve achieving it at the expense of others.

Just as national identity and ethnic identity are independent yet strongly linked, we can find examples of ethnic or national conflict, as well as situations in which both forces are at work. In **ethnic conflict**, different ethnic groups struggle to achieve certain political or economic goals at each other's expense. However, this struggle does not imply nationalism. Neither side may seek to separate and form a sovereign state; instead, each may hope to increase its own position within the existing state, regime, or government. By contrast, in **national conflict**, one or more groups do develop clear aspirations for sovereignty, clashing with others as a result.

Around the world, we can find examples of both ethnic and national conflict. Afghanistan, for example, has seen frequent ethnic conflict. This conflict is not national, however; the different Afghan groups are seeking not independence but greater power over each other within the country. In contrast, the American Revolution can be seen as a national rather than an ethnic conflict. The American colonies broke away from Great Britain to form a separate country, but this separation was not based on ethnic differences. Rather, it was based on conflicts over political rights and the desire for sovereignty.

Not only can conflict arise out of different objectives, but it can also emerge in different ways. Political scientists disagree about whether ethnic and national conflict originates primarily from the top down or from the bottom up—in other words, whether conflict begins among political leaders and then spreads down to society or whether conflict begins among the people and spreads up to the government and the state. In reality, both paths have been

IN FOCUS

Two Views of Ethnic Conflict

Top-down view	Conflict is generated by elites.
	Conflict could be stopped by controlling political leaders responsible.
	Use of outside force can be effective.
Bottom-up view	Conflict is generated by long-standing friction between groups.
	Animosity must "burn itself out."
	Use of outside force will be ineffective.

evident in cases of ethnic and nationalist conflict, sometimes simultaneously. Political leaders often foster ethnic or national conflict as a way to divide the population and rally support. In other cases, ethnic or national conflict may emerge from long-standing grievances between different groups and/or changes in the distribution of resources or particular political rights. In the case of Iraq, we can see conflict as a product of old animosities that have been given a chance to resurface as the balance of power shifts from Sunnis (who had historically dominated the country) to Shiites and Kurds; at the same time, this conflict is intentionally stoked by political actors intent on feeding the flames of conflict and division.

How can such intractable problems be solved? Often it is assumed that one of the main solutions can be found in national borders. In many countries around the world, national boundaries are largely arbitrary, drawn by former colonial masters under imperialism. Some ethnic groups were bifurcated by colonial borders and thus wound up in different countries after decolonization; in other cases, different and often hostile groups were forced together in the same country. This arbitrary gathering and dividing of peoples, some observers argue, set the stage for later conflict. This was evident in the case of Iraq, which was cobbled together out of three provinces of the Ottoman Empire after World War I. But although it is true that in many cases borders certainly could have been better drawn to more accurately reflect ethnic divisions, there are few examples where simply changing the borders would solve problems. In many countries, divisions on ethnic lines would lead to the creation of multiple states, and even these borders could not so easily be drawn, since many groups often share the same territory. The level of ethnic fragmentation throughout the postcolonial world can be seen in the map in Figure 3.1; in many parts of the world, the largest ethnic group makes up less than 50 percent of the population.

Ethnic and national conflict may thus emerge from a number of different forces operating either in isolation or in combination. Conflict may be generated by elites to solidify their own power through conflict or to favor one group over another. Conflict may also result from long-standing friction between groups, catalyzed by economic or political changes. And in some situations, conflict is fueled by both the top and the bottom, locked in a cycle of violence. Each type of conflict presents different challenges in the search for peace and stability. Finally, ethnic and nationalist rivalries are exacerbated by the inherent heterogeneity of much of the world. Clear borders between groups are more the exception than the norm. In much of the world, the territories in which people find themselves, and even the ethnicities they claim, are legacies of imperialism. We will turn to these ideas in more detail in Chapter 9, which looks at less-developed and newly industrializing countries.

Figure 3.1 **LEVELS OF ETHNIC FRAGMENTATION**

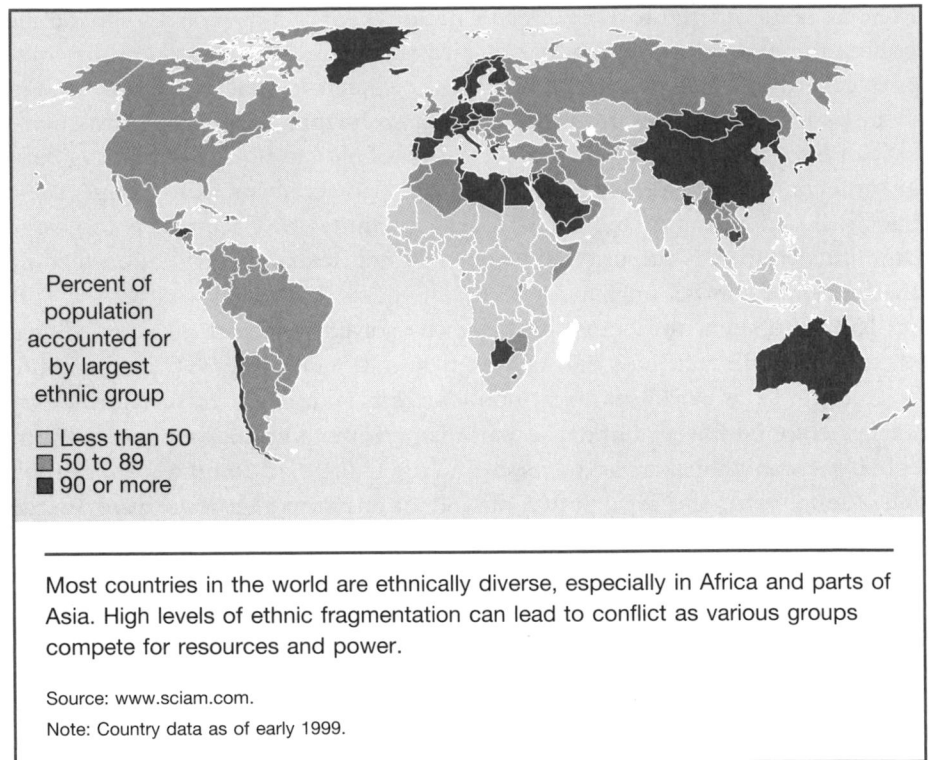

Percent of
population
accounted for
by largest
ethnic group

☐ Less than 50
▣ 50 to 89
■ 90 or more

Most countries in the world are ethnically diverse, especially in Africa and parts of
Asia. High levels of ethnic fragmentation can lead to conflict as various groups
compete for resources and power.

Source: www.sciam.com.

Note: Country data as of early 1999.

Political Attitudes and Political Ideology

We have covered a great deal of ground so far in our discussion of the ways
in which societies are organized and the identities they construct. As we have
seen, ethnicity, national identity, and citizenship are all ways in which people view themselves in relationship to one another, vis-à-vis other groups, and
in their relationship to the state. In addition to these basic forms of group
identity, people also hold individual views regarding the relationship between
freedom and equality within their own country and in the wider world. These
views are not defined by birth or by the state, although they may be influenced by either. Nor are the boundaries between such views as clear or evident as they are with ethnicity, national identity, or citizenship; people may
freely modify or combine values, in spite of the wider pressures or expectations of state or society.

In the rest of this chapter, we will categorize these views into two different types: political attitudes and political ideology. Political attitudes are
concerned with the speed and methods to achieve political change. Political
ideology comprises the basic values held by an individual about the funda-

mental goals of politics regarding freedom and equality. Although political attitudes focus on the specific context of political change in a given country, political ideologies are more universal, as they assume that there is one way to balance freedom and equality that should apply to people everywhere. Let's look at each concept in detail and distinguish further between the two.

Political Attitudes

Political attitudes describe views regarding the necessary pace and scope of change between freedom and equality. The attitudes are typically broken up into the categories of radical, liberal, conservative, and reactionary and are often arrayed on a spectrum, from left to right.

Radicals are placed on the extreme left. **Radicals** believe in dramatic, often revolutionary change of the existing political, social, or economic order. Radicals believe that the current system is broken and cannot simply be improved or repaired but must be scrapped in favor of a new order. As a result, most radicals do not believe in slow, evolutionary change. Politics will only be improved, they believe, when the entire political structure has been fundamentally transformed, remaking the political institutions of government, regime, and state. As a result, radicals may be more inclined to favor violence as a necessary or unavoidable part of politics. The institutions of the old order, in some radicals' view, are maintained through inertia and will not change willingly; they will have to be destroyed, if necessary through force. These views are not held by all radicals, however. Some may argue that radical change can be achieved through peaceful means, by raising public consciousness and mobilizing mass support for wide-ranging change.

Liberals, like radicals, believe that there is much that can be changed for the better in the current political, social, and economic institutions, and liberals, too, support widespread change. However, instead of *revolutionary* transformation, **liberals** favor *evolutionary* transformation. In the liberal view, progressive change can happen through changes within the system; it does not require an overthrow of the system itself. Liberals believe that although there may be a need for change, the system is not fundamentally unjust or broken, and change can be pursued through the

IN FOCUS

Political Attitudes Are . . .

- Concerned with the speed and methods of political change.
- Generally classified as radical, liberal, conservative, or reactionary.
- *Particularistic*: relative to the specific context of a given country. A view that is "radical" in one country may be "conservative" in another.
- Distinct from political ideologies.

political process. Liberals may favor a change in government or even in regime, but they do not demand sudden transformation. Moreover, liberals part from radicals in their belief that the state can be an instrument of positive change. Liberals also believe that change can, and sometimes must, occur over a long period of time; they are skeptical that institutions can be replaced or transformed within a short period of time and believe that only constant effort can create fundamental change.

Conservatives break with both radicals and liberals in this view of the necessity of change. Whereas radicals and liberals both advocate change, disagreeing only on the degree of change and the tactics to achieve it, **conservatives** question whether any significant or profound change in existing institutions is necessary. Conservatives are skeptical of the view that change is necessarily good in itself and instead view it as disruptive and leading to unforeseen outcomes. Conservatives see the state and the regime as important structures that provide basic order and continuity to politics, economics, and society, and they view unnecessary tinkering with this system as dangerous. Should too much change take place, conservatives argue, the very legitimacy of the system might be undermined, destroying the basic values and norms that hold society together. Conservatives also question the extent to which the problems that radicals and liberals point to can ever really be solved. At best, they believe, change will simply replace one set of problems with another, and at worst, it will actually create more problems than it solves.

Reactionaries are similar to conservatives in their opposition to further evolutionary or revolutionary change, yet unlike conservatives and similar to radicals, they view the current order as fundamentally unacceptable. Rather than a transformation of the system into something new, however, **reactionaries** seek to restore political, social, and economic institutions that once existed. Reactionaries advocate a restoration of older values, a change back to a previous regime or state that they believe was superior to the current order. Some reactionaries do not even look back to a specific period in history, but instead seek to "return" to an envisioned past ideal that never really existed. Reactionaries, like radicals, are more willing to use violence to advance their cause.

The left-right continuum on which these attitudes are typically illustrated gives the impression that the further one travels from the center, the more polarized politics becomes. By this logic, then, radicals and reactionaries are miles apart from one another, with nothing in common (Figure 3.2, top). But our preceding discussion indicates that in many ways this interpretation is incorrect. Thus, some political scientists believe that viewing left and right as a single continuum is misleading, for the closer one moves toward the extremes, the closer the attitudes become. These political scientists have devised an alternative way to envision the spectrum of political attitudes. They

Figure 3.2 **TWO VIEWS OF POLITICAL ATTITUDES**

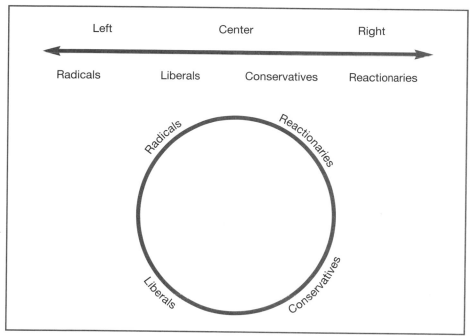

bend the straight continuum into a circle, bringing the two ends, radical and reactionary, close together (Figure 3.2, bottom). And in fact, radicals and reactionaries share much in common. Both believe in dramatic change, though in different directions, and both contemplate the use of violence to achieve this change. Although their ends may be quite different, the means of both groups can often be similar. In fact, just as liberals sometimes become conservatives and vice versa, radicals and reactionaries often cross over into each other's camps. For example, many reactionary fascists in Europe became supporters of radical communism after World War II.

One thing you might have noticed by this time is that our discussion of the political spectrum of attitudes has not provided any specific examples, such as welfare, civil liberties, or defense—common sources of political division that separate right from left in most industrialized democracies. But these specific policy areas belong instead to the concept of political ideology, those basic beliefs about how politics should be constructed. It is important to emphasize again that ideology and political attitudes are not interchangeable. The attitudes of radicals, liberals, conservatives, and reactionaries often take on different ideological content in different societies, depending on the context. What might be considered radical in one country could be conservative in another.

Consider some examples. In the United States, Canada, or Western Europe, radicals are viewed as those who seek to fundamentally transform or overthrow the current capitalist democratic order, replacing it with a system of greater economic and social equality. Radicals believe that by ending economic injustice and inequality, blights such as racism, sexism, and war would disappear, deprived as they would be of their financial underpinnings. Liberals in these countries are sympathetic to some of these ideas but believe in pursuing gradual changes within the current system. Rather than believing that politics is part of the problem, they believe that existing government, regime, and state institutions can be part of the solution. Income inequality or discrimination, for example, can be solved through income redistribution, affirmative action, and laws against discrimination. Conservatives believe that the current economic and social structures are fine as they are and do not wish to tamper with the political order. In their mind, discrimination and inequality, although unfortunate, will always exist; governments cannot make these problems go away, so it is up to individuals to overcome these obstacles themselves. Reactionaries, meanwhile, reject the very idea that discrimination or inequality is bad, viewing as natural the hierarchy between people and advocating that it should be restored, through violence if necessary. The foregoing is a simplified but accurate description of how political attitudes are manifested in the United States and much of the West.

These same political attitudes would manifest themselves quite differently in a country such as China, however. China is an authoritarian country still controlled by a communist party, even though dramatic economic (if not political) reforms have taken place in China over the past twenty years, creating a system with some elements of capitalism. Given this context, a Chinese radical, defined as someone who seeks the destruction of the current system, would advocate the overthrow of communist rule and its replacement, perhaps by a democracy like those found in the West. Students who were active in the Tiananmen Square protests for democracy in 1989 were frequently described or condemned by observers and the Chinese government as "radicals" for their demands for sweeping change in the communist system. Chinese liberals are also likely to favor many of the changes that were advocated in Tiananmen Square, although they would approach these reforms much more slowly and in a less confrontational manner, favoring a process of gradual change within the existing political system. In 2000, secret Chinese government documents concerning the crackdown against the Tiananmen Square protesters were leaked to the international media by someone presumed to be an inside government source. Many assumed that this was the work of liberals within the Communist Party who hoped that the documents would discredit their conservative and reactionary opponents, who had directed the massacre of the protesters. Chinese conservatives, those individuals suspicious of change, continue to resist calls for democratic reform or for an admission that the use of violence in 1989 against nonviolent protesters was a mistake. They may support or tolerate some market reforms, but they do not view these steps as leading down an inevitable path to democracy or capitalism. Finally, Chinese reactionaries strongly oppose any reforms that might jeopardize communist rule, viewing the Tiananmen Square events as proof that communism had been undermined by reforms carried out over preceding decades. These hard-liners favor a return to earlier, "purer" communist values and policies, bringing reforms to an end and rolling back changes that have already taken place.

Clearly, American or Western European radicals would have little to say to Chinese radicals; both are united by their attitudes toward the scope and speed of political change, but in terms of their political values and goals—their ideologies—they are dramatically different. Indeed, Chinese radicals might have more in common with American or European conservatives in terms of their support for democracy and capitalism. Chinese reactionaries, on the other hand, might have more in common with American or European radicals: the former wish to return to communism as it existed before recent reforms, and many of the latter seek to achieve the same kind of outcome in their own countries.

Political Ideology

The preceding discussion of the importance of context in understanding political attitudes might lead one to conclude that making any meaningful attitudinal comparisons between countries is difficult: what is radical in one country might be conservative in another. To move past these particularistic differences between countries, political scientists also speak about political ideologies. Like much of modern politics, the concept of ideology is relatively recent, with the term first coming into usage during the French Revolution to speak of a "science of ideas."[4] This meaning is important, for it alludes to the fact that ideologies emerged with the construction of modern secular states to provide a means to guide practical politics. Ideologies were thus viewed as alternatives to traditional sets of values such as religion; they were seen as based on rational thought rather than spiritual notions of good and evil. For our purposes, **political ideologies** are defined as sets of political values held by individuals regarding the fundamental goals of politics. Rather than being concerned with the pace and scope of change in a given context, as political attitudes are, ideologies are concerned with the ideal relationship between freedom and equality for all individuals and the proper role of political institutions in achieving or maintaining this relationship. Supporters of each ideology work to ensure that their values become institutionalized as the basic

---

IN FOCUS

Political Ideologies Are . . .

- Sets of political values regarding the fundamental goals of politics.
- Exemplified by five dominant modern ideologies: liberalism, communism, social democracy, fascism, and anarchism.
- *Universalistic*: not specific to one country or time.
- Distinct from political attitudes.

---

regime, or rules of the political game. In the modern world, there are five primary ideologies (Table 3.1).

Liberalism as an ideology (rather than as a political attitude) places a high priority on individual political and economic freedom. Adherents of a liberal ideology believe that politics should seek to create the maximum degree of liberty for all people, including free speech, the right of association, and other basic political rights. This goal requires a state with a low degree of autonomy, so that it can be easily controlled or checked by the public should it begin encroaching on individual rights. For liberals, the lower the ability of the state to intervene in the public's affairs, the greater the scope and promise of human activity and prosperity. As Thomas Jefferson said, "The legitimate powers of government extend to such acts only as are injurious to others. But it does me no injury for my neighbor to say there are twenty gods, or no God. It neither picks my pocket nor breaks my leg."[5]

It is from these ideas of liberalism that we take our current definition of democracy, which is often defined as **liberal democracy**—a system of political, social, and economic liberties, supported by competition, participation, and contestation (such as voting). To be sure, liberals do recognize that not all individuals will succeed if left to their own devices and that there will inevitably be great economic inequality between the wealthiest and the poorest. In spite of this shortcoming, liberals argue that a high degree of freedom will produce the greatest amount of general prosperity for the majority.

As a final point, we should note that liberalism as an ideology and liberalism as a political attitude are very different things; in China, the ideology of liberalism would be considered a radical political attitude; in the United States, the ideology of liberalism is essentially a conservative political attitude, since it represents the current status of the U.S. regime. Ideologically, the United States is a liberal country, founded on free markets, individualism, and a state with relatively low autonomy.

Communism differs greatly from liberalism in its view of freedom and equality. Whereas liberalism enshrines individual freedom over equality, communism rejects the idea that personal freedom will ensure prosperity for the majority. Rather, it holds that in the inevitable struggle over economic resources, a small group will eventually come to dominate both the market and the state, using its wealth to control and exploit society as a whole. Prosperity will not be spread throughout society but will be monopolized by a few for their own benefit. The gap between rich and poor will widen, and poverty will increase. For communists, liberal democracy is "bourgeois democracy"— of the rich, by the rich, and for the rich. Such institutions as free speech and voting are meaningless when a few control the wealth of society.

To eliminate exploitation, communism advocates that the state control all economic resources in order to produce true economic equality for the community as a whole. This goal requires a powerful state in terms of both autonomy and capacity, able to restrict those individual rights (such as owning property or opposing the current regime) that would hinder the pursuit of economic equality. Individual liberties must give way to the needs of society as a whole, creating what communists would see as a true democracy. The

INSTITUTIONS IN

ACTION

LIBERALISM, A CONFUSING TERM

The ideology and political-economic system of liberalism favors a high degree of individual freedom and a weak state in order to ensure the greatest prosperity, even if this means tolerating inequality. Yet this definition flies in the face of the term *liberal* as used in the United States and Canada, as it typically implies a stronger state and greater state involvement in economic affairs. This confusion stems in large part from historical developments: over time, liberals who once placed their faith in the market to expand freedom and equality came to believe more and more that state intervention was necessary. Liberals in North America essentially became what many other countries would refer to as "social democrats."

This kind of ideological transformation did not occur in many other countries, however. Outside of North America, liberalism has retained its original meaning. Some political scientists therefore use the term *classical liberalism* to refer to the original tenets of the ideology. Others, particularly critics of the ideology, often use the term *neoliberalism* instead, indicating that the original ideas of liberalism (free markets and greater individualism along with a tolerance for inequality) are resurgent around the world.

So the term *liberal* can have many different meanings:

1. As a political attitude: favoring slow, evolutionary change
2. As a political ideology in North America: favoring a greater state role in limiting inequality, or what many outside of the region would call "social democracy"
3. As a political ideology outside of North America: favoring free markets and individualism, accepting greater inequality
4. As a political economy: favoring a limited state role in the economy

Soviet Union from 1917 to 1991 and China since 1949 are examples of countries where this communist ideology has been installed as the political regime through revolution, creating what these countries call (or called) "people's democracies." Thus, democracy can be a slippery concept, defined differently, depending on a person's ideology. We will turn to this problem in greater detail in Chapter 6.

Social democracy (sometimes called **socialism**) shares some early influences with communism but over time has been influenced by liberal values to form its own quite distinct ideology. Unlike communism, social democracy accepts a strong role for private ownership and market forces while still maintaining an emphasis on economic equality. A state with strong capacity and autonomy is typically considered important to social democrats to ensure greater economic equality through specific policies, but this commitment to equality, while limiting freedom to a greater extent than under liberalism, recognizes the importance of individual liberty. In much of Europe, social democracy, rather than liberalism, is the guiding political regime. Many environmental parties, which seek to balance human and environmental needs, also have social democratic influences.

Fascism, like communism, is antiliberal in its focus and hostile to the idea of individual freedom. However, although it favors a collective approach to human organization, fascism rejects the notion of equality. Instead, fascism rests on the idea that people and groups can be classified in terms of inferiority and superiority. Particular nations and ethnic groups are deemed superior to others, thus justifying a hierarchy among them. Neither freedom nor equality is possible or desirable under fascism; individual freedom must submit to the collective will, and the superior must rise above the inferior through a process of struggle and will to dominate. Whereas liberals and communists both see inherent potential in every person (although they disagree on the best means to unleash this potential), fascists do not. The metaphor of fascism is one of the society as an organic whole, a single living body, with a few leaders serving as its brain and controlling its actions. Fascists view the state as a vital instrument for molding society and the economy to best strengthen the nation against inferior people within and without. State autonomy and capacity must therefore be high, and democracy, no matter how defined, is rejected as anathema, just as freedom and equality are rejected. No fascist regimes currently exist in the world, although fascism is well remembered from the Nazi system that ruled Germany from 1933 to 1945. Fascist political parties and movements still do exist, however, such as white supremacist groups in North America and Europe.

Anarchism departs from these other ideologies quite drastically. If liberalism, communism, and fascism differ over how powerful the state should be, anarchism rejects the notion of the state altogether. Anarchists share with communists the belief that private property leads to inequality, but they are opposed to the idea that the state can solve this problem; power in the hands of the state, in the anarchist view, would not necessarily eliminate inequality and would certainly eliminate freedom. As the Russian anarchist Mikhail Bakunin (1814–1876) once stated, "I am not a communist, because communism unites all the forces of society in the state and becomes absorbed in it; because it inevitably leads to the concentration of all property in the hands of the state, while I seek the complete elimination of the principles of authority and governmental guardianship, which under the pretence of making men moral and civilizing them, has up to now always enslaved, oppressed, exploited, and ruined them."[6]

Thus, like liberals, anarchists view the state as a threat to freedom and equality rather than as their champion. Accordingly, anarchists believe that both individual freedom and equality can be achieved only if the state is eliminated entirely. Without a state to reinforce inequality or limit personal freedom, argue anarchists, people would be able to freely cooperate as true equals. Moreover, without the state to reinforce private property and economic exploitation, these would also disappear. Economic activity would instead take place in a society of relative equality. In short, anarchists believe that in the absence of a state and a capitalist economy, people would be free to pursue their own lives and individual desires.

Given that we live in a world of states, anarchism is the one ideology of the five primary ideologies that has never been realized. No society has ever adopted anarchism as a political regime and dispensed with the state, although anarchist groups, movements, and collectives have appeared in many societies throughout modern history. Anarchist ideas played a role in the Russian Revolution (1917) and in the Spanish Civil War (1936–1939). Some point to new technological innovations such as the Internet as potential sources of anarchist politics in the future.

Fundamentalism and the Crisis of Ideology

Ideologies emerged alongside the modern secular state in many ways as an alternative or rival to religion. If religion had in the past helped describe and prescribe the world, including issues of freedom, equality, and power, then ideologies were seen as nonspiritual guides to that same end. Accordingly, ideologies and religions are in many ways similar, with their assertions about the fundamental nature of humans and society, the key to a good life and an ideal community, a host of core texts and prophets, and a promise of salvation.

For the past two centuries, ideologies have increasingly replaced religion in public life. Whereas faith was central to public affairs, including politics,

IN FOCUS

Ideology and Political Attitudes

Ideology	Tenets	Corresponding Political Attitude in North America
Liberalism	Favors a limited state role in society and economic activity; emphasizes a high degree of personal freedom over social equality.	Conservative
Communism	Emphasizes limited personal freedom and a strong state in order to achieve social equality; property is wholly owned by the state and market forces are eliminated; state takes on task of production and other economic decisions.	Radical
Social democracy	Supports private property and markets but believes that state has a strong role to play in regulating the economy and providing benefits to the public; seeks to balance freedom and equality.	Liberal
Fascism	Stresses a low degree of both personal freedom and equality in order to achieve a powerful state.	Reactionary
Anarchism	Stresses the elimination of the state and private property as a way to achieve both freedom and equality for all; believes that a high degree of personal freedom and social equality is possible.	Radical

in the premodern world, the rise of ideology led to what has been termed "the privatization of religion," where faith was pushed out of the public sphere and relegated to private life. To be certain, this was never complete or uniform from country to country. But the emergence of modern states and ideology was central to the development of secularism and the retreat of religion. This process was described by Max Weber as "the disenchantment of the world," where faith in the mystical and spiritual was replaced by faith in the material world, in human-made institutions, and in the notion of progress.

In the past few decades, the claims and power of ideologies have themselves come under attack. In the past the vibrancy of ideologies lay in the intensity of conflict between them. But slowly these battles have disappeared as many ideologies have fallen by the wayside. Fascism and communism have been largely discredited and defeated, while anarchism has never been able to establish a lasting presence or a major following. This has left only social democracy and liberalism as the major ideological players, and even between the two, the differences have narrowed over time. This is what the scholar Francis Fukuyama meant by "the end of history"—that major ideological struggles had come to an end, with no new ideological alternatives on the horizon.

Related to this decline of ideological alternatives has been the declining appeal of ideology in general. In the West, where liberalism and social democracy first originated and have been dominant for decades, the relative success of these ideologies has also contributed to their decline. To many people, politics now seems focused on the distribution of public benefits and the solution of technical issues rather than on any grand ideals. Outside the West there has been a similar disenchantment, but for different reasons. Many individuals in less-developed countries who put their faith in Western ideology as a means of development and prosperity have been deeply disappointed. Communism, fascism, liberalism—none of these values have helped lift billions of people out of misery and tyranny. For all societies, rich or poor, the utopian claims associated with many ideologies—that modernity, science, and rationalism would usher in a golden age—have been discredited. Ideologies have contributed to development and democracy for some, but they have also failed to solve many pressing problems while fueling and justifying war, genocide, and the possible annihilation of the earth itself. It is in this vacuum of ideals that fundamentalism has appeared.

Before we proceed further, we should be clear about what we mean by the term *fundamentalism*. As with many politically charged words, *fundamentalism* is a term bandied about and used indiscriminately, often to describe someone holding strong views that repel us. Some scholars dislike the very use of the term beyond its original meaning, which described a particular kind of movement among Protestant Christians in the nineteenth century. But in spite of these problems or concerns, the term is useful and can describe a similar pattern across many religions, whether Jewish, Christian, Muslim, Hindu, or other faiths.

The scholar Bruce Lawrence has defined fundamentalism as "the affirmation of religious authority as holistic and absolute, admitting of neither criticism nor reduction; it is expressed through the collective demand that specific creedal and ethical dictates derived from scripture be publicly recognized and legally enforced."[7] Following from this, **fundamentalism** can be viewed as an ideology that seeks to unite religion with the state, or rather, to make faith the sovereign authority. This definition implies several things. First, fundamentalism is not the same as religiosity, puritanism, or religious conservatism. For example, Orthodox Jews or the Amish are by definition not fundamentalists; any group that retreats from public life and politics hardly fits with our definition. Nor is merely a belief in a greater role for spirituality in politics or society by definition fundamentalism. Second, fundamentalism is not a premodern view. As we mentioned earlier, in the premodern world, religion played a central role in public life. The rise of the modern state pushed faith into the private realm, replacing it in part with ideology. But fundamentalism seeks not to return to a premodern role of faith, but rather restructure religion as an ideology—to make faith the sole foundation for a modern regime, a concrete and inerrant guide for politics in the contemporary world.

To that end, fundamentalists base their beliefs on the failures of ideology. Through ideology, people sought to create heaven on earth, believing that they could deny the authority of God and seize control of their own destinies. The result has been, in the fundamentalists' view, not only greater human misery but spiritual malaise. Even for those who have benefited materially, they are still truly disenchanted, spiritually empty, and morally adrift, forced to fill their lives with mindless distractions—consumption, entertainment, sex—to avoid confronting this terrible truth. Fundamentalism, religion as a form of ideology, is thus a very modern phenomenon.[8]

As a political attitude, fundamentalism can often appear as a reactionary or radical view or a combination of the two. Fundamentalists will often make claims to return to some golden age of faith, but they also seek to solve the problems of the modern world, not simply turn back the clock. This mixture of reactionary and radical attitudes also explains why fundamentalism is often associated with violence and terrorism. However, we should be clear that only a small number of fundamentalists embrace such an approach. We will delve into this issue in depth in Chapter 11 when we consider political violence. To reiterate, we should not confuse religiosity or piety with fundamentalism, or fundamentalism with violence.

How does fundamentalism fit the relationship between freedom and equality? It depends in part on the religious foundation of the fundamentalism under consideration, but even within fundamentalist trends in a single religion, there is a great diversity of ideas. Some fundamentalist views emphasize collective equality but reject individual freedom in favor of submission to God; others posit an expression of individual freedom made possible through a political system based on faith and are less concerned with inequalities between people. There are also views that reject freedom and equality in favor of hierarchy and the domination of believers over nonbelievers or the more faithful over the less so. It is thus a mistake to think of fundamentalism as a single ideology; rather it is a pattern across many religions that have produced various ideological forms. In some cases, these remain nebulous and with few adherents. In other cases, they are well defined and exercise significant political power.

For example, in Islamic fundamentalism, we find arguments that states and nations where Muslims live should return to the Koran (the central holy book) as the source for national laws, constitutions, and government policies. Other arguments advocate the creation of an Islamic empire covering some or all Muslim peoples and lands and headed by a **theocracy**—a combined religious and political ruler. Still others are skeptical of either a national or supranational approach, seeing national identities and theocratic leaders as incompatible with Islam and favoring a more decentralized political order. Just as these goals differ widely, so do the ends. Some call for a military struggle, or *jihad*, to defend or expand the faith, while others believe that their goals should be achieved only through peaceful means.[9] In the end, these diverse views are bound by one commonality—that faith and politics are inseparable and to separate them, as modern states have done, breaks humanity's relationship to God. Similar debates can be found across Christian, Jewish, Hindu, and other fundamentalisms, though each debate is shaped by the existing institutions of the faith itself, as well as the political institutions where that fundamentalism is found. As the politics of fundamentalism continue to develop, this "return of God" may well prove to be one of the most important developments in future global politics meaning not the end of history, but its resumption in a new ideological form.[10]

Political ideologies differ according to where they believe the proper balance between freedom and equality lies and what role the state should have in achieving that balance. Building on the preceding chapters' discussion of freedom and equality and state strength, Figure 3.3 shows how liberalism, social democracy, communism, fascism, and anarchism each try to reconcile freedom and equality with state power. These ideologies do not prescribe a solution or ideal simply for one country or one point in time, but for all people everywhere and for the future if not forever. These values are not particularistic, like political attitudes, but are universal in their outlook. And although ethnic and national identities and citizenship may form the lines of conflict between groups, ideologies and attitudes shape the arena of political conflict within groups. How much change should there be? How fast? How peaceful or violent? And to what end? This is the essence of political life, as

Figure 3.3 **POLITICAL IDEOLOGIES VARY ACCORDING TO THE BALANCE THEY STRIKE BETWEEN FREEDOM AND EQUALITY**

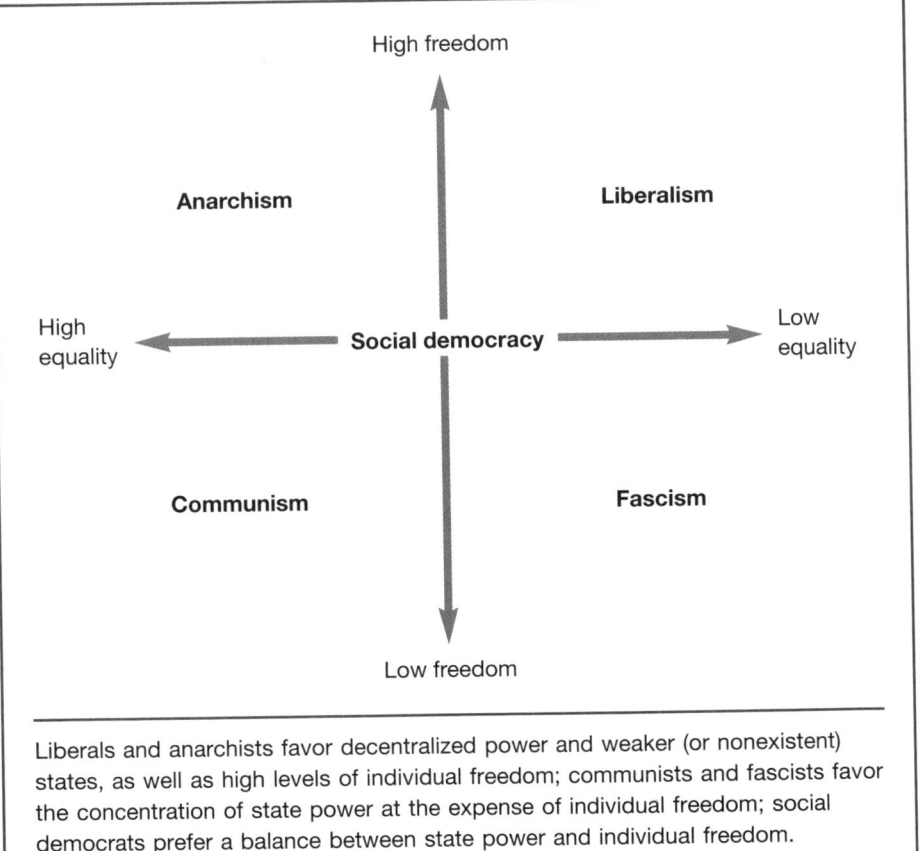

Liberals and anarchists favor decentralized power and weaker (or nonexistent) states, as well as high levels of individual freedom; communists and fascists favor the concentration of state power at the expense of individual freedom; social democrats prefer a balance between state power and individual freedom.

ideologies rise and fall in prominence, clash peacefully or violently, and pass from the scene as new ones take their place—as fundamentalism may now be doing. In 200 years, the ideas of liberalism or communism or fascism may make no more sense than the idea of a powerful monarchy does today.

Political Culture

So far, we have discussed how the ways in which societies identify themselves can have important implications for politics. Ethnicity, nationality, and citizenship provide collective identities with relatively clear boundaries, catego-

An important thing to keep in mind is the fact that Germany is very aware. It's not always clear if their efforts are misguided, but they don't try to hide their ~~distorted~~ history... at the same time it's kinda become a contradiction. ex. Can. camp — how is that beneficial and to whom? why & why not?

rizing people and generating questions about the nature of freedom and equality between different groups. In contrast, political attitudes and ideologies shape debates over the pace and scope of political change and ultimately about the ideal relationship between freedom and equality for all groups. These differences in turn create political conflict, competition, and cooperation within societies and help us to understand how societal differences can profoundly shape politics within countries.

But a final question remains. All of these forms of identification help set the arena for political struggles over freedom and equality. But what explains why countries differ so dramatically in their ideological outcomes? Why, for example, is the regime in the United States based on liberalism, with communist ideas considered radical by the public, whereas in China, communism forms the ideological core of the regime and liberalism is considered a radical notion? There are a number of possible explanations for these differences; some of these explanations look to such factors as the level of economic development in society or the power of particular individuals or groups to spread or impose their political values. But a societal explanation also exists, embodied in a concept known as "political culture."

Before we discuss this concept any further, however, we need to understand what is meant by "culture" in general. If society is a complex collection of people bound by shared institutions, as it was defined at the start of this chapter, then **culture** comprises those basic institutions that help define a society. Culture acts as a kind of social road map, telling people what is and is not acceptable and providing guidelines and priorities for how people should organize their lives. In some societies, for example, alcohol may be viewed as a normal part of cultural activities, whereas in other societies it may be frowned upon or taboo. Cultures can differ profoundly in their attitudes toward work, leisure, sex, and politics. Culture stands somewhere between the group identities of ethnicity, national identity, and citizenship on the one hand and individual political attitudes and ideologies on the other. Culture binds groups together, serving as part of the fundamental content of a society—of what makes the French different from Peruvians or Cambodians—yet at the same time it is a personal set of norms that people may choose to accept or reject.

In short, if ethnicity or nationality or citizenship is the definition of what group an individual belongs to, then culture is the activity that group

---

IN FOCUS

Political Culture Is . . .

- The basic norms for political activity in a society.
- A determining factor in what ideologies will dominate a country's political regime.
- Unique to a given country or group.
- Distinct from political attitudes and ideologies.

considers proper and normal for its members. **Political culture**, in turn, refers specifically to the basic norms for political activity in a society.[11]

Initially, it might be hard to believe that any society shares one specific set of political views that are somehow distinct from that of other countries. In fact, the discussion of political attitudes and ideologies so far in this chapter would seem to have taught us exactly the opposite—that people within countries differ widely in their views. Some political scientists in fact agree with this view, believing that political culture is not a useful concept. In their view, people everywhere are essentially rational and respond toward politics in roughly similar and predictable ways. Others, however, argue that in each society fundamental political views and values are shaped by cultural institutions, and observers cannot accurately understand politics in a country if they do not grasp its political culture. In this view, ideologies and political attitudes rest on a foundation of political culture that gives meaning to political debates.

Survey research done by political scientist Ronald Inglehart and his colleagues indicates that across the globe, societies can be arrayed by the extent to which they are guided by values that fall along two axes: traditional versus secular-rational values and survival versus self-expression values (Figure 3.4). Traditional values emphasize such things as religion, family, and nation, while secular-rational values are less deferential to authority in favor of individual autonomy. Survival values focus on economic and physical security and emphasize group conformity to that end, while self-expression values emphasize greater diversity among people and tolerance for their behavior. As Inglehart's map of political culture shows, countries appear to group in certain cultural sets across these two axes, with African, Latin American, English-speaking, postcommunist, or historically Protestant countries falling in close proximity to one another. Interestingly, the United States shows a strong emphasis on self-expression values like much of Europe, but gives much greater emphasis to traditional values. Such differences can help explain why Europeans and Americans see eye to eye on many issues but seem worlds apart on others.[12]

At a broader level, some scholars have argued that political culture can be used to explain important historical puzzles, such as the rise of fascism in Germany or communism in Russia. These arguments assert that in both cases, authoritarian and anti-individualist elements of German and Russian political culture allowed fascist and communist movements to take root. This argument has recently become connected to research on norms of reciprocity and trust between people, or what has been termed *social capital*. This scholarship hypothesizes that different political cultures exhibit varying degrees of social capital, and this variation in trust and reciprocity is correlated with how politics is viewed and institutions constructed.[13] Some go even further, arguing that there is in fact a culture of democracy and that certain cultural systems (Islam or Confucianism are frequently cited) are inherently incompatible with

Figure 3.4   CULTURAL VALUES AROUND THE WORLD

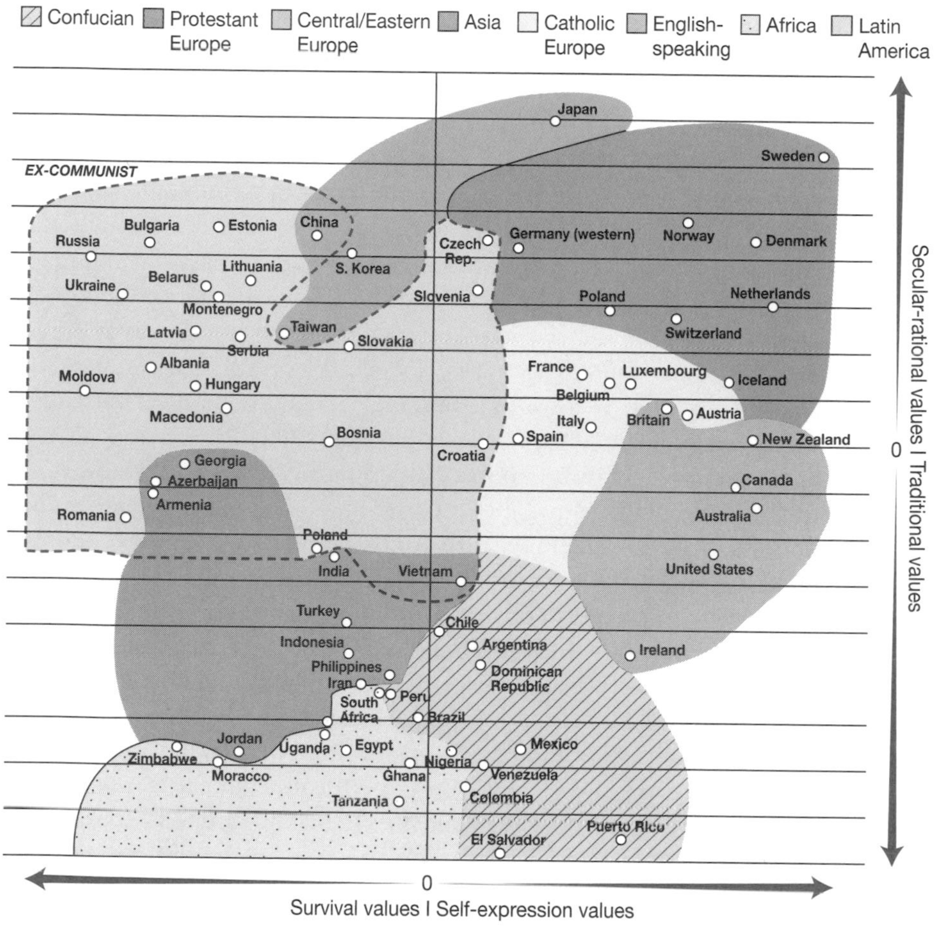

World values map. This figure charts cultural values of countries around the world. The figure shows not only that societies have distinct cultural differences, but that they tend to cluster based on religious, economic, geographical, or other shared experiences and institutions.

Source: http://www.worldvaluessurvey.org/statistics/index.html.

democracy as it has developed in the West. In the case of Islam, it has been argued that the central religious tenets of the faith have led to the rise of a particularly powerful fundamentalist movement and resulting conflict with liberal democratic states. Other scholars of political culture reject this view, but emphasize instead Arab political culture rather than Islam (the majority of whose adherents are not Arab and do not live in the Middle East). This is a hotly debated topic. Used badly, political culture arguments can veer into stereotypes if not outright racism. With that said, we can hypothesize that countries that fall into the zone of traditional and survival values are going to be much more resistant to democracy, since these values are more hostile to individual freedom and pluralism. However, in all four corners of the world values map shown in Figure 3.4, we can find examples of democracies, even where traditional and survival values are both predominant, such as India, South Africa, and Turkey. Thus, we should be careful not to overstate the claims of political culture. For our purposes, it is enough to say that the ideological debates that take priority and the kinds of ideologies that dominate a country's political regime may be shaped by that country's political culture.

Assuming that this argument is correct, how resilient is political culture? Political culture, like culture in general, is subject to change over time. Some political scientists, while they believe that political culture is an important factor in comparative politics, expect that different cultures will continue to transform, perhaps even merging into a common global culture. They predict that as societies modernize, democratize, and interact as a result of economic globalization and technological innovation, their cultures will grow closer together, exchanging ideas, values, habits, and preferences, eventually leading to a fusion of cultures. They hypothesize that postmodern (secular-rational and self-expression) values, including environmentalism, individualism, human rights, and tolerance, will develop as a result of greater global awareness and a growing consensus regarding the balance of freedom and equality.

Others are more skeptical. Culture, political or otherwise, does not easily change, they argue, and even the most developed countries around the world still remain distinct in how they approach and view politics. Indeed, some argue that in the aftermath of the Cold War and the rise of dramatic technological changes, basic cultural identities will in fact supplant political ideologies as the main dividing lines of global politics. These will grow increasingly important as social change increases in scope and pace, leading people to retreat into old identities as a source of constancy and certainty. Change, if it does come, may only lead to greater cultural divergence. The terrorist attacks of September 11, 2001, are often cited as horrible proof of this potential "clash of civilizations."[14]

In Sum: Society and Politics

Societies are complex and often difficult to unravel, but in this chapter, we have unraveled them somewhat. In looking at how societal organization shapes politics, we have found that individuals have a number of identities that they hold simultaneously: ethnicity, national identity, citizenship, political attitude, ideology, and political culture. Ethnicity provides a group identity, binding individuals to a group and separating them from others. National identity provides a political aspiration for that group, a desire for self-government, while citizenship establishes a relationship between that group and a state. Although each of these identities is distinct, they are often strongly connected, and some see the three as almost interchangeable. Such identities may bind people together; but they also can be the source of conflict when different groups see each other as threats to their freedom and equality.

Whereas group identities establish differences between groups, political attitudes, ideologies, and culture all help position an individual within a group. These three identities help clarify an individual's view of the ideal relationship between freedom and equality for society and of how fast and through what means change, if any, should be achieved.

Society's role in politics is clearly complicated, shaped by an array of factors that affect the ongoing debate over freedom and equality. Not long ago, many social scientists dismissed social identities such as nationalism and religion as outdated forms of identification that were giving way in the face of modernization and individualism. However, there is a growing belief that collective identities are more resilient than was once thought and that they may in fact sharpen in the face of new societal challenges. More broadly, politics is not simply the sum of individual actions but the product of a rich array of institutions that overlap one another, providing meaning to our lives and informing the ideas, viewpoints, and values that we carry within us. We will consider this idea further in the next chapter as we turn to a new set of institutions and ideas that shape the struggle over freedom and equality: those concerned with economic life.

NOTES

1. For more on nationalism, see Benedict Anderson, *Imagined Communities* (London: Verso, 1983).
2. Charles Tilly, ed., *The Formation of National States in Western Europe* (Princeton, NJ: Princeton University Press, 1975). See also Reinhard Bendix, *Nation-Building and Citizenship* (Berkeley: University of California Press, 1964), and Douglass C. North and R. P. Thomas, *Rise of the Western World: A New Economic History* (New York: Cambridge University Press, 1997).
3. For an excellent overview, see David Horowitz, *Ethnic Groups in Conflict* (Berkeley: University of California Press, 2000).
4. Destutt de Tracy, *A Treatise on Political Economy* (New York: Kelley, 1970).
5. *Notes on the State of Virginia*, chap. 17, available at www.xroads.virginia.edu.

6. Quoted in George Plechanoff, *Anarchism and Socialism* (Chicago: Kerr, 1909), 80.

7. Bruce Lawrence, *Defenders of God: The Fundamentalist Revolt against the Modern Age* (New York: Harper & Row, 1989), 78.

8. For an excellent discussion of fundamentalism in Christianity, Islam, and Judaism, see Karen Armstrong, *The Battle for God* (New York: Ballantine, 2001).

9. "Understanding Islamism," International Crisis Group, Middle East/North Africa Report no. 37, March 2, 2005. www.crisisgroup.org.

10. Gilles Kepel, *Revenge of God: The Resurgence of Islam, Christianity and Judaism in the Modern World*, trans. Alan Brayley (University Park, PA: Pennsylvania State University Press, 1994); Daniel Bell, *The End of Ideology on the Exhaustion of Political Ideas in the Fifties "with The Resumption of History in the New Century"* (Cambridge, MA: Harvard University Press, 2000).

11. Gabriel A. Almond, "The Study of Political Culture," in *A Discipline Divided: Schools and Sects in Political Science* (Newbury Park: Sage, 1990), 138–156.

12. For more on the World Values Survey, see www.worldvaluessurvey.org.

13. See Francis Fukuyama, *Trust: The Social Virtues and the Creation of Prosperity* (New York: Free Press, 1996).

14. Samuel P. Huntington, *The Clash of Civilizations and the Remaking of World Order* (Simon & Schuster, 1996).

4 POLITICAL ECONOMY

Like politics, economies are made up of many different institutions—rules, norms, and values—that strongly influence how the economic system is constructed. People often think about economic systems as somehow "natural," with functions akin to the law of gravity. In reality, an economy relies on an array of institutions that enable individuals to exchange goods and resources with one another. Moreover, economic institutions, like political ones, are not easy to replace or change once they have been constructed. They become self-perpetuating, and people have a hard time imagining life without them.

Economic institutions directly influence politics, and vice versa. The economy is one of the major arenas in which the struggle over freedom and equality takes place. Some view the economy as the central means by which people can achieve individual freedom, whereas others view the economy as the central means by which people can achieve collective equality. These values clash when different groups or ideologies have different expectations about how the economy should function and what kinds of societal goals should be pursued. Inevitably, this struggle involves the government, the state, and the regime. How this balance between freedom and equality is struck directly influences such things as the distribution of wealth, the kinds of economic activity and trade that citizens may conduct, and the overall degree of security, insecurity, and prosperity that people enjoy. In short, the interactions between political institutions and economic institutions in any country will have a profound impact on the prosperity of each and every citizen. The study of how politics and economics are related and how their relationship shapes the balance of freedom and equality is commonly known as **political economy**.

In this chapter, we will address these issues through an investigation of the relationship between freedom and equality. We will start by asking what role states play in managing an economy. There are a number of different areas in which states commonly involve themselves in economic life; depending on such things as the dominant ideology and regime, the scope and impact of these actions can vary dramatically. Just as there are different ideologies concerning the ideal relationship between the state and society, as we saw in Chapter 3, there are different ideological views regarding the ideal rela-tionship between the state and the market, each of which leads to a different political-economic system. We will explore each of these political-economic systems and their ideological origins. Once we have compared these differing views, we will consider how we might measure and compare their relative outcomes. In the process, we will look at some of the most common stan-dards by which to measure wealth and its distribution. Finally, with those concepts in hand, we will consider the future of the relationship between state and market and how their interaction shapes the balance between freedom and equality.

The Components of Political Economy

Before we compare the different types of relationships between states and economies around the world, we should first familiarize ourselves with the basic components of political economy. All modern states are strongly involved in the day-to-day affairs of their economies, at both the domestic and the global level. In shaping the economy to achieve their stated ideological goals, states and regimes use a variety of economic institutions.

Markets and Property

The most fundamental place to begin is with markets and property. These are terms that we come across all the time. When people speak of markets, one of the first things that may come to mind is a physical place where individu-als buy and sell goods. For as long as human beings have lived in settled com-munities that were able to produce a surplus of goods, there have been mar-kets. Markets are closely connected with the rise of cities; people would settle around markets, and markets would often spring up around fortifications, where commerce could be conducted with some sense of security. Such places still exist around the world. In Istanbul, Turkey, for instance, the Grand Bazaar, which dates back to the fifteenth century, is an enormous covered market comprising thousands of shops that sell everything from gold jewelry and carpets to T-shirts and postcards. No prices are fixed—everything must be negotiated between buyer and seller. Interestingly, the emergence of Inter-net auctions such as eBay has reintroduced the notion of the bazaar to much of world, albeit in a "virtual" location.

When social scientists speak of a market, they are speaking of these same forces at work, though without a specific location. **Markets** are the interac-tions between the forces of supply and demand, and they allocate resources through the process of that interaction. As these two forces interact, they create values for goods and services by arriving at specific prices. What is amazing about markets is the way they can be so decentralized. Who decides how many cars should be built this year? Or what colors they should be? Who knows what the price of a candy bar should be? Or the cost of this textbook? These decisions are made not by any one person or government, but by millions of individuals, each making decisions about what he will buy and what she will sell. If I produce a good and set its price at more than people are willing to pay, I will not be able to sell it and turn a profit. This will force me to either lower my price or go out of business. Similarly, if I produce a good that no one wants, I must change it, lower its price, or face economic ruin. Sellers seek to create products that people will desire or need, and buyers seek to buy the best or the most goods at the lowest price. Because more than one seller or producer typically exists for a product, this tends to generate competition and innovation. Sellers seek to dominate a market by offering their goods at the cheapest price or by offering a good that is innovative and therefore superior to any alternative.

In short, markets emerge spontaneously as a community of buyers and sellers in constant interaction through the economic choices that they make. Where there is demand, a market will emerge, whether people like it or not. Because of this spontaneity, states must determine how and if they wish to regulate the market by controlling the supply or demand of certain goods and services. For example, by setting a minimum wage, a state is controlling to some extent the price of labor. By making certain drugs or prostitution illegal, the state is attempting to stamp out a certain part of the market altogether for social or political reasons. Yet these goals are not always easily achieved. Minimum wages can be subverted by illegal immigrants, and "black" or underground markets appear where drugs and prostitution are illegal. Markets have a life of their own, and each state must decide in what way, and to what extent, it will involve itself in them.

Property is a second element critical to any economy. Just as markets are the medium through which goods and services are exchanged, **property** refers to the ownership of those goods and services. Property can refer to land, buildings, businesses, or personal items, to name some of the most common forms. In addition, a certain set of property rights can go along with ownership,

IN FOCUS

Markets

- Sellers seek to create products that will be in demand.
- Buyers seek to buy the best or most goods at the lowest price.
- Markets are the medium through which buyers and sellers exchange goods.
- Markets emerge spontaneously and are not easily controlled by the state.

such as the right to buy and sell property or the right not to have it taken away by the state or other citizens without a good reason (just cause) and compensation. These rights, a core component of individual freedom, require the state to create and enforce them.

In many people's minds, property, unlike markets, has a physical presence. I can see a car, buy it, own it, and sell it when I want a new one. However, property is not always tangible. Intellectual property, for example, refers to ownership of a specific type of knowledge or content—a song, a piece of software code, or a treatment for diabetes. As economic developments center more and more on such intangible forms of information and knowledge, the concept of property and property rights becomes just as fuzzy as that of markets, with no physical entity to speak of. Anyone who has downloaded a song, a movie, or software from the Web knows exactly what we are speaking of.

States vary in how they construct and enforce property rights, both between people and between the state and society. States may fail to enforce the rights of individuals to protect their own property from other individuals—by failing, for example, to enact or enforce laws against counterfeiting or theft. States may also assume certain property rights for themselves, claiming ownership over property such as airwaves, oil, land, or businesses. Airlines, for example, are a common form of state-owned business in many countries. Wherever these rights lie, it is important to understand that such rights do not automatically exist. In fact, many less-developed countries enjoy a wealth of property but a poverty of property rights, with states that are unable to establish or enforce such rules. We will speak about this more in Chapter 9.

Public Goods

Property as just described typically refers to goods that individuals obtain in a market and own and benefit from themselves. Yet some desirable goods cannot be easily created and traded in this manner. Take, for example, roads or military defense. Although both of these goods can exist in the private realm—in the form of toll roads and mercenaries or bodyguards—some societies question the moral and practical implications of allowing these goods to belong only to a narrow few. The limitation of such goods may limit economic development: a network of privately held roads might impede trade; a system of private protection may leave many insecure. Because of such concerns, all states provide some level of **public goods**, which we define as those goods, provided or secured by the state, available for society and indivisible, meaning that no one private person or organization can own them. Unlike private goods, with their inherent link to individual freedom, public goods generate collective equality, as the public is able to share broadly in their benefits.[1]

In many countries, roads, national defense, health care, and primary education are public goods, and everyone within the country may use them or benefit from their existence. But states do differ greatly in the extent to which they provide public goods, in large part because of the role of ideology in the relationship between states and markets. In the United States, health care is not a public good; it remains in private hands, and not everyone has equal access to it. In Canada, however, health care is a public good, provided by the state in the form of publicly owned hospitals and equal, universal benefits for all citizens. In Saudi Arabia, oil is a public good, owned by the state; revenue from its sale is spread (although not equally) among society. In Cuba, most businesses are owned by the state, making them public goods as well. The goods and profits of these firms belong not to a private owner, but to the state, to be distributed as the government sees fit.

Social Expenditures: Who Benefits?

This discussion of public goods leads us into the broader subject of **social expenditures**—the state's provision of public benefits, such as education, health care, and transportation, or what is commonly called "welfare" or the "welfare state." For many people, the very word *welfare*, like *taxes*, has an inherently negative connotation; it calls up images of freeloaders living off the hard work of others. To be certain, the redistribution of wealth in this manner is controversial and has become more so in many advanced industrial democracies over the past two decades. Often critics assert that social expenditures lead to counterproductive behavior. High unemployment benefits, they argue, may discourage people from seeking work. Moreover, alternative forms of social security that people have relied on in the past, such as the family, the community, or churches, may be weakened by too broad a welfare system.[2] These critics charge that the quest for collective equality has trumped individual freedom.

Even if one disagrees with these arguments, one practical problem that does remain for many countries is that social expenditures can be very costly and particularly hard to fund in countries with an aging population—a common phenomenon in many parts of the world. Because many countries fund social expenditures through income taxes, an aging population means that a greater proportion of a country's workers have retired and are no longer paying income taxes while still collecting pension and health-care benefits. As a result, many countries have in recent years sought to reduce their level of social expenditures or at least to reduce the rate by which those expenditures increase over time. We will explore this issue further in Chapter 7 as we consider the problem in the advanced democracies in particular.

Who benefits from social expenditures? If we use a strict definition, social expenditures are provided by the state to those who find themselves in adverse circumstances: the unemployed, the elderly, the poor, and the disabled. Such expenditures include health care, job training, income replacement, and housing. However, many of these and other social expenditures can also be defined as public goods. For example, a national health-care system treats employed and unemployed, wealthy and poor alike. Highways, public higher education, and cultural institutions such as museums may primarily benefit the well-off. In fact, if we define social expenditures to include all those public goods that the state provides, we find that in many countries, the majority of funds spent benefit the middle class, not the poor. In this sense, the modern welfare state is less a structure whereby the middle class and the rich are taxed to benefit the poor than one in which the middle class and the rich are taxed for services that benefit themselves.

Taxation

Over the past fifty years, public goods and social expenditures have become major and increasing responsibilities for states. How do states pay for these expenses? One of the major sources of funds is taxation. As with social expenditures, taxation generates passionate opinions: some view it as the means by which a greedy state takes the hard-earned revenues of its citizens, whereas others see it as a critical tool for generating a basic level of collective equality. Regardless of one's opinion of taxation, states are expected by societies to provide a number of public goods and services. Roads, health care, defense, schools, police, and welfare or social security (benefits for retirement, old age, unemployment, and other social needs) all cost money. Taxation is the means by which the state collects the funds to pay for public goods and services—which, in the end, benefit the public directly.

How much tax is collected varies from country to country. Figure 4.1 illustrates this variation, showing that in some countries, taxes consume a large portion of the gross domestic product of the country (a term we will discuss in more detail shortly). Many European countries with large social expenditures tend to have high overall tax rates to fund those expenses. In addition, countries differ in where this revenue comes from. Some countries rely on high personal taxation, while others rely on taxes on businesses or goods and services. All countries struggle with finding the right mix and level of taxation, aiming to extract needed funds without stunting economic growth by taking too much.[3]

Money, Inflation, and Unemployment

It should be getting clearer that many political-economic processes are tightly interlinked. States must form a relationship with markets and property, decid-

Figure 4.1 **TAXATION**

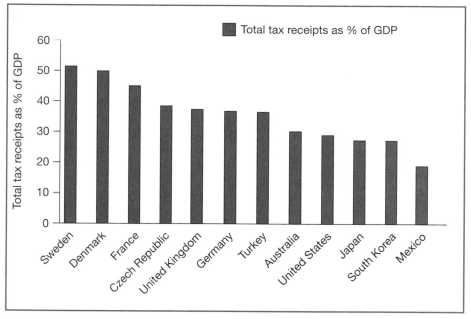

Source: Organization for Economic Cooperation and Development.

ing which goods should remain in private hands, which should be public, and what kinds of rights exist for each. They must also determine which goods and services should become publicly distributed to ensure a basic standard of living and security for all citizens. This distribution requires funds, for which states must draw on the public's resources through taxation. But a successful and productive tax base needs a dynamic and growing economy, which is also necessary to meet the public's needs and demands. So the state is also charged with fostering economic growth.

One basic way the state does this is through the creation and management of money. Money is nothing more than a medium of exchange; unlike wealth, which consists of property that has value, money is an instrument through which people conduct economic transactions. Money represents only a tiny fraction of the wealth in the world, most of which is tied up in houses, factories, land, and other property. But without money, economic transactions are difficult. States thus play a critical role in providing money as a means to secure and stimulate economic transactions.

Long ago, money did not exist. People had few goods that they wished to exchange, and what transactions did take place would occur through barter. As goods became more specialized and market forces spread over a greater distance through trade, barter began to be conducted through a limited number of goods that were widely desired, portable, or durable—in other words, products that themselves had some inherent value. Goods such as gold, silver, beads, salt, and tea, to name just a few, gradually replaced other forms of barter. These items were the first forms of money—a basic unit for economic transactions. Money in turn allowed for a system of prices to emerge, as one could gauge the value of various items against a single standard (how many beads is one pig or a chicken worth?).

These forms of money were not created by states. Their value existed only in the worth of the items themselves. As complex political systems began to take shape, however, they began to establish some basic monetary relationships through such things as taxes or fines, as well as the weights and measures of currency. From here, states then began to take responsibility for the creation of money, minting coins and thus ensuring the quality and value of the money. By the twelfth century C.E., the Chinese Empire moved beyond metal coins to issue paper money, which many centuries later became the standard practice around the world. Within the past century, money has completely lost any of its intrinsic worth, comprised of low-value metals, paper, or little more than an electronic representation in credit and debit accounts. With these transformations, people have come to place their faith in a state's currency on the basis of their trust in that state. A person accepts payments in dollars or euros or yen because he or she knows that others will accept them in turn. The society functioning under that currency trusts that money only so long as it also trusts its state.

As a result of their control over money, states have a great deal of influence over their domestic economies. Part of this power comes through what is known as a **central bank**, an institution that controls how much money is flowing through the economy, as well as how much it costs to borrow money in that economy.[4] One of the main ways a central bank affects these two areas is by changing a national interest rate, that is, the rate charged to private banks when they need to borrow funds from the central bank or one another. When the central bank lowers the interest rate charged to banks, those banks in turn lower their own interest rates for businesses and individuals. Loans become less expensive and saving becomes less lucrative, prompting people to borrow more and spend more. This in turn increases the amount of money active in the economy and thereby stimulates economic growth. If the central bank raises interest rates, on the other hand, people are likely to borrow less and save more to take advantage of the higher interest their savings can earn. The money supply in the economy contracts as a result, and economic growth is likely to slow. Thus, in 2001, when the U.S. Federal Reserve (the U.S. central bank) cut interest rates eleven times, lowering the national rate from 6 percent to less than 2 percent, it was trying to stimulate the economy in the face of an economic downturn.

The actions of a central bank are also closely tied to two other important factors in any economy, inflation and unemployment. Given the previous discussion, you might be wondering, If low interest rates stimulate development, why not just keep interest rates low? When the money supply is increased through inexpensive credit, an economy can wind up with too much money chasing after too few goods—an imbalance of supply and demand. In such circumstances, prices begin to rise and money loses its value—a problem known as **inflation**. Although small levels of inflation are not a problem, inflation can become problematic when it is too high. Savings rapidly lose their value, and workers and those on fixed incomes, such as the retired, find that their salaries or pensions buy less and less. People then press for higher wages or benefits to offset higher prices, and this in turn feeds inflation further.

IN FOCUS

A Central Bank . . .

- Controls the amount of money in the economy.
- Controls the cost of borrowing money.
- Lowers interest rates to stimulate the economy.
- Raises interest rates to check inflation.

In extreme cases, countries can experience **hyperinflation**, defined as inflation that is more than 50 percent a month for more than two months in a row. (By comparison, the U.S. inflation rate in 2005 was about 3 percent per year, while that of the European Union was around 2 percent.) Hyperinflation usually occurs when governments find themselves lacking the tax revenues needed to carry out basic tasks, such as paying state employees or funding public goods—in other words, when the government has produced a budget deficit. Under these conditions, many governments go into debt, borrowing from the public, from international private banks, or from institutions such as the International Monetary Fund. For wealthy countries, lenders are not hard to find. But for poorer or more unstable countries, people and institutions may be unwilling to loan funds. The government in question may therefore decide to simply print money to pay for its own expenditures. When large amounts of money are printed and dumped into the economy, however, that money's value quickly erodes. This in turn leads people to spend their money as quickly as possible, driving inflation even higher. As you can imagine, under such conditions, normal economic processes quickly become impossible: Why accept money for any transaction when it will be virtually worthless tomorrow? For example, in Yugoslavia in the 1990s, the government, suffering from war and an international embargo against it, printed huge amounts of money to cover state expenses. As a result, between 1993 and 1995, prices increased by 5,000,000,000,000,000 (5 quadrillion) percent.

You might now conclude that a high interest rate is best; after all, it fends off inflation. Indeed, some countries that have experienced hyperinflation have since kept fairly tight control over their money supply. Yet the trade-off of high interest rates can be higher rates of unemployment and low rates of economic growth. If money becomes too expensive to borrow, businesses may be unable to create new jobs because their supply of credit for additional investment is limited. Individuals may also avoid borrowing and spending, leaving their money in the bank to earn interest at attractive rates. This can lead to deflation, where there are too many goods chasing too little money. While dropping prices might sound like a good thing, they can be devastating for businesses if they are unable to make a profit, leading to more unemployment, less spending as a result, and even more deflation. This is a problem in Japan, where prices dropped each year between 1998 and 2005. States thus walk a very fine line in managing the money supply, trying to create an economy with low inflation and low unemployment, yet knowing that these two factors may work against each other.

Given the difficulty of this balance and the temptation for governments to use the central bank for their own political ends (such as printing money to cover expenses or lowering interest rates around election time), many countries have insulated central banks from the government by making it difficult for elected leaders to dismiss the directors of the central bank. This is typically done by guaranteeing the head of the central bank a fixed term of office.

Regulation

So far, our discussion has dealt with the state's role in fostering the development of markets and property—what is to be provided, by whom, and at what cost. But states must concern themselves not only with economic output, but also with the means by which that output is created. As with public goods, moral and technical issues often affect a state's approach in this area. Are some economic processes inherently counterproductive in creating goods and services? Are there economic processes that generate "public bads," problems that affect all of society? Whose rights are most important in these cases— the individual's or the group's? These concerns draw states into the realm of economic regulation.

Regulations—rules or orders that set the boundaries of a given procedure— may take a number of different forms. Many regulations are indirect, such as safety or environmental regulations that affect the way in which a business may operate. Other regulations may be more specific, such as those in the area of competition and innovation. One problem encountered in modern economies is the emergence of a single producer of a good or service that is able to dominate the market—otherwise known as a **monopoly**. With the rise of capitalism in the nineteenth century, large corporations came to control national and even international markets for some goods; new technological developments had suddenly made such economic reach possible. States and societies began to fear that domestic economies would soon become dominated by a few huge monopolies, unfettered by competition and able to charge whatever prices they pleased for their goods. Another similar arrangement that emerged to dominate markets is what is known as a **cartel**, a group of producers that, although individually unable to dominate a market, try to do so in collaboration with one another. Microsoft is often viewed by its critics (and some countries) as a monopoly that controls the computer software market, whereas the Organization of Petroleum Exporting Countries (OPEC), whose members control some 40 percent of the world's oil supply, is an example of an international cartel.

Because monopolies and cartels can control prices by limiting supply, some states believe that such entities stifle competition, increase prices, and limit innovation. As a result, states often try to break up such entities when possible. Recently, the European Union ordered Microsoft to sell its Windows operating system unbundled from its media player to allow for greater competition from other rivals, such as RealNetworks and Apple. But there is no consensus that this is a proper activity for the state. Many argue against such regulation, believing that if monopolies do emerge, they will grow complacent, fail to innovate, and eventually be unseated by some new upstart rival. Microsoft's open source rival, Linux, could be cited here, an interesting example of new forms of property that are owned by no one and freely distributed. Cartels, many believe, will similarly fail owing to internal disagreements and the temptation for members to cheat and produce more than the cartel wishes. Others believe that monopolies and cartels are able to crush competition even before it emerges, keeping rivals and new technology out of the market. Finally, some may advocate the creation of domestic monopolies or international cartels for the very reason that others decry them: they are powerful businesses and may be able to dominate international markets. Each of these views is consistent with a different ideological perspective on the relationship between states and markets, which we will explore later in this chapter in our discussion of political-economic systems.

Trade

States must grapple with the challenge of regulating economic production not just within their country, but between their citizens and the outside world. In most economies, markets are no longer only local; goods and services come from all over the world. States can influence the degree of competition and access to goods within their own country by determining what foreign goods

---

IN FOCUS

Arguments over the Regulation of Trade

Why regulate trade?	Why not?
• To generate state revenue	• To promote competition
• To foster local industry	• To keep the costs of goods low
• To protect local jobs	• To stimulate domestic innovation in areas of comparative advantage
• To keep wealth in the country	

---

and services may enter the domestic market.

The way in which a state structures its trade can have a profound impact on its own economic development. States have a number of tools to use to influence trade: **tariffs**, which are basically taxes on imported goods; **quotas**, which limit the quantity of a good coming into the country; and other **non-tariff barriers**, which may create health, packaging, or other restrictions and whose ostensible purpose is to protect its citizens but which in reality make it difficult or expensive for foreign goods to be sold in the local market. For example, in Canada, 35 percent of all music on AM and FM must be of Canadian origin, and for television, 60 percent. This initially created conflicts with American satellite radio companies like Sirius and XM, since they did not conform to such programming, and as a result, neither service was allowed to legally operate in Canada until they offered increased Canadian content.

Why regulate trade? States may favor tariffs as a way to generate revenue, and they and local manufacturers may see such barriers against foreign competitors as a way to reduce the competitiveness of foreign goods by increasing their prices, thereby stimulating local production as a result. As in the case of regulating competition, limiting trade is a matter of hot debate. Those in favor of tariffs and other trade barriers argue that the jobs of those producing local goods are at stake and that the profits from the sale of imported goods will go to foreign producers, transferring national wealth in the process. Those who oppose trade barriers counter that a few jobs do not justify higher costs for the public as a whole. In fact, they believe that greater competition drives weaker firms out of business, stimulating domestic innovation in new areas in which the country can gain a **comparative advantage**—the ability to produce a particular good or service more efficiently relative to other countries' efficiency in producing the same good or service.[5]

We've covered a great deal in this section, so let's quickly review what we have discussed. The most basic "building blocks" of political economy are markets and property; states oversee how goods and services are produced, delineating basic economic rights and limitations. States step into the market when the private sector cannot or should not provide or control certain products, creating public goods and other social expenditures. To fund such expenses, states must not only develop a system of taxation but also help stimulate and secure the economy. Expanding and contracting the money supply helps increase economic development and provide jobs, but states must be careful not to overstimulate or retard the economy, which can generate inflation or deflation. To prevent such mishaps, many states insulate their central banks from government interference. In addition to overseeing and drawing revenue from the creation of private and public goods, states must also concern themselves with regulating the means of their production. Managing competition, both within the country and between countries, is a contentious task. All of these responsibilities are part of a complex web of cause and effect that can shape freedom, equality, and the generation of wealth. Which mixture of policies across these areas will result in economic prosperity and state power? As we shall see in the next section, there is no easy answer to this question. States have taken radically different approaches to the ideal relationship between state and market, leading to a variety of distinct political-economic systems around the world.

Political-Economic Systems

A **political-economic system** can be defined as the actual relationship between political and economic institutions in a particular country, as well as the policies and outcomes they create. Various types of political-economic systems view the ideal relationship between state and market, and between freedom and equality, in different ways. Political-economic systems are often classified as liberalism, social democracy, communism, or mercantilism.

Three of these political-economic systems match the political ideologies we discussed in Chapter 3. This should not be too surprising: political-economic systems can be seen as the attempt to realize an abstract ideology in the form of real economic institutions and policies. There is always a disjuncture, however, between theory and practice. For example, some subscribers to a liberal ideology would say that existing "liberal" political-economic systems around the world do not live up to liberal ideals. Many communists similarly condemned the communist political-economic system that was practiced in the Soviet Union as a betrayal of "true" communist thought. In addition, the ideologies of fascism and anarchism do not have a political-economic counterpart to speak of. In the case of fascism, this is because the fascist political-economic systems that arose in the 1930s were destroyed by World War II. Anarchism, meanwhile, has never been realized in politics or economics. The absence of fascism and anarchism from current political economies does not mean, however, that they could not reappear in the future.

These basic typologies simplify the complexity of political economy. In reality, of course, there are many different variations within and among these categories. Each of these categories strikes a different balance between state power and the economy, thereby shaping markets and property, public goods and social expenditures, taxation, regulation, and trade.

Liberalism

Recall from Chapter 3 that as a political ideology, liberalism places a high priority on individual political and economic freedom; it advocates limiting state power in favor of greater freedoms for the individual and the market. Liberalism assumes that individuals are best suited to take responsibility for their own behavior and well-being. Liberal scholars such as Adam Smith put their faith in the market and in private property: if people are allowed to harness their own energies, sense of entrepreneurialism, and, yes, greed, they will generate more prosperity than any government could produce through "top-down" policy making and legislation.

For liberals, then, the best state is a weak one, constrained in its autonomy and capacity. Markets and property should be regulated as little as possible, they believe, to encourage competition and innovation and produce **capitalism**—a system of production based on private ownership and free markets. The state should provide public goods only in such critical areas as defense or education; social expenditures, like most public goods, should be dramatically restricted to prevent free riding and to encourage individual responsibility. Regulations and taxation should be kept to a minimum and property rights expanded and protected. Central banks should have a limited ability to intervene in the market, and unemployment should be accepted as an inevitable outcome that cannot be eliminated. Free trade should be promoted to encourage global competition and innovation. Taxation should be kept to a minimum so that wealth will remain in the hands of the public and be reinvested into the economy. Overall, the state should by and large act as a sort of night watchman, intervening to defend the public only when crises arise. These conditions describe the liberal tenet of **laissez-faire**, which holds that the economy should be "allowed to do" what it wishes.

Under these minimalist conditions, liberals believe, economic growth will be maximized. Moreover, under such conditions, people will enjoy the greatest amount of personal and political freedom. Liberals would in fact stress that democracy requires a free market. If too much economic and political power is concentrated in the hands of the state, they believe, this monopoly would endanger democracy. In their view, private, individual economic power must act as a check on the political power of the state. As Adam Smith, one of the fathers of liberal ideology, argued in 1755, "Little else is requisite to carry a state to the highest degree of opulence from the lowest barbarism but peace, easy taxes, and a tolerable administration of justice: all the rest being brought about by the natural course of things."[6]

Liberalism as a political-economic system, then, is defined by its emphasis on individual freedoms over collective equality and on the power of markets over the state. The political economies of many countries around the world are founded on these essential liberal values. If we stretch the definition, we can even argue that any capitalist democracy is an example of liberalism at work. However, to remain true to the essential values of liberalism, this book will confine its definition to those countries where state involvement in the economy and society is relatively low.

As you might imagine, the United States is typically touted as a paragon of liberal values. The U.S. Constitution, for instance, explicitly attempts to separate and weaken state power as a check on the possible growth of tyrannical government. Regulations are often much weaker and social expenditures and taxation tend to be lower in the United States than in other industrialized democracies, and the American public is largely skeptical of state power. For many critics of American liberalism, however, this emphasis on individual rights over the needs of society appears amoral and irresponsible, a celebration of selfishness over community that only increases the gap between the rich and the poor.[7]

But the United States is not the only country in the camp of liberalism. The United Kingdom, the intellectual wellspring for much of liberal thought, is also viewed as a liberal country, as are Canada, Australia, and New Zealand (all, like the United States, former British colonies). Other countries around the world, ranging from Chile to Estonia, have over the past twenty years embraced the "neoliberal" economic model and are noted for their low levels of government regulation, taxation, and social expenditures and for their protection of property rights. Yet even though liberal ideology would argue that a free market and democracy are inseparable, we do find countries with liberal political-economic systems that nevertheless restrict democratic rights. Singapore, for example, is regularly noted for having one of the freest economic systems in the world, and yet individual political and civil rights in Singapore are sharply limited. This is similarly true of Hong Kong, which since 1999 is under the authority of China and whose democratic rights are curtailed. Critics of liberalism often highlight this contradiction, pointing out that the free market sits easily with political repression. We will discuss this contradiction further when we turn to authoritarianism in Chapter 5.

Social Democracy

In Chapter 3, we noted that social democracy draws from liberalism and communism in an attempt to temper the extremes of too much freedom or too much equality. Like liberalism, social democracy functions on a foundation of private property and open markets, but it has only come to accept this system over time. Social democrats broke with communists by rejecting the radical call for revolution and state appropriation of private property and wealth. Most notable among early social democratic thinkers was Edward Bernstein (1850–1932). In his 1898 work *Evolutionary Socialism*, Bernstein rejected Karl Marx's belief in inevitable revolution, concluding instead that democracy could evolve into socialism through the ballot box rather than through the gun.[8]

Based on this rejection of revolution and embrace of democracy, social democracy has gradually come to accept a role for private property and market forces, but it remains ambivalent about their ultimate benefits to society. Unchecked economic development produces great inequality, social democrats argue, by concentrating wealth in the hands of a very few. This in turn can polarize society, pitting owners against laborers, rich against poor, city against countryside. In this way of thinking, the state is seen less as a threat to society (as liberals tend to view it) than as a creator of certain positive social rights, basic foundations of collective equality that social democrats feel are lost in the vicissitudes of the market. The manifesto of the Party of European Socialists explains:

> For socialists and social democrats, a modern economy can only be developed in close cooperation with social partners. We know that economies are stronger when societies are just. The poverty of some diminishes the lives of all who live in a divided society. . . . That is why we say "yes" to a market economy, but "no" to a market society.[9]

These problems of economic injustice and instability can be ameliorated by the state, say social democrats, in a number of different ways. Markets and property should be encouraged by the state but controlled to prevent individual profit at the expense of society as a whole. A wide array of public goods, such as health care and transportation, should be made available by the state. Money and inflation should be actively managed by a central bank that responds to the government's need to combat and eliminate unemployment. The need for competition should not stand in the way of state regulation or even ownership of certain sectors of the economy, and trade should similarly be promoted in such a way that it does not endanger domestic businesses and jobs. Finally, the goal of equality requires a higher level of social expenditures to ensure basic benefits for all. Taxes make these social expenditures possible while also redistributing wealth from the rich to the poor. Thus, taxes tend to be higher in a social democratic system.

In addition to these policies, another element common in social democratic systems is the use of **neocorporatism**, a system of policy making involv-

ing the state, labor, and businesses. In the liberal model,
economic decisions are made
through the competitive interaction of business and labor;
workers demand higher wages
or better safety conditions,
striking or quitting their jobs
when necessary, and employers
hire, fire, and negotiate with
workers as they see fit. In some
cases, this relationship can be
quite antagonistic, leading to

IN FOCUS

**How Do Social Democracies Seek
to Achieve Greater Equality?**

- Through taxes, which make high levels of social expenditure possible while redistributing wealth from rich to poor.
- Through trade, which is promoted but balanced with preserving domestic industry and jobs.
- Through government regulation and even ownership of
  important sectors of the economy.

conflict that can hurt businesses and result in violence. Thus, even in liberal
societies, a certain level of business and labor regulation exists to protect both
workers and businesses from each other. But overall, this conflict is seen by
liberals as a necessary and positive part of human economic relations.

In contrast, a neocorporatist system as used by social democrats rejects
this combative relationship and the limited role played by the state. Instead,
neocorporatism uses policy to build consensus over competition by creating
a limited number of associations that represent a large segment of business
and labor. Good examples of such associations can be found in Germany,
where the German Federation of Trade Unions comprises eleven different
trade unions and more than 8 million workers. The Confederation of German
Employers' Associations includes nearly every large or medium-sized
employer in the country. These associations are in turn recognized by the state
as legitimate representatives of their members, and together these associations and the state decide on such important economic policy issues as wages,
unemployment compensation, and taxation.

In other words, many decisions that under liberalism are left to the state
alone or that result from the interaction of business and labor are decided
under neocorporatism in a cooperative and organized fashion. The result, supporters argue, is a system that is much less prone to conflict and that provides a greater role for both business and labor in state economic policies.
Liberals would retort that such structures harm the economy in the long run
by hindering the flexibility of business and labor, making it difficult to fire
employees, to close unprofitable factories, or to hire additional workers.

Finally, social democratic systems often involve themselves in the economic system through state ownership of firms. Even liberal countries have
some basic services under public ownership, such as mail services or public
transportation, but social democratic states may own part or all of a much
wider set of businesses that provide what they view as public goods. These

can range from extractors of natural resources such as oil, timber, and the like, to various large industries, including steel, banking, or automobile production, which are seen as too large or economically important to be left in the hands of a few private owners. As a result, the social democratic state assumes control, believing that it can better serve society by directly owning and managing the firms. Until 2002, the French state owned more than 40 percent of the auto manufacturer Renault (it is now around 16 percent); and in Sweden, all iron mines are owned by the state, having been purchased from private businesses decades ago.

Social democratic systems are most common in Europe; they include France, Germany, Sweden, and Denmark. These states generally have more autonomy and capacity than do liberal states, since they are able (and expected) to actively intervene in the economy in order to guide it toward cer-

---

IN FOCUS

Contributors to the Theories of Political Economy

System	Thinker	Contribution
Liberalism	Adam Smith	*The Wealth of Nations* (1776), considered one of the first texts on modern economics. Articulated the idea that economic development requires limited government interference.
Social democracy	Edward Bernstein	*Evolutionary Socialism* (1898). Rejected Marx's belief in the inevitability of revolution, arguing that economic equality can be achieved through democratic participation.
Communism	Karl Marx	*Das Kapital* (1867). Asserted that human history is driven by economic relations and inequality and that revolution will eventually replace capitalism with a system of total equality between people.
Mercantilism	Friedrich List	*National System of Political Economy* (1841). Rejected free-trade theories of liberalism, arguing that states must play a strong role in protecting and developing the national economy against foreign competitors.

INSTITUTIONS IN

ACTION

WEALTH AND PROSPERITY IN THE UNITED STATES AND EUROPE

One of the major debates between the United States and Europe has been over their rival visions of prosperity and economic development. At first glance, the issue appears rather simple. Although Europe's per capita gross domestic product (GDP) might at first appear higher than that of the United States, when converted into purchasing-power parity, it drops below the U.S. GDP by about a third. Similarly, many observers in both the United States and Europe have noted the latter's lower growth rate. Europe would seem to be falling behind the United States in wealth and prosperity. But is this correct? It depends on how one measures wealth. According to some research, when one looks more closely at the numbers, the major differences between Europe and the United States in terms of productivity or growth are in fact not as different as they first appear. This, however, would make the differences in GDP even more puzzling. The answer may lie in how Europeans and Americans choose to take that wealth. In the United States, the rise in GDP has been accompanied by an increase in working hours, to the extent that Americans work five or six weeks more a year than workers in Europe. More hours worked, of course, means a higher GDP. In Europe, the trend has been toward greater leisure, longer vacations, and earlier retirement. Such leisure is typically supported by social expenditures and state regulations. While this does not count toward GDP, it can certainly be seen as an important component of prosperity. Thus, while Americans on average may be wealthier, they work longer and harder for it. The remaining puzzle is why there is this difference in the first place. Is it due to cultural values? The power of trade unions? The specific effects of particular political-economic systems?

Source: Alberto Alesina, Edward Glaeser, and Bruce Sacerdote, "Work and Leisure in the US and Europe: Why So Different?" NBER Working Series 1128 (April 2005). www.nber.org.

tain social goals. Social democrats laud these systems for their attempt to balance market forces with societal needs; liberals view them as overly regulated, inflexible, and thus a drag on economic growth.

Communism

Whereas social democracy departs from liberalism in its attempt to balance individual freedom and collective equality, the political-economic system of communism chooses to effectively eliminate the former to fully achieve the latter. We will discuss communism in much greater detail in Chapter 8, when we look at communist and postcommunist countries; for now we will focus on its basic institutions. Communist thinkers such as Karl Marx began with the premise that private property and a free market cannot truly serve the needs of society as a whole. Communists view private property as a form of power that inevitably leads to control over others. Economic competition between people creates exploitation and the development of social classes in which a small group of the wealthy dominate and benefit from the labor of the poor majority. Both domestically and internationally, this exploitation opens an ever-wider gap between those who control the economy and those who merely labor in it. Such inequalities, Marx argued, will inevitably lead to a revolution, during which a single communist party will take control of the state on behalf of all people.

Given this interpretation of markets and property, communist systems choose to transform both. Private property is fully nationalized, placed in the hands of the state on behalf of the people. Through nationalization, communism seeks to eliminate the economic differences between people and the instruments of exploitation. In other words, the entire economy becomes a public good, existing for the benefit of all. In addition, market forces are eliminated by the state; almost all private transactions are considered black markets. In stark contrast to the "invisible hand" of liberalism's market and the guided economies of social democracy, communism's economic decision making is entrusted entirely to the state, which is assumed to make the most rational economic decisions that produce the greatest benefits for the whole of society.

Because all economic decision making and ownership are centralized under state control, many of the essential tasks of states in other political-economic systems are fundamentally different under communism. Taxation, for example, takes an indirect form through fixed prices and wages; any profit produced by a worker or a firm goes to the state for public expenditures (which include guaranteed employment). Because all firms are owned by the state, competition is also eliminated, and regulations, although present, may be much weaker—since the state winds up regulating itself. Finally, trade is highly restricted; the only imports are those the state deems necessary that cannot be produced domestically. State capacity and autonomy are extremely high; the state can operate without the interference of either the public or private economic actors.[10]

As you would expect, supporters of private property and market forces argue that states lack the ability to make the kinds of economic decisions made by a decentralized market. Inefficiency and waste are likely in such a state-dominated system. Moreover, supporters of democracy argue that so much power in the hands of the state would guarantee authoritarian rule. If there are no property rights left with the people and if all economic decisions are made by the state, there is no separation between public and private. States

Political Economic Systems

IN FOCUS

	Liberalism	Social Democracy	Communism	Mercantilism
Role of the state in the economy	Little; minimal welfare state	Some state ownership, regulation; large welfare state	Total state ownership; extensive welfare state	Much state ownership or direction; small welfare state
Role of the market	Paramount	Important but not sacrosanct	None	Limited
State capacity and autonomy	Low	Moderate	Very high	High
Importance of equality	Low	High	High	Low
How is policy made?	Pluralism	Corporatism	State/party	State
Possible flaws	Inequality, monopolies	Expense of welfare state, inefficiency	Authoritarianism and inefficiency	Can tend toward authoritarianism; can distort market
Examples	U.S., UK, former British colonies	Western Europe (Germany, Sweden)	Cuba, Soviet Union, China	Japan, South Korea, India

wind up controlling the fates of people—where they live and work, what they earn, what they may buy. In response, communists would say that what they offer is total equality for all; their system emphasizes equality and sacrifices individual freedom, just as liberalism does the opposite. And even if such a system is inefficient, its supporters might argue, better that economic resources are wasted in the attempt to provide for all than squandered on luxuries for a wealthy few, as is common in market economies.

Mercantilism

The final political-economic system, **mercantilism**, stands quite apart in the debate over freedom and equality that separates liberalism, social democracy, and communism. Whereas all three systems we have studied so far theoretically emphasize the needs of society, albeit in different ways, mercantilism focuses on the needs of the state; it is much less concerned with either individual freedom or collective equality. Instead, national economic power is paramount. As a result, mercantilism views the domestic economy as an instrument that exists to serve the needs of the state by generating wealth that can be used for national power. Mercantilist states focus in particular on their position in the international system, for they believe that economic weakness undermines national sovereignty. Political power must be backed by wealth, in the mercantilist view, and that wealth should be directed toward national ends.[11]

Although this system may seem a strange outlier in the debate between freedom and equality, as it seems to emphasize neither, as a political-economic system mercantilism is the oldest of the four we have covered. At the advent of modern economies in Europe centuries ago, most countries engaged in mercantilist practices. The building of empires, in particular, was an outgrowth of mercantilism, a way in which a state could use its political power to gain control over resources and markets, shutting out its rivals. The creation of British colonies in North America and elsewhere and the requirement that they trade only with the home country are good examples of mercantilist practices at work. And in spite of the challenges posed by other political-economic alternatives, mercantilism continues to be an attractive system for countries around the world, some of which have used it to great effect, particularly in Asia. China, which is quickly abandoning communist economic practices, is moving along what could be called a mercantilist direction, and Russia, too, has shown mercantilist tendencies since the collapse of the Soviet Union. These contemporary policies are often referred to as *neomercantilism*, to distinguish them from the earlier imperial forms.

One way that mercantilist states attempt to achieve state economic power is through an active industrial policy. Economic ministries seek to direct the economy toward certain industries and away from others through such policies as taxation and subsidies. In some cases, mercantilist states, like social democracies, may rely on partial or full state ownership of specific industries (sometimes called **parastatals**), attempting to create certain businesses that are viewed as critical for international competitiveness. Capitalism is guided by the state toward goals set by the government.

Another complementary method to boost the domestic economy under mercantilism is the strong use of tariffs, nontariff barriers, and other trade regulations. Here the rationale is that goods that are not locally produced lead to a loss of national profits and an increased dependency on foreign economies. High tariff barriers are a common way to shield and promote domestic industry. For example, after World War II, the Japanese government relied on its Ministry of International Trade and Industry to steer the economy toward exports such as electronics and automobiles. High tariff barriers kept foreign competition at bay, and subsidies were provided to certain industrial sectors, such as producers of semiconductors. South Korea subsequently followed a similar set of policies.

In its emphasis on state power, mercantilism does not typically focus on social expenditures in the way that social democracy does. Welfare benefits tend to be much lower. Indeed, there is a logic to this policy: if benefits are low, the public knows that it must bear the burden for retirement and health care. This can encourage higher public savings, providing more capital that can be borrowed by the state or businesses. Lower levels of expenditure are also likely to translate into lower taxes. Finally, the central bank is a critical mercantilist tool: it promotes industrialization through such policies as low interest rates to encourage borrowing. State capacity and autonomy are much higher in mercantilist political economics than in liberal or social democratic systems. However, unlike under communism, markets and private property remain powerful under mercantilism, even though they are administered by state policy.

Supporters of mercantilism cite its ability to direct an economy toward areas of industrial development and international competitiveness that the market, left on its own, might not pursue. For developing countries, such direction is particularly attractive, and Japan and South Korea are cited as exemplars of mercantilism's strengths. Critics of mercantilism respond that states are not well suited to decide what kinds of industries are likely to be successful in the long run and that putting so much economic power into states' hands while limiting competition is a recipe for waste and corruption. Even though Japan and South Korea are examples of successful mercantilism, some critics argue, the economic downturns in both countries during the 1990s were the inevitable result of overly tight connections between the economy and the state. Using many other examples, such as postcolonial India and Nigeria, critics assert that mercantilist policies have failed to reap significant rewards.

IN FOCUS

How Do Mercantilist States Seek to Achieve Economic Power?

- By directing the economy toward certain industries and away from others through the use of subsidies and taxation.
- Through partial or full state ownership of industries that are considered critical (parastatals).
- With the strong use of tariffs, nontariff barriers, and other regulations.
- By limiting social expenditures and thereby keeping taxation to a minimum.
- With low interest rates set by the central bank to encourage borrowing and investment.

Finally, critics note that in its most extreme form, mercantilism is connected to the ideology of fascism, with the state directing the economy in the same way it seeks to direct society. Fascist Germany and imperial Japan both employed extreme forms of mercantilism and used war as a means to conquer and control important economic resources such as land, food, and oil. Mercantilism is not inherently incompatible with democracy, however; postwar Japan and India are examples of democratic countries that have industrialized using mercantilist methods. Overall, though, mercantilism is more commonly correlated with authoritarian systems than with democracies.

Political-Economic Systems and the State: Comparing Outcomes

Having gained an understanding of the different political-economic systems used around the world and the different ways they approach their tasks, we next should consider how to compare them. Since each system is founded on a different ideological approach and set of institutions to reconcile freedom and equality, it might seem that trying to compare them would be difficult, like comparing apples and oranges. However, there are criteria we can use to compare these systems. These criteria are by no means the only ways to make comparisons and draw conclusions, but they are useful tools for our purposes.

Gross Domestic Product (GDP)

One basic criterion for comparison we can use is the level of economic development. The most common tool that economists use to measure economic development is **gross domestic product (GDP)**, defined as the total market value of all goods and services produced within a country over a period of one year.* GDP provides a basic benchmark for the average per capita income in a country. However, GDP statistics can be quite misleading. For one thing, a given amount of money will buy more in certain parts of a country than in others. A salary of $30,000 a year will go a lot further in Boise, Idaho, than it will in New York City, where a home costs many times more. The same problem arises when one compares countries: people may earn far more in some countries than they do in others, but those raw figures do not take into account

---

*Another common measure of a country's wealth is gross national product (GNP), which is similar to GDP, except that it counts the value of goods and services produced by the residents of a country, including income from abroad. For example, if a French company earns profits from producing goods in China, those profits would be included in France's GNP but not in its GDP. Conversely, those profits would be included in China's GDP but not in its GNP. As international trade has become more important, many countries have switched from GNP to GDP as the primary way of measuring output. For that reason, and in the interests of consistency, GDP is used throughout this text.

the relative costs of living in those countries, especially when trying to convert different economies into a single currency, such as the U.S. dollar. As exchange rates rise or fall between countries, this can make countries look richer or poorer in comparison, which is misleading. To address these difficulties, economists often calculate national GDP data on the basis of what is known as purchasing power parity. **Purchasing-power parity (PPP)** attempts to estimate the buying power of income in each country by comparing similar costs, such as food and housing, using prices in the United States as a benchmark. When these data are factored in, comparative incomes change rather dramatically, as shown in Table 4.1. For example, without PPP, Japan's national income is higher than that of Canada, but when the cost of living in each country is factored in through PPP, the reverse is true. Incomes in poorer countries such as China and India also rise quite dramatically when PPP is taken into account.

Although GDP can be a useful way to measure wealth, it has its limitations. For example, since these figures capture economic transactions, a coun-

Table 4.1 Measuring the Size of Economies, 2005		
	GDP Per Capita (in U.S. $)	**GDP Per Capita (PPP, in U.S. $)**
United States	42,075	42,075
Sweden	38,451	29,544
United Kingdom	36,977	28,876
Japan	36,486	29,164
France	33,125	28,145
Germany	33,099	29,204
Canada	32,072	33,103
South Korea	14,649	19,515
Mexico	6,566	9,726
Russia	4,749	10,300
South Africa	3,885	10,585
Brazil	3,310	8,594
Iran	2,607	7,630
China	1,352	5,791
India	651	3,018
Nigeria	527	959

Sources: Central Intelligence Agency, World Bank.

try that suffers a natural disaster may see its GDP go up as a result of increased activity to rebuild the damage. High crime might also increase GDP if more police are hired and prisons built. Nor does GDP take into consideration the costs of economic growth, such as pollution, or other indicators of social development, such as life expectancy (though these, too, can be measured, as we will see shortly). Material transactions alone do not easily capture the overall well-being or happiness of a society.

Gini Index

Perhaps more problematic is the fact that GDP does not tell us how wealth is distributed among a population (the issue of inequality). A more sophisticated approach that does so is the **Gini index**, a mathematical formula that measures the amount of economic inequality in a society. Perfect equality is given a Gini ranking of zero, and perfect inequality gets a ranking of 100. Thus, the greater the Gini index, the greater the inequality within a given economy. As Table 4.2 reveals, there is a correlation between the amount of wealth held by the poorest 10 percent of the population and the concentration of wealth in the hands of the richest 10 percent. In countries where those at the bottom hold less wealth, those at the top (as opposed to those in the middle) tend to hold more. These greater inequalities in turn lead to a higher Gini rating. Interestingly, China and the United States, one a relatively poor, communist country and the other a rich, liberal one, have similar levels of income inequality. What explains this? For one thing, over the past twenty years, China has been rapidly undertaking market reforms that have increased inequality. In 1985, China's Gini index was 29, similar to that of social democratic Germany. Meanwhile, Japan and Sweden, one mercantilist and the other social democratic, have two of the lowest levels of income inequality in the world.

What conclusions can we draw from the Gini index? One is that social democratic countries tend to have the lowest Gini ratings, which is not surprising given their emphasis on equality. Some mercantilist countries, such as Japan and South Korea, have similarly low rates of inequality. One can see a high level of inequality in some liberal countries, such as the United States, but other liberal countries, such as Canada and Ireland, exhibit much more equal income distributions. Less-developed countries tend to have the worst levels of inequality.

We should note that inequality is not the same thing as poverty.[12] While poverty tends to be measured by some absolute material standard, inequality can be measured in very different ways. We should therefore be careful about confusing the two. If, for example, those making $10,000 a year and those making $100,000 a year find that their incomes are rising at the same rate

Table 4.2   Distribution of Wealth

Percentage of Total National Income Held by Segment of Population

	Poorest 10% of Population	Richest 10% of Population	Gini Index
Japan	4.8	21.7	24.9
Sweden	3.6	22.2	25.0
Germany	3.2	22.1	28.3
Russia	3.3	23.8	31.0
South Korea	2.9	22.5	31.6
India	3.9	28.5	32.5
France	2.8	25.1	32.7
Canada	2.5	25.0	33.1
United Kingdom	2.1	28.5	36.0
United States	1.9	29.9	40.8
Iran	2.0	33.7	43.0
China	1.8	33.1	44.7
Nigeria	1.6	40.8	50.6
Mexico	1.0	43.1	54.6
South Africa	1.4	44.7	57.8
Brazil	0.7	46.9	59.3

Source: World Bank. Data for Russia is from 2002; for Brazil and China, 2001; for Germany, India, Mexico, South Africa, Sweden, and United States, 2000; for the United Kingdom, 1999; for Canada, Iran, and South Korea, 1998; for Nigeria, 1997; for France, 1995; for Japan, 1993.

(say, 10 percent), overall poverty may drop while relative inequality stays the same—the latter group will still be making ten times more than the former. However, in absolute terms, a 10 percent increase in a $10,000 income is only $1,000, whereas a 10 percent increase in a $100,000 income is $10,000; thus, in absolute terms, the difference in inequality has grown. For some, these issues lead to the conclusion that poverty and inequality are zero-sum; to reduce poverty, there must be economic growth, but such growth will inevitably create inequality. However, our Gini examples show that the richest countries are also those that tend to be the most equal, and some economists suggest that a reduction in relative inequality does correlate with reduced poverty.[13] In terms of global poverty, there appears to be a consen-

IN FOCUS

Measuring Wealth

Gross domestic product (GDP)	Total production within a country, regardless of who owns the products.
Gross national product (GNP)	Both production and the flow of wealth into and out of a country, with attention to national versus foreign ownership.
Purchasing-power parity (PPP)	Takes cost of living and buying power into account.
Gini index	Assesses inequality.
Human development index (HDI)	Assesses health, education, and wealth of population.

sus that in total numbers and as a percentage of the global population, poverty has declined over the past twenty years. In contrast, whether inequality across the globe as a whole has increased is strongly debated, depending on the data used as well as whether it is absolute or relative inequality that is being measured. Thus, some studies show that world inequality, both relative and absolute, is rising; others dispute this, arguing that such figures are not properly weighted to take into account such large countries as China and India, where economic growth has been strong.[14]

Human Development Index (HDI)

Poverty, inequality, relative or absolute—how can we make sense of any of this if we want to simply determine whether people are better off? There is a final measurement that might help. The **human development index (HDI)**, developed by the United Nations Development Program, looks not only at the total amount of wealth in a society, as GDP does, nor even at its distribution, as with the Gini index, but at the overall outcome of that wealth—the well-being of a country's people. The HDI takes into consideration such factors as adult literacy, life expectancy, and educational enrollment, as well as GDP. By looking at such data, we can consider whether the wealth generated in a country is actually used in a way that provides a basic standard of living for all, whether through public or private means. All 162 countries in the world are ranked on the HDI; in 2004, Norway was ranked at number one, and Sierra Leone, wracked by civil war, came in at the very bottom.[15]

The HDI does show a strong correlation between standard of living and a country's GDP, as shown in Table 4.3. Those countries with the highest national incomes also show the highest levels of education and life expectancy in the world. Interestingly, the HDI lists social democratic systems such as Sweden right alongside more liberal countries such as Canada and the United States and mercantilist ones such as Japan and South Korea. Across these countries, HDI scores have consistently increased over the past twenty years. Each of these political-economic systems, it would seem, can create its own path to high standards of living. Communist and postcommunist states, however, generally show lower and more varied results, and in recent years, their scores have moved in divergent directions. China, for example, has shown a dramatic increase in its HDI score over the past decade, though it lags far behind many other states, while over the same period, Russia's HDI score has actually declined.

Table 4.3 Comparing Wealth and Prosperity		
	GDP Per Capita (PPP, in U.S. $)	**HDI Rank**
Sweden	29,544	2
Canada	33,103	4
United States	42,075	8
Japan	29,164	9
United Kingdom	28,876	12
France	28,145	16
Germany	29,204	19
South Korea	19,515	28
Mexico	9,726	53
Russia	10,300	57
Brazil	8,594	72
China	5,791	94
Iran	7,630	101
South Africa	10,585	119
India	3,018	127
Nigeria	959	151

Sources: Central Intelligence Agency, United Nations Development Program.

Note: HDI rank is out of a total of 177 countries in 2002; GDP data are for 2005.

The Future of Political Economy

For a century, our four major models of political economy have rivaled one another as they have sought to strike the ideal relationship between freedom and equality. In the early years of modern capitalism, mercantilism was a dominant force, but by the nineteenth century, liberalism had spread alongside democracy across Europe and North America. In the early twentieth century, liberalism, too, began to falter, challenged by fascism and communism and their alternative forms of political and economic organization. For many observers in that period, the extreme mercantilist systems practiced in Germany and Japan under fascism or in the Soviet Union under communism were attractive alternatives to a liberalism that appeared economically and ideologically bankrupt.

Yet as we stand at the beginning of the twenty-first century, the world is a quite different place. The most extreme forms of fascist mercantilism were destroyed by World War II, and even more limited neomercantilist policies have in recent years been challenged by internal difficulties and a changing international economy. Communism has largely vanished; it survives in only a few countries and often in name only. Social democracy, too, faces challenges, struggling with the high costs of the public goods it provides, especially as the population it serves grows older.

For some, then, the twenty-first century represents the triumph of liberalism, a victory for private property and free markets over state regulation of the economy. Individual freedom, it would seem, has trumped the quest for collective equality. The world we live in now is one dominated by a liberal political economy.

To what extent are these cries of victory borne out by evidence? One interesting study is summarized in Table 4.4, which compares the overall level of economic changes around the world consistent with liberalism, taking into account such factors as government expenditures, price controls, taxes, individual property rights, and trade. Changes in these areas that limit the power of the state over that of private property and market forces are commonly referred to as economic liberalization. The ratings in the table are given on a 10-point scale, with 10 being the most liberal and 1 being the least. The study (conducted by a liberal organization) concluded that from 1980 to 2002, there has been a steady move toward greater **economic liberalization**, from an average global score of 5.1 in 1980 to 6.4 in 2003.[16] Even its critics acknowledge that economic liberalization has grown, in some cases dramatically, around the world.

So is liberalism now the only game in town? It may still be too early to write the epitaph for any of the other political-economic systems. Although other forms of political economy may be down, they are not necessarily out.

Table 4.4 Increasing Levels of Economic Liberalization, 1980–2003			
Country	1980	2003	Change
United States	7.4	8.2	0.8
United Kingdom	6.1	8.1	2.0
Canada	7.0	8.0	1.0
Germany	7.1	7.5	0.4
Sweden	5.6	7.3	1.7
South Korea	5.7	7.0	1.3
Japan	6.4	7.2	0.8
South Africa	5.4	6.9	1.5
France	5.7	6.9	1.2
Mexico	5.1	6.5	1.4
India	4.9	6.4	1.5
Brazil	3.7	5.9	2.2
Iran	3.4	6.1	2.7
China	3.8	6.0	2.2
Nigeria	3.5	5.9	2.4
Russia	N/A	5.1	

Note: 10 = most liberal.
Source: Fraser Institute.

Just as liberalism seemed on the edge of extinction in the 1930s, only to reemerge, so, too, might any of these other political-economic arrangements reemerge—rethought, revamped, and reenergized. Moreover, across the globe there are continuous pressures against liberal economic policies, whether in the form of protests against cuts to social services, support for increased trade barriers, or calls for "fair trade" in favor of free trade. Many of these forces have been compounded by globalization. We will discuss this at length in Chapter 10. Finally, in spite of its victories, liberalism remains burdened with concerns that it has not yet been able to resolve: inequities between rich and poor, boom-and-bust cycles of economic development, and, some believe, an overemphasis on material goods over the intangible elements of society, such as community, morality, environment, and leisure. Whether money can buy happiness is an important challenge for liberalism, since individual material wealth is liberalism's primary product. Studies indicate that past a certain point, increased wealth and individual consumption do not make people any happier.[17] At what point might people say that enough is enough?

In Sum: The End of Economic History?

As we have seen, states play a large role in the domestic and international economy. They must deal with and manage markets and property, with an eye toward generating societal wealth and revenue so that basic political tasks can be funded. This is no small task, as it goes to the heart of freedom and equality: How should freedom and equality be reconciled through economic policy, and what mixture of the two will create the greatest degree of wealth? Different political-economic systems give very different answers to those questions. Economic liberalism has weathered various challenges to emerge as the dominant system in much of the world. As we shall see in the next two chapters, this "triumph" of liberalism has occurred alongside political liberalization as well, as many authoritarian regimes around the globe have given way to democracy.

But in spite of these dramatic changes, it would be foolish to assume that political economy has reached its endgame. We cannot know what other economic challenges, opportunities, and ideas lie on the horizon. The modern industrial economy and the various political-economic systems that describe and manage it are all relatively new, having formed only in the past few centuries—the blink of an eye in terms of human history. Can we be so certain that in a world of rapid economic change our current assumptions about markets and property, freedom, and equality will remain valid for long? Dramatic transformations are certain to come.

NOTES

1. For a discussion of the difficulties inherent in providing public goods, see Mancur Olson, *The Logic of Collective Action: Public Goods and the Theory of Groups* (Cambridge: Harvard University Press, 1965).
2. For a discussion of this problem as it relates to the United States, see Charles Murray, *Losing Ground: American Social Policy, 1950–1980* (New York: Basic Books, 1984).
3. See Sven Steinmo, *Taxation and Democracy: Swedish, British, and American Approaches to Financing the Modern State* (New Haven: Yale University Press, 1993).
4. A good comparative discussion of central banking can be found in Majorie Deane and Robert Pringle, *The Central Banks* (New York: Viking, 1995).

5. The arguments in favor of free trade can be found in Jagdish Bhagwati, *Free Trade Today* (Princeton: Princeton University Press, 2003); for a protectionist view, see Patrick Buchanan, *The Great Betrayal: How American Sovereignty and Social Justice Are Being Sacrificed to the Gods of the Global Economy* (New York: Little, Brown, 1998).

6. Adam Smith, *Essays on Philosophical Subjects* (Indianapolis: Liberty Classics, 1980), 1xxx.

7. See, for example, Robert Kuttner, *Everything for Sale: The Virtues and Limits of Markets* (Chicago: University of Chicago Press, 1999); for a European perspective, see Emmanuel Todd, *After the Empire: The Breakdown of the American Order* (New York: Columbia University Press, 2003).

8. Edward Bernstein, *Evolutionary Socialism: A Criticism and Affirmation* (New York: Schocken, 1961).

9. Party of European Socialists, *Manifesto for the 1999 European Elections*, 3.

10. For a discussion of communist political economies, see Robert W. Campbell, *The Socialist Economies in Transition: A Primer on Semi-Reformed Systems* (Bloomington: Indiana University Press, 1991).

11. The classic work on mercantilism is Friedrich List, *The National System of Political Economy* (New York: Kelley, 1966).

12. For data and discussion on global poverty, see the World Bank Poverty Net Website, www.worldbank.org/poverty/.

13. Martin Ravallion, "A Poverty-Inequality Trade-Off?" Development Research Group, World Bank, Policy Research Working Paper WPS 3579, April 2005; www.worldbank.org.

14. For global poverty data, see the World Bank, World Development Report 2005; www.worldbank.org; a more optimistic view of global poverty and inequality can be found in Xavier Sala-I-Martin, "The World Distribution of Income," National Bureau of Economic Research Working Paper No. 8933, May 2002; www.nber.org.

15. See the United Nations Human Development Report 2004, available at undp.hdr.org.

16. Fraser Institute, Economic Freedom of the World Annual Report 2004, available at www.fraserinstitute.ca/.

17. Robert Frank, "How Not to Buy Happiness," *Daedalus* (Spring 2004): 69–79.

5 AUTHORITARIANISM AND TOTALITARIANISM

"Man is born free but everywhere he is in chains," wrote Jean-Jacques Rousseau in 1762. Since his time, democracy has emerged and flourished in many places throughout the world. However, according to Freedom House, an American nongovernmental organization that monitors and promotes open markets and democratic institutions around the world, over half of the world's population still live in societies defined as either "partly free," where some personal liberties and democratic rights are limited, or "not free," where the public has little individual freedom.[1] In neither case can these regimes be described as democratic.

In this chapter, we will look at the internal dynamics and origins of nondemocratic regimes. After defining these regimes and their relationship to freedom and equality, we will look at their sources, addressing the puzzle of why a nondemocracy is the dominant regime in some countries but not in others. Behind this puzzle lies the broader question of whether society's natural political state is one of democratic or nondemocratic rule. We will specifically look at competing societal and economic explanations. What circumstances, if any, are more likely to promote authoritarian or totalitarian rule? This discussion of the possible sources of nondemocratic regimes will lead us into an examination of how their rulers maintain their hold on power. Nondemocratic regimes display a great diversity; nevertheless, we can identify and contrast a number of common features. Finally, we will consider the future of nondemocratic rule. After 1989 and the end of the Cold War, many assumed that liberal democracy was the wave of the future. In recent years, however, some question whether, in the face of tremendous political, social, and economic obstacles, democracy is ever going to spread to all people. Such issues will set the stage for Chapter 6, where we will look at democracy.

Defining Authoritarianism and Totalitarianism

Scholars define **authoritarianism** as a political regime in which a small group of individuals exercises power over the state without being constitutionally responsible to the public. In authoritarian regimes, the public does not play a significant role in selecting or removing leaders from office; thus, political leaders in authoritarian regimes have much greater leeway to develop policies that they "dictate" to the people (hence the term *dictator*). As one can imagine, authoritarian regimes by their nature are built around the restriction of individual freedom. At a minimum, they eliminate people's right to choose their own leaders, and they also restrict to varying degrees other liberties, such as the freedom of speech or of assembly. Authoritarianism's relationship to equality is less clear. Some authoritarian regimes, such as under communism, limit individual freedom in order to produce greater social equality. Others seek to provide neither freedom nor equality, existing only to enhance the power of those in control.[2]

Various types of ideologies and institutions can be found in authoritarianism. Authoritarian leaders do not always rule completely arbitrarily; indeed, authoritarianism can have a strong institutional underpinning of ideology. As ideologies, fascism and communism, for instance, explicitly reject liberal democracy as an inferior form of social organization, favoring instead a powerful state and restricted individual freedoms. This ideology provides the set of norms that fascist or communist authoritarian leaders follow. But other authoritarian regimes are not ideological, and their politics are often driven largely by the whims of those in power. In this case, it becomes difficult to even speak of a regime. Indeed, under such conditions, the term is often used pejoratively by critics, coupled with a leader's name (such as "the Castro regime" in reference to Cuba or "Saddam Hussein's regime" in Iraq). This terminology reflects the critics' view that all decisions flow from the ruler, unfettered by political institutions of any sort. The leader, in essence, *is* the regime.

Many people use the terms *totalitarian* and *authoritarian* interchangeably to describe political regimes that severely limit individual freedom. This has led to controversy, as *totalitarianism* became a highly charged word, often used during the Cold War to describe the Soviet Union or any particularly repressive (or detested) political regime. Some thus called for abandoning the term altogether. But political scientist Juan Linz, long the most prominent scholar of nondemocratic regimes, has argued strongly that totalitarianism is an important concept in its own right and one distinct from

IN FOCUS

Authoritarianism

- A small group of individuals exercises power over the state.
- Government is not constitutionally responsible to the public.
- Public has little or no role in selecting leaders.
- Individual freedom is restricted.
- Authoritarian regimes may be institutionalized and legitimate.

authoritarian rule. **Totalitarianism** refers to a highly centralized regime that possesses some form of strong ideology that seeks to transform and absorb fundamental aspects of state, society, and the economy. Unlike authoritarianism, totalitarianism seeks to use power to transform the total institutional fabric of a country according to some ideological goal. Finally, because of the ambitious goals of totalitarianism, violence often becomes a necessary tool to destroy any obstacle to change.[3] The use of terror not only destroys enemies of the totalitarian ideology, but, as political philosopher Hannah Arendt pointed out, also shatters human will, destroying the ability of individuals to create, much less aspire to, freedom.[4] Under these conditions, the use of terror and violence is common in order to break down existing institutions and remake them in the leadership's own image. This is not to say that a violent regime is totalitarian. The central issue is to what end that violence is used. Totalitarianism often emerges in cases where those who have come to power profess a radical or reactionary political attitude, both of which reject the status quo and see dramatic change as indispensable and violence as necessary or even positive.

Many countries in history have been controlled by leaders with totalitarian aspirations, but few of these leaders have been able to put their theories to practice. The Soviet Union under the rule of Josef Stalin from the 1930s to the 1950s is commonly viewed as totalitarian, with most domestic institutions radically restructured, most aspects of private life controlled by the state and the Communist Party, and millions imprisoned and executed toward those ends. Nazi Germany is also commonly viewed as a totalitarian regime, although in some areas, such as the economy, changes were relatively few. Other fascist regimes, such as Italy during World War II, lacked the capacity and power to be totalitarian, even though they openly aspired to be so. Similarly, while China during the Cultural Revolution of the 1960s experienced widespread violence against people and institutions, the fragmentation of the Communist Party and its ideology raises questions as to whether this was truly a totalitarian state. As we see, in spite of a more precise definition, we find the term difficult to apply (and thus subject to pejorative, rather than objective, use).

In the modern world, only communist North Korea can still be properly described as totalitarian, dominated by an elaborate ideology that covers all aspects of life and is backed by violence, widespread fear, and the absence of even small

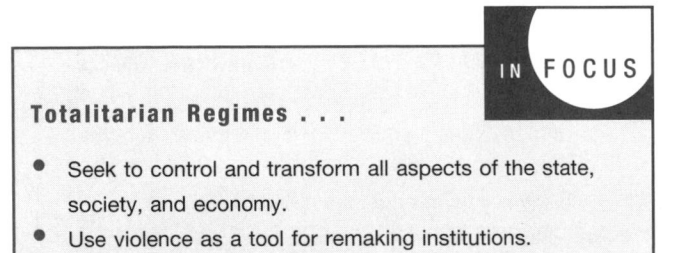

IN FOCUS

Totalitarian Regimes . . .

- Seek to control and transform all aspects of the state, society, and economy.
- Use violence as a tool for remaking institutions.
- Have a strong ideological goal.
- Have arisen relatively rarely.

personal freedoms. By way of comparison, a country such as Iraq under Saddam Hussein, although highly oppressive, cannot be described as totalitarian because it lacked a clear ideology and in many ways was less centralized than outsiders imagined. Saddam Hussein's primary goal as Iraq's leader was simply to maintain and expand his political power as an end in itself. Violence, then, was a means to one end alone—keeping Hussein in control—and not the transformation of society.

To sum up, authoritarian rule is a political regime in which power is exercised by a few, unbound by any public or constitutional control. The public lacks not only the right to choose its own leaders but also other personal liberties that those in power may see as a threat, such as freedom of speech or assembly. In contrast, totalitarianism adds to this greater state centralization an ideology that seeks the fundamental transformation of most domestic institutions and the use of violence toward that end.

Sources of Nondemocratic Rule

Now that we have defined authoritarianism and totalitarianism, we might consider their sources. Naturally, there is no single or simple explanation, and political scientists do not agree on what factors are most important in explaining nondemocratic regimes. These issues will become clearer as we look at the most prominent economic and societal explanations for nondemocratic rule.

Economic Sources of Nondemocratic Rule

Many observers argue that authoritarianism and totalitarianism are essentially an expression of economic forces and institutions. For example, a great deal of scholarship argues that there is a strong connection between markets and regimes. Economic growth, which distributes wealth, eliminates widespread poverty and creates a middle class. This inevitably undermines nondemocratic rule. Not only is such a society more educated and able to formulate and articulate its own political goals, but as it gains this awareness, society inevitably seeks to assert its own political rights.[5] The wealthier the society, the greater the desire to couple public economic power with greater political power, especially to limit the greed of those in office. Where there is no middle class, however, and where poverty and inequality are great, an authoritarian or totalitarian regime is much more likely to develop and persist, either to defend the economic wealth of the few who possess it against the majority (producing a regime that is elite focused) or to forcibly distribute that wealth among the majority population (producing a regime that is mass focused). Consistent with our earlier discussion of political ideology, liberals thus view capitalism as a powerful weapon against nondemocratic rule. Social democrats, too, would agree with much of this argument, though they would counter that a state focused on redistribution and social expenditures is a better instrument toward the creation and protection of a middle class and the undermining of nondemocratic regimes.

Are such arguments borne out by evidence? It depends. One powerful argument in favor of this economic hypothesis is the correlation between development and regime type. Studies indicate that the poorer the country, the less likely it is to be democratic. Approximately 50 percent of all states at $5,000 per capita GDP PPP are democratic, while at $8,000, the figure is around 90 percent.[6] However, in spite of this correlation, there are important caveats and exceptions. First, we can find examples where the failures of economic development have ushered in nondemocratic rule. Periods of hyperinflation, discussed in Chapter 4, can quickly destroy the wealth of the public, generating widespread insecurity and poverty and leading to calls for drastic action, where the public is willing to give up some freedom in favor of greater economic security. The rise of Nazi rule in Germany in the 1930s, for example, was preceded by devastating hyperinflation that wiped out the savings of the middle class. When members of the middle class believe that economic insecurity, rather than those who hold political power, is the greatest threat to their wealth, they may become the greatest supporters of authoritarianism or totalitarianism.

There is also the question of causality versus correlation. We see that nondemocratic rule is associated with lower levels of development. But which is the cause and which is the effect? Certainly, we can cite countries where democracy has taken root in spite of weak economic development; India, with over 1 billion people, is a powerful counterexample. At the other end, many nondemocratic regimes have persisted in spite of economic development or have even been justified by their economic claims. In this view, by restricting political rights, the government can focus on constructing the necessary environment for a market economy and attract investment by limiting the kind of turmoil that might come about in a new or weak democracy. Many nondemocratic regimes have used this argument to justify their regime, arguing that democracy is a "luxury" that their country cannot yet afford—bread first, ballots later. For example, South Korea, Taiwan, and Singapore experienced long periods of authoritarian rule during which they rapidly industrialized; all three are now fast-growing and powerful economies. Only in the 1980s and 1990s did Taiwan and South Korea democratize, and Singapore shows no signs of following their lead. Other regimes with existing wealth, such as Saudi Arabia, have been able to use this economic power specifically to stave off demands for greater individual rights. In this light, it has been argued that where autocrats are weak or divided, the public is more likely to assert their rights.[7] In short, while economic factors may be critical, it is not obvious that they are either a necessary or sufficient condition in determining the kind of regime in power, and they may in fact be an effect, rather than a cause.

Societal Sources of Nondemocratic Rule

Economics is not the only possible explanation for nondemocratic rule, and many political scientists do not view wealth or inequality as key issues. They believe instead that cultural factors are central. According to this argument, culture has the capacity to either encourage or constrain democratic development, depending on whether the existing culture embodies norms and values that are consistent with democratic practices. Thinking back to our earlier discussion of political culture in Chapter 3, we recall the idea that societies with more traditional and survival-based values might be more prone to hierarchical, authoritarian, anti-individualist, and thus nondemocratic rule. A more region-specific argument asserts that certain sets of political cultures are important. For example, a common argument is that democracy is a unique product of interconnected historical experiences in Europe, such as Christianity (particularly Protestantism), the emphasis on individualism and secularism, the development of the nation-state, ideology, early industrialization, and the development of capitalism, among others. These factors, the argument goes, allowed for the creation of democracy as a regime built on liberal values that emphasize freedom— what we typically call "Western" societies. According to some scholars, these liberal values are not universal, and other societies are constructed around norms and institutions that do not fit easily in with Western democratic practices. As evidence, they would note that the further one travels from the West (meaning North America, Western Europe, and Japan), the fewer democracies one finds, even in societies that over the past few decades have seen a dramatic rise in wealth, such as the oil states of the Middle East (Figure 5.1).[8]

Some have further asserted that under Islam, the relationship between religion, the nation, and the state has profound implications for the likelihood of nondemocratic rule. In such societies, political power and religious power are one and the same: laws are seen not as societal institutions to protect or advance individual rights, but as codes handed down by Allah that are to be observed and defended. Similarly, nationality and citizenship are defined not by allegiance to a collective group or state, but by faith. Thus, some would argue, Western ideas of competing political ideologies, of societies divided by ethnicity and citizenship, and of state power separated from religious authority are alien in Islamic society. In this view, Westerners' assumptions that all societies seek to be democratic are not only misguided but dangerous. Other societies may not only view their own authoritarianism or totalitarianism as a superior form of politics, but may also view Western liberal democracy as something inherently egocentric, atomized, ungodly, and destructive.

Figure 5.1 **REGIONS AND POLITICAL SYSTEMS, 2005**

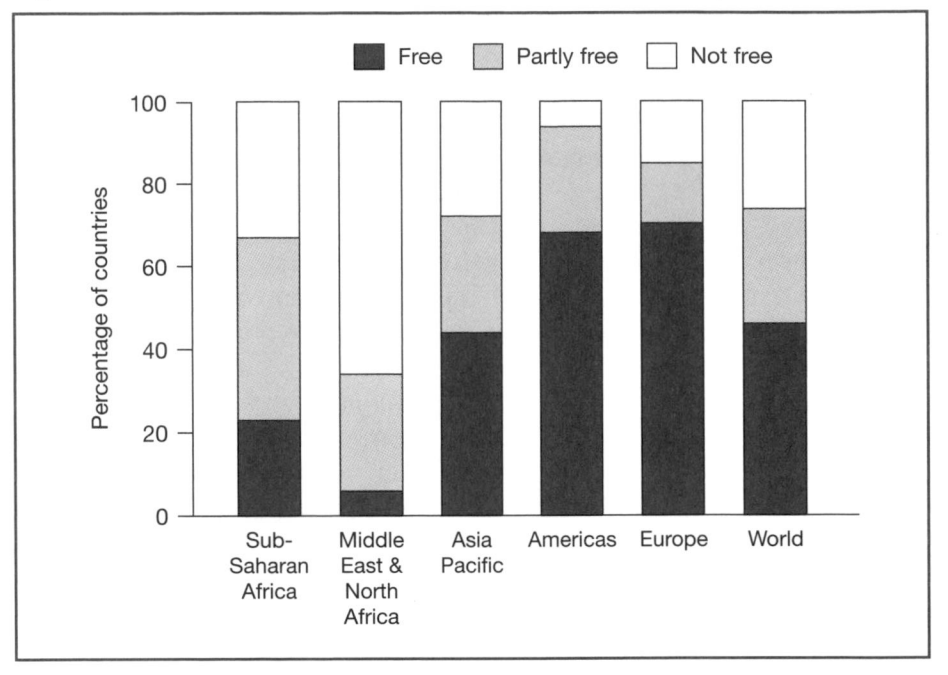

Source: Freedom House.

This debate over the relationship between nondemocratic regimes and culture can be seen beyond the case of Islam. It is also illustrated by what is commonly called the "Asian values" debate, which essentially asks to what extent there are particular cultural values in eastern Asia that conflict with Western notions of individualism, democracy, and liberty. Proponents of the idea of Asian values argue that Asia's cultural and religious traditions stress conformity, hierarchy, and obedience, which are more conducive to a political regime that limits freedom in order to defend social harmony and consensus. The philosophy of Confucianism is frequently cited in this regard. Confucianism, they assert, with its emphasis on obedience to hierarchy and its notion of a ruler's "mandate from heaven," promotes authoritarian rule; the ruling elite acts as a parental figure over the people, acting in the public's best interest but not under its control. As Malaysian prime minister Mahathir Mohamad, one of the major proponents of "Asian values," has put it,

> When citizens understand that their right to choose also involves limits and responsibilities, democracy doesn't deteriorate into an excess of freedom. . . . These are the dangers of democracy gone wrong, and in our view it is precisely the sad direction in which the West is heading.[9]

As you might imagine, there are many both inside and outside of Asia that reject the notion of "Asian values" and the supposed natural tendency of Asians toward authoritarianism. Critics point out that Asia, like any other part of the world, is far too diverse to speak of one set of values; differences in history, religion, social structure, and other institutions have led to very different political values from country to country. Asia has no clear set of cultures or civilizations, they assert, but rather an array of different and overlapping ideas that are in a continuous process of interaction and reinterpretation. Confucian thought, just like the Bible in the West or the Koran in Islamic countries, can be interpreted in very different ways. Thus, the very notion of "Asian values," critics argue, is a misinterpretation by observers who fail to grasp the complexity of Asia or who use the idea simply to justify nondemocratic rule. As Kim Dae Jung, former president of South Korea, argued, "The biggest obstacle is not [Asia's] cultural heritage but the resistance [to democracy] of authoritarian rulers and their apologists. . . . Culture is not necessarily our destiny. Democracy is."[10] These same criticisms can also be applied to those arguments that view democracy and Islam as incompatible. In short, while culture may matter, it may also be more amenable to change, including democracy.

A look at history may shed some light on these debates. In the past, it was often argued that "Latin" cultures, those strongly influenced by Roman Catholicism, were also inherently nondemocratic in nature (as opposed to cultures steeped in Protestant forms of Christianity). The reasons given for this were very similar to those just discussed: an emphasis on hierarchy, a lack of tolerance for other views, and a focus on community versus individual rights. This has also been claimed, for similar kinds of reasons, for societies where Orthodox Christianity was predominant. In fact, several decades ago, this argument would have had strong empirical support. In Europe, predominantly Catholic Italy gave birth to fascism, and after World War II, nondemocratic regimes persisted in Catholic Spain and Portugal and in Orthodox Greece and the Soviet Union. Latin America, long influenced by Catholicism, also had a strong history of authoritarian rule. However, by the 1970s, the last authoritarian regimes in Western Europe moved to democracy, and similar processes have been under way in Latin America and Eastern Europe since the 1980s, to such a point that the majority of states in both regions are now democratic.

A final consideration is thus in order. Both economic and societal explanations of nondemocratic regimes tend to be institutional in nature—that is, they argue that existing institutions, whether social or economic, profoundly influence the nature and persistence of nondemocratic regimes. People are seen as less important. But some scholars argue that such an approach is overly deterministic and that people and individual leaders do make a huge difference in exploiting or overcoming economic or societal factors. Just as nondemocratic regimes are often associated with particular leaders (Stalin, Hitler, Mao), so, too, is the end of a nondemocratic regime often associated with the bold steps of individuals (Gorbachev, Gandhi, Mandela). Would the political regimes of any of these countries have been the same without these figures? Leadership may be key to both the birth and death of nondemocratic regimes, with institutions only shaping the political field on which these battles are fought.[11]

Nondemocratic Regimes and Political Control

There is no consensus about what brings about nondemocratic rule. Economic arguments emphasize economic development and the distribution of wealth, whereas cultural arguments emphasize the societal institutions that may foster or hinder the concentration of power. Both arguments may overemphasize institutions at the expense of individual leaders or the public in general. But even if we cannot be certain how nondemocracies come to power, we can carefully examine how they stay in control. As with all political systems, a number of different state, regime, and government activities and institutions perpetuate political control. Some of these use fear and violence; others do not. In fact, in this section, we will need to answer a difficult question from earlier in the chapter: Do all nondemocratic regimes by nature rely on force to intimidate a hostile public, or can such rule be accepted or even embraced by the people? But first we should outline some of the most common features of nondemocratic rule.

Coercion and Surveillance

One feature that we may initially associate with authoritarianism and especially with totalitarianism is the use of **coercion**, which can be defined as compelling behvavior by threatening harm. Compliance and obedience with regime goals are often enforced through close observation of and the use of force against the population, sending a clear signal that those who oppose the regime or government will be identified and dealt with harshly. Nondemocratic regimes commonly use coercion as a mechanism of public control, threatening those who challenge the political order with severe retribution: arbitrary arrest, detention without trial, torture, and even death. In several authoritarian regimes in Latin America in the past, "death squads" made up of police or military troops targeted individuals suspected of harboring political views opposed to the regime. These individuals were abducted by the death squads and murdered, frequently after torture. In some cases, their bodies were dumped in the open, as a warning to others who dared to question the regime; in other cases, the victims became one among thousands who "disappeared," never to be seen again.

In other regimes, violence has been used even more indiscriminately. When Stalin consolidated his totalitarian rule in the Soviet Union in the 1930s, he carried out what are known as "purges," widespread arrests

IN FOCUS

Authoritarian Means of Control

- *Coercion*: public obedience is enforced through violence and surveillance.
- *Co-optation*: members of the public are brought into a beneficial relationship with the state and government, often through corporatism or clientelism.
- *Personality cult*: the public is encouraged to obey the leader based on his or her extraordinary qualities and compelling ideas.

that decimated the ranks of the Communist Party and the state bureaucracy. Former leaders of the 1917 revolution, city mayors and local party bosses, high-ranking officers in the army and navy, university professors, scientists, diplomats, and many others were detained, tortured, coerced into confessing during "show trials," forced to implicate others in their supposed crimes, and either sent to forced labor camps or executed. The targets of the purges were not limited to the party or the state; writers, artists, students, farmers, and workers were also among those accused of political sabotage and anti-Soviet views. It is not known how many died in these purges; estimates range from 5 million to 20 million. Undoubtedly, in the vast majority of these cases, the victims were innocent; yet this was unimportant to Stalin's regime. By making everyone fear that they, too, can be arrested, the public can be controlled and even turned against itself, with everyone fearing that they will be denounced by someone else. Stalin's tactics have not been forgotten; Saddam Hussein was apparently a great student of Stalinism and applied the use of terror to great effect, shattering much of Iraqi society in the process.

Another important means of control is the ability to maintain a close watch over the population. Surveillance allows the government to prevent opposition from organizing and also instills uncertainty among the population—are they being watched? Surveillance may be conducted through the use of an internal security force, or "secret police," charged with monitoring public activity, spying on individuals, and interrogating members of the public suspected of political activity hostile to the regime. In some countries, surveillance has included widespread telephone tapping and the creation of a huge network of public informers, where nearly anyone may be the eyes and ears of those in power.

Co-optation

The prevalence of coercion and surveillance in some nondemocratic regimes may give the impression that those in power must be ever vigilant against the public to prevent opposition or revolution that might spring up at any time. But not all regimes need to or choose to rely on fear or surveillance as a central means of control. Another method they may use is **co-optation**, the process by which individuals outside of an organization are brought into a beneficial relationship with it, making them dependent on the regime for certain rewards. Although co-optation is not unique to nondemocratic regimes, it tends to be much more widespread under such regimes than under democracy, which is usually more suspicious of such favoritism.

Co-optation can take many forms. The most structured form of co-optation is corporatism. Recall from Chapter 4 the term *neocorporatism*, a structure in which business, labor, and the state engage in bargaining over economic policy. In its earliest form, however, modern **corporatism** emerged as a method by which authoritarian and totalitarian regimes attempted to solidify their control over the public by creating or sanctioning a limited number of organizations to represent the interests of the public and restricting those not set up or approved by the state. These organizations are meant to replace independent organizations with a handful that alone have the right to speak for various sectors of society. For example, under a corporatist regime, churches, labor unions, agricultural associations, student groups, neighborhood committees, and the like, would all be approved and funded by the state. Nonsanctioned, alternative organizations would not be allowed. For example, in China, the Catholic Church is not allowed to have official ties to the Vatican, as this would presume an external authority over that of the regime. Nonsanctioned religious groups are similarly banned.

Unlike the overlapping memberships, competition, and ever-changing nature of organizations and political parties in a pluralistic society, corporatism arranges society such that each organization is empowered by the state to have a monopoly of representation over a given issue or segment of society (meaning that no other organization may act in that area or speak on that issue). State, society, and the market under corporatism are viewed as a single organic body, with each element cooperating and performing its own specific and limited role. This is quite different from a view of politics that is centered on the individual and that values competition and conflict.

Corporatism can be an effective form of control, as it gives the public a limited influence (or at least the pretense of influence) in the policy-making process. Farmers or students have an official organization with elected officers and resources that are meant to serve their interests. In return, the regime is able to better control the public through these institutions, which are funded and managed by the state. For the average individual, a state-sanctioned organization is better than none at all, and many willingly participate in the hope that their needs will be met.

Many modern countries have displayed elements of corporatism while under nondemocratic rule. Corporatism is an integral part of totalitarianism, but it exists in authoritarian regimes as well, including fascist Italy and Germany as well as Spain and Portugal up to the 1970s. In Spain, for example, a single political party organized most business and labor interests together into a limited number of "syndicates" that represented both owners and workers in different sectors of the economy. Communist regimes are similarly corporatist. In Cuba, for example, all labor is organized under a single union directly controlled by the state, and independent unions are illegal. Although different in form and degree, in all corporatist regimes we see the presence of a limited number of organizations used to represent and direct societal interests, bringing the public under organized state control.

A less structured means by which states may co-opt the public is through **clientelism**, whereby the state co-opts members of the public by providing specific benefits or favors to a single person or small group in return for public support. Unlike corporatism, clientelism relies on individual patronage rather than organizations that serve a large group of people. In other words, clientelism creates a patron-client relationship between the state and individual members of the public.

INSTITUTIONS IN

ACTION

CLIENTELISM AND AUTHORITARIANISM IN MEXICO

Mexico's economy is based in part on a large number of street vendors who operate in open-air markets around the country. The authoritarian, one-party regime of the Institutional Revolutionary Party (PRI), which controlled the government from 1915 to 2000, recognized the potential value of such a large group of individuals, whose ability to function depended entirely on the permission of the government (since the vendors did not own land or shops of their own). Starting in the 1950s, the PRI began to pressure street vendors in Mexico City to provide donations to political campaigns or provide public support at rallies; in return, the state would not crack down on their activities. Local "bosses" acted as intermediaries between the state and the vendors, collecting funds and mobilizing vendors in return for a share of the wealth. With the failure of the PRI in the 2000 presidential elections and the subsequent democratization of Mexico, this system may now break down, though such forms of clientelism often resist political and even regime change.

The state has a number of perquisites it can use in co-opting individuals. Jobs within the state or in state-run sectors of the economy, business contracts or licenses, public goods such as roads or schools, and kickbacks and bribes are a few of the tools in its arsenal. Such largesse often leads to **rent seeking**, a process in which political leaders essentially rent out parts of the state to their clients, who as a result control public goods that would otherwise be distributed in a nonpolitical manner. For example, leaders might turn over control of the national postal system to political supporters, providing them with jobs and the ability to siphon off public funds from that branch of the state.

In general, co-optation may be much more successful than coercion at maintaining nondemocratic regimes, since many in the public may actively support the regime in return for the benefits they derive. Political opposition is dealt with not through repression and violence, but by simply incorporating one's opponents into the system and making them dependent on it. Such a regime, however, faces limitations. Corporatist and clientelist institutions run the risk of running out of benefits with which to pacify the public. In addition, in a regime where economic resources are doled out for political reasons, problems may emerge as productive resources are siphoned off to secure the acquiescence of the public. At its worst, such a regime can decline into a kleptocracy (literally, "rule by theft"), where those in power seek only to further fill their own pockets and drain the state of assets and resources. As these resources dry up, co-optation may quickly unravel.

Personality Cults

Authoritarian and totalitarian leaders may also reinforce their rule through what are known as personality cults. First used to describe Stalin's rule in the Soviet Union, a **personality cult** refers to the promotion of the image of a leader not merely as a political figure but as someone who embodies the spirit of the nation, possesses endowments of wisdom and strength far beyond those of the average individual, and is thus portrayed in a quasi-religious manner— all-wise, all-seeing, all-knowing. In other words, personality cults attempt to generate a charismatic form of authority for the political leader from the top down by convincing the public of the leader's admirable qualities. In recent times, Saddam Hussein can be seen as a leader who attempted to build a personality cult around himself.

The media and culture play a vital role in this regard, promoting the cult of personality through all aspects of daily life—news reports, public rallies, art, music, films, and other imagery of the leader. All successes in the country are attributed to the power of the leader, and mistakes are blamed on the mortal flaws of the public or on external enemies. Whether the public actually believes in the personality cult is, of course, another issue.

Cults of personality may also function largely through terror; the public may not believe the praise, but no one is willing to say so. This is especially the case where charismatic power has faded over time to become little more than a facade, held up only by force. Under these conditions, there is always the chance that the cult will crack and the public will turn against the leadership. This occurred in Romania in 1989, when Nicolae Ceausescu, the self-styled "conductor" of his country, was shown on national television reacting in a stunned and confused manner when attendees at a public rally he was addressing suddenly turned against him. Within hours, revolution had swept the country, and within three days, Ceausescu and his wife had been executed by firing squad.

Nondemocratic Regimes and Legitimacy

Nondemocratic regimes thus rely on a range of tools to maintain power: some are "carrots" (tempting rewards), others "sticks" (threatened or actual punishments). It also follows that some people may view such a regime as legitimate because they agree with the regime's ideology, are direct beneficiaries of its rule, venerate its leaders, or simply fear political change. The idea of nondemocratic legitimacy may be hard for some to accept. Particularly in Western democracies, there is the assumption that in every nondemocratic regime, the people are simply waiting for the chance to depose their rulers and install democracy. This belief is an exaggeration. Authoritarian or totalitarian regimes can be just as institutionalized—and therefore as stable and legitimate—as any democratic regime, enjoying some, or even a great deal of, public support.

Max Weber's discussion of the forms of legitimacy (discussed in Chapter 2) can help explain this idea further. Nondemocratic regimes may rely on charismatic authority, as the preceding discussion of personality cult indicated. The public may strongly support and venerate its leaders, as was seen in the cases of Mao Zedong, Josef Stalin, and Adolf Hitler, and may see their leadership as indispensable. In spite of the violence used by each of these leaders, their publics venerated them as nearly divine figures. Such forms of legitimacy can produce a tremendous personal following and power.

Other regimes may be based on traditional authority. In the case of North Korea, Kim Jong Il's legitimacy rests not just on a personality cult meant to project charismatic power, but on the fact that he is the son of the founder of the country, Kim Il Sung. In fact, this claim to traditional, hereditary authority may be a greater source of power than any charisma that Kim Jong Il hopes to project. That North Korean totalitarianism weathered the death of Kim Il Sung may have much to do with the fact that his son was waiting in the wings, able to establish continuity in the regime. Similar institutions that support the idea of traditional authority are also present in much of the Middle East, where hereditary monarchies are still powerful and command popular support.

Rational authority may also play a role. Authoritarian and totalitarian regimes often claim that they are "scientific" or "technocratic" (the latter meaning, literally, "rule by expertise"), that they alone possess the knowledge and skills necessary to guide the country. The institutions that support non-democratic rule may stress a "rational" and "objective" approach to rule, implying that democracy is an emotional, inefficient, and thus inferior means of rule. In the past, both communism and fascism laid claim to rational legitimacy, arguing that their rule was based not just on ideology but on the laws of science. In the case of communism, revolution and the downfall of capitalism and liberalism were seen as inevitable laws of development; theories regarding the superiority or inferiority of peoples and races legitimized fascist rule. More recently, political regimes in Asia and Latin America used claims of technocratic expertise to legitimize authoritarian rule.

Types of Nondemocratic Rule

By now it should be clear that nondemocratic regimes may emerge for different reasons and may persist in different ways by using, to different degrees, tools of fear and support. Based on these characteristics, political scientists often classify these regimes into a number of specific forms of rule. The most commonly seen forms are personal and monarchical, military, one-party, theocratic and illiberal regimes. Personal rule is based on the power of a single strong leader who typically relies on charismatic or traditional authority to maintain power. Under military rule, in contrast, the monopoly of violence that characterizes militaries tends to be the strongest means of control. One-party rule is often more corporatist in nature, creating a broad membership as a source of support and oversight. Theocracies, though limited in number, derive their power from their claim to rule on behalf of God. Finally, in illiberal regimes, the basic structures of democracy exist but are not fully institutionalized and often not respected. Because these classifications are by necessity somewhat abstract, many nondemocratic regimes combine elements of different categories rather than fitting easily into any one. In spite of this limitation, these categories make for useful comparisons.

Personal and Monarchical Rule

Personal and monarchical rule is what usually comes to mind when people think of nondemocratic rule, perhaps because long before modern politics, states, or economies came into being, people were ruled by powerful figures—

kings and Caesars, emperors and sultans, chiefs and caudillos. Drawing from charismatic or traditional legitimacy, **personal rule** rests on the claim that one person is alone fit to run the country, with no clear regime or roles to constrain that person's rule. Under personal rule, the state and society are commonly taken to be possessions of the leader, to be dispensed with as he (or, occasionally, she) sees fit. The ruler is not a subject of the state; rather, the state and society are subjects of the ruler. Ideology may be weak or absent, as the ruler justifies his control through the logic that he alone is the embodiment of the people and therefore uniquely qualified to act on the people's behalf. This claim often necessitates a strong personality cult or a reliance on the traditional authority of bloodlines. While personal rule is still widespread, monarchies have largely faded from the scene. However, they continue to be important in the Middle East in particular, where countries such as Saudi Arabia, Jordan, Morocco, Kuwait, and Bahrain still have monarchies that are not fully or even partially bound by a constitution.

In some cases, personal rule relies less on charismatic or traditional authority than on what is referred to as **patrimonialism**, under which the ruler depends on a collection of supporters within the state who gain direct benefits in return for enforcing the ruler's will. The state exists not as a body of trained officials but as a close group of supporters of the ruler, who in return for their allegiance seek personal profit (that is, a kleptocracy). This is a form of co-optation, although under patrimonialism, it is only the ruler's own personal followers who benefit. All others in society tend to be held in check by force, and legitimacy does not extend past the leader's own circle.

An example of personal rule based on patrimonialism was found in Zaire (now the Democratic Republic of Congo) under the rule of Mobutu Sese Seko from 1965 until 1997. Although he once commanded a great deal of charismatic legitimacy, over time Mobutu increasingly used patrimonialism as a way to maintain his power. In particular, Mobutu built his patrimonial regime around Zaire's abundant natural resources, such as diamonds, gold, copper, and cobalt. These resources were used by the regime not to benefit the country as a whole, but as Mobutu's personal treasury; he siphoned off the profits from these resources to enrich himself and his followers. The result was a coterie of supporters who were willing to defend Mobutu in order to maintain their economic privileges.[12] This system of dependence and economic reward helps explain how Mobutu maintained power for more than three decades while Zaire's per capita GDP dropped two-thirds from the 1970s to the 1990s.

Military Rule

A second form of nondemocratic rule is **military rule**. Once considered relatively unusual, military rule has become much more common over the past half century, particularly in Latin America, Africa, and parts of Asia. Where governments and states are struggling with legitimacy and stability, and where there are high levels of public unrest or violence, the military may choose to intervene directly in politics, seeing itself as the only organized force able to ensure stability. This view may be combined with a sense among military leaders that the current government or regime threatens the military's or the country's interests and should be removed. Military rule may even have widespread public support, especially if people believe that the strong arm of the military can bring an end to corruption or political violence, prevent revolution, and restore stability.

Military rule typically emerges through a **coup d'etat**, in which military forces take control of the government by force. In some cases, military actors may claim that they have seized control only reluctantly, promising to return the state and government to civilian rule once stability has been restored. Often, under military rule, political parties and most civil liberties are restricted, and civilian political leaders or opponents of military rule are arrested and may be killed or disappear. The use of terror and surveillance is a common aspect of military rule, since by their nature, militaries hold an overwhelming capacity for violence.

Military rule typically lacks a specific ideology, although some military leaders espouse radical or reactionary political attitudes. Military rule also tends to lack any charismatic or traditional source of authority, meaning that if they seek legitimacy in the eyes of the people, they often must fall back on rational authority. One particular variant of military rule that reflects this logic is known as **bureaucratic authoritarianism**, a regime in which the state bureaucracy and the military share a belief that a technocratic leadership, focused on rational, objective, technical expertise, can solve the problems of the country—as opposed to "emotional" or "irrational" ideologically based party politics. Public participation, in other words, is seen as an obstacle to effective and objective policy making and so is done away with. In the 1960s and 1970s, bureaucratic authoritarianism emerged in a number of less-developed countries as rapid modernization and industrialization generated a high degree of political conflict. State and industry, with their plans for rapid economic growth, clashed with the interests of the working class and peasantry, who sought greater political power and a larger share of the wealth. This increasing polarization in politics often led business leaders and the state bureaucracy to advocate military rule as a way to prevent the working class and the peasantry from gaining power over the government.[13]

Military rule, like any form of nondemocracy, may lead to a variety of outcomes. Military rule in South Korea, Taiwan, and Chile occurred alongside high levels of economic growth that in turn helped pave the way for democracy in the 1990s. However, in many more cases, military rule has simply meant more instability and violence and little or no improvement over the governments that were replaced. Even in the most successful cases, as in the three countries named here, progress occurred alongside great loss of life. In the first years of military rule in Taiwan, for instance, tens of thousands of students, intellectuals, political figures, and community leaders were executed. In South Korea, protests by labor unions and students in 1980 lead to a military crackdown during which several hundred were killed. And in Chile, debate still rages over the legacy of Augusto Pinochet, the military leader from 1973 to 1990. During his rule, thousands were arrested, tortured, killed, or "disappeared." We also do not know whether military rule can be credited for the economic successes of these countries, since we cannot determine how they might have developed had the military not intervened in the first place.

One-Party Rule

A form of rule often associated with totalitarianism in particular is **one-party rule**, under which a single political party monopolizes politics, with other parties banned or excluded from power. The ruling party serves several functions. The party helps to incorporate the people into the political regime through membership and participation. Typically, the party only incorporates a small minority of the population—in most communist countries, for instance, party membership was less than 10 percent—but this still means that hundreds of thousands or millions of people are party members. One-party rule is often also combined with a larger corporatist regime of public control.

Through membership, the party can rely on a large segment of the public that is willing to help develop and support the policies of authoritarian or totalitarian rule, as well as to transmit information back to the leadership on developments in all aspects of society. Single-party regimes are often broken down into smaller units or "cells" that operate at the university, workplace, or neighborhood level. These units report back to higher levels of the party, help deal with local problems and concerns, and keep tabs on society as a whole. No area is untouched by the presence of the party, and this helps to maintain control over the public.

In return for their support, members of the party often are granted privileges that are otherwise denied to the public at large. They may have access to certain resources (better health care or housing, for instance) that nonmembers do not; positions in government and other important areas of the economy or society may also be restricted to party members. One important result of such membership is that a large group of individuals in society directly benefits from the regime and is therefore willing to defend it. This pragmatic membership, however, can backfire: those who embrace party membership only for the personal benefits and not out of any ideological conviction may quickly desert the leadership in a time of crisis.

Finally, the party serves as a mechanism of mobilization. The leadership uses the party as an instrument to deliver propaganda that extols the virtues of the current regime and government; it relies on its rank-and-file members, through demonstrations and mass rallies, to give the appearance of widespread public support and enthusiasm for the leadership. If necessary, it also uses party members to control and harass those who do not support the regime. Although such terror or surveillance may be important to one-party rule, co-optation is the primary mechanism that ensures compliance and support.

One-party regimes are often associated with communism and fascism and were present in all cases of totalitarianism. However, they also can be found around the world as part of a variety of authoritarian regimes. In some cases, other parties may exist, but they typically are highly restricted by the government so that they cannot challenge the current regime. For many years, this was the case in Mexico, which was dominated by the Institutional Revolutionary Party, or PRI. In Zimbabwe, the ruling Zimbabwe African People's Union–Patriotic Front (ZANU-PF) has held power since 1980. Cuba, North Korea, China, Vietnam, and Laos are other examples of one-party regimes, each controlled by a single communist party.

Theocracy

Theocratic rule is probably the hardest form of nondemocratic rule to describe and analyze. Although **theocracy** can be defined as, literally, "rule by God," where the faith is the foundation for the political regime, such a regime can be founded on any number of faiths and variations within them. Thus, in theory, a Christian theocracy might look completely unlike a Jewish one, drawing on very different texts, traditions, and interpretations of the faith. Moreover, there are very few examples of theocracies around the world—indeed, some scholars would say there are none. However, we can suggest some commonalities and elements of theocratic rule, even if such a system does not exist in pure form. In Chapter 3, we noted that one of the recent challenges to ideology has been the rise of fundamentalism, which we defined as the fusion of religion and politics into an ideology that seeks to merge religion and the state. Such a merger of religion and state, where faith is the sole source of the regime, would render democratic institutions as subordinate or in contradiction to the perceived will of God. In the vast majority of cases, such a goal remains hypothetical. Yet we can note cases where theocratic institutions are present and powerful.

Iran is the best example of a country that could be described as a theocracy. In 1979, revolution overthrew the existing secular monarchy, ushering in a new government headed by the cleric Ayatollah Khomeini. For many years, Khomeini had the idea of an Islamic government, which was put to practice in Iran. Most importantly, in the Iranian system, the traditional forms of secular government (executive, legislature, judiciary) are mirrored by unique institutions that are controlled by religious leaders. Thus, the Supreme Leader, a religious figure, holds power over the president, while a Guardian Council can reject legislation and candidates for office for being insufficiently Islamic. Afghanistan, too, could be described as a theocracy between 1996 and 2001, lacking any constitution and relying on local clerics to rule on judicial matters based on their interpretation of Islamic law.

In a more mixed form, Saudi Arabia combines both monarchical and theocratic forms of rule. Politics is monopolized by the ruling family, and the king also acts as the supreme religious leader. Judicial and other matters must conform to Islamic law and are enforced by the *Mutawwai'in*, or morality police. Conversion from Islam is punishable by death, and other faiths, even sects within Islam, are not allowed to practice. Many worry that Iraq might move toward a theocracy in the coming years, though surveys indicate that while

IN FOCUS

Types of Authoritarian Rule

Type	Definition	Primary Tools of Control
Personal and monarchical rule	Rule by a single leader, with no clear regime or rules constraining that leadership	Patrimonialism: supporters within the state benefit directly from their alliance with the ruler (corruption)
Military rule	Rule by one or more military officials, often brought to power through a coup d'état	Control of the armed forces, sometimes also allied with business and state elites (bureaucratic authoritarianism)
One-party rule	Rule by one political party, with other groups banned or excluded from power	Large party membership helps mobilize support and maintain public control, often in return for political or economic benefits
Theocracy	"Rule by god"; regime based on holy texts as foundation for regime and politics	Religious leadership and political leadership fused into single sovereign authority
Illiberal regimes	Rule by an elected leadership, though through procedures of questionable democratic legitimacy	Manipulation of democratic procedures, such as vote rigging or harassment of opposition

many Iraqis believe that Islam should be an important component of their political system and oppose the separation of faith and state, less than a quarter favor a political system under the control of religious leaders.[14] As with fundamentalism, we should not confuse religiosity, or even greater religion in politics, with theocracy or nondemocratic rule, though that can be one outcome.

Illiberal Regimes

Finally, some political regimes feature a few or many of the familiar aspects of democracy but remain in essence authoritarian regimes. In fact, Figure 5.1, shown earlier, includes a large group of countries that are categorized as neither "free" nor "not free," but as "partially free," falling somewhere between democracy and authoritarianism. These regimes go by a number of names, such as semiauthoritarian, quasi-democratic, or hybrid regimes. We will group these terms under the concept of **illiberal regimes.** Illiberal regimes may appear like other established democracies—people are given the right to vote, elections take place, and political parties compete. Procedurally, then, these regimes are nominally democratic. However, many democratic rights are not institutionalized or respected.

Most importantly, illiberal regimes usually restrict the democratic process to a great degree, and those rights that do exist are often insecure, subject to arbitrary change or sudden withdrawal. For example, the government may control which political organizations may participate in politics, banning any it thinks might threaten the government's hold on power. Access to the media is also often restricted, with the ruling political elites able to dominate the airwaves while opposition forces have little chance to make their views known. Important state institutions, such as the judiciary, the military, or state-run industries, are likely to be under the direct control of the government and used to control political opposition. Under such conditions, open elections can often be tolerated, since the opposition functions at a great disadvantage. Nigeria is a good example of an illiberal regime. After decades of military rule, the country has moved toward civilian rule, but is plagued by political violence, voter fraud, and limited control over the armed forces.

In short, illiberal regimes in many ways represent a gray area between nondemocratic and democratic rule. Although the mechanisms of democracy may be in place, they remain weakly institutionalized, operating in an uncertain and hostile environment. The big question here is whether illiberal regimes are transitional, in the process of moving from nondemocratic to democratic rule (or vice versa), or a new form of nondemocracy that uses the trappings of democracy to perpetuate its control. Both may in fact be true. In the future, the world may look more democratic, but many of these "democracies" may be so in name only.[15]

In Sum: Nondemocratic Regimes in Retreat?

Although nondemocratic regimes exhibit an amazing diversity and flexibility in maintaining political control, the global trend over the past half century has been away from this form of rule. In the early part of the last century, democratic countries were few and beleaguered, wracked by economic recession, whereas authoritarianism and totalitarianism, backed by communist and fascist ideologies in particular, seemed to promise radically new ways to restructure states, markets, and societies. The German philosopher Oswald Spengler summarized these views in his 1922 work *The Decline of the West:*

> The era of individualism, liberalism and democracy, of humanitarianism and freedom, is nearing its end. The masses will accept with resignation the victory of the Caesars, the strong men, and will obey them. Life will descend to a level of general uniformity, a new kind of primitivism, and the world will be better for it.[16]

Yet the exact opposite has taken place. Indeed, Figure 5.2 shows that the number of countries classified as "not free" and "partly free" has declined dramatically over just the past thirty years, from nearly three-quarters of the

Figure 5.2 **AUTHORITARIANISM IN DECLINE, 1974–2004**

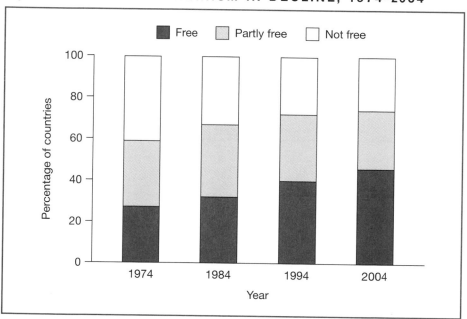

Source: Freedom House.

countries in the world to just over half. The number of fully free countries has increased by almost 20 percent. If we look at the data in terms of population instead of countries, the data are similar (though the number of people living in "not free" countries is higher).

Why this decline in nondemocratic regimes? Various economic, political, and societal arguments have been advanced that are tied to our earlier discussion regarding the sources of nondemocratic rule. Yet one simple explanation may be that nondemocratic rule has lost much of its appeal. Fifty years ago, ideologies predicated on authoritarianism or totalitarianism could mobilize people with visions of a world to be transformed. However, in the aftermath of World War II and the Cold War, there is no longer any strong ideology that combines the absence of individual freedom with some broader goal. Leaders may claim that limitations on political rights are necessary for political stability or economic development, but they no longer offer any real alternative vision for politics. It is increasingly difficult to justify nondemocratic regimes through any universal set of ideas.

Does this mean that the days of nondemocratic regimes are numbered? Perhaps. There may in fact come a time when all societies are democratic, and the nondemocratic regime, like slavery, is an aspect of human behavior consigned to history and the margins of global society. However, we cannot know what new visions may emerge that again give power and purpose to nondemocratic rule. Will rising inequality eventually clash with increased freedom? Will people someday come to see the absence of freedom as a benefit rather than a form of bondage? Might a new religious or secular vision of human life reject democracy as antiquated or profane? Perhaps what we now enjoy is simply a brief aberration in the long human history of nondemocratic rule.

NOTES

1. See the Freedom House website at www.freedomhouse.org.
2. For an excellent discussion of the bewildering variety of authoritarian rule, see Juan Linz, *Totalitarian and Authoritarian Regimes* (Boulder: Lynne Rienner, 2000). This work was originally published in Fred I. Greenstein and Nelson W. Polsby, eds., *Handbook of Political Science* (Reading, MA: Addison-Wesley, 1975).
3. Linz, *Totalitarian and Authoritarian Regimes*.
4. Hannah Arendt, *Totalitarianism* (New York: Harcourt, Brace and World, 1951).
5. For a discussion of the role of the relationship between the middle class and democracy, see Barrington Moore, *Social Origins of Dictatorship and Democracy: Lord and Peasant in the Making of the Modern World* (Boston: Beacon, 1966).
6. Adam Przeworski, Limongi Neto, and Fernando Papaterra, "Modernization: Theories and Facts," *World Politics* 49, no. 2 (January 1997): 156.

7. Mancur Olson, "Dictatorship, Democracy and Development," *American Political Science Review* 87, no. 3 (September 1993): 567–576.

8. Samuel Huntington, *The Clash of Civilizations and the Remaking of World Order* (New York: Simon & Schuster, 1996). See also Francis Fukuyama, "The Primacy of Culture," in Larry Diamond and Mark Plattner, eds., *The Global Resurgence of Democracy* (Baltimore: Johns Hopkins University Press, 1996), 320–327.

9. Mahathir Mohamad and Shintaro Ishihara, *Voice of Asia: Two Leaders Discuss the Coming Century* (Tokyo: Kodansha International, 1996), 82.

10. Kim Dae Jung, "Is Culture Destiny? The Myth of Asia's Anti-Democratic Values," *Foreign Affairs* 73, no. 6 (November–December 1994): 194.

11. Jung, "Is Culture Destiny?"

12. For details, see Michael Bratton and Nicholas Van de Walle, "Neopatrimonial Regimes and Political Transitions in Africa," *World Politics* 46, no. 4 (1994): 453–489.

13. Guillermo O'Donnell, *Modernization and Bureaucratic Authoritarianism: Studies in South American Politics* (Berkeley: Institute of International Studies, 1973).

14. This is based on public opinion surveys taken in 2004 and 2005. See "Iraqi Public Rejects Iranian Model But Wants Major Role for Islam in Government," Program on International Policy Institute, June 14, 2005. www.pipa.org.

15. Marina Ottaway, *Democracy Challenged: The Rise of Semi-Authoritarianism* (Washington, DC: Carnegie Endowment for International Peace, 2003).

16. Oswald Spengler, *The Decline of the West* (New York: Knopf, 1928), 347.

6 DEMOCRACY

Democracy is a type of regime that has risen and fallen in prominence over time. For most of human history, people have not been organized in a way that we would consider democratic; in most political systems, few people have been able to exercise power. But in recent centuries, democracy has emerged in various parts of the world. With the collapse of rival, nondemocratic ideologies such as fascism and communism, democracy has been on the rise. Around the globe, political leaders and publics have sought and gained greater democratic rights, from South Africa to South Korea and from Poland to Chile, pushing aside other ideologies and regimes. From the perspective of those already living in a democratic society, the spread of this political system may appear natural or inevitable: Who wouldn't want to live in a democracy? But we must ask ourselves why this should be the case. Why would democracy be an attractive or effective form of government? How does democracy actually work? What sorts of things can democracy provide, and what are its limitations? Does democracy by definition reconcile freedom and equality in a single way, or does democracy allow for different mixtures of the two?

This chapter will speak to these questions in some detail, as we consider the origins, structures, strengths, and weaknesses of democracy. We will begin by defining democracy itself, since different ideologies use the term in very different ways. From there we will investigate democracy's origins in modern politics. Why did it first emerge in the modern world? We will attempt to answer this question by looking at the political development of the United Kingdom, often considered the birthplace of modern democracy. Next we will consider the various institutions that represent democracy itself: participation, competition, and liberty. As we shall see, none of these institutions is ironclad; various democracies construct each institution rather differently, shaping freedom, equality, and the locus of power. Democracies are more diverse than one might expect. Finally, we will consider some of the challenges to democracy around the world as we move into the next set of chapters in the text.

What Is Democracy?

Before we proceed, we must nail down our terminology, a particularly difficult task when dealing with the concept of democracy because the word itself
is so loaded with meaning. The word *democracy* has, for many people, an
inherently positive connotation: things that are "democratic" are good,
whereas things that are "undemocratic" are inherently bad. Of course, in reality, this is far from the truth: a university is not a democratic institution, but
that does not mean that it is bad or somehow deficient. But because of the
word's symbolism, many individuals and organizations describe themselves
as democratic, although they then define the term in very different ways. For
example, in Chapter 3, we noted that for communists, democracy means collective equality and not individual freedom. Countries such as the Soviet Union
thus saw themselves as "true" democracies, which they defined as featuring,
among other things, full employment, universal education, and the elimination of economic classes. These societies saw democracy in the United States
or Europe as little more than the struggle within a small elite over who would
dominate the populace. Naturally, capitalist countries viewed communist systems, with their single-party control and lack of civil liberties, as anything but
democratic. As you can see, each side is using different criteria to define
democracy. For communist systems, collective outcomes are the gauge of
democracy, while for the West, the process by which individuals seek particular outcomes is what matters.

How can we make any comparisons if democracy is in the eye of the
beholder? One way to begin is to go back to the origins of the word itself. The
word *democracy* comes from the Greek words *demos*, meaning "the common
people," and *kratia*, meaning "power" or "rule." Democracy at its most fundamental is a system where power resides with the people. Based on this origin, we can begin by defining democracy as a system where political power
resides with the people. The people, in turn, may exercise that power either
directly or indirectly, and the exercise of power typically takes three forms:
participation, such as through voting and elections; competition, such as that
between political parties; and liberty, such as freedom of speech or of assembly. **Democracy**, then, can be fully defined as political power exercised either
directly or indirectly through participation, competition, and liberty.

This definition is subjective; it clearly emphasizes individual freedom and
is in keeping with the ideology of liberalism. Indeed, many political scientists
use the more specific term **liberal democracy** to indicate that they are referring specifically to a political system that promotes participation, competition, and liberty. Liberal democracies are rooted in the ideology of liberalism,
with its emphasis on individual rights and freedoms.[1] This can, for example,

be contrasted with our earlier discussion of "illiberal" democracy in Chapter 5, where such values and practices are limited or unprotected.

But liberal democracy is not found only where a liberal ideology and a liberal political-economic system are predominant. Many liberal democracies have social democratic regimes, which place a much higher emphasis on collective welfare over individual rights, tempering individual freedoms in favor of greater equality. But social democracies nevertheless continue to respect the basic liberal democratic tenets of participation, competition, and liberty. Social democrats accept not just the role of markets and property, but also the importance of the democratic process and individual freedom. Mercantilism, too, emphasizes a strong role for the state and lower personal freedoms as a result, but this has not prevented countries such as Japan, Taiwan, and South Korea from developing liberal democratic institutions.

To sum up, liberal democracy presumes a basic set of institutions for participation, competition, and individual liberties. Some democracies go much further in their emphasis on individual freedoms, whereas others limit freedoms in order to achieve social or national objectives. In all cases, however, the basic conditions of liberal democracy—participation, competition, and liberty—are met. When the term *democracy* is used in the remainder of this chapter, we, in fact mean liberal democracy. It is also important to remember what is not being said here about democracy. This book is not saying that democracy is the only or even the best way to organize politics. All it is saying is that democracy is a particular system of institutions that have developed over time and out of liberal thought. Each person must decide for himself or herself whether the particular goals enshrined in liberal democracy are those that are most important and whether society is best served by being organized in this manner. We will speak more about this at the end of this chapter.

The Origins of Liberal Democracy and the Rule of Law

Where did democracy come from? In the past, when most humans lived in very weakly organized societies in which the issues of freedom and equality were less relevant, many decisions were probably made through some consensus or through the force of a single leader. But as societies became sedentary and developed more complex technologies and human relations, struggles over freedom and equality necessitated political organization and the centralization of power. In many cases, this involved coercion, with order imposed from the top down—that is, nondemocratic rule. But consensus has always been an important element as well, and it eventually sparked democratic development.

Athenian Democracy and Roman Republicanism

Truly complex democratic practices have their roots in ancient Greece, specifically Athens and its government of public rule. But Athenian and other early Greek democracies were quite different from modern liberal democracies. They were forms of direct democracy. Typically found in small communities, ancient Greek **direct democracy** allowed the public (excluding women, children, and slaves) to participate directly in the affairs of government, choosing policies and making governing decisions. The people were the state.[2] In contrast, in its modern form, democracy is one of representative rule, often called **indirect democracy** or republicanism. Republicanism has its origins in the Roman Empire. Broadly defined, **republicanism** emphasizes the separation of powers within a state and the representation of the public through elected officials (as opposed to the unaccountable powers of a monarchy or the direct participation of the people). It is from Rome that we get the idea of legislation and legislative bodies such as the Roman Senate. But while the Roman republicanism advocated wider control over monarchs (a system of checks and balances), power was granted only to the upper classes of society. Thus, we see that in their earliest forms, neither Greek democracy nor Roman republicanism would be defined as liberal democracies by today's standards. Both emphasized certain democratic elements but restricted them in fundamental ways. As political rights and institutions have expanded over the centuries, republicanism and democracy—Roman and Greek thought and practices—have become intertwined to produce the modern liberal democratic regime we know today.

These modern democracies, and the ideas that gave birth to them, originated in Europe. Why? In short, liberal democracy is closely connected to the rise of the modern state, which, as we saw in Chapter 2, first emerged in Europe.

England: The Birthplace of Liberal Democracy

The origins of modern democracy can be traced back to 1215 C.E. in England. At that time, English nobles forced King John to sign the Magna Carta, a doc-

---

IN FOCUS

Two Forms of Democracy

Direct democracy	Public participates directly in governance and policy making; historically found in small communities such as ancient Athens.
Indirect democracy	Public participates indirectly through its elected representatives; the prevalent form of democracy in the modern age.

ument that sought to curb the rights of the king and laid the foundation for an early form of legislature in which the king would consult the barons over such matters as the levying of taxes. The most often noted aspect of the Magna Carta was its assertion that all freemen (at the time, only the aristocracy) should enjoy due process before the law; this assertion set the stage for the idea of civil rights. The Magna Carta states:

> No freeman shall be taken, imprisoned, . . . or in any other way destroyed . . . except by the lawful judgment of his peers, or by the law of the land. To no one will we sell, to none will we deny or delay, right or justice.

Although the Magna Carta was limited in its goals and application, it presented the idea that no individual, not even the king, was above the law. Thus, it was the first attempt at limiting state autonomy and establishing the concept of the rule of law. By **rule of law**, we mean a political system that all individuals are subject to regardless of their position or power. The law, rather than any one person, has sovereignty. This concept thrived in England over the centuries as democratic practices expanded and an ever-greater proportion of the public was given political rights. Periodic attempts by the monarchy to expand its power led to violent resistance, most notably in the 1642 English Civil War between King Charles I and Parliament, in which the king eventually lost (and lost his head).

The emergence of democracy in England was thus incremental, developing across centuries. In fact, one notable aspect of British democracy is that as a result of this incremental process, the country still lacks a formal, written constitution. Although various historical documents, such as the Magna Carta or the 1689 Bill of Rights, have helped deepen and define British democracy, there is no single document that lays out the rules of British politics or the rights of British citizens. This often strikes outsiders as amazing—that a country can maintain democracy in the absence of clearly written rules that define the regime.

Was there something special about England that allowed democracy to flourish there in the first place, when it was not emerging elsewhere? Several factors may have been important in this regard, and all are linked to the development of the state. As noted in Chapter 2, there was a strong connection between early political organization and warfare: in Europe, states emerged out of centuries of conflict as rival warlords slowly concentrated their holdings and extended their power. In this regard, England enjoyed both relatively early unification and the defensive benefits of being an island; the need to maintain a large army to unify and defend the country was much lower for isolated England than for the many other European states that had to defend land borders. This lower need for an army meant that the state did not have

TIME LINE / MILESTONES IN THE RISE OF DEMOCRACY

18th century B.C.E.	Babylonian ruler Hammurabi establishes the earliest known legal code
6th century B.C.E.	Autocratic rule overthrown and first democracy established in Athens
5th century B.C.E.	Democracy collapses in Athens as it is undermined by war and economic crisis
1st century B.C.E.	Roman philosopher Cicero writes of *res publica,* or "affairs of the people," viewing the public as an important source of political power
5th–10th century C.E.	European dark ages: power in Europe is fragmented, fostering intense competition among rulers and setting the stage for the emergence of the nation-state
1215	Writing of the English Magna Carta, an early precedent for establishment of the rule of law
1646	Treaty of Westphalia asserts the right of European states to choose their own religion, enforcing the notion of state sovereignty
1689	Bill of Rights is passed in England, establishing parliamentary supremacy
1690	English philosopher John Locke writes *Two Treatises of Government,* arguing that government's job is to protect "the right to life, liberty, and the ownership of property"
1762	Jean-Jacques Rousseau writes *The Social Contract,* arguing that if a government fails to serve its subjects, the populace has the right to overthrow it
1787	U.S. Constitution and Bill of Rights codify the separation of powers and civil rights
1832–84	Reform Acts in the United Kingdom expand voting rights to much of the male population
1893	New Zealand grants women the right to vote
1945	Defeat of the Axis powers eliminates fascism as a threat to democracy in Europe and Japan
1948	United Nations approves the Universal Declaration of Human Rights, setting the stage for the internationalization of civil rights
1989–91	Soviet Union disintegrates, leading to democratization in Russia and Eastern Europe
1994	First democratic elections in South Africa, ending racial restrictions on voting

to extract great amounts of revenue from the people in the form of high taxes, a fact that further reduced the need for a strong coercive force to take taxes from a less-than-willing public. England's position as an island country also meant that economic development was strongly linked to international trade, which also helped generate state revenues through port taxes. Trade provided an easier means for the state to gain income and lessened the need to forcibly extract taxes from the people.

As a result of these factors, England developed without needing a large, land-based military force to quell threats inside and outside the country and therefore without the powerful state that would have been necessary to construct and wield such an army. This relative decentralization of power in turn helped foster individual freedom through the assertion of such notions as civil liberties and economic rights—ideas that would eventually give shape to the ideology of liberalism. It is no accident that an ideology that emphasized individual freedom and private property emerged in a country where the state was historically weak. The public, able to gain the upper hand against the state early on in England's political development, could check attempts by the state to increase its power. This public power paved the way for an expansion of rights over time, culminating in the modern liberal democracy.[3]

Institutionalizing Democracy

We now have an understanding of the origins and basic elements of liberal democracy. But once those elements of democracy emerge, how are they made to last? What are the most effective ways to encourage and safeguard them? How is each reconciled with individual freedom and collective equality? The world's liberal democracies do not answer these questions in the same way. Each country creates its own unique form of liberal democracy, shaped by state, societal, and economic factors. Through these unique combinations, liberal democracies create a rule of law—a condition in which the public and those in power respect and abide by the rules and norms of the democratic regime. Democracy is thereby institutionalized. The following sections will take us through the institutions of participation, competition, and liberty, showing how each can vary in building a democratic order and the rule of law.

Participation: Voting and Elections

Participation is central to liberal democracy; it is hard to imagine a regime as democratic if people have no say in politics. Of the many ways in which democratic participation can be expressed, one of the most basic is voting and elections. Voting and elections allow the public to have control over their public officials and policies through a process of competition in which leaders can be turned out of office. Elections are not the only way in which the public can influence politics (they may also rely on lobbying, letter writing, or public demonstrations, for instance), but they are an important structure in which people are given a say in the staffing and direction of government and thereby in the relationship between freedom and equality. Elections also prevent any one individual or group from maintaining its power indefinitely, and as such they limit the possibilities for leaders to abuse their power.

In a liberal democracy, the right to vote, or **suffrage**, needs to be open to all adult citizens, with few restrictions. In many democracies up until the latter half of the twentieth century, women, individuals from lower classes, and certain ethnic groups were not allowed to vote—something that would no longer be considered acceptable. New Zealand was the first country to give women the right to vote—in 1893—but in the United States, women did not gain this right until 1920, and in France not until 1944. In Australia, restrictions on the rights of the indigenous aboriginal people to vote lasted until the 1960s. In the United States, literacy tests as a prerequisite to voting rights were used as a mechanism to discriminate against African Americans, who had little access to education. At the opposite end of the spectrum, some countries view suffrage as more than a right—it is a formal responsibility. In Australia, Belgium, Brazil, and a number of other democratic countries, voting is actually compulsory, and those who fail to vote can be fined.

Beyond the basic right to vote is the more complicated question of how votes should be cast and counted. **Electoral systems** are the rules that decide how votes are cast, counted, and translated into seats in a legislature, and these systems vary widely around the world. Such systems matter, for how electoral rules are constructed makes a huge difference in the distribution of political power. Differences in electoral systems affect which individuals or parties gain power and even the degree to which people vote.

All democracies divide their populations into a number of electoral boundaries or constituencies (a **constituency** is a geographical area that an elected official represents) that are allocated a certain number of legislative seats. The total number of constituencies may vary widely: Norway is broken up into 19 constituencies that correspond to the country's 19 coun-

IN **FOCUS**

Participation

- One of the most basic ways in which the public participates in politics is through voting and elections.
- The two main types of electoral systems are the single-member district (SMD) and proportional representation (PR). The majority of democratic countries today use PR. Many use a mix of SMD and PR.
- Voters may also participate in political decision making through referenda, initiatives, and plebiscites.

ties, whereas in Nigeria there are 360 constituencies for elections to their House of Representatives. How these boundaries are drawn matters, too. For example, a small minority group might be concentrated in one region but be divided by electoral boundaries, diluting its voting power. Or different districts may have very different population sizes but the same number of legislative seats; such circumstances give those in less populated districts more power. How governments draw electoral boundaries thus can have a huge impact on who gets elected.

Electoral Systems

A second distinction is how votes are cast and counted.[4] There are essentially two broad forms of electoral systems in use in liberal democracies today. The first are plurality and majority systems, often called **single-member district (SMD)** systems for reasons that will become clear in a moment, and **proportional representation (PR)** systems. Let us consider each one in turn.

A minority of democratic countries around the world, including the United Kingdom, Canada, the United States, India, Nigeria, and other former British colonies, rely on plurality-based single-member district systems, or what is often (confusingly) called **first past the post**. In these systems, electoral constituencies are structured as single-member districts, by which we mean that there is only one representative for that constituency. In elections, the candidate with the largest number of votes wins the seat. This need not be a majority of votes; a plurality of votes (the largest share of the total) is sufficient. Those votes cast for other candidates are "wasted"; that is, if the candidate for which a vote is cast does not win, that vote does not count toward anyone getting into office. Plurality SMD is thus "winner take all" and can therefore amplify the political power of some parties while weakening the political power of others.

By way of illustration, let's look at the outcome of the 2005 elections for the House of Commons (the lower legislative house) in the United Kingdom. As Table 6.1 shows, the Labour Party won 35 percent of the vote but 55 percent of the seats. Meanwhile, the Conservatives, who came just 3 percent behind Labour, won only 30 percent of seats. Why this disparity? The answer is because Labour came in first place in a larger number of districts than the Conservatives, and thus many of the votes cast for the Conservatives were effectively wasted.

Not surprisingly, SMD is seen by political scientists as having a profound impact on the number of parties in the legislature. A French political scientist, Maurice Duverger, argued that under SMD, most people are unwilling to vote for smaller parties. Since such parties are unlikely to win first place, voters feel that a vote cast for a small party will be wasted and that they would be better off giving their vote to a stronger party that has a chance of coming in first.[5] The example of the Liberal Democrats, who won 22 percent of the vote but less then 10 percent of the seats, bears this concern out. As a result, SMD is much more likely to produce a legislature dominated by two parties, as in the United States and the United Kingdom, where smaller parties are for the most part unrepresented in the legislature.

However, it is possible to alter the impact of SMD with a small modification in the electoral rules. Majority SMD systems function largely the same as plurality systems, with the exception that certain mechanisms ensure that the winner is elected by a majority of the voters in the district. The simplest way to do this is by having two electoral rounds, where the two top vote getters go on to a runoff. This is used in France and in several mixed electoral systems (discussed shortly). In a more complicated variation, a majority can be generated by having voters rank candidates by preference. If no candidate wins an outright majority, the candidate with the lowest number of first preferences is eliminated, and her or his ballots are then reassigned on the basis of their second preferences. This elimination of the lowest-ranking candidates continues until one candidate has a majority. This system, called alternative, preferential, or instant runoff vote, is currently used in Australia, Fiji, and Papua New Guinea, as well as in local elections in several other countries. Advocates have supported its adoption for national elections in the United Kingdom, United States, Canada, and elsewhere.[6] Supporters believe that this system would increase the chances for smaller parties to gain office, since voters would worry less about wasting their vote, and would also encourage alliances and bargaining between different groups in order to pool their support (such benefits can also apply to a two-round system). Critics, however, doubt that majority SMD would actually lead to a much greater diversity of parties in office, since in the end it is still a winner-take-all form of election, where a large number of the votes will be wasted. In fact, in France and Australia, in spite of majority SMD, politics is dominated by two large parties. This concern will make more sense as we look at proportional representation.

Quite different from plurality and majority SMD is proportional representation (PR), which is used in some form by a majority of democracies around the world. PR generally attempts to decrease the number of votes that are wasted, thus increasing the number of parties in the legislature. Rather than relying on single-member districts, PR relies on **multimember districts (MMDs)**; in other words, more than one legislative seat is contested in each district. In PR systems, voters cast their ballots for a party rather than for a candidate, and the percentage of votes a party receives in a district determines how many of that district's seats the party will gain. Theoretically, if a party wins 17 percent of the vote in a district, it will receive 17 percent of that dis-

Table 6.1 Electoral Systems and Outcomes: The United Kingdom and South Africa					
Plurality Single-Member District (First Past the Post) United Kingdom, House of Commons, 2005				**Proportional Representation: South Africa, National Assembly, 2004**	
Party	**Percentage of Votes Won Nationally**	**Percentage of Seats Won in Legislature**	**Party**	**Percentage of Votes Won Nationally**	**Percentage of Seats Won in Legislature**
Labor Party	35	55	African National Congress	70	70
Conservative Party	32	30	Democratic Alliance	12	13
Liberal Democrats	22	10	Inkatha Freedom Party	7	7
Scottish National Party	2	1	United Democratic Movement	2	2
Democratic Unionist Party	1	1	Independent Democrats	2	2
Sinn Fein	1	1	New National Party	2	2
United Kingdom Independence Party	2	0	African Christian Democratic Party	2	2
Green Party	1	0	Freedom Front	1	1
			United Christian Democratic Party	1	1
			Pan-African Congress	1	1

Source: Electionworld.org

trict's seats; if it wins 100 percent of the vote in a district, it will receive all of the seats. As opposed to plurality and majority systems, where a large proportion of votes cast in an electoral district may not count toward any particular candidate being elected, in PR, even small percentages of the vote can result in winning seats. The 2004 elections in South Africa, also detailed in Table 6.1, show how votes under PR can correspond much more closely to the percentage of seats won in the legislature. Small parties that would not have won a single seat under plurality or majority systems are in fact represented in the South African National Assembly.

Because PR is based on multimember districts, elections are not centered on competitions between individuals. Instead, political parties draw up in advance a list of their candidates for each electoral district, often proposing as many candidates as there are seats. If a district has ten seats and a party wins 50 percent of the vote in that district, the party will send the first five candidates on its party list to the legislature. As you can imagine, one result of this system is that political parties have tremendous power over who will get on the list and at what rank. A candidate would want to be listed as high up on the list as possible in order to gain a seat even if the party gets a small share of the district vote.

PR can have several effects. Most importantly—and in contrast to plurality or majority systems, in which voters tend to support only those parties with a chance of winning a large share of votes in a district—PR voters are more willing to vote for small parties, since they stand a better chance of winning at least some seats in the legislature. Even if a party wins less than 10 percent of the vote, it may well gain seats, as the 2004 South African elections showed. As a result, countries with PR are likely to have many more parties in the legislature. Israel's legislature, for example, has twelve parties, some of which are coalitions of several smaller parties. Some PR systems try to limit the number of small parties by establishing a threshold or minimum percentage needed by any party in order to gain seats in the legislature; in Germany, it is 5 percent, in Turkey, 10 percent. Of course, this also leads to wasted votes, since voters choosing parties that do not make it over the threshold will not have their vote count (in Turkey's elections in 2002, this counted for nearly half the vote). Still, the degree of wasted votes tends to be much smaller than in SMD.

Which system better serves participation: SMD or PR? This is a controversial question. Supporters of PR argue that it is a more democratic form of electing officials, since it wastes votes to a much smaller degree and in so doing allows for a greater range of political interests to be expressed.[7] PR widens the number of parties able to win seats in the legislature, helping specialized parties concerned with narrow or minority interests to have a greater

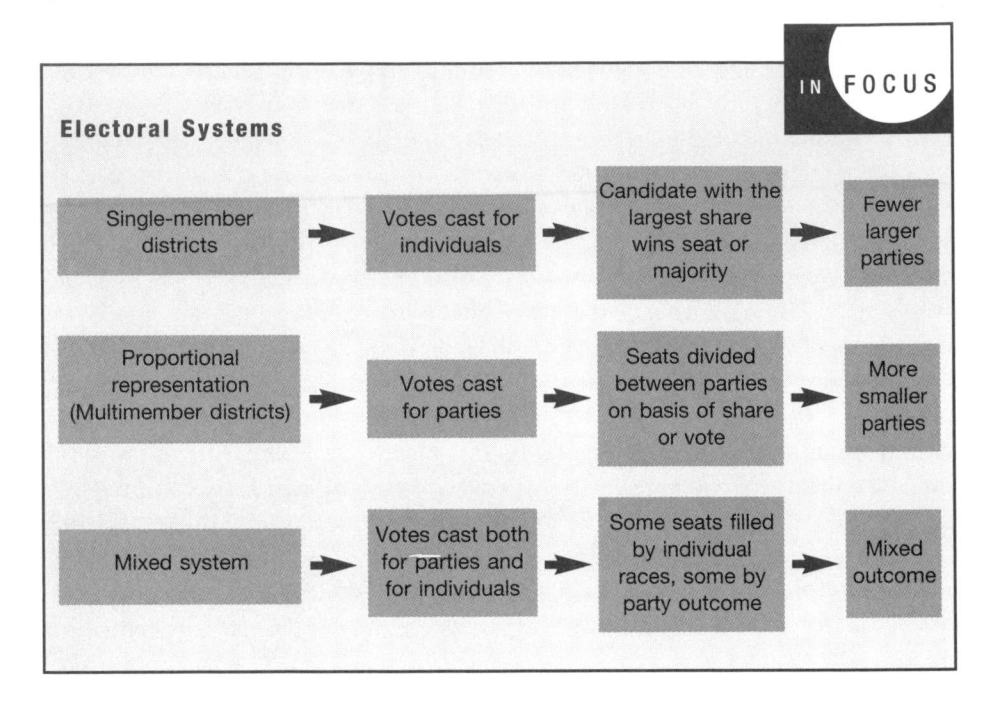

IN FOCUS

Electoral Systems

Single-member districts	→ Votes cast for individuals	→ Candidate with the largest share wins seat or majority	→ Fewer larger parties
Proportional representation (Multimember districts)	→ Votes cast for parties	→ Seats divided between parties on basis of share or vote	→ More smaller parties
Mixed system	→ Votes cast both for parties and for individuals	→ Some seats filled by individual races, some by party outcome	→ Mixed outcome

say in policy making. Imagine, for example, what kinds of parties there might be in the United States if the U.S. electoral system were based on PR: a Pacific Northwest Party? An African American or Native American Party? In addition, with a larger number of parties in the legislature, it is often necessary for parties to form ruling coalitions to muster a majority of votes, thus building consensus across a range of views. PR can also make it easier for parties to establish a quota of underrepresented groups to run for elections, such as women or minorities, thus ensuring more diversity in the legislature.

Those who favor SMD emphasize the benefits of single-member districts and winner-take-all elections. Such a system can make it easier for individuals to connect with their elected representatives than under PR, since voters express their support or rejection of a particular candidate in a way not possible with PR party lists. Indeed, in PR, a candidate no longer liked by the public can still be elected simply because he or she has the backing of the party and is placed high on the party list. In other words, supporters of SMD argue that it increases accountability on the part of individual representatives. Supporters also note that SMD (especially plurality SMD) eliminates fringe parties from the political scene, allowing for the creation of large parties that are able to muster the majorities needed to govern without being held hostage by smaller ones. The flip side of party diversity under PR, critics argue, may be fragmentation and political instability. For SMD, then, representative accountability and majority control over the legislature are the major strengths; for proportional representation, a greater diversity of representation and coalition building are key. Clearly, there is no correct side to this debate, because it turns on different perceptions of what makes a system more or less democratic or effective.

Given the advantages and disadvantages of these two basic forms, some countries have combined the two. For example, Germany, Hungary, and Mexico use what is known as a **mixed electoral system** that combines plurality or majority SMD with PR. Voters are given two votes—one for a candidate and the other for a party. Candidates in the single-member districts are elected on the basis of plurality or majority, while party votes are allocated using proportional representation. The actual percentage of the seats allotted for each electoral method varies from country to country. For example, in Germany, the seats in the lower house of the legislature are divided evenly, whereas in Japan, the breakdown is 60 percent SMD and 40 percent PR. Under this system, voters not only get two votes, but also have the option to split their choice, voting for a candidate from one party in the SMD portion of their ballot while choosing a different party for their PR vote. For example, in Germany, one might vote for the large left-wing Social Democratic Party for the plurality SMD portion of the ballot (since only a large party is likely to get the plurality of votes needed to win), while reserving the PR portion of the ballot for the small environmentalist Green Party.

Referendum and Initiative

In addition to shaping how one's participation is counted, electoral systems can also affect policy. Although national ballots are typically used to choose parties or candidates for office, many countries also have the option of allowing a public vote on a particular policy issue. Such a national ballot is commonly known as a **referendum**. In contrast to the more indirect impact that elections have on politics, referenda allow the public to make direct decisions about policy itself by putting certain issues before the public and allowing them to decide. National referenda are unknown in the United States and Canada (although they exist in some local and state governments), but they are used in many other democracies. Recently, Italy and New Zealand used national referenda to dramatically restructure their electoral and legislative systems, and in Switzerland, where the political system comes closest to the idea of direct democracy than in any other country, many of the most important national decisions are regularly decided by referenda.

Strictly defined, referenda can be called only by the government or members of the legislature. In some countries, the public may have the power of **initiative**, which is essentially a publicly initiated national referendum. In this

INSTITUTIONS IN

ACTION

NEW ZEALAND CHANGES
ITS ELECTORAL SYSTEM

New Zealand is a good example of the differences between SMD and PR because it is one of the few examples where a country has shifted from the former toward the latter. In the late 1970s and early 1980s, national elections in New Zealand produced a result where one party gained an outright majority of seats in the legislature even though it had won fewer votes than the other major party. As a result, in the mid-1980s, the government commissioned a study on electoral reform that proposed that the country shift from plurality SMD to a mixed electoral system similar to that of Germany, with a 5 percent threshold. Two referenda on this electoral change received majority public support, and the first election under this mixed system was held in 1996.

What has been the effect? One important change is something we should have expected: since 1996, no one party has been able to gain a majority of seats in the legislature, in contrast to the previous fifty years. Instead, the two major parties now find themselves having to contend with additional parties in the legislature. In the 2002 elections, some seven parties gained seats. A second related effect is coalition government. With no one party able to muster a majority, parties have been forced to form coalitions (both stable and unstable) to elect a prime minister. Finally, representation has become more diverse. Under the mixed system, new parties were able to form and win seats representing the indigenous Maori people, environmentalism, libertarianism, and anti-immigration views. The share of women and minorities in the legislature also increased. One might conclude that New Zealand's electoral change has thus been an unqualified success. Yet the public has complained that the reform has made politics more confusing, given too much power to small parties, and made members of Parliament less accountable to the public.

process, those organizing the initiative must propose an issue for a nationwide vote and collect a certain number of supporting signatures from the public; if they are able to do so, the government is obliged to schedule a ballot. Initiatives and referenda raise the question of whether the government is obligated to act in accordance with the outcome of a national ballot. In some cases, governments may call a ballot to consult public opinion rather than to make a final, binding decision about some aspect of policy, law, or citizenship. These are known as nonbinding referenda, sometimes called **plebiscites**.

Initiatives and referenda are thus variations on the same theme, that of a nationwide ballot concerning some particular issue. Does such a system make a country more democratic? People who favor greater participation in government policy making support such direct mechanisms, while others argue that the public is ill qualified to make major changes to national policy or institutions. In some societies, national referenda or initiatives might help legitimize democracy through direct participation, while in others they might polarize the public and weaken the notion of republicanism and representative democracy.[8]

As you can see, democratic participation is rather complex. When we speak about the right to vote, we must also consider how that vote is cast and counted. Electoral boundaries and electoral rules strongly influence the power of one's vote, shaping the number of parties in government and the kinds of interests they may represent. Referenda and initiatives also widen the scope for public participation by giving the people a direct say in policy. Using these institutions, liberal democracies can secure the participation of their citizens.

Competition: Political Parties and the Separation of Powers

If participation is a vital part of liberal democracies, it stands to reason that such a right is limited if the public is denied any choice. An election in which there is only one candidate or party to choose from is not a democracy. Therefore, in addition to participation, a democracy requires competition between groups, individuals, and ideas, each seeking to realize their own political goals regarding freedom and equality. In this section, we will focus on two important elements in democratic competition: political parties and the separation of powers. Political parties compete against one another to gain control over the government and state, and the separation of powers makes certain that no one party is able to exercise this control completely. Paradoxically, then, liberal democracies must encourage, but also frustrate, the quest for political power.

Political Parties

Among the many political actors engaged in this competition, political parties are the most organized, the most powerful, and seemingly inevitable. As James Madison once wrote, "In every political society, parties are unavoidable."[9] He did not say that political parties are desirable; since the early days of democracy, many people have viewed them as little more than a necessary evil. Why must we have parties at all? Could we have a democracy in which people could choose between candidates but not political parties? Isn't political choice, rather than parties per se, the most important thing? This is an important question and one that political scientists don't often consider.

Observers have offered several reasons why political parties are vital to liberal democracy.[10] For one thing, parties are important organizations that bring together diverse groups of people and ideas. These organizations serve two functions. By bringing together different people and ideas into a single group, they help establish the means by which the majority can rule. In other words, without political parties that provide candidates and agendas for politics, the political process would be too fragmented and it would be impossible to enact policy or get much else done. But although political parties bring individuals and ideas together, they remain relatively loose, with differences and factions within them. This relative heterogeneity prevents a tyranny of the majority. No one party can easily impose its will undemocratically on the people, since the very diversity within parties prevents the kind of unanimity necessary for tyranny. Parties in liberal democracies are thus homogeneous enough to create majority rule but too weak to facilitate a tyranny of the majority.

Political parties also create the means by which politicians can be held accountable by the electorate and fellow political elites. By articulating an ideology and a set of goals, parties hold their members responsible for achieving those goals. Voters are able to evaluate a group of politicians on the basis of these goals and promises: Did they do what they promised? Lacking parties, the public would have a difficult time evaluating the goals and achievements or failures of each candidate. Parties can thus serve as a political symbol, a shorthand for a set of ideas and objectives, and voters can distill complex decisions into questions of whether to vote for party A or party B. Political parties thus play a key role in encouraging democratic competition. They help articulate broader coalitions while preventing domination by any one group, provide a means to hold elected officials accountable, and thereby encourage democratic debate and the evolution of ideas.

The Separation of Powers

The competition for political power, although vital to democracy, raises the danger that someone might win that competition. More specifically, if too much power rests in any one group's hands, there is the possibility that democracy could be undermined. The loose nature of political parties helps limit this threat, but the problem remains that a particular branch or segment of government may wield too much power and that those who control that branch might be tempted to abuse that power. Through the **separation of powers**, democracies diffuse democratic power by giving specific branches the ability to check the political power of other actors within government.[11] Such power may also slow politics by requiring oversight of various branches of government, limiting hasty decision making that might polarize the public or lead to ill-considered policies. Although it is possible to have democracy without formal checks and balances (the United Kingdom, for example, lacks such structures), they are widely accepted as valuable safeguards. The mere existence of separate branches of government does not ensure an effective separation of powers, however. Each branch must have an independent base of authority outlined in a constitution, embedded in the regime, and respected by politicians and the public.

Democracies typically encompass three major branches of government: executives, legislatures, and constitutional courts. As with electoral rules, each of these institutions may be constructed in very different ways in different liberal democracies, reflecting unique conditions and circumstances.

EXECUTIVES: HEADS OF STATE AND HEADS OF GOVERNMENT We begin with what is the most prominent office in any country, the **executive**, the branch that carries out the laws and policies of a state. When we think of this office, what first comes to mind is a single person in charge of leading the country and setting a national agenda—such as a president. But in fact, the executive comprises two distinct roles. The first is that of **head of state**, a role that symbolizes and represents the people, both nationally and internationally, embodying and articulating the goals of the regime. In contrast, the role of the **head of government** is to deal with the everyday tasks of running the state, such as formulating and executing policy. This distinction is an old one that goes back to the days when monarchs reigned over their subjects, leaving others in charge of ruling the country.

In many countries, this distinction between head of state and head of government still exists in two executive offices. As head of government we find a prime minister, a member of the legislature who has been elected by that body to serve as the executive. Because the prime minister is elected by the legislature, he or she is usually the head of the largest political party, since that party wields the most votes in the legislature. The prime minister and the cabinet (the other chief ministers or officials in government, in charge of such policy areas as defense and agriculture) are charged with formulating and executing policy. As head of state in such systems, one finds a monarch or a president. In most liberal democracies, this position is largely ceremonial. The Japanese and British emperor or the Indian

IN FOCUS

Competition

- Political parties encourage democratic competition by articulating broader coalitions while simultaneously preventing domination by any one group.
- The separation of powers between different branches of government prevents abuses of power by any one branch.

president have little power, though each serves an important symbolic role, representing the nation and the regime. This type of system, in which the head of state and the head of government are separate individuals, is typically known as a **parliamentary system**, since the prime minister, as a member of parliament, is the chief executive.

In contrast, some countries fuse the roles of head of state and head of government into a single office in what is known as a **presidential system**. These systems feature a directly elected president who is entrusted with all executive powers and roles in both domestic and international affairs. The president's function is thus symbolic and practical; in many ways, the office embodies charismatic legitimacy, albeit within a modern rational-legal framework of elections and constitution. The United States is a presidential system, as is Nigeria, Brazil, Mexico, and many other countries.

Political scientists find advantages and flaws in each type of system. One important advantage of the parliamentary system derives from the fact that the prime minister is elected from the legislature. This support reduces the degree of conflict between the executive and the legislature and in turn increases the possibility that legislation can be passed. Prime ministers thus may make for more effective government. Moreover, if prime ministers do lose the support of the legislature, they often can be removed through a "vote of no confidence" by the legislature; a new prime minister is then chosen or new elections called. In other words, the prime minister and the legislature do not serve fixed terms in a parliamentary system. Supporters view this as a great source of flexibility should the government lose the people's confidence.

Some critics of parliamentary systems, however, view the lack of separation between the prime minister and the legislature as a dangerous concentration of power, since both are controlled by the same party. Furthermore, when a single party does not hold a majority in the legislature (which, as we noted, can often occur under proportional representation), it is necessary to build a coalition government that involves several parties. Although coalitions may help generate political consensus, they can also create problems. For example, a party with a plurality of seats in the legislature may bring smaller parties into the cabinet in return for their support in electing a prime minister. But such an arrangement can give smaller parties an inordinate amount of power in the government and the ability to stymie politics altogether. After the 2003 elections in Israel, there were fifteen parties in its legislature and four parties represented in cabinet, and two of those were coalitions of several smaller parties themselves. In short, parliamentary government may limit competition between the executive and the legislature but instill too much competition within the executive itself, especially when combined with a PR electoral system.

Supporters of a presidential system point first to its direct mandate from the people. This means that presidents serve fixed terms, ensuring stability, as they cannot be removed by the legislature except for criminal activity. The fusion of head of state and head of government gives the office additional legitimacy and may increase executive power. Finally, supporters of the presidential system see it as more democratic, because the head of the country is directly chosen by the people. This echoes the argument in favor of SMD, and presidential elections are, in essence, a form of SMD, with candidates winning either through plurality or majority (with a runoff between the top two candidates), depending on the country. Critics, of course, are more doubtful of the presidential system's merits.[12] By fusing heads of state and government, too much power is placed in one person's hands, which can limit competition and threaten democracy. This problem is further compounded by an inability to easily remove the president. Finally, because the executive and the legislature are elected separately, divided government (in which the executive is controlled by one party and the legislature by another) is much more likely, leading to deadlock. For these reasons, some political scientists have gone so far as to say that presidential systems are more likely to undermine democracy, especially where they are weakly institutionalized. However, the direct role played by the people in choosing their leader still makes it an attractive option for many.

In part because of this dispute, some countries have tried to reconcile presidential and parliamentary systems. In such cases, a prime minister coexists alongside a president who is directly elected by the people and who holds a significant degree of power. This power typically includes control over foreign affairs, the ability to dismiss the prime minister or the legislature under certain conditions, and the ability to call national referenda. This combination, known as a **semipresidential system**, can be found in France, Russia, South Korea, and Taiwan, among other countries. Which of the two executives is more powerful under this system depends on the particular issue and the country itself.

A final point about executives and their relationship to the legislature is in order. There is no direct connection between the electoral system for the legislature and the kind of executive system, such as presidential or parliamentary, in any given country. A country may have a directly elected president and use PR for its legislature; it may be parliamentary and use SMD; or it may have any other combination of the two systems. What kind of executive system a country has and how its legislature is elected are entirely separate mechanisms.

LEGISLATURES: BICAMERAL OR UNICAMERAL As with executives, legislatures are an important arena in which people compete for power. Unlike executives, which are charged with carrying out policy, legislatures serve as the main arena in which national politics is debated. The **legislature** is the branch of government charged with making laws. As with all the institutions we have studied so far in this chapter, legislatures vary in their political powers and construction, again reflecting the particular nature of democracy in a country. One major distinction is that between bicameral and unicameral systems. As you might guess from their names, **bicameral systems** have two houses in the legislature, whereas **unicameral systems** have only one. Bicameral systems can be traced back to England and other European states, where two or more chambers were created to serve the interests of different economic classes. The upper house represented the aristocracy; the lower house served the merchant class. In the United Kingdom, this distinction is still evident in the names of the two houses, the lower house being the House of Commons and the upper house the House of Lords. Over time, as the powers of the middle class expanded, the powers of the aristocracy in most countries' legislatures were reduced or eliminated.

Yet the idea of upper and lower houses still remains. Why have two chambers if the old class distinctions that gave rise to bicameralism no longer apply? In fact, in the United Kingdom, the House of Lords lost the last of its remaining powers nearly a hundred years ago, and in 1999, the House of Commons stripped the House of Lords of most of its aristocratic members as well, and yet it chose to maintain the upper house as an institution. It would seem, then, that bicameralism is not like one's appendix, an organ that has lost its function through political evolution. Indeed, bicameralism can play several roles in fostering democratic competition.

First, in many liberal democracies, bicameralism is a part of federalism, which was discussed in Chapter 2. Under federalism, bicameralism allows for one house (usually the upper chamber) to represent regional governments and local interests. Local legislatures may appoint the members of that chamber, or those members may be directly elected. In the United States, the Senate was indirectly elected by local legislatures until 1913. Consistent with the idea of federalism, the goal of bicameralism is to strike a balance of power between national and local government, giving the latter the ability to approve or reject national legislation. Bicameralism can also counterbalance disproportionate power in the hands of any regional government. Whereas seats in the lower house are typically allocated by population, in the upper house, representation may be uniform. For example, in Brazil, each state is given three seats in the Senate, irrespective of the size of each state's population. In the United States, each state has two seats in the Senate. Bicameralism as an expression of federalism can be especially important in countries that are large and where there are many disparate and regional interests.[13]

Even where federalism does not exist, bicameralism may serve to create competition between the two houses as a means to slow down the legislative process. When both houses are required to approve legislation, it becomes difficult to quickly pass laws; such systems therefore force consensus build-

Branches of Government

Branch	Functions, Attributes, and Powers
Executive	Head of state / head of government
	Parliamentary, presidential, and semipresidential systems
	Term length may be fixed (president) or not (prime minister)
Legislative	Lawmaking
	Unicameral or bicameral
Constitutional court	Determines the relative constitutionality of laws and acts
	Judicial Review (abstract and concrete)

ing between the upper and lower houses. In this rationale for bicameralism can be seen echoes of the old aristocratic logic: upper houses are sometimes viewed as a body that must check the passion of the lower house, which may be stirred to sudden and hasty action by members with little political experience. This logic arose in the debates between the Federalists and the Antifederalists during the drafting and ratification of the U.S. Constitution. Many upper houses still reflect this logic through longer terms of office and specific input on changes to the constitution. Different terms of office between the two houses may also serve to increase political stability by preventing a sudden and complete turnover following an election.

Of course, these advantages come at a price. Bicameralism, like any separation of powers, may weaken the legislature by creating too many obstacles to passing legislation, lowering government efficiency. As a result, many countries, especially those that are unitary rather than federal, have opted for relatively weak upper houses or no upper house at all. Sweden, for example, abandoned its upper house in 1971. But the majority of liberal democracies do retain some form of bicameralism.

CONSTITUTIONAL COURTS Our discussion of the separation of powers takes us to the last major branch of government in liberal democracies. The **constitutional court** is the highest judicial body that rules on the constitutionality of laws and other government actions. Over the past half century, many democracies have seen the growth of judicial power, and constitutional courts have played an ever greater role in the realm of politics. At one time, the idea of a strong court overseeing the activities of the legislature and the executive would have been seen as unusual and undemocratic; but in most liberal democracies, constitutional courts are now viewed as important safeguards against abuse. Still, this development has not been without its share of controversy. Because constitutional courts are not directly elected, some view them as failing to represent and often thwarting the direct will of the people. In addition, members of the court tend to serve long terms in office, meaning that turnover is infrequent and that politicians are unable to influence the court as easily as they might like. Of course, this is precisely the point.

Constitutional courts serve to defend the democratic principles of a country against infringement by public or private actors. The court's powers center on the concept of **judicial review**, the mechanism by which the court can review laws and policies and overturn those that are seen as violations of the constitution. Judicial review may take two forms. **Concrete review** is the power by which the court can rule on constitutional issues on the basis of disputes brought before it. In other words, the court has power but is reactive and must wait for a legal dispute before it can rule on the constitutionality of any law or state action. **Abstract review**, in contrast, allows a court to decide on questions that do not arise from actual legal cases, sometimes even before legislation actually becomes law. Some constitutional courts have only concrete power, as with the Supreme Court in the United States; others have only abstract power, as with the Constitutional Council in France (the French court does not hear specific cases between disputants). Some courts have both powers at their disposal, as in the case of the Constitutional Court in Hungary.

The growth of judicial power over the past century has been spurred in part by the desire to protect human rights. In the aftermath of World War II, many world leaders and groups realized that democratic electoral systems could nonetheless give rise to authoritarian leaders. Judges who lacked the power to interpret and defend the democratic provisions and spirit of a constitution could not strike down undemocratic laws if they were promulgated in a technically legal manner. Courts, in other words, have grown in strength as guardians of constitutions and regimes, giving them wider latitude to interpret the law as they see fit. To what extent this growing power interferes with participation and competition by overturning the decisions of elected representatives, however, remains an open question.

Liberty: Civil Rights, Civil Liberties, and Civil Society

The last component of liberal democracy is liberty itself. One thing we have noted in our previous chapters is that the concept of liberty exists to some extent independent of democracy. For example, democracy can exist in an electoral form but otherwise be limited, leading to what we termed illiberal regimes.

Thus, to speak of liberty, we must go beyond democratic process and speak about the substance of democracy itself. In this sense, liberty can be viewed in two distinct but related forms. The first takes the form of civil rights and civil liberties. **Civil rights** typically refer to the promotion of equality, whereas **civil liberties** refer to the promotion of freedom, though there is clearly an overlap between two. Civil rights and liberties include free speech and movement, the right to religious belief, the right of public assembly and organization, equal treatment under the law, the prevention of inhumane punishment, the right to a fair trial, the right to privacy, and the right to choose one's own government. These go back to our earlier discussion of the rule of law—that there exist legal institutions that everyone is subject to, thus preventing the violation of liberty. This facet of liberty flows from the state downward.

Some liberal democracies include civil rights in the area of social or economic outcomes, such as universal education, health care, or retirement benefits. Such rights are particularly strong in social democratic regimes. For example, the Swedish constitution states that "it shall be incumbent upon the public administration to secure the right to work, housing and education, and to promote social care and social security and a good living environment." In addition to differences in how far civil rights should be collectively expanded, liberal democracies also differ in the range of individual liberties. For example, all liberal democracies uphold the rights of free speech and association. Yet in some countries, such as Germany, the democratic constitution outlaws antidemocratic activity, meaning that the state can ban political parties that are seen as hostile to democracy. The South African constitution limits freedom of expression by forbidding "advocacy of hatred that is based on race, ethnicity, gender, or religion, and that constitutes incitement to cause harm."[14] Similar issues are at work regarding the right of individuals to possess firearms. What are the limits to rights or liberties? At what point do the rights of the individual threaten democracy itself? No one has a concise answer to this question, and what is the accepted norm at one point in time can change in the future. But that itself is one of the great strengths of democracy—its ability to evolve.

This leads to our second form of liberty. In our discussion, we see that liberty is not simply freedom or the absence of controls over our scope of action. Rather, liberty is something that must be created, institutionalized, and defended. The state, government, and regime are thus central to fostering and furthering liberty for the citizens. But it would be a mistake to conclude that liberty is simply the product of state action. As our discussion of nondemocratic regimes indicates, states and governments can and do act in ways that are quite illiberal and that encroach on public rights. Indeed, some would argue that the quest for power is a natural tendency of states, and thus even the most liberal state will crowd out liberty over time unless somehow held at bay. But what acts as this check? If liberal institutions are enshrined within the state, they are given life and substance by the people themselves. This is where our sense of the words *public* and *civic* come from—the people's relationship to and role in politics and community affairs. In the past few decades, political scientists have come to speak of this relationship though the concept of **civil society**. Basically, civil society can be defined as organized life outside of the state, or what the French scholar Tocqueville called the "art of association."[15] These are not necessarily political organizations. On the contrary, civil society is a diverse fabric of organizations created by people to help define and advance their own interests, whatever those interests may be, and may include clubs, environmental groups, churches, and even bowling leagues. What is important here is that although such groups may be inherently unpolitical, they serve as a cornerstone of liberty by allowing people to articulate, promote, and defend what is important to them. Civil society is thus the fuel of the democratic process and pluralism, a collective process that helps sustain individual liberty. Moreover, while civil society gives substance to politics and also checks the power of the state, at the same time the very diversity of civil society helps prevent a tyranny of the majority by creating a diverse set of cross-cutting groups and views. This reflects and is linked to our earlier discussion of political parties, which themselves build on civil society.

Where does civil society come from and how is it sustained? This is, not surprisingly, uncertain and controversial. Many would observe that civil society can exist in the absence of a democratic regime; the very term itself gained currency in reference to movements in Eastern Europe in the 1970s that organized independent of, and often in opposition to, communism.[16] Civil society could thus be seen as a precursor to democracy, the foundation that liberal democratic institutions are built on. Yet this begs the question of its origins. Is civil society fostered by economic development? Culture? The rise and widespread embrace of certain ideas? Can democratic institutions create civil society where none exists? These questions are all at play in Iraq, where earlier forms of civil society were largely destroyed by Saddam Hussein's regime. Even in long-established democracies, the state of civil society is a major concern, with some scholars arguing that civic life is on the wane, replaced by an atomized and detached public that has lost interest in the art of association.[17] If true, the impact on democracy could be profound.

In Sum: Future Challenges to Democracy

As we have seen, democracy is one way to manage the dilemma of individual freedom and collective equality, one that this chapter has traced back to ancient Greece, Rome, and early modern England. In its modern liberal form, democracy emphasizes individual freedom and the need to create rules that place political power in the hands of the people. Liberal democracy does this through three basic sets of institutions: participation, competition, and liberty. Participation, such as elections, helps provide the public a means of control over the state and the government; competition ensures an open arena of ideas and prevents too great a centralization of power; and liberty creates a basic set of rights made possible by the state and civil society. When these elements are institutionalized—valued for their own sake, considered legitimate by the public—democracy is institutionalized, and we can speak of the existence of a rule of law. No one stands above the democratic regime.

In the remaining chapters, we will look at the struggle between individual freedom and collective equality in different parts of the world and in the face of different challenges. We shall look at democracy and prosperity in the advanced democracy, the postcommunist world, and in the newly industrializing and less-developed countries. In each case, freedom and equality have moved down a distinct path, leading to very different political institutions. And each faces its own unique set of challenges in creating a political order that generates participation, prosperity, and stability. Moreover, while these challenges may be distinct to each group, they are increasingly interconnected and bound by international ties, or what we commonly call globalization. Freedom and equality are no longer simply domestic concerns; increasingly, they are strongly influenced beyond the state. Finally, we shall consider how these issues relate to political violence. Under what conditions do these struggles escape the realm of normal politics into violent action, such as revolution and terrorism? And how do such actions shape the fates of all countries around the world? The answers to such questions concern us all.

NOTES

1. C. B. MacPherson, *The Life and Times of Liberal Democracy* (New York: Oxford University Press, 1977).
2. Christopher Blackwell, ed., *Demos: Classical Athenian Democracy*. www.stoa.org/projects/demos/home.
3. For details, see Charles Tilly, "War Making and State Making as Organized Crime," in Peter B. Evans, Dietrich Rueschemeyer, and Theda Skocpol, eds., *Bringing the State Back In* (New York: Cambridge University Press, 1985), 165–91.
4. An exhaustive discussion of the different forms of electoral systems and other facets of voting and elections can be found at the Administration and Cost of Elections website at www.aceproject.org.
5. Maurice Duverger, *Political Parties: Their Organization and Activity in the Modern State* (New York: Wiley, 1964).
6. Advocates for majority SMD in the United States can be found at www.fairvote.org/irv/.

7. An extensive argument in favor of adopting PR in the United States can be found at the website of Professor Douglas Amy of Mount Holyoke College: www.mtholyoke.edu/acad/polit/damy/prlib.htm.

8. For a critique of the use of direct democracy, see Fareed Zakaria, *The Future of Freedom: Illiberal Democracy at Home and Abroad* (New York: Norton, 2003).

9. William T. Hutchinson et al., eds., *The Papers of James Madison*, vol. 14 (Chicago: University of Chicago Press, 1985), 197–98.

10. John Aldrich, *Why Parties? The Origin and Transformation of Political Parties in America* (Chicago: University of Chicago Press, 1995).

11. This idea was first elaborated by Baron de Montesquieu in *The Spirit of the Laws*, trans. Thomas Nugent (New York: Hafner, 1949).

12. See Juan Linz and Arturo Valenzuela, eds., *The Failure of Presidential Democracy* (Baltimore: Johns Hopkins University Press, 1994).

13. Alberto Alesina and Enrico Spolaore, *The Size of Nations* (Cambridge, MA: MIT Press, 2003).

14. The South African and other constitutions of the world can be found online at www.uni-wuerzburg.de/law/home.html.

15. Alexis de Toqueville, *Democracy in America* (1840), available at http://xroads.virginia.edu/.

16. Vladimir Tismaneanu, *In Search of Civil Society: Independent Peace Movements in the Soviet Bloc* (London: Routledge, 1990).

17. Susan J. Pharr, Robert D. Putnam, and Russell J. Dalton, "A Quarter Century of Declining Confidence," *Journal of Democracy* 11, no. 2 (2000): 5–25.

7 ADVANCED DEMOCRACIES

So far in this book, we have moved through various concepts that help us compare politics. With these tools now in hand, we can begin to investigate some specific parts of the world. The areas we will study are not themselves geographical locations, but rather groups of countries that are in some way similar in their political institutions. (Recall the discussion in Chapter 1 about the comparative method: by looking at similar countries, we can hope to control our variables so as to better pose questions and test possible answers.) Our first group of countries is commonly known as the **advanced democracies**. This term is problematic, since it is value laden and also teleological—that is to say, it makes it sound as if advanced democracies represent some "end stage" that other countries are heading toward. Recalling the hubris and disappointment of the behavioral movement, we should emphasize that while for many advanced democracy does represent a goal to strive toward, it can cover a diverse set of countries that may get only more diverse in the future. With that said, we here use the term to refer to countries that have institutionalized democracy and a high level of economic development and prosperity.

In this chapter, we will look at the basic institutions and dynamics that characterize advanced democracies, applying the concepts we have studied so far. We will start by categorizing advanced democracies: What do they have in common? What differences exist between them? This comparison will lead us to a discussion of the role of individual freedom and collective equality in the advanced democracies. How do these countries reconcile the two? Once we have a grasp of these ideas, we will move on to consider political, economic, and societal institutions in advanced democracies, particularly the challenges those institutions face in contemporary politics. The forces of integration and devolution—transferring power to international institutions or down to local ones—challenge the very notion of state sovereignty that has been at the core of modern politics. Whether this is the trend of the future is open to question. In economics, too, the emergence of postindustrial societies is transforming the very nature of wealth and labor, providing new opportunities to some while marginalizing others. Similar changes can be seen in societal institutions: new social values may be emerging as a reflection of political and economic change, reshaping ideology in the advanced democracies and the debate over freedom and equality. All of these issues are further compounded by demographic issues as the populations of the advanced democracies become older and more diverse.

Are the advanced democracies on the brink of dramatic transformation? If so, is this change a harbinger of things to come around the globe? This chapter will lay out some of the evidence so that we can consider the possibilities.

Defining Advanced Democracy

What, exactly, are advanced democracies? In the past, scholars typically spoke of these countries as belonging to the "First World," meaning that they were economically developed and democratic. They were contrasted with the countries of the "Second World," or communist states, and those of the "Third World," meaning the vast body of less-developed countries. Categorizing countries into these three "worlds" was always somewhat problematic, since various factors in various combinations around the world often confounded these categories. The rise of oil-based economies in the Middle East, for example, created countries with a great degree of wealth, but this wealth was based on natural resources controlled by the state rather than on private property and free markets. The rise in wealth in these countries also did not coincide with a move toward liberal democracy—so they did not really fall into the Third World, yet were not at all part of the advanced First World, either. With the end of the Cold War and the collapse of communism, the three-worlds approach became even more confusing, as many industrialized, formerly communist countries embraced capitalism and liberal democracy, while others experienced economic decline and continued authoritarianism. They had little left in common except history.

Instead of using this problematic three-worlds approach, this book will refer to *advanced democracies, communist and postcommunist countries,* and *developing and less-developed countries.* These categories, too, have their limitations, and critics might say they differ from past approaches only in name. One difference, however is that our groupings imply that movement is possible between the categories—that countries can industrialize or democratize, can move to or from communism, can develop or remain less developed. In fact, we will place some countries in more than one category, especially those that lie in a transitional area from one category to the next.

So, how do we determine which countries belong to the category of advanced democracies? In the area of democracy, we can rely on the factors discussed in Chapter 6, looking at the degree and institutionalization of participation, competition, and liberty in each. In the area of economic development and prosperity, we can consider those issues raised in Chapter 4: the presence of private property, open markets, and the level of gross domestic product (GDP) at purchasing-power parity (PPP). We might also consider the kind of economic output that countries produce. In general, advanced democracies tend to have a relatively small portion of their GDP arising from agriculture and industrial production. During the Industrial Revolution and after, industry displaced agriculture in many of today's advanced democracies; but today, that industry itself is increasingly being displaced by the service sector, which includes such things as retail sales, computer programming, and education. Finally, we should also consider the output of that wealth in terms of prosperity by looking at the overall well-being of society (such as is measured by the human development index)

Table 7.1 lists a few countries that can be classified as advanced democracies, with a few nonadvanced democracies listed for comparison. The advanced democracies share in common not only liberal democratic regimes, but also capitalist economic systems (liberal, social democratic, or mercantilist) in which the service sector dominates and a high HDI ranking. This contrasts with countries such as Saudi Arabia, China, India, and Nigeria, which are poorer, have low HDI rankings, and lack a strong industrial and service sector or institutionalized liberal democracy or both.

Given our definition of advanced democracies, the countries that we place in this category are rather diverse—a diversity that has grown particularly strong over the past decade. For example, countries such as Poland and South Korea were historically categorized as part of the Second and Third Worlds, respectively. But with economic and political changes in both countries, it makes less and less sense to think of them in these terms. Postcommunist Poland now has much more in common economically and politically with Western European countries such as Germany and France than with many other countries that also were once part of the communist world; South Korea has more in common with Japan and the United States than it does with other, less-developed countries around the world.

The countries listed as advanced democracies in Tables 7.1 and 7.2 have high levels of economic development (GDP PPP of over $7,000) and small agricultural sectors. They also are institutionalized democratic regimes and are among the top fifty-five countries on the HDI, or what the United Nations classifies as "high human development." Note that within this category are several recent democratizers and postcommunist countries that also exhibit the hallmarks of economic development and democracy. This group is not meant to be exhaustive, certain, or definitive. Scholars continue to debate whether these and other countries should or will be categorized as advanced

Table 7.1 Advanced Democracies, 2006

North and South America	Europe	Asia	Middle East and Africa
United States	*European Union members:*	Australia	Israel
Canada	Austria	Japan	
Bahamas	Belgium	New Zealand	
Barbados	Cyprus		
Bermuda	Denmark	*South Korea*	
	Finland	*Taiwan*	
Argentina	France		
Chile	Germany		
Mexico	Greece		
Uruguay	Ireland		
	Italy		
	Luxembourg		
	Malta		
	Netherlands		
	Portugal		
	Spain		
	Sweden		
	United Kingdom		
	Czech Republic		
	Estonia		
	Hungary		
	Latvia		
	Lithuania		
	Poland		
	Slovakia		
	Slovenia		
	EU non-members:		
	Norway		
	Switzerland		
	Iceland		
	Croatia		

Note: Countries in italics have recently undergone democratization.

democracies, since their economic and political advances are still relatively new, incomplete, and not fully institutionalized. Indeed, these countries will be discussed again in the chapters on postcommunist and developing and less-developed countries. In spite of this uncertainty, their presence indicates that as a result of recent global economic and political changes, the camp of

Table 7.2 Economic Portraits, 2005

Country	Percentage of GDP Contributed by			GDP (PPP, in U.S. $)	Institutionalized Democracy?	HDI Ranking
	Agriculture	Industry	Services			
Advanced Democracies						
United States	1	23	76	40,100	Yes	6
Japan	5	25	70	29,400	Yes	9
Canada	3	23	74	31,500	Yes	3
Sweden	2	29	69	28,400	Yes	2
South Korea	3	40	66	19,200	Yes	27
Poland	3	31	66	12,000	Yes	37
Other Countries (for Comparison)						
Saudi Arabia	4	67	29	12,000	No	71
China	14	53	33	5,600	No	96
India	23	28	48	3,100	Yes	124
Nigeria	36	31	33	1,000	No	148

Source: CIA, United Nations Development Program.

advanced democracies appears to be expanding well beyond its traditional provinces of Western Europe and North America.

One result of using a broad definition for advanced democracies is the inclusion of countries that have come to this category by very different means—countries that were early industrializers and early democratizers, as well as countries that have moved into both categories more recently. Indeed, the paths to the realm of advanced democracy have been varied. Some countries experienced democratic and economic development early and simultaneously, as did the United States and the United Kingdom in the late eighteenth and early nineteenth centuries. In other cases, economic development did not lead directly to democratization. For example, in Germany, capitalist industrialization in the nineteenth century occurred under the guidance of a powerful authoritarian regime. This was also the case somewhat later in Japan and subsequently in countries such as South Korea and Taiwan. In these cases, democracy came only in the latter half of the twentieth century. Finally, countries in Eastern Europe saw their industrialization carried out primarily by authoritarian communist regimes; their transitions to capitalism and democracy occurred only since the early 1990s.

Freedom and Equality in Advanced Democracies

How do advanced democracies reconcile the dilemma of freedom and equality? All countries that fall into this category share in common an institutionalized liberal democracy, private property, free markets, and a high level of economic development based on industry and services. However, this similarity does not mean that these countries' approaches to reconciling freedom and equality are identical. Advanced democracies differ in how they reconcile freedom and equality while remaining capitalist and liberal democratic. Countries with liberal regimes are focused more on individual freedoms than on collective equality, whereas the focus of social democratic systems tends toward the opposite. Mercantilist systems, meanwhile, have policies that tend to be more development oriented, with freedom and equality issues of less direct concern to the state. In spite of this wide variation, however, these countries are united by common democratic and economic institutions.

First consider the role of freedom: all advanced democracies are institutionalized liberal democracies, sharing in common a belief in participation, competition, and liberty. Yet there are real differences in how countries define each of these categories. For example, civil rights and/or liberties may be expanded or restricted without calling into question the democratic nature of a country. Take the case of abortion. Some advanced democracies, such as Sweden, Japan, the United States, Hungary, Canada, France, and Austria, allow abortions during a pregnancy's first trimester with relatively few restrictions. In others countries, such as South Korea, Argentina, and Poland, abortions are more restricted. And some countries ban abortions altogether or allow them only to save a woman's life (in Chile, Malta, and Ireland, for example). We can find similar distinctions in the regulation of prostitution, drugs, or hate speech or in the degree to which privacy is protected from state or economic actors.

Advanced democracies also vary in their levels of political participation. The different electoral systems discussed in Chapter 6 can all be found among these countries, alone and in combination. The use of referenda and initiatives differ greatly across these countries; most advanced democracies do use them to some degree, although a few countries allow for such votes only at the local level (the United States, Canada, Germany, and Japan), and still others make no provision for such ballots at any level of government (Israel). Another difference can be found in voter registration; in most advanced democracies, it is the responsibility of the state to ensure that all eligible voters are automatically registered to vote; yet in a few (the United States and France), it is contingent on the individual voter to register. Voting rights and obligations may also differ. In Norway, Sweden, the Netherlands, and Denmark, any foreigner who has taken up permanent residence may vote in local elections. In Australia, Argentina, Uruguay, and Belgium, voting is mandatory, though with varying degrees of enforcement and sanction.

Nor is competition uniform across the advanced democracies. Its variations include the ways in which political parties and campaigns are funded: some countries impose specific limits on the amount of money that can be contributed by private actors to any political party or candidate and require the disclosure of the source of private political contributions. The separation of powers also varies greatly, with unicameral and bicameral systems, strong and weak constitutional courts, presidents and prime ministers.

In short, the advanced democracies are politically diverse. All advanced democracies guarantee participation, competition, and liberty, but they differ in where the boundaries of these freedoms are defined or how these freedoms are exercised. Freedom is a basic guarantee, but the form and content of freedom varies from case to case.

In addition to a commitment to freedom, advanced democracies also share a similar approach to equality that emphasizes capitalism, that is to say, private property and free markets. This approach appears to have generated a great deal of economic prosperity—overall basic standards of living are higher in the advanced democracies than elsewhere in the world, and average life expectancy is high, at over seventy years—yet this wealth exists alongside inequality, with the wealth sometimes concentrated disproportionately among certain ethnic groups.

Yet here, too, we see variation. Recall from Chapter 4 that the Gini index, a measurement of inequality around the world, found a surprising degree of difference between countries even when their levels of economic development were roughly the same. For example, Germany and the United States have comparable levels of economic development as measured by GDP, but very different levels of inequality as measured by the Gini index.

This difference in equality is in part a function of the role of the state. Across advanced democracies, states differ greatly in their economic functions, including their role in the distribution of wealth. In liberal and mercantilist countries such as the United States and Japan, the state provides relatively low levels of social expenditure. Individuals or families have a greater responsibility for funding basic needs, and the total tax burden on the public in these countries is typically lower as a result. This is not to say, however, that inequality is necessarily the end result; in Japan, Estonia, and South Korea, a small welfare state coexists alongside a higher level of economic equality than in the United States. In social democratic systems, such as those found in much of Europe, taxation is much higher, and these resources are used for income redistribution through a strong system of social expenditures. However, these variations in the state's approach to inequality do not change the fact that in each of these countries, private property and free markets are fundamental institutions (Table 7.3).

In short, the advanced democracies hold in common a basic set of institutions to reconcile freedom and equality. These institutions include liberal democracy, with its emphasis on participation, competition, and liberty, and capitalism, with its emphasis on free markets and private property. Yet each of the advanced democracies has constructed these institutions in different ways, resulting in quite significant variations among them.

Table 7.3 Income Redistribution in Advanced Democracies, 2001

Country	Political-Economic System	Taxes as a Percentage of GDP, 2001	Gini Index
Sweden	Social democratic	51	25
Denmark	Social democratic	50	24.7
France	Social democratic	45	32.7
Germany	Social democratic	37	30
United Kingdom	Liberal	37	36.8
Canada	Liberal	35	31.5
United States	Liberal	29	45
Japan	Mercantilist	27	24.9

Sources: CIA, Organization for Economic Cooperation and Development.

IN FOCUS

Political Diversity in Advanced Democracies

Participation

- Standards of voter eligibility differ.
- Referenda and initiatives are used in varying degrees.
- Some, but not all, states automatically register all eligible voters.
- Voting is compulsory in some nations, but voluntary in most.

Competition

- Different methods and levels of funding for political parties and campaigns.
- Separation of powers varies greatly and is based primarily on the relative strength of different branches of government.

Liberties

- Distinctions in the regulation, allowance, or prohibition of activities such as abortion, prostitution, and hate speech.
- Different degrees of individual privacy from state and corporate intrusion.

Advanced Democracies Today

The institutions that the advanced democracies share are part of what makes these countries **modern**—that is, secular, rational, materialistic, technological, bureaucratic, and placing a greater emphasis on individual freedom than on collective equality. But like any other set of countries, the advanced democracies are not static; their institutions are subject to change under the influence of domestic and international forces. Indeed, many argue that the advanced democracies are currently undergoing a profound set of social, political, and economic changes. In the eyes of some, many of the advanced democracies are entering into a new era, characterized by a new set of values that view freedom and equality and the balance between them in a fundamentally different way. If true, this would mean that existing modern institutions are also giving way to new ones as these countries make a transition from modernity to postmodernity. Such a change, if it is indeed happening, is likely to be profound. Others, however, either doubt that such changes are under way or are as widespread as claimed or argue that the kinds of changes being witnessed are more a retreat back into older modern values. These are big questions that lie in the realm of speculation and rely on fragmentary evidence, so we must be careful. To get some answers, we need to look at how political,

societal, and economic institutions may be changing in the advanced democracies and in what direction so that we may draw our own conclusions about
whether modernity, as we understand it, is really giving way to something new.

States and Sovereignty: Challenges and Opportunities

In Chapter 2, we discussed a number of ways in which states can be analyzed
and compared. In particular we spoke about state sovereignty and the way in
which state power can be viewed in terms of autonomy and capacity. Although
advanced democracies differ in their levels of autonomy and capacity, they
are all distinguished by the ability to formulate and carry out the basic tasks
expected of them by society. In other words, advanced democracies are notable
for their sovereignty, or their ability to act independent of outside actors,
which ever since the rise of the modern state has been a hallmark of power.

Yet in recent decades, these concepts have come under challenge. In particular, within the advanced democracies we have seen a movement toward
greater integration between countries and greater devolution within countries.
Integration is a process by which states pool their sovereignty, surrendering
some individual powers in order to gain political, economic, or societal benefits in return. Integration blurs the line between countries by forging tight
connections, common policies, and shared rules that bind them together. In
contrast, **devolution** is a process by which political power is devolved, or "sent
down," to lower levels of government. This process is intended to increase
local participation, efficiency, and flexibility, as tasks once handled at the
national level are managed by local authorities. These two processes differ in
the direction in which power is flowing—either "above" the state in the case
of integration or "below" the state in the case of devolution. But in both cases,
state capacity, autonomy, and sovereignty are affected, influencing the relationship between freedom and equality. Although both integration and devolution can be found to varying degrees around the world, it is among the
advanced democracies that such processes are the most advanced and profound. While many have expected this twin process of integration and devolution to effectively transform the modern state as we know it, there are also
countervailing processes that may limit, or even end, these movements.

The European Union: Integration, Expansion, and Resistance

The most important example of integration is the European Union (EU), a
project without precedent and whose possible long-term implications are both

awesome and completely uncertain. Following World War II, a number of European leaders argued that the repeated conflicts in the region were caused by a lack of interconnection between the countries themselves—which in turn fostered insecurity, inequality, and nationalism. These leaders believed that if their countries could be bound together through economic, societal, and political institutions, they would reject war against each other as an irrational act. Moreover, they argued, a common political agenda would give European states greater international authority in a postwar environment that had become dominated by the Soviet Union and the United States. With these motivations, a core of Western European countries began the process of integration in the early 1950s. As you can imagine, this was a radical step away from sovereignty and not an easy one for any state or society to swallow. As a result, integration moved forward slowly.[1]

As the time line on page 172 shows, the EU developed incrementally over time. This was intentional; the EU was from the start an ambitious project, but one that its supporters realized could be achieved by moving slowly and cautiously. Thus, the EU began its life as a small agreement between a handful of countries that dealt primarily with the production of steel and coal, only to expand over time to become a body that included many more members and vastly greater responsibilities. Out of these changes a basic set of institutions has developed, with increasingly sovereign power in many areas over the member states themselves. While there are now a huge number of EU bodies and subgroups, four institutions are central. The European Commission, made up of representatives appointed by the member states' governments, develops legislation. The Council of Ministers, made up of cabinet ministers from the countries' respective national governments, approves or rejects this legislation (with each minister voting in accordance with his or her country's concerns). A third body, the European Parliament, is directly elected by the member states' citizens. In other words, EU citizens vote in elections both for their national legislatures and for the European Parliament. The European Parliament is able to modify or reject most legislation that comes from the Commission, as well as approve the addition of new members to the EU. Finally, the European Court of Justice plays an important role in resolving disputes over legislation once it has been adopted; it also decides matters of EU law. These statelike institutions have gained power over time, so much so that now many people no longer speak of the EU as an **intergovernmental system**, with countries cooperating on issues, but as a **supranational system**, with its own sovereign powers over the member states themselves. As a result, the reconciliation of freedom and equality has become as much an international task as a domestic one.

Each of the individual states of the EU has had to weigh the benefits of integration against the loss of sovereignty. For example, Sweden is a relative

TIME LINE / EUROPEAN INTEGRATION	
1951	European Coal and Steel Community founded by Belgium, France, Germany, Italy, Luxembourg, and the Netherlands
1957	European Economic Community created
1967	European Community (EC) created
1973	Denmark, Ireland, and the United Kingdom join EC
1979	Direct elections to the European Parliament
1981	Greece joins EC
1986	Spain and Portugal join EC
1993	European Union (EU) created
1995	Sweden, Finland, and Austria join EU
1999	Monetary union created between most EU member states
2002	Euro currency enters circulation; most EU national currencies eliminated
2004	EU accepts ten new members
2005	EU constitution rejected by France and the Netherlands in referenda

latecomer to the EU, having joined only in 1995. Its long resistance toward membership stemmed in part from its tradition of political neutrality (Sweden did not take sides during World War II) and from the fear that membership would require changes in domestic institutions and policies in order to conform to EU standards. Of greatest concern were Sweden's large social expenditures, created to ensure greater collective equality. However, the end of the Cold War changed Swedish thinking about neutrality, and in the 1990s, the government moved to apply for membership, although public skepticism remained. A few European countries, such as Norway and Switzerland, have chosen to stay out of the body altogether, their publics having rejected membership in referenda.

The growing breadth and depth of the EU have been further underscored by three recent projects, each of which changed (or hoped to change) the EU in fundamental ways. The first has been monetary union. On January 1, 1999, the majority of EU member states linked their currencies to the euro, a single currency eventually meant to replace those of the member states as a means to promote further economic integration and growth. The logic of monetary union was that member states would benefit through a single currency, as it would allow for one measure of prices and values across the EU, increasing competition (and thus lowering prices) by stimulating trade and cross-border investment within the EU. More generally, the euro was hoped to help foster a true European identity, with a single currency to bind these countries together. Finally, a single currency backed by some of the world's wealthiest countries would increase the EU's power in the international system by creating what could become a "reserve currency" for other countries—that is, a currency with global legitimacy that central banks would use as part of their monetary holdings. Reserve currencies are also the main monetary standard for businesses and individuals around the world. While the U.S. dollar has been the global reserve currency for decades, giving the United States certain benefits as a result, the euro represented a real challenge to its global authority. In short, monetary union was promised to have both domestic (intra-EU) and international benefits.

Figure 7.1 **EUROPEAN UNION MEMBERSHIP**

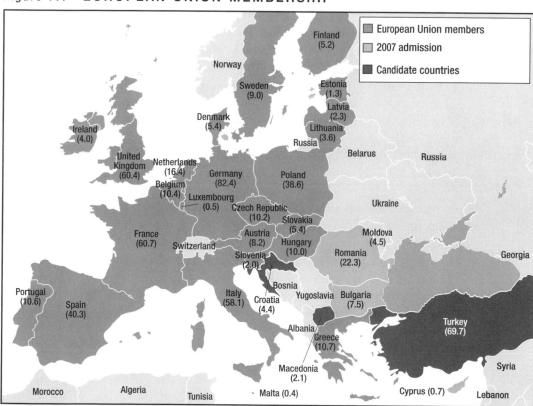

Source: British Parliament.

Note: Numbers in parentheses indicate population size, in millions.

On January 1, 2002, all EU member states that joined the monetary union withdrew their own currencies from circulation and replaced them with the euro. In Chapter 4, we noted that one important facet of a state's power is its ability to print money and set interest rates; in the European monetary union, this power has been surrendered to the European Central Bank. This monetary union represents the largest single transfer of power to date within the EU; it has also been extremely contentious. Some EU members, such as Sweden, Denmark, and the United Kingdom, have declined to join the monetary union. These countries, while quite different in their domestic political and economic systems, share a similar fear that the single currency would force their state to align their political economic systems more with the other EU member states. More generally, each sees monetary union as an important loss of sovereignty that is unacceptable to their publics. In Denmark and Sweden, referenda on euro membership have failed, while in the United Kingdom, the Labour government, which favors joining the euro, has promised a referendum but has so far failed to schedule it (probably because polls show that it would clearly be rejected).

For those counties that have joined the euro, the results depend on the objective. The hope to make the euro a reserve currency seems to have been borne out, and the currency has become a serious rival to the U.S. dollar, dramatically appreciating in value in the process. But this has been of less interest to EU citizens, many of whom complain that the euro's introduction has led to higher, rather than lower, prices. EU surveys also show that the majority find that the euro has not increased their sense of a greater European identity, though support for the currency remains strong in most countries that adopted it.[2] Economists, meanwhile, warned that the EU is made up of very different kinds of countries in terms of their economic systems and patterns of growth. A single currency would essentially straightjacket all members into a single set of monetary policies, such as interest rates. A high interest rate might be good for Ireland, while a low interest rate might be more suitable for Germany. But with a single currency and central bank, one rate now has to apply for all member states. Some have argued that this has contributed to relatively lower levels of economic growth and higher unemployment in the EU than in the United States, though this is disputed.

A second important development has been the ongoing expansion of the EU (Figure 7.1). From 1951 to 2004, the EU grew from six member states to fifteen, and with the collapse of communism in Eastern Europe, a new wave of countries eagerly sought out membership as a part of their "return to Europe." After a long period of negotiation, in 2004 the EU accepted an additional ten countries, adding an additional 75 million people to the EU (an increase of 20 percent, to over 450 million—larger than the U.S. population, which is less than 300 million) and an additional 750 billion euro in GDP (an increase of 9 percent), bringing the EU and U.S. economies to roughly the same size.

While enlargement has certainly made the EU a much bigger body, this has created new issues and concerns. One is economic. Many of the new member states are much poorer than the past EU average. Per capita GDP for the fifteen EU members that belonged before 2004 is approximately 22,500 euro; all the new members fall below this, ranging from 18,000 euro to as low as 7,000, or less than one-third of average.[3] Because of this, the EU spent large sums of money trying to improve the economic and social conditions of these nations in advance of membership, and with membership, these new states should be eligible for special EU funds that are directed toward development and agriculture. However, older members of the EU have opposed this wholesale redirection of support toward the new members, especially France, whose agricultural sector is heavily supported by EU subsidies. This has increased conflict between and within old and new members—over how much support the EU should provide to member states, where these funds should come from, and who should receive it. Related to this, the relative poverty of new members has increased fears in the EU that European businesses will move their firms eastward to take advantage of lower wages, while East European workers will move en masse westward looking for jobs, compounding unemployment problems. Whether true or not, enlargement has played into existing concerns among member states about economic growth and globalization in general (we will speak more of this in Chapter 10).

These economic considerations have been compounded by political ones. The majority of the new member states spent the last half century under communist rule, several of them as part of the Soviet Union itself. As a result, among many of them, there is great support for EU membership, but also skepticism toward large bureaucratic institutions that seek to direct economic, societal, and political institutions and policies at the national level. These states only recently regained their sovereignty and are less eager to surrender it once again. Many of the new members also have pursued much more liberal economic politics than is the norm in Western Europe. The U.S.-led war against Iraq brought many of these tensions out in the open when a number of postcommunist countries publicly declared their support for U.S. action, much to the anger of Germany and France, who have historically been seen as the driving force behind the EU.

A last element of enlargement is that it is far from over. Bulgaria and Romania are on track to join in 2007 or 2008, and there are a number of other countries that are either in the negotiation process or interested in beginning negotiations in the next decade. Most important among these is Turkey. After years of seeking membership, Turkey has finally been allowed by the EU to formally enter into negotiations. Turkey has a population of over 65 million people (almost as many people as all ten states that joined in 2004 combined) and a relatively low GDP (less than 7,000 euro, or a third of EU average), and it is Muslim. The possibility of Turkish membership has acted as a lightning rod for a number of reasons: Where does Europe end? What will it mean to have a Muslim state alongside a community of Christian ones and have the borders of the EU stretch to Iraq and Syria? Is it possible to have integration when the membership of the EU is increasingly diverse along economic, historical, cultural, and religious lines? EU membership and enlargement was easier when the members had relatively similar institutions and experiences. This is no longer so.

This brings us to a third development, alongside monetary union and enlargement: constitutional reform. As a statelike body, the EU has created a number of documents over time to deal with its structure, powers, and scope, dating back to the Treaty of Rome in 1957. However, there has never been a single document that codified the functions and role of the EU. With monetary union and enlargement, it was clear that the old institutions, originally created to serve a half-dozen countries, could no longer effectively function in a body of twenty-five members, with more to come. In 2002, the EU held a special convention with the goal of creating a true single constitution for the EU that would reform the existing structure and set forth its future tasks and responsibilities. As one can imagine, this was a difficult and acrimonious process. Member states had different notions about the degree and kind of reform necessary, as well as the extent to which additional sovereign powers should be vested with the EU. The final draft attempted to balance these competing views and desires, producing a document that ran over 250 pages and moving the EU in a more federal direction. Expectations were that the new constitution, in spite of various national concerns, would pass in all the member states (with perhaps the exception of the "Euroskeptic" United Kingdom). This was not the case. In June 2005, referenda in France and Holland delivered a shock, with their publics rejecting the constitution. This was especially surprising given that France and Holland were founding members and had been traditionally strong supporters of the EU. This has effectively stopped the process in its tracks.

What happened? Observers have given several reasons for why the constitution failed to gain public support. For some, the constitution became a symbol of the rapid changes going on inside and outside the EU—such as enlargement, globalization, and the loss of sovereignty. Indeed, one could easily find opponents of the constitution who feared that it was an instrument of liberal economic policies, while others saw it as communism in disguise. The sheer opacity and length of the constitution did not help matters. Finally, for many the rejection was evidence of the long-discussed "democratic deficit" in the EU. That is, many see the EU as lacking a direct connection to the citizenry, as a bureaucracy unconnected to the needs and anxieties of the public. For many, opposition to the constitution represented their only way to give voice to these concerns.

What happens next is uncertain. The EU may attempt to revive the constitution at some point in the future. It may move to a more multitiered organization, with different levels of integration for different members. It may also proceed more warily toward further enlargement, especially with countries like Turkey. A shift away from a federal vision may help foster an EU that is more flexible, able to deal with a diversity of members. Less optimistically, it may lead to a period of drift that only compounds uncertainty and rancor among its citizens, members, and countries in waiting. The lessons here extend beyond Europe. The attempt of the United States to expand its free-trade agreements to Central and South America has faced similar resistance by many who fear a loss of sovereignty and see such integration as an instrument of globalization.

Devolution and Democracy

Integration continues to exert a strong pull on many advanced democracies, in spite of resistance. At the same time, many advanced democracies also face the tug of devolution from below. As mentioned earlier, devolution is a process by which powers and resources are transferred away from central state institutions and vested at a lower level. What is interesting about this process is that it is a reversal of the historical development of the state, which is noteworthy for its centralization of power over time. Over the decades, ever greater power has moved from the local level to the national level on issues such as social welfare. Yet across the advanced democracies, powers have been flowing in the opposite direction.

Why this apparent reversal? Many political leaders in advanced democracies are concerned that the public mistrusts the state, viewing it as too large, too distant, and too inflexible. Devolution is viewed as a way to counteract this distrust by bringing government closer to the public, thereby increasing local control and participation. By increasing the public voice and the public's capacity to shape politics, it is hoped, democracy can be reinvigorated.[4]

How does devolution take shape in reality? One way is through the transfer of responsibility and funds to local authorities, giving them greater say in how policies are crafted and executed. When local institutions have more control and responsibility, they can craft policy to meet their own particular conditions. One example of such devolution occurred in the United States in the 1990s, when welfare reform created bulk transfers of funds to the states, which

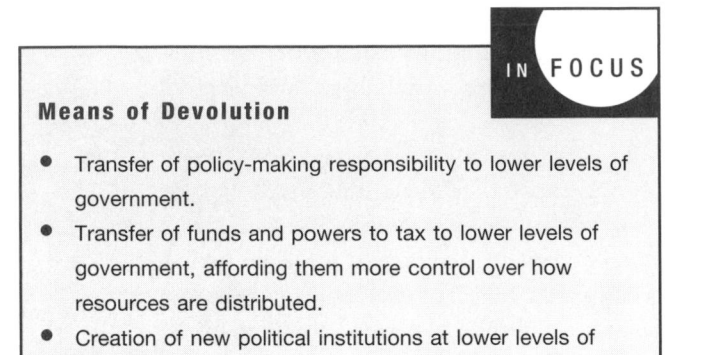

IN FOCUS

Means of Devolution

- Transfer of policy-making responsibility to lower levels of government.
- Transfer of funds and powers to tax to lower levels of government, affording them more control over how resources are distributed.
- Creation of new political institutions at lower levels of government.

could then use this money to design and implement their own particular social welfare policies. Another is through the creation of wholly new political institutions to provide a new level of public participation. An example of such innovation was seen in Canada in 1999, when an entirely new province, Nunavut, was created out of a portion of the Northwest Territories. The creation of this new province was intended to give the native Inuit people self-government and control over the natural resources in the region where they live. Similarly, in 1999, the United Kingdom created new, directly elected assemblies for the regions of Scotland, Wales, and Northern Ireland. In fact the EU, as part of its integration process, encouraged devolution as a way to give local and regional interests a greater voice in government.

As with integration, it is not certain whether devolution is a trend among the advanced democracies that will continue to spread and deepen in the future, nor is it clear what the long-term implications of such a process would be. Devolution may be a means to rebuild democratic participation by making people more directly responsible for policy making. However, it may also undermine the capacity and autonomy of the central state, especially if coupled with integration. Some of this may be overstated; in the aftermath of September 11, a number of advanced democracies moved away from devolution in important ways, centralizing and increasing capacity and autonomy as a way to fight the threat of terrorism. As with integration, external and internal conditions can influence devolution's pace and strength. Not long ago, observers saw integration and devolution as inexorable processes that states and citizens could not stop. That may not be the case.

Social Change and Conflict

Just as advanced democratic states are undergoing a number of challenges and changes in the new millennium, societies are in transition as well. As with states, societies seem to be pulled from two directions. Some political scientists point to a new set of shared norms and values emerging across the advanced democracies, while others point to greater emphasis on local identities that are turning these same societies inward. These processes are strongly connected to the struggle over integration and devolution. Whether these social forces are complementary or contradictory, and whether such developments are a sign of greater cooperation or conflict, is still a matter of debate.

Postmodern Values and Organization

In recent years, a number of political scientists have begun to track the emergence of what they see as the development of postmodern values in the advanced democracies.[5] As we have noted, in premodern societies, people were focused to a greater extent on traditional forms of authority and on basic survival; this focus often led to authoritarian systems with clear standards of obedience and collectivism. Starting in the eighteenth century, those countries that would become the advanced democracies began to embrace the notions of rationality and science, individualism, and autonomy. The modern state, society, and economy promised a world of progress, development, and limitless possibilities, and it did enable unprecedented economic growth, material abundance, and improved standards of living for hundreds of millions of people.

Yet by the 1960s, modern values came under attack, just as they themselves had challenged premodern ones more than two centuries earlier. These challenges took several forms. Economic development came into question because of the environmental damage that it causes. Modern values stressed the environment as an instrument for achieving material goals, but critics argued that the environment should be valued for its own sake—a public good to be shared by all. Science, too, was similarly viewed with greater skepticism. Technological innovation did not lead to unmitigated benefits, but rather carried with it risks and uncertainty. Fears over nuclear power and chemical contamination underscored the belief among many that the very notion of "progress" was a questionable goal. In politics, too, postmodern values challenged nationalism and patriotism, questioning authority, hierarchy, and deference to the state. In general, these criticisms indicated the possible emergence of a new set of social norms and values.

Postmodern values differ from modern ones in a number of ways. As already indicated, **postmodern** values are much less focused on the idea of progress as embodied by material goods, technological change, or scientific innovation. Instead, postmodern values center on what have been called "quality of life" or "postmaterialist" issues, which give primary attention to concerns other than material gain. These include concerns over the environment, health, and leisure as well as a greater focus on personal equality and diversity. At the same time, postmodern values are skeptical of state power while supportive of democracy, especially in the form of direct participation and

action. These values in many ways reflect both integrationist and devolu-
tionary tendencies, with their concern for greater tolerance among people
(integration) and their greater hostility toward centralized power (devolution).
Turn back to our map of political culture in Chapter 3 (Figure 3.4 on page 73).
Postmodern values can be located in the upper right-hand corner, a combination of secular-rational and self-expression values.

    We must be careful not to overstate these findings, however. As Figure 3.4
shows, many countries grouped as part of the advanced democracies show much
more traditional values, which cannot be explained away by economic development. These include the United States, Canada, Chile, Ireland, and Australia.
These differences indicate that domestic factors in each country remain important in shaping the value systems of societies, even as they undergo a general
process of development and consequent change. The central question then
becomes whether there is a shared set of postmodern values that all advanced
democracies are converging toward, and if so, whether these values will inex-
orably spread to new members of this community.[6] At one time, scholars
answered both questions in the positive; more recently, however, doubts regarding the inevitability of postmodern values have surfaced.

Diversity, Identity, and the Challenge to Postmodern Values

There are reasons why scholars have become more tentative about the spread
of postmodern values. Questions have been growing for a number of years,
but September 11 in many ways served to bring them into the open, not just
in the United States but across the advanced democracies as a whole. People
are asking themselves whether their different societies are truly as similar as
once thought and whether the shared values within their respective countries
will survive in the long run.

    Perhaps the most important factor influencing this debate is the almost
unprecedented wave of immigration that has impacted most of the advanced
democracies. In 1960, the foreign-born population of the United States stood
at around 4 percent; today, that number is 12 percent. In Western Europe,
the percent of foreign born averages around 7 percent, and it stands at over
18 percent in Canada. These waves of migration are changing the ethnic, religious, and racial compositions of these countries; for example, forecasters
have concluded that by the middle of this century, whites of European origin
will make up half of the U.S. population, compared to nearly 90 percent in
1960.[7] Moreover, the makeup of the immigrant population is quite different
across the advanced democratic countries. In the United States, a large number of immigrants come from Latin America; in Canada, they come from India
and Pakistan; in Australia and New Zealand, from Asia; and in Europe, from
North Africa and Turkey. Thus, while many advanced democracies are expe-

riencing immigration, the nature of that immigration and the challenges or opportunities it brings are very different.[8]

In many countries, increasing numbers of immigrants have increased xenophobic tendencies—that is, fear of foreigners. This takes on economic, societal, and political dimensions. The economic dimension is perhaps most familiar to us. Although supporters of immigration note the benefits of new sources of labor and skills that can come from immigrants, critics view immigrants as a threat to existing workers, competing for scarce jobs and depressing wages. The debate in Europe over the EU constitution turned in part on the "Polish plumber" issue—that economic immigrants from Eastern Europe and Turkey—Polish plumbers, Hungarian waiters, Czech auto mechanics—would move west and displace local workers. Immigration has been a similar sticking point in U.S.-Mexican relations, and Australians, Canadians, and New Zealanders express concern over an influx from Asia. Some countries, like Japan, have avoided this issue by limiting immigration, though this brings with it its own problems, as we shall discuss shortly.

A more complicated issue turns on societal institutions. As more and more diverse groups of immigrants enter the advanced democracies, they raise questions about what it means to be American, Canadian, French, or European. Advanced democracies are struggling with questions of assimilation and multiculturalism. How much should new groups be accommodated in their relationship with national institutions and identities? At one end, arguments for multiculturalism claim that societies should help foster and maintain these new groups, preserving what is distinct about them as a positive contribution to a diverse society. At the other end, arguments for assimilation hold that immigration implies an agreement to accept and adapt to the existing culture, values, and norms of that society. For countries like the United States, Canada, or Australia, multiculturalism may be somewhat easier to embrace, because the vast majority of people have come from somewhere else within the last two or three generations. Yet even here there are strong tendencies toward assimilation and fears that the sheer numbers of immigrants and their relative lack of diversity (Mexicans in the United States, for example) mean that assimilation, even if desired, is simply not possible.[9]

If multiculturalism is a source of controversy in traditionally immigrant countries, it is an even more explosive subject in countries where ethnic and national identity are much more tightly fused, as in much of Europe. There, the influx of non-Europeans, especially Muslim North Africans and Turks, has raised similar and perhaps even greater fears. Racial, religious, and ethnic homogeneity in Europe must now confront people whose geographical, cultural, religious, and historical traditions are quite different. Indeed, the paradox that has emerged is one of postmodernism itself. In the past, many European states prided themselves on their high degree of secularism and tolerance for different lifestyles. But how do they tolerate immigrant groups that may be much more religious and socially conservative—immigrants coming from societies that are quite removed from postmodern values?

Such economic and social concerns translate into politics. In many advanced democracies, growing ethnic and religious diversity has fueled the rise of anti-immigration, nationalistic, and xenophobic movements that seek to restrict immigration, increase assimilation, and assert ethnic and national primacy. The New Zealand First Party, which seeks a drastic reduction in immigration and a greater commitment to assimilation, took 10 percent of the 2002 vote. In France, Jean Le Pen's National Front regularly calls for the deportation of immigrants and withdrawal from the EU, a platform that also took over 10 percent of the vote in the 2002 elections. Le Pen himself came in second in the 2002 presidential elections with nearly 20 percent of the vote. More generally, there are calls to limit the use of second languages or regulate religion, especially Islam in Europe. This in turn causes immigrant groups to feel marginalized or humiliated. Europeans, in particular, fear that incorporating Muslim immigrants will lead to domestic terrorism, making Europe in future a more likely target than the United States. This has already come to pass in Spain in 2004, when a terrorist attack on a commuter train, carried out in part by immigrants from Morocco, left nearly 200 dead. The London subway bombings in 2005 are another example, one that has contributed to a heated debate about the future of multiculturalism in Europe.

A final issue is how these changes will affect relations between the advanced democracies. Although most of these countries face similar questions regarding immigration and its effects, as we already noted, the source of migration differs from country to country or region to region. This diversity can become a source of growing difference between the advanced democracies, pulling the West apart by shaping different cultural values and external orientations. In North America, migration from Central America and Asia may reorient these countries south and east, away from Europe, while in Europe, larger Muslim communities will draw these countries closer to the Middle East. Faith may also come into play, with Hispanic immigrants into the United States bringing with them more conservative Roman Catholic, Evangelical, or Pentecostal religious values, while Islam will grow more central to European life. Advanced democracies may see less and less of themselves in each other. This need not be a source of conflict; democratic values and a commitment to prosperity have linked very different countries together in the past (think of Japan, South Korea, and Eastern Europe, which not long ago were not considered part of the democratic West). But some speculate that a growing divergence of the advanced democracies may eventually create barriers that a shared commitment to democracy cannot overcome.

Economic Change

Our discussion so far has asked to what extent postmodernity is changing state and societial institutions. Our last area of interest is that of economic development, the area that is perhaps most obvious and widespread. Dramatic changes have taken place in the economic structures of the advanced industrialized democracies over the past generation, to such an extent that it may no longer be logical to refer to them as "industrial" at all. At the same time, long-standing assumptions about the role of the state in such areas as the redistribution of income and social expenditures have come under question, challenging the welfare state. This may lead to an overturning of existing ideas and policies regarding the proper balance of freedom and equality in the advanced democracies.

Postindustrialism

So far, we have considered postmodernity and how it may affect advanced democratic states and societies. In both of these arenas, the evidence and implications of change are largely unclear and open to debate. But in the economic realm, the advanced democracies have experienced a clear and dramatic shift during the last half century, from economies based primarily on industry and manufacturing to postindustrial economies. In **postindustrialism**, the majority of people are employed in and the bulk of profits made in the **service sector**—work that involves not the creation of tangible or physical goods, such as cars or computers, but such industries as finance, insurance, real estate, education, retail sales, transportation, communication, high technology, utilities, health care, and business and legal services. Just as modern economies made the transition from agriculture to industry, they are now moving away from their industrial orientation. As Table 7.4 indicates, this shift has been occurring across the advanced democracies over the past several decades. In these countries, around three-quarters of the working population are now employed in the service sector. This shift has occurred for a number of reasons. Much industrial production has migrated outside of the advanced democracies in search of lower labor and other costs. Globalization is accelerating these tendencies. Furthermore, technological innovation in the advanced democracies is changing the requirements of labor. Employees are expected to have higher levels of education than they were forty years ago; whereas in 1960 only 8 percent of Americans had completed college, that figure now stands at over 25 percent.

Postindustrialism in some ways reflects and may reinforce the political and social trends discussed earlier. The emergence of an information-based economy, for example, may contribute to a greater devolution of power within

Table 7.4 Employment by Economic Sector, 1960–2004

	Percentage of Total National Employment in		
	Services	Industry	Agriculture
United States			
1960	58	33	9
2004	78	20	2
Canada			
1960	55	32	13
2004	75	22	3
Japan			
1960	41	29	30
2004	68	28	4
France			
1960	39	38	23
2004	73	23	4

Source: Bureau of Labor.

the economy as firms become less hierarchical and more decentralized, less physical and more "virtual," less national and more international (something we will speak about more in Chapter 10), and with much greater individual autonomy and flexibility. This shift, in turn, may well reinforce postmodern values that question hierarchical structures and authority. However, for those without specialized training and education, postindustrialism may mean less freedom and equality; the growing importance of knowledge could marginalize these workers, creating an educational underclass whose prospects for upward mobility are limited.

As always, we should be careful not to overestimate postindustrialism's impact. Although it is clear that the advanced democracies are moving toward economies centered more on information and less on industry, this does not automatically mean that the old economic system will disappear. The rise of the Internet does not mean that "bricks and mortar" businesses are doomed; the demise of many dot-com businesses only underscores this argument. Nor does it mean that hierarchical forms of organization have outlived their usefulness. Finally, the elimination of industrial jobs does not automatically mean that those without education will no longer find work—only that the nature of unskilled labor will change, bringing different advantages and problems. As these transformations proceed, states will be called on to manage the marketplace in new ways, reconciling freedom and equality in the face of social and economic change.

Maintaining the Welfare State

This leads us to the final aspect of economic transformation in the advanced democracies: the future of the welfare state. As we discussed in Chapter 4, for the past half century, a defining element of the advanced democracies has been the development of social expenditures as a way to reduce inequality and provide public goods through such programs as national pension plans, public health care, education, and unemployment benefits—programs collectively known as the welfare state. There can be no doubt that the welfare state has provided a wide array of benefits among the advanced democracies: extreme poverty, especially among the elderly, has been reduced; infant mortality has declined and life expectancy has increased; and literacy and education have improved dramatically. Social expenditures have played an important role in socializing risk—that is, making the uncertainties that come with work, health, and age a community, rather than an individual, concern.

The welfare state has also brought costs and controversies. First, although social expenditures have been lauded as an essential part of a humane society, they are increasingly expensive. During the early part of the twentieth century, social expenditures typically amounted to around 10 to 15 percent of advanced democracies' GDPs. By the late 1990s, however, in most of these countries, social expenditures consumed a quarter or more of GDP. This increased spending has required higher taxes: in Western Europe, taxes in 1965 consumed around one-quarter of GDP; now they average more than half of GDP. Even in more liberal or mercantilist countries, such as the United States and Japan, public expenditures have risen dramatically over the past half century, requiring new taxes or government borrowing.

This trend will be magnified by important demographic changes within the advanced democracies. It is not just immigration that will shape these countries, but the age of their populations as well. One contributing factor is increased health. In 1900, residents of these countries had an average life expectancy of around forty to fifty years; by 2000, they could expect to live seventy to eighty years. Life expectancy in the advanced democracies is expected to increase to over eighty years by 2050. A second factor is lower birthrates. In most of the advanced democracies, the birthrate is below the replacement level, leading to fewer children (the United States is an interesting exception).[10] As a result of increased longevity and fewer births, many advanced democracies face a growing elderly population. According to some estimates, by 2050, a quarter to over a third of the population in the advanced democracies will be over sixty years old, compared with one-fifth (20 percent) of the population in 2000.[11] As an ever larger proportion of the population, this older segment of society will seek more welfare benefits, but there will be fewer and fewer working-age individuals to fill needed jobs and pay into these systems.

The solutions are not easy. Increased immigration is one obvious solution, though we have already seen the complex issues there, which become even more complicated when social expenditures come into play. For example, the United Nations estimates that to prevent population decline in Japan, the country would need to accept nearly 400,000 immigrants a year until the year 2050. By that time, nearly 20 percent of the Japanese population would be made up of immigrants and their descendants—a huge demographic shift in a country noted for its ethnic homogeneity. As can be imagined, there is little desire in Japan to follow such a course, though the alternative is for the country to significantly shrink in population and wealth. A second course would be to cut back on benefits. However, politicians face well-organized

INSTITUTIONS IN ACTION

DIVERSITY AND THE WELFARE STATE

We have considered how many advanced democracies face the issues of increased immigration, demographic shifts, and costs of maintaining the welfare state. It may turn out that each of these is tightly connected, making the problem that much more complicated. A puzzle we mentioned in Chapter 3 is why the United States is such a small welfare state compared with Europe, lacking, for example, national health care, which is a norm in the advanced democracies. Many arguments have been put forth to explain this, but one explanation may have to do with ethnic and racial diversity. The argument is that societies that are more diverse have a more difficult time building social institutions to redistribute income and distributing public goods for the simple reason that people are less comfortable giving up some of their money if they perceive the benefits going disproportionately to people unlike them. Equality and solidarity is in part a function of homogeneity. Racial divides in the United States thus limit the extent to which the majority is willing to accept redistribution. Contrast this with strong social democratic countries in Europe, such as Scandinavia, that are highly homogenous. If true, the question then becomes what will happen to the welfare state in countries where the immigrant population is growing? If more individuals come from places that racially, culturally, or by religion are quite different, will this engender resentment and conflict over those social expenditures that have been a cornerstone of society? Is there a trade-off between diversity and social solidarity? Already the issue has been raised in the United Kingdom, with a resulting furor and charges of racism. Such concerns can also be seen at work in opposition to the EU constitution. Certainly, the issue will become more contentious in the coming years.

Source: David Goodhart, "Too Diverse?" *Prospect* (February 2004): 30–37.

opposition, and in some countries, such as the United States, benefits have continued to increase even as the means to pay for them are nowhere to be found. A third solution would be to expand one's working years, such that as people live longer, they are expected to work longer. Yet in many countries, where retirement is akin to a constitutional right, such a suggestion is hardly welcome. If solutions are not found, however, many advanced democracies will find themselves unable to sustain some of the most basic elements of prosperity they have constructed over the past century.

In Sum: The Advanced Democracies in Transition

Advanced democracies are in many ways unique, both in their institutions and in the challenges they face. Although there is variation among them, these countries are characterized by liberal democracy and high levels of economic development. They represent, in many ways, what we consider modern social, economic, and political life. Yet none of these institutions is set in stone. State sovereignty is confronted by the twin dynamics of devolution and integration, transferring power above and below. Social norms are similarly in flux, as postmodern values challenge the status quo and are in turn being challenged. Modern industrial structures have given way to a new, information-based economy that empowers some and dislocates others, and demographic changes will affect how countries provide public goods to their people. All of these factors challenge the existing balance of freedom and equality.

In the coming chapters, we will turn to these same issues as they exist outside the advanced democracies. Communist and postcommunist, less-developed and newly industrializing countries all confront issues of state sovereignty, social values and ideology, industrialization, and the welfare of the public. What unique challenges each group faces in these areas will be the focus of the next two chapters. Will these countries eventually join the ranks of the advanced democracies in a convergence of political, economic, and social institutions around the globe? This question will remain with us through the next two chapters and our discussion of the prospects for globalization.

NOTES

1. For details on the historical development of the EU, see *The Community of Europe: A History of European Integration since 1945* (New York: Addison-Wesley, 1995).
2. See "The Euro, 3 Years Later," *Flash Eurobarometer Report*, no. 165 (December 2004): 40; and *Eurobarometer* 62 (May 2005): 156–158; http://europa.eu.int/.

3. See European Union, "Enlargement: Frequently Asked Questions," at europa.eu.int.

4. For a broader discussion of devolution, see Larry Diamond with Svetlana Tsalik, "Size and Democracy: The Case for Decentralization," in Larry Diamond, ed., *Developing Democracy: Toward Consolidation* (Baltimore: Johns Hopkins Press, 1999).

5. Robert Cooper, *The Postmodern State and the World Order* (London: Demos, 1996).

6. For further discussion, see Ronald Inglehart and Marita Carballo, "Does Latin America Exist? (And Is There a Confucian Culture?): A Global Analysis of Cross-Cultural Differences," *PS: Political Science and Politics* 30, no. 1 (March 1997): 34–46.

7. U.S. Census Department, *Projected Population by Race and Hispanic Origin, 2000–2050*, www.census.gov

8. *World Economic and Social Survey 2004: International Migration* (New York: United Nations, 2004).

9. For two controversial works on this topic, see Samuel Huntington, *Who Are We? The Challenges to America's National Identity* (New York: Simon & Schuster, 2004), and Victor David Hanson, *Mexifornia: A State of Becoming* (San Francisco: Encounter, 2004).

10. For data on population trends worldwide, see Population Reference Bureau, *World Population Data Sheet*, www.prb.org.

11. United Nations, *World Population Prospects: The 2004 Revision*, www.un.org.

8 COMMUNISM AND POSTCOMMUNISM

The advanced democracies we studied in Chapter 7 have become the wealthiest and most powerful countries in the world. In spite of this success, however, these countries continue to struggle with a number of issues, among them economic inequality—both within their societies as well as between themselves and the rest of the world. Their dilemma is no small matter: Must freedom always come at the expense of equality? Particularly with the rise of economic and political liberalism and the apparent retreat of the welfare state, it would seem that the answer is yes. But throughout history humans have struggled to find a way in which equality might be secured, providing benefits for all. This concern goes to the heart of communism in both theory and practice, for communism seeks to create a system that limits individual freedoms in order to divide wealth in an equitable manner. This vision of a world without economic distinctions drove the formation of communist regimes around the world, eventually bringing hundreds of millions of people under its banner.

Yet in spite of the lofty ideals of communist thought, and in spite of its dramatic emergence as a political regime in the early part of the twentieth century, within less than a century the majority of the world's communist regimes began to unravel. Why? What brought the quest for collective equality to a dead end? Was there a mistranslation of theory into practice, or were the theories themselves inherently suspect, unable to be realized in any practical manner?

In this chapter, we will look at how communism attempted to reconcile freedom and equality and why communist systems have largely failed at that endeavor. We will begin by looking at the original theories of modern communism, particularly the ideas of Karl Marx. From there we will investigate how communism was changed from theory into practice as communist regimes were built around the world, most notably in the Soviet Union, Eastern Europe, and China. How did these systems seek to create equality and bring Marx's ideas to life? Our answer will discuss the nature of government, regime, and state under communism.

After examining the dynamics of communism in practice, we will study its demise. What were its shortcomings, and why could these limitations not be corrected? Why did attempts at reform in the Soviet Union and Eastern Europe turn into a rout? And what lessons can we draw from this when we look at the only major remaining communist country (at least in name), China? Our look at the downfall of communism will take us to our last issue: What comes after it? In addressing each of these questions, we will uncover the enormous scope and vision of communist thought, the tremendous challenges of putting it into practice, the serious flaws and limitations that this implementation entailed, and the daunting work of building new political, social, and economic institutions from the rubble of communism's demise.

Communism, Equality, and the Nature of Human Relations

Communism is a set of ideas that view political, social, and economic institutions in a fundamentally different manner than most political thought, essentially challenging much of what we have studied so far. At its most basic level, we can define it as an ideology that seeks to create human equality by eliminating private property and market forces.

In modern politics, communism as a political theory and ideology can be traced primarily to the German philosopher Karl Marx (1818–1883).[1] Marx began with a rather straightforward observation: human beings are able to create objects of value by investing their own time and labor into their cre-

Table 8.1 Communist Regimes in the 1980s			
Europe	**Asia**	**Africa and the Middle East**	**Latin America**
Albania	Afghanistan	Angola	*Cuba*
Bulgaria	Cambodia	Benin	
Czechoslovakia	*China*	Ethiopia	
East Germany	*Laos*	Mozambique	
Hungary	Mongolia	South Yemen	
Poland	*North Korea*		
Romania	*Vietnam*		
Soviet Union			
Yugoslavia			

Note: Communist countries as of 2006 are shown in italics.

Terms in Marxist Theory

Surplus value of labor: the value invested in any human-made good that can be used by another individual. Exploitation results when one person or group extracts the surplus value from another.

Base: the economic system of a society, made up of technology (the means of production) and class relations between people (the relations of production).

Superstructure: All noneconomic relations in a society (for example, religion, culture, national identity). These ideas and values derive from the base and serve to legitimize the current system of exploitation.

False consciousness: Failure to understand the nature of one's exploitation; essentially "buying into" the superstructure.

Dialectical materialism: Process of historical change that is not evolutionary but revolutionary. The existing base and superstructure (thesis) would come into conflict with new technological innovations, generating growing tensions between the exploiters and the exploited (antithesis). This would culminate in revolution, overthrowing the old base and superstructure.

Dictatorship of the proletariat: Temporary period after capitalism has been overthrown during which vestiges of the old base and superstructure are eradicated.

Proletariat: The working class.

Bourgeoisie: The property-owning class.

Communism: According to Marxists, the final stage of history once capitalism is overthrown and the dictatorship of proletariat destroys its remaining vestiges. In communism, state and politics would disappear, and society and the economy would be based on equality and cooperation.

Vanguard of the proletariat: Lenin's argument that an elite communist party would have to carry out revolution, because as a result of false consciousness, historical conditions would not automatically lead to capitalism's demise.

ation. That "surplus value of labor" stays with the object, making it useful to anyone, not just the maker. It is this ability to create objects with their own innate value that sets people apart from other animals, but it also inevitably leads to economic injustice, Marx concluded. He argued that as human beings develop their knowledge and technological skills, an opportunity is created for those with political power to essentially extract the surplus value from others, enriching themselves while impoverishing others. In other words, once human beings learned how to produce things of value, others found that they could gain these things at little cost to themselves simply by using coercion to acquire them.

For Marx, then, the world was properly understood in economic terms; all human action flowed from the relations between the haves and the have-nots. Marx believed that structures, rather than people or ideas, made history. Specifically, Marx spoke of human history and human relations as being based on what he termed the *base* and the *superstructure*. The base is the system of economic production, including the level of technology (what he called the "means of production") and the kind of class relations that exist as a result (the "relations of production"). Resting on the base is the superstructure, which represents all human institutions—politics and the state, national identity and culture, religion and gender, and so on. Marx viewed this superstructure as a system of institutions created essentially to justify and perpetuate the existing order. People consequently suffer from "false consciousness," meaning that they believe they understand the true nature of the world around them, but in reality they are deluded by the superstructure imposed by capitalism. Thus, liberal democracy was rejected by Marx and most other communists as a system created to delude the exploited into thinking they have a say in their political destiny, when in fact those with wealth actually control politics.

Revolution and the "Triumph" of Communism

Having dissected what he saw as the nature of politics, economics, and society, Marx used this framework to understand historical development and to anticipate the future of capitalism. Marx concluded that human history developed in specific phases, each driven by the particular nature of exploitation at that point in time. In each historical case, he argued, the specific form of exploitation was built around the existing level of technology. For example, in early agrarian societies, feudalism was the dominant political and economic order; the rudimentary technology available tied individuals to the land so that their labor could be exploited by the aristocracy. But although such relations may appear stable, technology itself is always dynamic. Marx recognized this and asserted that the inevitable changes in technology would increase tensions between rulers and ruled as new forms of technological development empowered new groups who clashed with the base and the superstructure. Again, in the case of feudalism, emerging technology empowered an early capitalist, property-owning middle class or *bourgeoisie*, whose members sought political power for themselves and the remaking of the economic and social order in a way that better fit capitalist ambitions.

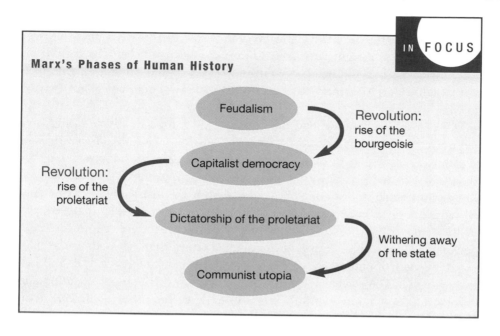

IN FOCUS

Marx's Phases of Human History

Feudalism

Revolution: rise of the bourgeoisie

Capitalist democracy

Revolution: rise of the proletariat

Dictatorship of the proletariat

Withering away of the state

Communist utopia

Eventually, this tension would lead to revolution; those in power would be overthrown, and a new ruling class would come to power. In each case, change would be sudden and violent and would pave the way for a new economic base and superstructure. This entire process is termed *dialectical materialism.* The dialectic portrays history as a struggle between the existing order (the thesis) and the challenge to that order (the antithesis), resulting in historical change (the synthesis). Revolutions inevitably come about as a result of this tension between economic classes.

On the basis of these ideas, Marx concluded that capitalist democracy, which had displaced feudalism, would itself eventually be overthrown by its own internal flaws. As capitalism developed, competition between firms would intensify. The working class, or *proletariat,* would find itself on the losing end of this process as firms introduced more and more technology to reduce the number of workers and as unprofitable businesses began to go bankrupt in the face of intense competition. The bourgeoisie would grow smaller and smaller as the wealth of society became concentrated in fewer and fewer hands, and large monopolies would come to dominate the economy. The wages of the working class would decline in the face of increased competition (an oversupply of labor as technology reduces the number of workers needed), and the ranks of the unemployed would swell.

Alienated and driven to desperation by these conditions, eventually the proletariat would "gain consciousness" by realizing the true source of their poverty and rise up in rebellion. They would carry out a revolution, seizing control of the state and the economy. Marx saw this process not simply as a national phenomenon, but as an international one. When the conditions were right, he hypothesized, revolution would spread among all the capitalist countries, sweeping away this unjust order in a relatively short period of time.

Once world revolution had taken place, Marx foresaw, there would be a temporary "dictatorship of the proletariat," during which the last vestiges of capitalism, particularly the old remnants of the superstructure, would be swept away. After the institutions of capitalism had been decisively eliminated, the institutions of the state itself would begin to "wither away." There would be no more need for laws or police, because all people would share equally in the fruits of labor. No longer would there be a need for armies or flags, because people would be united in equality rather than blinded by the false consciousness of nationalism. People would live in a stateless world, and history, which in Marx's view had been fundamentally driven by exploitation and class struggle, would essentially come to an end. Only then could one actually speak of "communism"—which is why communist parties would usually speak of their own countries as being "socialist," since they were still controlled by the state. Adding to this confusion is the fact that in the advanced democracies, the word *socialism* is used interchangeably with social democracy. However, for most contemporary social democrats, socialism is seen as an end stage, where the state exercises significant but not total control over the economy. For communists, however, socialism is a transitional phase toward an outcome where private property no longer exists.

Putting Communism into Practice

Communism thus provides an entire worldview, explaining the course of human history and the inevitable ascent into utopia as the product of economic interaction. As one might imagine, such a sweeping theory has proved extremely convincing for many people, including those who sought to put Marx's ideas into practice. Two of the most notable followers of Marx's ideas were Vladimir Ulyanov, more commonly known as Lenin, and Mao Zedong, who came to lead communist revolutions in Russia (1917) and China (1949), respectively. Yet although both Mao and Lenin were inspired by Marx, they departed from his ideas by seeking to carry out revolution in two countries that were weakly industrialized and far from being capitalist. Marx had argued that revolution would occur only where and when capitalism was most advanced and thus most prone to collapse; however, at the end of his life, he did hold out the possibility that revolution could occur in less-developed Rus-

Important Figures in Communism

Karl Marx (1818–1883) First philosopher to systematically construct a theory explaining why capitalism would fail and be replaced by communism; father of modern communist thought.

Lenin (Vladimir Ulyanov) (1870–1924) Applied Marxist thought to Russia, leading successful revolution in 1917; modified Marxist ideas by arguing that revolution would occur not in most developed societies, but rather in struggling countries such as Russia.

Stalin (Josef Dzhugashvili) (1879–1953) Succeeded Lenin as leader of the Soviet Union; embarked on rapid industrialization of the country, modifying Marxism to argue that socialism could be built in a single country; extended communism to Eastern Europe after World War II; denounced by Nikita Khrushchev in 1956 for his use of a personality cult and terror.

Mao Zedong (1883–1976) Led Chinese Communist Party and fought against Chinese rivals and Japanese occupiers during World War II; modified communism to focus on peasantry instead of working class, given primarily agrarian nature of China; unleashed Cultural Revolution in 1966 to weaken party and increase his own power.

Fidel Castro (1926–   ) Led Cuban revolution in 1959 and defended the communist system against anticommunist forces and U.S. opposition; continues to defend Cuban socialism in spite of the collapse of the Soviet Union and other communist regimes in Eastern Europe.

Deng Xiaoping (1905–1997) Fought with Mao Zedong against Chinese nationalists and Japanese invaders during World War II; named general secretary of the Chinese Communist Party in 1956; stripped of all posts during the Cultural Revolution, but emerged as country's leader after death of Mao; pursued economic liberalization in 1980s and supported repression of Tiananmen Square protests.

Mikhail Gorbachev (1931–) Made general secretary of the Communist Party of the Soviet Union in 1985; initiated twin policies of perestroika (economic restructuring) and glasnost (political liberalization), which eventually led to increasing discord within the country and a failed coup attempt by hard-line communists who opposed further reform; the resulting dissolution of the Soviet Union left Gorbachev without a country to lead.

sia, in contradiction to his own theories.[2] Lenin and Mao had believed that revolution could be carried out in less advanced countries if leaders constructed a "vanguard of the proletariat"—Lenin's term for a small revolutionary movement that could seize power on behalf of the people.[3]

This approach meant that in reality, communism spread where the level of economic development was relatively low—exactly the opposite of what Marx had originally theorized. Whereas communism made no headway in the developed countries, it continued to spread in much of the less-developed world, often with the backing of the Soviet Union and China. By the 1980s, communist regimes accounted for approximately one-third of the world's population.

Yet even as it expanded, communist countries faced a common dilemma: How exactly did one go about building communism? Marx had left no blueprint for that task—for what to do once the revolution had succeeded.

In part because Marx provided no specific outline for how communism would be built, the systems that were created varied widely, shaped by domestic economic and political conditions, historical context, cultural factors, and the ideas and authority of those in power. But beyond these differences, they shared a basic set of institutions, first developed in the Soviet Union after 1917. Because of the desire to so fundamentally reshape human relations, communist states accrued a high level of autonomy and capacity; their authoritarian regimes have at times become totalitarian in their desire to transform virtually all basic human institutions, from work to prayer to gender to art.

The task of this transformation was entrusted to the communist elite who came to direct and staff the state.[4] At its apex, political power rested within the Communist Party, a relatively small "vanguard" organization (typically comprising less than 10 percent of the population) whose leading role in the country was typically written directly into the constitution—meaning that there was no constitutional way to remove the party from power. Because the Communist Party embodied what it saw as the "correct" view of human history and future relations, alternative organizations and ideologies making up civil society were seen as hostile to communism and repressed.

But as we discussed in Chapter 5, no system of authoritarian rule can survive through the threat of force alone. Communist parties maintained control over society not only through repression, but also by carefully allocating power throughout the country's various political, social, and economic institutions—a thorough form of co-optation. This can be seen clearly in the ***nomenklatura***, politically sensitive or influential jobs in the state, society, or economy that were staffed by people chosen or approved by the Communist Party. The *nomenklatura* encompassed a wide range of important positions: the head of a university, the editor of a newspaper, a military officer, a film director. Not surprisingly, party approval often required party membership, making joining the party the easiest way to prove one's loyalty and rise up the career ladder. Party membership could also bring other benefits: better housing, the ability to travel abroad, or access to scarce consumer goods. As a result, party membership was often driven more by opportunism than by idealism; many joined so that they could pursue certain careers or simply gain the benefits that party membership could buy.[5]

The dominant role played by the Communist Party and the *nomenklatura* created a power relationship different from those in democratic and many other authoritarian systems. Power, rather than being centered within the state and government, rested within the party. For example, when observers referred to the "leader" of a communist country, they were usually referring not to a government official but to the general secretary of the Communist Party. Indeed, top party leaders often did not hold any important position within the state. Communist countries by and large resembled political systems we see elsewhere in the world, typically with a prime minister or president, a parliament, a judiciary, and local government—all encompassing positions that were part of the *nomenklatura* and thus staffed by party members. Although trappings of democracy, such as parliamentary elections, typically existed, electoral candidates were almost exclusively Communist Party members with no real competition. Moreover, parliaments and other organs of power were little more than "rubber-stamp" institutions, approving of decisions sent down the party hierarchy.

As for the party itself, in many ways it intentionally mirrored the state, with a general secretary serving as chief executive, and a **Politburo** (short for "Political Bureau") and **Central Committee** acting as a kind of cabinet and legislature, respectively, shaping national policy and confirming the decisions of the party leadership. Below the Central Committee, various other bodies extended all the way down to individual places of work or residence, where party members were organized into basic party organizations called "cells." These cells were ostensibly intended to represent the interests of the people, but they were primarily mechanisms by which the party could closely monitor the population. Traditionally, the party held a congress every few years, at which its leadership was elected by delegates sent from the party cells, but these elections were little more than confirmations of those already in power.

While the party and its *nomenklatura* controlled key organizations, communist ideology shaped policy and sought to legitimize authoritarian control. Based fundamentally on the theories of Marx as adapted by Lenin, communist ideology focused on the elimination of inequality and the promotion of economic development. Because of the expansive nature of communist ideology and its promise of a future utopia, it was, perhaps more than the other ideologies we discussed in Chapter 3, a secular "religion," requiring unquestioning faith in a set of beliefs and sacrifice for a future reward and boasting its own collection of saints, martyrs, and devils. In this view, adherents venerated charismatic leaders who served as prophets of communism, such as Lenin, Mao, Josef Stalin, and Fidel Castro. Many charismatic communist leaders reinforced their position through elaborate personality cults (discussed in Chapter 5).

The quest for and exercise of this monopoly on power, as expressed through the *nomenklatura* and the deep penetration of the state and society by the party, down to the most basic level of home and work, proved to be dangerous and lethal. In the first decades of communist rule in the Soviet Union, China, and Eastern Europe, terror was used to eliminate opposition and to maintain control. Tens of millions perished in such campaigns, especially in the Soviet Union under Stalin and in China under Mao. Under the rule of Stalin, many people were purged from within the Soviet Communist Party itself and executed for imaginary crimes. These were not cases of mistaken punishment: Stalin used terror and victimized symbolic "criminals" as a way to cow the Communist Party and the population as a whole.[6] Similarly, in China, Mao unleashed the Cultural Revolution in the late 1960s, encouraging the public (students, in particular) to attack any institution or individual that was either a remnant of precommunist China or lacked revolutionary zeal. Mao's targets included the **party-state**, which he believed had grown conservative over time and was restricting his power. During the next decade, not only did countless Chinese die (estimates are over 1 million), but books were burned, art destroyed, and cultural relics demolished—all for the crime of being "reactionary."[7]

Communist Political Economy

If the Communist Party's singular quest for power led in the cases of Stalin and Mao to its gross abuse, the centralization of economic power similarly created problems that Marxist theory did not anticipate. Communist political-economic systems shared a set of institutions fundamentally different from liberal, mercantilist, or social democratic alternatives, as both markets and property are essentially absorbed by the state.[8] With the means of production held by the state, many of the typical aspects of capitalism that we take for granted—individual profit, unemployment, competition between firms, bankruptcy—were eliminated. Individuals lost their right to control property, including their own labor; the party-state made the decisions about how these resources should be used. In turn, communist leaders redirected national wealth toward the goal of collective equality through such mechanisms as industrialization and social expenditures. But none of this was painless. Rapid industrialization and the collectivization of agriculture under the Great Leap Forward in China (1959–1961) led to some 30 million famine deaths.[9]

Alongside the elimination of private property, communist systems also eliminated the market mechanism, believing that it was incapable of equitably distributing wealth. Communist countries by and large chose to replace the market with the state bureaucracy, which explicitly allocated resources by

planning what should be produced and in what amounts,
setting the final prices of these
goods, and deciding where they
should be sold. This system is
known as **central planning**.

As one might imagine, planning an entire economy is an
extremely difficult task. A market economy responds to the
relationship of supply and
demand in a spontaneous and
decentralized manner. If there
is a market for something, a
producer will often come along
to fill that need in the hope
of making a profit. In a centrally planned economy, however, bureaucrats must central-

Communist Political Economy

- Markets and property are wholly absorbed by the state.
- Central planning replaces the market mechanism.
- Individual property rights, individual profit, unemployment, competition between firms, and bankruptcy are all virtually eliminated.
- Most of the nation's means of production are nationalized.
- The economy functions in essence as a single large firm, with the public as its sole employees.
- The state provides extensive public goods and social services, including universal systems of public education, health care, and retirement.

ize these decisions. How much steel should be produced this year? How many
women's size eight shoes? How many apartments? Determining needs for each
and every good produced in a country requires huge amounts of information.

As communist planners found, matching up all these inputs and outputs
is overwhelming. There are simply too many things to plan—in the Soviet
Union, for instance, there were some 40,000 to 50,000 physical items—and
too many unforeseen outcomes, such as a factory failing to deliver its full output, or a change in demand. Because most entities in an economy are inter-
dependent, small problems can have a huge effect on the entire plan. A mis-
calculation resulting in the underproduction of steel, for example, would have
disastrous effects on all those goods dependent on steel, some of which would
themselves be components in other finished goods—such as nails or bolts.
Any mistakes or changes in the central plan, and production begins to go out
of balance.

Another problem encountered in centrally planned economies was the lack
of worker incentives. Factories and farms were unconcerned about the quality of their goods, since central planners simply indicated a numerical quota
they had to fulfill. Workers did not have to fear losing their jobs or factories
going out of business as a result of shoddy work, because under communism,
employment was guaranteed and firms, being owned by the state, could not
go bankrupt. This explains in part why all communist countries eventually
fell behind economically. In the absence of competition and incentives, innovation and efficiency disappeared, leaving these systems to stagnate.

Societal Institutions under Communism

In addition to reengineering politics and economics to eliminate the inequality and exploitation associated with capitalist systems, communist parties also sought to reorder human relations, hoping to sweep away the old superstructure held responsible for generating false consciousness. Individual freedoms were also repressed, since they were viewed as an expression of false consciousness and therefore a threat to communist goals.

One example of this hostility can be seen in communism's view of religion. Marx is known for his oft-cited statement that "religion is the opiate of the masses," meaning that it is part of the superstructure that serves to perpetuate inequality and legitimize suffering in return for rewards in some afterlife. As a result, in most communist countries, religion was strongly suppressed. In the Soviet Union, most places of worship were closed, converted to other uses, or torn down. In China during the Cultural Revolution, most temples and other religious shrines were destroyed. Even where religion was tolerated to a greater extent, it was still harassed or directly controlled by the Communist Party.

Traditional gender relations were also seen by Marxists as a function of capitalism; specifically, gender relations were seen to be class relations in microcosm. Men exploit women through the family structure, just as the bourgeoisie exploit the proletariat, and sexual morality serves as a means to perpetuate this gender inequality. Communism envisioned complete economic, social, and political equality between men and women. Even the repressive institution of marriage, like the state, would fade away, replaced by what Marx called "an openly legalized community of free love."[10] This was quite a radical view of gender relations for its time; after all, Marx was writing in the late nineteenth century, when women did not even have the right to vote anywhere in the world.

In spite of Marxist ideals, gender relations only partially changed under communist rule. In most communist countries, women were given much greater opportunities than they experienced previously. To promote industrialization, communist parties encouraged women to enter the workforce and to increase their education. Most countries also enacted liberal divorce and abortion laws and provided social benefits such as state-run child care. In spite of these changes, however, women's traditional roles as housekeepers and mothers did not change. The "new socialist woman" was not complemented by a "new socialist man"; traditional patterns of sexism persisted, and women found themselves burdened by the double duty of work inside and outside the home. In addition, while many women worked in important occupations, few rose to positions of any significant political or economic power. The top ranks of the party membership, the state, and the economy remained dominated by men.[11]

IN FOCUS

Societal Institutions under Communism

Ideal	Reality
Religion, the "opiate of the masses," will disappear.	Religion was suppressed but not eliminated.
Men and women will be economically, socially, and politically equal.	Opportunities for women increased, but women were still expected to fulfill traditional duties in the home.
Repressive institutions such as marriage will be replaced by "an openly legalized system of free love."	Many communist countries remained sexually very conservative.
Nationalism, exposed as part of the elite's "divide and conquer" strategy, will be eliminated.	Though discouraged from doing so, people clung to old national and ethnic identities.

A final aspect of society that communist countries sought to change was national and ethnic identity. As part of the superstructure, nationalism and ethnicity were seen as mechanisms by which the ruling elite pit the working classes of different countries against one another in a tactic of divide and rule. With the advent of world communist revolution, such divisions were expected to disappear, to be replaced by equality and harmony among all peoples. As a result, communist parties tended to reject any overt expressions of nationalism, though such identities often lurked beneath the surface. For example, encompassed within the vast Soviet Union were many ethnic groups, although the Communist Party tended to be dominated by Russians, who made up the single largest ethnic group in the country. Many citizens of non-Russian ethnic groups resented this Russian domination. Many Eastern Europeans also viewed communist rule as little more than Russian imperialism; their national identity was therefore sharpened, not erased. This simmering nationalism played an important role in the fall of communism in Eastern Europe and the Soviet Union.

The Collapse of Communism

In retrospect, it may seem obvious that communism was bound to fail, and yet even in the mid-1980s, few expected that it would happen anytime soon. Two factors played an important role in bringing about its sudden decline.

The first was the reemergence of Cold War struggles between the Soviet Union and the United States. After the tense decades of the 1950s and 1960s, which were marked by international competition, arms races, and harrowing events such as the Cuban missile crisis, the United States and the Soviet Union settled into a period of détente in which peaceful coexistence became the main goal. But détente lasted less than a decade. The Soviet Union's invasion of Afghanistan in 1979 to prop up a failing communist regime there and the election of Ronald Reagan as U.S. president in 1980 soured relations between the two countries. Reagan, who viewed the Soviet Union as an "evil empire," embarked on a new policy of military buildup. But growing economic stagnation made it difficult for the Soviet Union to meet this expensive challenge.

At the same time as the United States and the Soviet Union entered a new and costly stage of the Cold War, a new generation of political leaders rose to power in the Soviet Union, among them Mikhail Gorbachev, who was chosen as general secretary of the Communist Party in 1985. Unlike his predecessors, Gorbachev recognized the stagnation of the Soviet system and understood that a new arms race would bankrupt his country. He thus proposed reforming both international and domestic relations, revitalizing both the Soviet Union and communist thought.

At the domestic level, Gorbachev initiated the twin policies of glasnost (openness) and perestroika (restructuring), intended to liberalize and reform communism. **Glasnost** encouraged public debate, with the hope that a frank discussion of the shortcomings of the system would help foster change and increase the legitimacy of the regime. **Perestroika**, or actual institutional reforms in the economy and political system, would flow from these critiques. These reforms were expected to include some limited forms of democratic participation and market-based incentives in the economy. Moderate reform, not wholesale transformation, was Gorbachev's goal.[12]

In the international arena, Gorbachev similarly proposed widespread, if moderate, changes. To reduce the Soviet Union's military burdens and improve relations with Western countries, he began to loosen his country's control over other communist states, particularly those in Eastern Europe, which had been under the thumb of the Soviet Union since the end of World War II. Gorbachev hoped that some limited liberalization in the region would ease tensions with Europe and the United States, enabling expanded trade and other economic ties.

But as Alexis de Tocqueville famously wrote with regard to the French monarchy, the most dangerous moment for a bad government is usually when it begins to reform itself. All of these policies wound up backfiring against Gorbachev and the Soviet Union. Glasnost encouraged public debate, but rather than simply criticize corruption or the quality of consumer goods (which is what Gorbachev expected), the public began to challenge the very

TIME LINE / COMMUNIST HISTORY

1848	Karl Marx and Freidrich Engels write *The Communist Manifesto*, a central document in communist thought.
1917	Lenin leads Russian Revolution, creating the Soviet Union as the world's first communist country.
1930s	Stalin begins to arrest and execute Soviet Communist Party members and others to consolidate power and terrorize the population.
1945	Soviet Army occupies Eastern Europe, imposing communist regimes; tensions between the United States and the Soviet Union lead to Cold War.
1949	Chinese Communist Party, led by Mao Zedong, gains control over mainland China after a long struggle against local opposition and Japanese occupiers.
1953	Stalin dies.
1956	Nikita Khrushchev denounces Stalin's use of terror and allows limited open debate; debate turns to unrest in parts of Eastern Europe; protests in Hungary lead to open revolution against communism; Hungarian revolution put down by Soviet army.
1966–76	Mao unleashes Cultural Revolution in China; student "Red Guard" attacks symbols of precommunism and party leaders accused of having grown too conservative; Cultural Revolution used to eliminate Mao's political rivals.
1976	Mao Zedong dies; China and the U.S. begin to improve relations; rise to power of Deng Xiaopeng, who enacts widespread economic reforms.
1979	Soviet Union invades Afghanistan, worsening relations between U.S. and Soviet Union; reintensification of the Cold War.
1985	Gorbachev becomes general secretary of the Soviet Communist Party and begins to carry out economic and political liberalization.
1989	Student protests for political reform in China's Tiananmen Square crushed by the military.
1989–90	East Europeans seize on reforms in the Soviet Union to press for dramatic political change; largely peaceful political protests lead to free elections and the elimination of communist rule in Eastern Europe.
1991	Increasing turmoil in Soviet Union leads communist conservatives to oust Gorbachev and seize power; coup fails due to weak military support and public demonstrations; Soviet Union breaks into fifteen separate states.

nature of the political system. Ethnic groups within the Soviet Union and citizens of Eastern European states used glasnost to agitate for greater freedom from Russian domination.

Perestroika had similarly unexpected effects. By seeking political and economic reform, Gorbachev threatened those within the party who had long benefited from the status quo. Political leaders, administrators, factory bosses, and many other members of the *nomenklatura* resisted reform, leading to infighting and instability. This problem was compounded by Gorbachev's actual reforms, which were largely halfhearted measures. Confusion deepened within the party, the state, and society as to where communism was heading.

Meanwhile, among the Soviet Union's satellite states, change was proceeding faster than anyone expected. In 1989, opposition movements across Eastern Europe used Gorbachev's new hands-off policy to oppose their countries' communist regimes, demanding open elections and an end to one-party rule. Eastern European Communist Party leaders, realizing that the Soviet Union would no longer intervene militarily to support them, had little choice but to acquiesce. As a result, by 1990, communists had been swept from their monopolies on power across the region. In most cases, this regime change was largely peaceful.

The Soviet Union would not be far behind. By 1991, the country was in deep turmoil: limited reforms had increased the public's appetite for greater change; the end of communism in Eastern Europe further emboldened opposition within the Soviet Union; and ethnic conflict and nationalism were on the rise as various groups sought political power.[13] Communist hard-liners eventually tried to stop the reform process through a coup d'état, seizing power and detaining Gorbachev. However, these leaders lacked the support of important actors such as the military and other segments of the state, and public demonstrations helped bring the poorly planned coup to an end.[14]

In the aftermath of the 1991 coup and in response to their own ethnic constituents, the individual republics that made up the Soviet Union broke up, forming fifteen new independent countries, of which Russia is one. Twelve of these countries (the Baltic states of Latvia, Lithuania, and Estonia refused to join) formed a loose confederation known as the Commonwealth of Independent States (CIS), but this body has held little power over its members.

But communism did not collapse everywhere. Although 1989 marked liberalization and the first moves toward democracy in Eastern Europe and the Soviet Union, similar protests in China that year, led by students and encouraged by Gorbachev's example, were met with deadly military force in Tiananmen Square. Communist leaders in China did not heed public demands for reform and political liberalization and showed themselves both willing and able to use the army to violently quell peaceful protests. Why this difference? One reason may be that in China, the Communist Party had already begun to carry out a set of wide-ranging economic reforms in the late 1970s. These reforms were not accompanied by simultaneous political reform, however. In fact, in China the Communist Party used economic reform as a way to stave off public discontent and increase the party's own legitimacy. Having been focused on economics and not politics and already involved in an extended period of reform, the Chinese Communist Party in 1989 did not confront the kind of rapid decompression and disarray that the Soviet Union or Eastern Europe did.

Political Institutions in Transition

So far, we have discussed the communist theory regarding the origins and solutions to inequality, the difficulties in translating theory into reality, and how eventually these institutions unraveled across most of the communist world. Yet although the downfall of communism was dramatic, what followed was no less awesome. Postcommunist countries faced, and continue to face, the challenge of building new political, social, and economic institutions to strike a new balance between freedom and equality. No country had ever made such a dramatic change in all three areas at once, and this task has met with varying degrees of success.

Reorganizing the State and Constructing a Democratic Regime

An underlying task in the transition from communism is to reorganize the state in terms of its autonomy and capacity. Under communism, the party-state was able to dominate virtually all aspects of human relations without any effective check. State autonomy and capacity were extremely high. But with the collapse of communism, the party was ejected from its leading role in political life, and new leaders had to change the very role and scope of the state. But reducing state power was not easy, as dramatic political change occurs alongside a substantial weakening of the state precisely when state power is most needed. Many postcommunist countries thus sought to narrow their states' capacity and autonomy without making them ineffective—a difficult task.

Another important aspect of postcommunist reform is the establishment of the rule of law. In Chapter 6 and elsewhere, we have seen that laws and regulations are essential institutions in political life; they are the basic "rules of the game" that the majority of people obey because it is in their best interest. Under communist systems, the rule of law was weak. The Communist Party could make, break, or change laws as it saw fit, and as a result, people came to view laws rather cynically. This attitude encouraged evasion and corruption, problems that expanded dramatically once the repressive power of the state was retracted or weakened. Those in power must now adhere to regulations and legal structures, not acting in a capricious manner or taking advantage of their authority. In society, too, the rule of law must be instilled in such a way that people willingly obey the system even when it is not in their personal interest to do so.

Alongside reconstructing state power and the rule of law, postcommunist countries have faced the prospect of building a democratic regime where authoritarianism has long been the norm. This project requires numerous tasks: revising or rewriting the constitution to establish civil rights and free-

---

INSTITUTIONS IN **ACTION**

PRESIDENTIALISM, PARLIAMENTARISM, AND POSTCOMMUNISM

Among the various issues that confronted postcommunist countries was that of executive-legislative relations. Recall that under communism, real executive authority rested with the general secretary of the Communist Party, while the positions of head of state and government had little power. However, with the end of the Communist Party's monopoly of power, the executive became a major source of conflict. As we have noted, most of Western Europe follows the parliamentary model, where power is vested with a prime minister who hails from the legislature and is beholden to them. However, in many postcommunist countries, there were strong pressures for presidentialism. For communist elites, a strong presidency was seen as a way to reinvest their power in a new institution that would be independent of the legislature. For opposition forces, too, a presidency promised the ability for the people to directly elect their leader and use the office to sweep away the vestiges of communist rule. In short, the concerns often raised about presidentialism—its insulation, lack of power sharing, and the difficulty in removing presidents from office—were precisely what made this office attractive. In the end, countries chose a variety of solutions. Most of postcommunist Europe opted for parliamentary government, with presidents that hold relatively little power (even in those cases where they are directly elected). In Russia and central Asia, however, more powerful semi- or purely presidential offices were created, giving these offices an extraordinary amount of power. Interestingly, presidentialism can be correlated with the absence of democracy in postcommunist countries; where democracy is weaker, presidencies are stronger. Cause and effect is not clear in these cases, however. Is it the creation of strong presidencies that have undermined democracy? Or is it weakness of democratic preconditions that helped create more authoritarian presidencies?

doms, creating a separation of powers between branches of government, revamping judicial bodies and high courts, generating electoral laws and regulating political parties, and doing all of this in such a way as to generate support on the part of the majority of actors in society.

Creating all of these institutions requires many decisions as to their final shape and form. For example, should these countries follow the European parliamentary model or opt for a presidential system like that of the United States? Most postcommunist countries in Eastern Europe opted for the prime ministerial model, while across the former Soviet Union, many adopted a semipresidential system or a purely presidential system. Another issue is that of electoral rules. Supporters of proportional representation (PR) favored that system as a way to include many different political ideologies and actors in the government, thus increasing legitimacy; opponents favored the use of single-member district (SMD) systems to create two large parties that they believed would be more effective in passing legislation. Many postcommunist countries opted for pure PR, but several opted for mixed PR and SMD.

Civil rights are a final area of concern. Under communism, constitutions typically established an elaborate set of civil liberties, though in reality these were largely ignored by those in power. With the collapse of communism, leaders were faced with deciding how civil liberties should be constitutionally protected. This meant not only strengthening the rule of law so that those once-hollow rights could be enforced, but also deciding what kinds of rights should be enshrined in the constitution and who should be the final arbiter of disputes over these rights. The role of constitutional courts became a major issue in countries where traditionally the judiciary had been neither powerful nor independent.

Evaluating Political Transitions

Over fifteen years have passed since the fall of communism in Eastern Europe and the Soviet Union. How have their political transitions fared? The picture is mixed. Freedom House, a liberal nongovernment organization that studies democracy around the world, ranks countries on a 1 to 7 freedom scale, with countries given a 1 being the most free and those given a 7 being the least free. This ranking is based on such considerations as electoral competition, freedoms of speech and assembly, rule of law, levels of corruption, and protection of human and economic rights.

As Table 8.2 shows, a number of postcommunist countries have made dramatic strides toward democracy and the rule of law, to such an extent that Freedom House now considers them consolidated democracies—meaning that their democratic regimes have been highly ranked on the Freedom House scale for a decade or so and are therefore stable and fully institutionalized. The majority of these consolidated democracies can be found in central

Europe (such as Hungary, Poland, and the Czech Republic) and the Baltics, areas that share a precommunist history of greater economic development, civil society, democratic institutions, and the rule of law and that enjoyed more contact with Western Europe and a shorter period of communist rule. All of these factors may help explain why democratic transition in these regions has been more successful, and the majority have now joined the European Union. Even the Balkans, which experienced widespread violence and civil conflict in the 1990s, have seen their democratic practices improve over this decade, with several next in line to enter the EU.

As we move eastward, however, the situation is less promising (Figure 8.1). In many of the former Soviet states, democracy is illiberal and weakly insti-

Table 8.2 Freedom in Selected Communist and Postcommunist Systems, 2005

	Political Rights	Civil Liberties	Regime Type
	(1 = most free, 7 = not free)		
Poland	1	1	Liberal democracy
Hungary	1	1	Liberal democracy
Estonia	1	1	Liberal democracy
Czech Republic	1	1	Liberal democracy
Latvia	1	2	Liberal democracy
Bulgaria	1	2	Liberal democracy
Croatia	2	2	Liberal democracy
Romania	3	2	Liberal democracy
Albania	3	3	Illiberal democracy
Moldova	3	4	Illiberal democracy
Georgia	3	4	Illiberal democracy
Ukraine	4	3	Illiberal democracy
Russia	6	5	Authoritarian
Tajikistan	6	5	Authoritarian
Kyrgyzstan	6	5	Authoritarian
Belarus	7	6	Authoritarian
China	7	6	Authoritarian
Uzbekistan	7	6	Authoritarian

Source: Freedom House.

Figure 8.1 **APPROVAL OF POSTCOMMUNIST POLITICAL CHANGES**

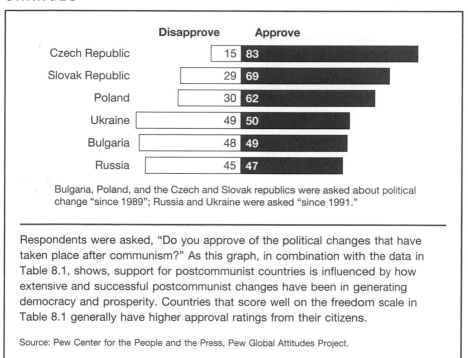

Bulgaria, Poland, and the Czech and Slovak republics were asked about political change "since 1989"; Russia and Ukraine were asked "since 1991."

Respondents were asked, "Do you approve of the political changes that have taken place after communism?" As this graph, in combination with the data in Table 8.1, shows, support for postcommunist countries is influenced by how extensive and successful postcommunist changes have been in generating democracy and prosperity. Countries that score well on the freedom scale in Table 8.1 generally have higher approval ratings from their citizens.

Source: Pew Center for the People and the Press, Pew Global Attitudes Project.

tutionalized or completely absent. These countries tend to be poorer, with little historical experience of democracy and a long period of Soviet control. In many of these countries, authoritarian leaders have consolidated power, many of them former members of the communist *nomenklatura*. Democratic rights and freedoms are still restricted, civil society is weak, and those in power have frequently enriched themselves through corrupt practices. In many cases, it is difficult to speak of the rule of law. Equally disturbing, many of these countries have become less democratic and less lawful over time, including Russia. There are a few hopeful signs; in recent years, mass movements have swept away entrenched leaders in Ukraine and Georgia. But similar protests in central Asia have been more violent and ambiguous in their goals and outcomes.

Outside of Eastern Europe and the former Soviet Union, democracy has been slow to spread; in fact, several communist regimes continue to hold on to power. China, Laos, Vietnam, North Korea, and Cuba remain steadfastly authoritarian, and only China has initiated significant economic reforms. Elsewhere in Asia and Africa, communist regimes have fallen, in many cases resulting in state collapse and civil war, as in Afghanistan. Upon the Soviet Union's withdrawal from that country in 1989, civil war raged until 1996, when the Taliban gained power over most of the country, thus paving the way for the eventual establishment of Al Qaeda. Thus, not everywhere has the end of communism been peaceful and democratic, and in some ways, the end of communism paved the path for the current global battle against terrorism.

Economic Institutions in Transition

In addition to transforming the state and the regime, transitions from communism have also confronted the task of reestablishing some separation between the state and the economy. This involves two processes: **marketization**, or the re-creation of market forces of supply and demand, and **privatization**, the transfer of state-held property into private hands. In both cases, decisions about how to carry out these changes and to what end were influenced by different political-economic alternatives. Let's consider the ways in which privatization and marketization can be approached before we investigate the different paths postcommunist countries have taken in each area.

Privatization and Marketization

The transition from communism to capitalism requires a redefinition of property. To generate economic growth and limit the power of the state, the state must reentrust economic resources with the public, placing them back into private hands. But the task of privatization is neither easy nor clear. In fact, prior to 1989, no country had ever gone from a communist economy to a capitalist one, so no model existed.

Among the many questions and concerns facing the postcommunist countries was how to place a price on the various elements of the economy—factories, shops, land, apartments. To privatize these assets, the state first must figure out their values, something difficult in a system where no market has existed. And who should get these assets? Should they be given away? Sold to the highest bidder? Made available to foreign investors? Each option has its own advantages in developing a thriving economy but also dangers in increasing inequality and generating public resentment.

Privatization was eventually carried out in a number of dif-

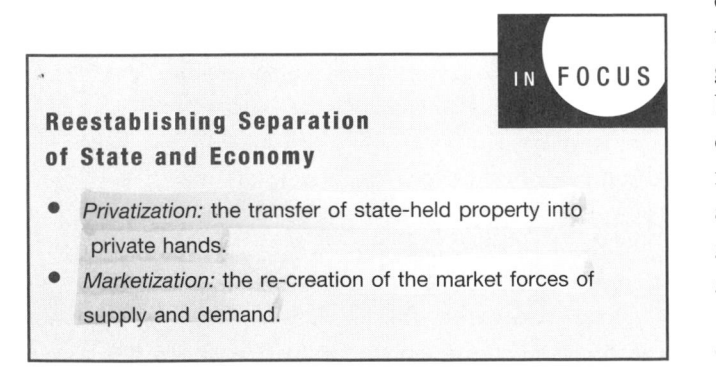

IN FOCUS

Reestablishing Separation of State and Economy

- *Privatization:* the transfer of state-held property into private hands.
- *Marketization:* the re-creation of the market forces of supply and demand.

ferent ways, depending on the country and the kind of economic assets. In many cases, small businesses were sold directly to their employees. Some countries did sell many large businesses to the highest bidder, often to foreign investors. Other countries essentially distributed shares in firms to the public as a whole. Scholars debated the benefits of each model, but in the end, there were examples where each one of these forms, whether alone or in combination, worked well (or badly).

No matter what the privatization process, in the end there were many firms in postcommunist countries that were overstaffed, outdated, and unable to turn a profit in a market economy. Most problematic were very large industrial firms, such as coal mines and steel plants built in the early years of industrialization; these antiquated behemoths are uncompetitive in the international market. Such firms often must be sold or radically downsized, leading to unemployment in a society where previously employment had been guaranteed. In some cases, such firms employed thousands of people and represented the main source of work in a city or region. To close down such firms is not an easy task for any politician, especially in a newly democratic system in which people are likely to vote with their pocketbooks and turn such leaders out of office. As a result, in some countries, privatization proceeded slowly for fear of widespread unemployment and resulting social unrest.

In addition to re-creating private property, states must re-create a market in which property, labor, goods, and services can all function in a competitive environment to determine their value. On the surface, marketization appears easier than privatization—a simple matter of eliminating central planning and allowing the market to naturally resurface. But marketization, too, is a complicated process. One issue of debate concerned how rapidly marketization should take place. Some argued that given the profound nature of the economic transformation in postcommunist states, changes should be gradual to minimize any social disruptions that might undermine these fledgling economies and democracies. In particular, supporters of this "gradualism" feared that sudden marketization would lead to a wild jump in prices as sellers became able to charge whatever they wanted for their goods. Inflation and even hyperinflation could result, undermining confidence in the transition process and generating widespread poverty. Others rejected these arguments, advocating rapid market reforms that would free prices and bring an end to central planning and state subsidies for businesses virtually overnight—a policy known as **shock therapy**. Such change would be painful and might initially involve a high degree of inflation, but the pain would be shorter than that accompanying gradualism.

In choosing particular forms of privatization and marketization, postcommunist countries adopted new political economic models—some gravitating toward the social democratic models of Western Europe, others the liberalism of the United States and United Kingdom, while still others opted for more mercantilist policies.

Evaluating Economic Transitions

How successful have all of these reforms been? The answer again depends on what country you are looking at.[15] Table 8.3 shows some of the results of ten

Table 8.3 Economic Indicators in the Communist and Postcommunist World, 1993–2004					
	Per capita GDP, 2004 (PPP, in U.S. $)	Percentage of GDP Privately Owned, 2002	Average Annual GDP Growth Rate, 1993–2004	Percentage of Labor Force Unemployed, 2004	2004 GDP as a Percentage of 1989 GDP
Czech Republic*	16,800	80	2.3	10.6	114
Hungary*	14,900	80	3.2	5.9	120
Estonia†	14,300	80	3.9	9.6	108
Poland*	12,000	75	4.4	19.5	142
Latvia†	11,500	70	3.7	8.8	90
Croatia*	11,200	60	3.3	13.8	94
Russia†	9,800	70	0.6	8.3	82
Bulgaria*	8,200	70	1.5	12.7	88
Romania*	7,700	65	2.5	6.3	99
Belarus†	6,800	20	2.4	2	111
Ukraine†	6,300	65	−1.9	9–10	57
China	5,600	60	8.6	20	307
Albania*	4,900	75	7.2	14.8	136
Georgia†	3,100	65	2.0	17	46
Moldova†	1,900	50	−1.6	8	44
Uzbekistan†	1,800	45	2.0	0.6	113
Kyrgyzstan†	1,700	60	0.5	18	80
Tajikistan†	1,100	50	1.0	40	69

*Former Communist country, Eastern Europe.
†Former republic of the Soviet Union.

Sources: CIA, World Bank, European Bank for Reconstruction and Development.

years of transition. In Eastern Europe and the Baltics, GDP is now on average a quarter higher than it was in 1989, with economic reforms now bearing fruit. In contrast, the Balkans have made no real progress economically, while the countries of the CIS have seen their GDP drop by an average of 20 percent. In countries like Moldova and Georgia, the drop has been by more than half. Why this variation? Those countries that did well benefited from many of the factors we discussed earlier: shorter periods of Soviet control; more precommunist experience with industrialization, markets, and private property; closer ties with Western Europe; and strong support from the European Union. Those countries that did more poorly experienced just the opposite. In these latter countries, freeing up markets often led to uncontrollable inflation and a rapid decline in the standard of living. These problems were compounded by the way in which privatization was carried out, with many of the most valuable assets falling into the hands of the old *nomenklatura* and/or a handful of private individuals, typically supported by corrupt political leaders. One theme that runs through all these cases is the correlation between economic growth and the rule of law. Where the rule of law is weak, economic transition is much less successful. Entrepreneurs (both domestic and international) lack a predictable environment in which to invest, while political leaders and state officials use their positions to siphon off resources for themselves.

Overall, postcommunist countries have seen an increase in inequality, relative poverty, and unemployment, which is to be expected as markets and private property become central economic forces. Where this has been balanced by economic prosperity for the majority of the population, support for change has been stronger. Where the majority of the population feels worse off, as in much of the CIS, economic change has bred resentment, nostalgia for the old order, and obstacles to democratization.

Outside of Eastern Europe and the former Soviet Union, economic transition is equally varied. Much attention has been focused on China, which historically had a much more weakly institutionalized system of central planning and control over property (which may in part explain China's early experimentation with reform). Since the 1970s, China's reforms have included a dramatic expansion of private business and agriculture, all with the support of the Chinese Communist Party. The slogan of this economic reform—"To get rich is glorious"—sounds anything but Marxist, but it is rooted in the practical realization that earlier drives for rapid economic growth led to disaster. Some observers argue that these reforms have succeeded where many other communist countries have failed, introducing economic transition while restricting political change so as to better manage the course of reform. Indeed, since 1989, the Chinese economy has grown by leaps and bounds, lifting hundreds of millions out of poverty and dramatically transforming the country, not to mention world trade.

Yet the Chinese model has its problems. Alongside economic growth and the development of a free market and private property, problems such as inflation, rampant corruption, unemployment, and growing inequality have also surfaced, often exacerbated by the still-powerful presence of the state in the Chinese economy. The lack of the rule of law only compounds these problems. China's rapid development has been profound; the question is to what extent this will continue into the future. Some see in China a growing economic superpower that will eclipse much of Asia and perhaps the world. This development could, in turn, foster a middle class that would pave the way for the democratization of one-fifth of the world's population.[16] Others believe that the Chinese "miracle" covers up serious problems, such as an unreformed industrial sector and large numbers of urban and rural unemployed. China could see a future of greater development, greater liberty, and greater conflict, all at the same time.

Societal Institutions in Transition

Like political systems and economies, societies, too, have been fundamentally transformed in postcommunist countries. Where once communist control asserted one interpretation of human relations, people now face a future much more uncertain and unclear. Postcommunist societies have the potential for greater individual action, but with this potential comes greater risk. The elimination of an all-encompassing ideology from people's lives has created a social vacuum that must be filled. In all of these countries, the transition from communism has been a wrenching process as people adjust to new realities and seek new individual and collective identities.

Re-creating Identities

This transformation of society has manifested itself in a number of different ways. Religion, once suppressed by Communist parties, has resurfaced in many countries. In Eastern Europe and parts of the former Soviet Union, Western evangelical movements have made many new converts, while in other parts of the former Soviet Union, such as central Asia, Islam has reemerged as a powerful force, with many thousands of mosques and religious schools built in part with funds from other Muslim countries, such as Saudi Arabia. In many countries, this return to religion has helped rebuild social norms and values and has also led to the emergence of fundamentalism and increased conflict between politics and religion. In China, too, new and old religious movements are gaining strength. For example, the spiritual group Falun Gong, which attracted somewhere between 70 million and 100 million followers in the 1990s, was the target of a harsh crackdown by government authorities, who feared any organization that could command greater loyalty than the regime.[17] Underground Christian churches in China may claim a similar number of members. In the face of economic hardship, corruption, and often still-oppressive regimes, this religious resurgence should not be surprising: religion can play an important role in providing people with a sense of community and purpose.

Like religion, ethnic and national identities have reemerged as potent forms of group identification. In many postcommunist countries, both leaders and publics have sought to reinstill national pride and resurrect the values, symbols, and ideas that bind people together. The scope of this task varies among the postcommunist countries. In much of Eastern Europe, a clear sense of ethnic and national identity has existed for many generations, and in spite of communist rule, many of these social structures not only remained intact but were reinforced by authoritarianism as a form of resistance. In contrast, across the diverse ethnic groups of the former Soviet Union, national identity has historically been much weaker. Many of these peoples have few ethnic or national institutions to draw on, and their identities are not so much being resurrected as they are being created from scratch, with new words, anthems, symbols, and myths. All such identities can be a double-edged sword, of course. Although they can help mobilize the public and provide stability in a time of great transition, religious, ethnic, and national identities can also generate division and conflict, particularly when several identities coexist in one country or in opposition to the state or regime.

The changes under way in social identities cannot help but affect gender relations as well. Recall our earlier discussion of how communist theory advances the radical notion of gender equality. Although equality was not truly realized in practice, women were incorporated into the workforce and provided with social benefits that generated new opportunities. With the end of communism, however, many of these policies and institutions have been weakened or challenged. Critics have attacked many communist-era practices such as easy access to abortions, while economic reforms have cut back much of the elaborate social safety net that once benefited women and families. The reemergence of religion has also challenged women's roles in society in some cases.

Evaluating Societal Transitions

New societies in postcommunist countries have developed in very different ways. In some cases, the emergence of new religious and national identities has contributed to violence and civil war. In Eastern Europe, the dissolution of Yugoslavia pitted ethnic and religious groups against one another, claiming more than 200,000 lives. Parts of the former Soviet Union, such as Tajik-istan, Chechnya (part of Russia), Uzbekistan, Moldova, Azerbaijan, and Arme-nia, also have seen violent conflicts with thousands killed. Finally, the almost endless wars in Afghanistan since the 1970s are yet another tragedy whose consequences have rippled throughout the domestic and international com-munities. In Afghanistan during the 1980s, volunteers from numerous Mus-lim countries, such as Osama bin Laden, fought alongside Afghan guerrillas against Soviet occupation in what they saw as a need to defend Muslims from atheist communism. Upon the end of that conflict and the dissolution of the Soviet Union, some of these fighters turned their attention toward the post-communist world, taking up the cause of Muslim populations in central Asia, the Caucasus, and the Balkans. What were regional and ethnic conflicts quickly became international and religious ones, feeding into the idea of a global war to defend Islam.[18] Other fighters would later regroup in Afghanistan, forming Al Qaeda—"the base"—under bin Laden's leadership as a launching pad for this international jihad. Thus, the current struggle against Al Qaeda and related groups has its origins in the collapse of communism. However, we should recall that much of the postcommunist world has been largely peaceful over the past decade, with ethnic and religious conflicts resolved or averted.

Gender relations in postcommunist countries also show signs of progress and setback as the rhetoric of equality espoused under communism has given way. For example, as parliaments have become more powerful, fewer women are winning seats, from an average of 21 percent in 1990 to 12 percent in 2004. However, these same countries show a growing number of women in ministerial positions in government.[19] By and large, women do not appear to have suffered disproportionately from unemployment, though there may be evidence of wage discrimination. Finally, the reduction in social expenditures has increased the burden on women for such things as child care.[20] These conditions tend to be worse in central Asia and China than in Eastern Europe, again highlighting the degree to which the postcommunist countries are mov-ing in very different directions in terms of freedom, equality, and prosperity.

In Sum: The Legacy of Communism

According to Marxist thought, capitalism inevitably led to great industrial-ization but also to great injustice, a contradiction that would result in its downfall. Communism would build on capitalism's ruins to generate a soci-ety of total equality. But constructing communism proved to be a daunting task. People within communist systems found little incentive for hard work and innovation and had few freedoms to express themselves individually.

For the Soviet Union and Eastern Europe, attempts to solve these problems led to outright collapse. One might use the analogy of renovating a dilapidated house only to find that the whole structure is unsound and that renovations are only making the situation worse. At that point, one has to either demolish the whole structure or be demolished by it. In 1989, people in a number of Eastern European countries chose to demolish the institutions of communism. Communist structures in the Soviet Union eventually collapsed on the Communist Party and Soviet society. China seems to be in a process of endless (and perhaps precarious) remodeling, while other communist countries, such as Cuba and North Korea, have yet to carry out any major reforms.

It is not clear what the coming decades will bring to the postcommunist world. All of these societies are attempting to grapple again with the dilemma of freedom and equality. New political, economic, and social institutions are needed, but in many cases they must be forged out of the rubble of the old order, a situation that is creating unique difficulties and contradictions. Over the past decade, both individual freedom and collective inequality have grown in many countries. Increased civil liberties have arisen alongside poverty, and the rebirth of society alongside conflict and hostility.

The results of this diverse process have been dramatically different across the communist and postcommunist world. In some countries, we see the institutionalization of democracy and capitalism; in others, authoritarianism and state-controlled economies remain in place. Moreover, it is apparent that over time, these countries will grow increasingly dissimilar. Democratic consolidation and economic growth in Eastern Europe appear to have placed many of these countries on the slow path to becoming advanced democracies. Within much of the former Soviet Union, however, economic stagnation or decline, political instability, and authoritarianism are more common; those countries are starting to resemble the less-developed world. China remains an enormous question mark. But whatever their paths, all these countries will continue to struggle to balance freedom and equality, a concern as pressing now as it was on the eve of the Russian Revolution in 1917.

NOTES

1. For a good overview of communist theory see Alfred Meyer, *Communism* (New York: Random House, 1984).
2. See Marx's 1882 preface to the Russian translation of the *Communist Manifesto*; www.marxists.org.
3. See V. I. Lenin, *What Is to Be Done? Burning Questions of Our Movement*, trans. Joe Fineberg and George Hanna (New York: International Publishers, 1969).
4. For a comparative discussion of different communist systems, see Stephen White,

John Gardner, George Schöpflin, and Tony Saich, *Communist and Post-Communist Political Systems* (New York: St. Martin's, 1990).

5. See Michael Voslensky, *Nomenklatura: Anatomy of the Soviet Ruling Class* (Garden City, NY: Doubleday, 1984).

6. See Robert Conquest, *The Great Terror: A Reassessment* (New York: Oxford University Press, 1990).

7. See Lowell Dittmer, *China's Continuous Revolution: The Post-Liberation Epoch, 1949–1981* (Berkeley: University of California Press, 1987).

8. Robert W. Campbell, *The Socialist Economies in Transition: A Primer on Semi-Reformed Systems* (Bloomington: Indiana University Press, 1991).

9. Dali Yang, *Calamity and Reform in China: Rural Society and Institutional Change since the Great Leap Famine* (Stanford: Stanford University Press, 1996).

10. Karl Marx and Friedrich Engels, *Manifesto of the Communist Party,* available online at www.marxists.org/archive/marx/works/1848/communist-manifesto/.

11. Joni Lovenduski and Jean Woodall, *Politics and Society in Eastern Europe* (Bloomington: Indiana University Press, 1987), 158.

12. Marcy McAuley, *Soviet Politics 1917–1991* (New York: Oxford University Press, 1992).

13. The best retrospective studies of the collapse of communism in Eastern Europe and its effects in the Soviet Union can be found in Mark Kramer, "The Collapse of East European Communism and the Repercussions within the Soviet Union," Parts 1–3, *Journal of Cold War Studies*, Fall 2003, Fall 2004, and Spring 2005.

14. On the collapse of communism in Eastern Europe, see Timothy Garton Ash, *The Magic Lantern: The Revolution of 1989 Witnessed in Warsaw, Budapest, Berlin and Prague* (New York: Random House, 1990); on the Soviet Union, see David Remnick, *Lenin's Tomb: The Last Days of the Soviet Empire* (New York: Random House, 1993).

15. *Transition Report Update 2005* (European Bank for Reconstruction and Development, 2005).

16. Bruce Gilley, *China's Democratic Future: How It Will Happen and Where It Will Lead* (New York: Columbia University Press, 2004).

17. See the website of Falun Gong at http://www.faluninfo.net/.

18. This idea is articulated in Abdullah Azzam, *Join the Caravan* (London: Azzam Publications, 2001).

19. See World Bank, *World Development Indicators 2001, 2005*; www.worldbank.org.

20. Pierella Paci, *Gender in Transition* (Washington, DC: World Bank, 2002).

9 LESS-DEVELOPED AND NEWLY INDUSTRIALIZING COUNTRIES

So far, we have investigated two major parts of the world—the advanced democracies, often described as the First World, and communist and postcommunist countries, or what had been known as the Second World. But these two categories leave out the majority of countries around the world, especially those in Latin America, Asia, and Africa. These regions are populated with countries that historically have had neither liberal democratic nor communist regimes. Moreover, the vast majority of these countries have levels of economic industrialization far below those in the advanced democracies or the communist and postcommunist world. The traditional labeling of these countries as belonging to the "Third World" unhelpfully grouped together a diverse range of people and political systems according to what they were not, rather than what they were.

How, then, should we understand this important and vast part of the world? Whereas the advanced democracies are noted for their early capitalist development and the possible emergence of a postmodern system, and the communist states for their later rapid modernization and industrialization directed by the state, the countries that are the subject of this chapter are characterized by their mixture of premodern and modern institutions and a hybrid of economic, societal, and political institutions both foreign and indigenous.

In this chapter, we will attempt to develop some ideas and categories to investigate and understand this part of the world. We will begin by distinguishing between newly industrializing and less-developed countries and examine how the relationship between freedom and equality is structured in each. From there we will look at some of the fundamental experiences and institutions that these countries share, particularly those associated with imperialism and colonialism. Although imperialism had different effects in different parts of the world, similar legacies resulted from this form of rule. Next we will consider what challenges and obstacles these countries have faced after gaining independence. How does a country reconcile freedom and equality when the conditions may favor neither? And how is it that some countries have managed to enjoy economic and political development while others have stagnated or declined? These topics will lead us into a final discussion of the prospects for political, economic, and societal development in this part of the world. What policies might help generate greater democracy, political stability, and economic prosperity in these countries? The difficulties they face are great and the tasks daunting. But out of such dilemmas can emerge new ideas and innovations with the potential for positive change.

Freedom and Equality in the Newly Industrializing and Less-Developed Countries

The countries of what was traditionally referred to as the "Third World" are in fact often divided into two groups that indicate differences in their levels of development. Over the past fifty years, some countries, particularly in Asia and parts of Latin America, have experienced dramatic rates of economic growth and democratization, to the point where they now resemble the advanced democracies in many ways. These are typically known as **newly industrializing countries (NICs)**. Although this name emphasizes their rapid economic growth, in recent years the newly industrializing countries have also shown a marked tendency toward democratization and political and social stability, such that many such countries are also listed in Chapter 7 as moving into the category of advanced democracies. South Korea is one such country. A relatively poor agricultural country in the early 1960s, divided and damaged by the Korean War, South Korea would over the next fifty years become one of the world's largest economies and slowly develop a set of democratic institutions alongside its growing wealth. In countries such as South Korea, one finds stable and democratizing political institutions, an expanding web of nongovernmental institutions and civil society, and a growing economy. Such countries, however, tend to be in the minority. In many other cases, economic and political structures have remained weak or grown weaker over the past decades; these countries are marked by economic stagnation or even decline, with some sliding into poverty, violence, and civil conflict. These countries are often referred to as the **less-developed countries (LDCs)**, a term that implies a lack of significant economic development or political institutionalization (Table 9.1). An example here might be the country of Ghana. Despite expectations in the 1960s that this newly independent country was on the road to rapid political and economic development, Ghana sank into economic stagnation, political instability, and authoritarian rule. Perhaps most curious, in the early 1960s, Ghana had a higher per capita gross domestic product (GDP) than did South Korea. This reversal of fortune will be explored later in this chapter.

Table 9.1 Less-Developed and Newly Industrializing Countries, 2006

Central and South America	Asia	North Africa and Middle East	Sub-Saharan Africa (continued)
Antigua & Barbuda	Afghanistan*	Algeria	Equatorial Guinea
Argentina	Bahrain	Egypt	Gagon
Belize	Bangladesh	Eritrea	Gambia
Bolivia	Bhutan	*Ethiopia*	Ghana
Brazil	Brunei	Iran	Guinea
Chile	Burma (Myanmar)	Iraq	Guinea-Bissau
Colombia	*Cambodia*	Jordan	Ivory Coast
Costa Rica	Cyprus	Lebanon	Kenya
Dominica	Fiji	Libya	Lesotho
Dominican Republic	India	Morocco	Liberia
Ecuador	Indonesia	Oman	Madagascar
El Salvador	Kiribati	Qatar	Malawi
Grenada	Korea (South)	Saudi Arabia	Mali
Guatemala	Kuwait	Syria	Mauritania
Guyana	Malaysia	United Arab Emirates	Mauritius
Haiti	Maldives	Yemen	*Mozambique*
Honduras	Marshall Islands		Namibia
Jamaica	Micronesia		Niger
Mexico	Nauru	**Sub-Saharan Africa**	Nigeria
Nicaragua	Nepal		Rwanda
Panama	Palau	Angola	Sao Tome and Principe
Paraguay	Pakistan	Benin	Senegal
Peru	Papua New Guinea	Botswana	Seychelles
St. Kitts & Nevis	Philippines	Burkina Faso	Sierra Leone
St. Lucia	Samoa	Burundi	Somalia*
St. Vincent & the Grenadines	Singapore	Cameroon	South Africa
Suriname	Solomon Islands	Cape Verde	Sudan
Trinidad & Tobago	Sri Lanka	Central African Republic	Swaziland
Uruguay	Taiwan	Chad	Tanzania
Venezuela	Thailand	Comoros	Togo
	Tonga	Congo (Republic of)	Tunisia
	Turkey	Congo (Democratic Republic of)	Uganda
Europe	Tuvalu		Zambia
Turkey	Vanuatu	Djibouti	Zimbabwe

Note: Former communist countries are shown in italics.

Although newly industrializing and less-developed countries seem in many ways to be increasingly dissimilar, what they still have in common is the relative weakness of both freedom and equality. Newly industrializing countries may have progressed toward greater democracy and economic development, but these processes remain incomplete and uninstitutionalized and could still be undermined. Indeed, in some cases, democratic and economic change has raised new problems in reconciling freedom and equality, particularly where gaps have grown between rich and poor and where politics have become polarized as a result. The situation is particularly bad in the less-developed countries, where both freedom and equality are often circumscribed, with economic and political power tightly held in the hands of a very few.

Why are freedom and equality so weak in these countries? Social scientists do not agree on the reasons, but many point to the important role played by imperialism and colonialism. Virtually all of the countries that we describe as newly industrializing or less developed were formerly part of much larger empires, possessions of more powerful states. This imperial rule, which in some cases lasted for decades or even centuries, dramatically and often rapidly transformed economic, political, and societal institutions in these countries. Although resistance eventually brought down imperial rule, the changes wrought by this system could not be unmade. To better understand these legacies, it is worth looking at this form of political control in some detail.

Imperialism and Colonialism

In the first three chapters of this book, we saw that over the past millennium, Europe, the Middle East, and Asia embarked on a series of dramatic societal, economic, and political changes that formed the outlines of what are now recognized as the hallmarks of modern society: ethnic and national identity, technological innovation, and political centralization. This growing power was soon projected outward to conquer and incorporate new lands and peoples that could contribute to this rapid development. The result was the emergence of **empires**, which are defined as single political authorities that have under their sovereignty a large number of external regions or territories and different peoples. Although this definition might lead one to conclude that any large, diverse country is an empire, central to the definition is the idea that lands and peoples that are not seen as an integral part of the country itself are nonetheless under its direct control. The term **imperialism** describes the system whereby a state extends its power to directly control territory, resources, and people beyond its borders. The term *imperialism* is often used interchangeably with the term **colonialism**, though they are different. Colonialism indicates to a greater degree the physical occupation of a foreign territory through military force, businesses, or settlers. Colonialism, then, is often a means to consolidate one's empire.

Although imperialist practices date back many thousands of years, modern imperialism can be dated from the 1500s, when technological development in Europe, the Middle East, and Asia—advanced seafaring and military technology in particular—had advanced to such an extent that these countries were able to project their military might far overseas. In Asia, the powerful Chinese Empire turned away from this path. Having consolidated power hundreds of years before the states of Europe did, the Chinese state had grown conservative and inflexible, interested more in maintaining the status quo than in striking out to acquire new lands. Indeed, at the same time that Europeans were setting out for the Americas, the Chinese were actually retreating from overseas voyages; by 1500, it had become illegal for Chinese subjects to build oceangoing vessels. Similarly, in the Middle East, the powerful Ottoman Empire expanded its power over much of the Arab world and into Asia, North Africa, and parts of Europe, nearly conquering Vienna in 1683. But the Ottoman Empire also turned inward and lost interest in technological innovation and in expanding power beyond the Islamic world, for reasons that are open to debate and will be discussed later. In contrast, the Europeans saw imperialism as a means to expand their resources, markets, subjects, and territory in order to gain the upper hand in their frequent battles with one another.

What should be clear is that those peoples who became subject to modern imperialism were not a blank slate, without any of their own institutions. On the contrary, many of the regions that were so dominated already possessed their own highly developed economic, political, and societal systems, in some cases surpassing those of Europe. Nevertheless, they could not withstand imperial pressure.

Thus, starting in the sixteenth century, Europe began a process of imperialism that would not end for nearly five centuries. Driven by economic and strategic motives, as well as by a belief that Christianity and Western culture needed to be brought to the rest of the world, European empires stretched their power around the globe. First, Spain and Portugal

IN FOCUS

Imperialism Is . . .

- A system in which a state extends its power beyond its borders to control other territories and peoples.
- Propagated by European powers from the sixteenth to the twenty-first centuries.
- Driven by economic, strategic, and religious motives.
- Often led to *colonialism*, the physical occupation of foreign territories.

gained control over South and Central America. By the seventeenth century, British, French, and other settlers began to arrive in North America, displacing the local population. In the eighteenth century, Europeans began to assert control over parts of North Africa and the Middle East, shocking Ottoman elites who had long viewed Europeans as technologically and culturally backward. This shock was shared by the Chinese in the nineteenth and early twentieth centuries as European imperialism rapidly expanded into Asia. Nearly all of Africa, too, was eventually divided up by the European states. This European imperialist expansion was joined briefly by Japan, which in the early twentieth century established its own empire across parts of Asia. In each of these cases, imperial powers possessed well-organized political systems, military structures, technological advances, and economic resources; these advan-

TIME LINE / MODERN IMPERIALISM	
1494	Following European discovery, Spain and Portugal partition the Americas between their two empires.
1519–1536	Indigenous groups (Aztecs, Incas) are defeated by imperial powers in South America.
1602–1652	Dutch begin to establish control over parts of Indonesian archipelago and southern Africa. English settlement begins in North America.
1810–1825	Wars of independence in Latin America; Spanish and Portuguese rule is brought to an end.
1839–1858	United Kingdom expands control into Asia, notably Hong Kong and India.
1884	The Berlin Conference: Africa is rapidly divided among European powers, notably France, Portugal, and Belgium.
1939–1945	World War II catalyzes the eventual decolonization of Asia and Africa.
1947	Independence of India; first major decolonization of twentieth century.
1956–1968	Independence of most British, French, and Belgian colonies in Africa after local rebellions against imperial rule.
1975	Independence of most former Portuguese colonies in Africa and Asia.
1999	Hong Kong (United Kingdom) and Macau (Portugal) returned to China.

tages were combined with a belief that imperial control was not only possible, but necessary and just.[1]

Institutions of Imperialism

The effect that imperialism had on those societies that came under foreign rule differs across time and place, but some common elements resulted from the imposition of modern political, societal, and economic systems onto largely premodern societies. As we shall see, the imposition of modern institutions onto premodern peoples had a traumatic effect that continues to the present.[2]

Exporting the State

One of the first major effects of imperialism was the transfer of the state to the rest of the world. Recall from Chapter 2 how the modern state that we take for granted today emerged as a result of a long historical process in Europe; prior to that time, political units tended to have much weaker control over land and their subjects, and territorial sovereignty was rather tenuous. States, however, eventually succeeded in consolidating power over other forms of political organization, eliminating their rivals, clearly delineating their borders, and establishing sovereignty.

When European empires began to expand around the world, new territories were incorporated into these state structures, territories carved up by rival states in the quest for economic resources and strategic advantages. The borders drawn by imperial states were often reflections of their own power rather than existing geographical, religious, or linguistic realities. In turn, many of these externally imposed boundaries would later become the demarcations for independent countries once imperial rule was overthrown. Even those countries that were able to resist direct imperial rule, such as Iran, nevertheless found themselves under the direct influence and pressure of these empires.

Having conquered these territories, imperial powers went about establishing state power and authority. In many empires, this meant establishing bureaucratic structures similar to those found in the home country in an attempt to "civilize"—to modernize—these premodern peoples. These structures commonly included a national language (typically that of the imperial power rather than a local language), police, taxation and legal systems, and basic public goods such as roads, schools, and hospitals. How this process was carried out and enforced differed. Some empires relied on local leaders to enforce their will, whereas others bypassed indigenous elites in favor of their own centralized forms of authority. In both cases, few if any democratic practices were introduced, even if they were the norm in the home country. Individuals under colonial rule were considered subjects, not citizens, and thus had few political rights.

This imposition of the state had mixed effects, the benefits of which are open to debate. Many subject peoples experienced increased education and the benefits of a basic infrastructure that improved communication and transportation. Life expectancies rose and infant mortality rates declined, although when those trends were combined with traditional family practices, they produced a population explosion that in many poor countries continues today. Traditional institutions such as local religions and customs were eroded and replaced by a greater awareness (and mimicry) of modern practices and institutions. This transition was incomplete and uneven. Imperial territories remained economically and politically underdeveloped, placing many subject peoples in a kind of limbo—no longer part of a premodern system but not fully incorporated into the modern one. The frustration that grew out of this conflict over identity helped fan the flames of anti-imperialism, the desire for freedom from foreign control.

Social Identities

The imposition of organizational forms from outside included various new identities that often displaced or were incorporated into existing social institutions. Among these were ethnic and national identities. In much of the world that came under imperial control, people identified themselves by tribe or religion, by economic position, or by vocation rather than by some ethnic or national identity. But just as empires brought their own political institutions with them, the concepts of ethnicity and nation were also introduced by the new ruling powers. Imperial elites, themselves shaped and defined by national and ethnic identities, took great interest in identifying and classifying different ethnic groups in the regions they came to occupy and structuring their political and economic control around these classifications.

Suddenly, people who had never thought of themselves as being part of an ethnic group found that their basic rights were tied to how they were ethnically defined by the empire.

Political and Social Institutions of Imperialism

- The state, as a form of political organization, was imposed on much of the world outside of Europe.
- Ethnic and national identities were created where none had existed prior to colonization.
- Gender roles from the imperial country were often imposed on colonies.

In some cases, this ethnic classification was tied to early modern notions of race, which held that certain ethnic groups were naturally superior to others. The European and Japanese empires were influenced by the assumption that the colonizing race was superior to the colonized and thus destined to rule them. Different peoples within the empire, too, were subject to hierarchical classification. Certain ethnic groups were promoted to positions of power and economic advantage while other groups were marginalized. Colonialism often further exacerbated these hierarchies as nonindigenous peoples migrated into colonies. Sometimes these migrants were settlers from the home country; in other cases, they were peoples from other parts of the empire or beyond it (for example, Indians migrating into Africa or African slaves brought to Brazil). These foreign presences further sharpened ethnic and racial divisions, especially when such groups were accorded specific economic or political privileges. In short, inequality and ethnicity, or race, became tightly interconnected.

In addition to ethnicity, imperial powers also introduced the idea of national identity. During the late nineteenth and early twentieth centuries, in particular, national identity grew to be a powerful force in the industrializing world, helping give shape to the imperialist cause. But the peoples brought under imperial control had little familiarity with national identity, little notion of any right to a sovereign state. This combination of nationalism and imperialism proved dangerous. Empires viewed the peoples living in their overseas possessions as inferior subjects and gave them only a limited ability to improve their standing within the empire. Yet the imperial powers' own concept of nationalism provided these subject peoples with the very means to challenge foreign rule. If nationalism meant the right for a people—any people—to live under their own sovereign state, did this not mean that subject peoples had a right to rule themselves? Empires would thus provide the very ideological ammunition that their subjects would eventually use to overturn imperialism.

Faith, too, was transformed in many societies by imperialism. Prior to European imperialism, Islam was spread across much of North Africa and the Middle East through contact and conquest, just as Christianity was later spread to Latin America and Africa—sometimes peacefully, sometimes through force. Tribal and local faiths gave way to these global faiths, though they often merged local traditional practices with these new values, creating an array of sects and schisms.

Colonialism also affected gender roles within the colonies. It is hard to make generalizations in this area, since in each region existing gender roles differed greatly and each imperial power viewed gender in a somewhat different way. Some scholars argue that on balance, imperialism brought a number of benefits to women, increasing their freedom and equality by improving their access to health care and education. Others reject this argument, asserting that quite the reverse occurred in many cases. In many premodern societies, gender roles may have been much less fixed than those found in the modern world, allowing women particular areas of individual freedom and relative equality with men. For example, in precolonial Nigeria, the women of the Igbo people wielded substantial political power. Under British imperialism, however, gender roles in Nigeria became much more rigid and hierarchical. Imperial powers brought with them their own assumptions regarding the subordinate status of women, views that were shaped in part by their religious values. These views were imposed through such policies as education and the legal system. The economic systems imposed by the colonizers marginalized women in many ways. On balance, although imperialism may have provided new avenues for women, this progress may have come at the cost of other freedoms or areas of equality that women once held in their premodern societies.[3]

Dependent Development

Just as imperialism transformed political and social institutions in colonial areas, creating an amalgam of premodern and modern forms, economic change similarly occurred in a dramatic and uneven way.[4] The first important change in most imperial possessions was the replacement of a traditional agricultural economy by one driven by the needs of the industrializing capitalist home country. Systems based largely on subsistence agriculture and barter were transformed into cash economies, in which money was introduced as a means to pay for goods and labor.

Alongside this introduction of a cash-based economy came the transformation of economic production. Using a mercantilist political-economic system (see Chapter 4), empires sought to extract revenue from their colonies while at the same time using these territories and their people as a captive market for finished goods from the home country. Free trade thus did not exist for the colonies, which were obliged to sell and buy goods within the confines of the empire. In addition, colonial production was organized to provide those goods that were not easily available in the home country. Rather than finished goods, local economies were

IN FOCUS

Economic Institutions of Imperialism

- Traditional agricultural economies were transformed to suit the needs of the imperialist power.
- Free trade was often suppressed as colonies were forced to supply goods only to the imperial country, creating extractive economies in the colonies.
- Economic organization under imperialism impeded domestic development in the colonies.

rebuilt around primary products such as cotton, cocoa, coffee, tea, wood, rubber, and other valuable commodities that could be extracted from the natural environment. Large businesses were established to oversee these so-called extractive economies, which were often dominated by a single monopoly. For example, in Indonesia, the United East India Company, a Dutch firm, gained control over lucrative spice exports while monopolizing the local market for finished goods from Europe, thereby destroying indigenous trade networks that had existed in the region for centuries. Similarly, the British East India Company functioned virtually as a state of its own, controlling a large portion of the Indian economy and much of its foreign trade. Export-oriented imperialism also led to the creation of large plantations that could produce vast quantities of rubber, coffee, or tobacco.

This form of economic organization was quite different from that of the home countries and in many respects ill suited to domestic development. Infrastructure was often developed only to facilitate effective extraction and export, rather than to improve communication or movement for the subject peoples; jobs were created in the extractive sector, but local industrialization and entrepreneurialism were limited; the development of agriculture for export instead of for subsistence damaged the ability of these peoples to feed themselves, and the creation of large-scale agricultural production drove many small farmers off the land. Many colonies saw a resulting boom in urbanization, typically centered around the colonial capital or other cities central to imperial politics and trade. By the late 1500s, for example, the Spanish had established more than 200 cities in Latin America, which to this day remain the central urban areas in the region.

Let us take a moment to summarize what we have considered so far. By virtue of their organizational strengths, modern states expanded their power around the globe, establishing new political, economic, and social institutions and displacing existing ones. In some cases, these institutions were reflections of the home country; in others, they were designed specifically to consolidate imperial rule. The result was an uneasy mixture of indigenous and foreign structures, premodern and modern. New political institutions and new societal identities were introduced or imposed while participation and citizenship were restricted; economic development was encouraged but in a form that would serve the markets of the home country. Imperialism thus generated new identities and conflict by classifying people and distinguishing between them— between rulers and ruled and between subject peoples themselves. At the same time, the contradictions inherent in this inequality and limitation on freedom became increasingly clear to subject peoples as they began to assimilate modern ideas and values. By the early twentieth century, the growing awareness of this system and its inherent contradictions helped foster public resistance to imperialism and would pave the way for eventual independence.

The Challenges of Postimperialism

Despite the power of empires to extend their control over much of the world, their time eventually came to an end. In Latin America, where European imperialism first emerged, Napoleon's invasion of Spain and Portugal in 1807–1808 led to turmoil in the colonies and a series of wars for independence, which freed most of the region by 1826. In Africa and Asia, where imperialism reached its zenith only in the nineteenth century, decolonization came after World War II. Numerous independence movements emerged within the Asian and African colonies, catalyzed by the weakened positions of the imperial powers and promoted by a Western-educated indigenous leadership able to articulate nationalist goals and organize resistance. Many imperial powers resisted bitterly: Portugal, for example, did not fully withdraw from Africa until 1975. Hong Kong was returned to China by the United Kingdom in 1997. For the most part, however, colonies in Africa and Asia gained independence in the 1950s and 1960s (Figure 9.1).

The elimination of imperialism, however, did not mean a sudden end to the problems of the newly industrializing and less-developed countries. Over the past half century, these countries have continued to struggle with political, social, and economic challenges to development and stability, freedom and equality. In many cases, these problems are a legacy of imperial rule, although in other cases they stem from particular domestic and international factors that have developed in the years since independence.

Building State Capacity and Autonomy

One central problem that many newly industrializing and less-developed countries have faced in the years after imperialism has been the difficulty in creating effective political institutions. In Chapter 2, we distinguished between weak states and strong states and noted that many scholars look at state power by distinguishing between state capacity and state autonomy. Recall that capacity refers to the ability of a state to achieve basic policy tasks, and autonomy refers to the ability of a state to act independently of the public. Both are necessary to carry out policy, and both have been difficult for the newly industrializing and less-developed countries to achieve.

In terms of capacity, states are frequently unable to perform many of the basic tasks expected by the public, such as creating infrastructure, providing education and health care, or delivering other public goods. This lack of capacity can often be traced to the absence of a professional bureaucracy to run the government. The foreigners who ran the imperial bureaucracies in the colonies typically left upon independence, precluding a gradual transition to a local bureaucracy. These initial problems of capacity have since been fur-

Figure 9.1 THE DECOLONIZATION OF AFRICA

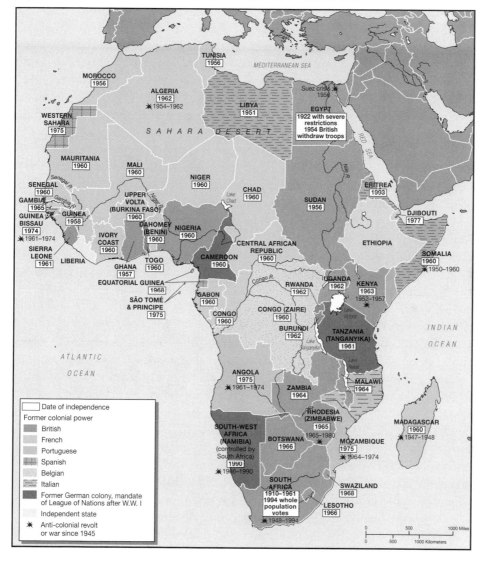

ther exacerbated by the politicization of the state; in many cases, the bureaucracy has become an important source of jobs, resources, and benefits that are doled out by political leaders as a way to solidify control. Civil servants thus become part of a system of clientelism, patrimonialism, and rent seeking, in which they assist in providing goods and benefits to certain members of the public in return for political support.[5]

Autonomy has been equally problematic in the postimperialist world. On the surface, many newly industrializing and less-developed countries appear to be highly autonomous, able to function without consulting the population at all. The prevalence of authoritarianism in much of the newly industrializing and less-developed world only seems to reinforce this impression. Indeed, many of these states can repress or terrorize the population as they see fit, but this autonomy is quite limited, built largely (and dangerously) around force alone. In many cases, the state is not a highly independent actor, but is instead penetrated by actors and organizations that see the state as a resource to be exploited rather than a tool for achieving policy. Frequently, the result of such penetration is high levels of corruption—what has been termed "kleptocracy," or government by theft. For example, during military rule in Nigeria in the 1990s, officials stole more than $1 billion from the state treasury. To be fair, not all newly industrializing and less-developed countries are corrupt; Chile, Singapore, and Botswana all rank among the least corrupt countries in the world. However, many more are concentrated toward the highly corrupt end of the spectrum. On a scale of 1 to 10, with 10 being the least corrupt and 1 the most corrupt, around three-quarters of the countries scoring 4 or below are newly industrializing and less-developed countries (the remaining quarter are communist or postcommunist). Table 9.2 lists a selection of countries and their scores on this corruption index.

In addition to constraints on autonomy from domestic sources, the states of the newly industrializing and less-developed world are often also limited in their autonomy by international factors. Less-developed and newly industrializing countries are subject to pressure from other, more powerful states and international actors such as the United Nations, the World Bank, multinational corporations, and nongovernmental organizations such as Amnesty International and the Red Cross. Frequently wielding much greater economic and political power than the states themselves, these actors can significantly influence the policies of these countries, shaping their military and diplomatic alliances, trade relations, local economies, and domestic laws.

These constraints on state autonomy and capacity have clear implications for freedom and equality. A state with weak capacity and autonomy is unlikely to be able to establish the rule of law. Laws will not be respected by the public if the state itself is unwilling or unable to enforce and abide by them. Freedom is threatened by conflict and unpredictability, which in turn hinder economic development. A volatile environment and the absence of basic public goods such as roads or education will dissuade long-term investment. Wealth flows primarily into the hands of those who control the state, generating a high degree of inequality. There is no clear regime, and no rules or norms for how politics is to be played.

Unfortunately, where instability is so high, there is often only one institution with a great deal of autonomy and capacity: the military. Where states

Table 9.2 Corruption Index, 2004	
Country	**Score** (10 = least corrupt)
Finland	9.7
United Kingdom	8.6
Canada	8.5
United States	7.5
France	7.1
Japan	6.9
Botswana	6.0
Taiwan	5.6
South Africa	4.6
South Korea	4.5
Mauritius	4.1
Brazil	3.9
Mexico	3.6
China	3.4
Iran	2.9
India	2.8
Mozambique	2.8
Russia	2.8
Philippines	2.6
Uganda	2.6
Ecuador	2.4
Venezuela	2.3
Bolivia	2.2
Kenya	2.1
Côte d'Ivoire	2.0
Angola	2.0
Indonesia	2.0
Nigeria	1.6

The corruption index is based on national surveys regarding the overall extent of corruption (size and frequency of bribes) in the public and political sectors.

Source: Transparency International.

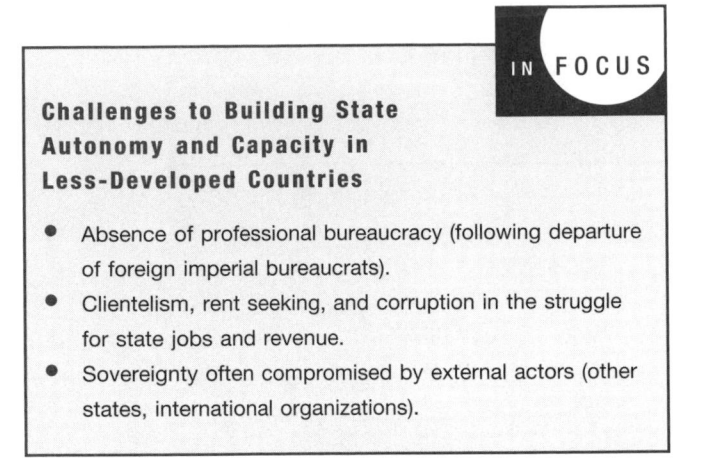

IN FOCUS

Challenges to Building State Autonomy and Capacity in Less-Developed Countries

- Absence of professional bureaucracy (following departure of foreign imperial bureaucrats).
- Clientelism, rent seeking, and corruption in the struggle for state jobs and revenue.
- Sovereignty often compromised by external actors (other states, international organizations).

are weak, military forces often step in and take control of the government themselves, either to stave off disorder or simply to take a turn at draining the state. Military rule has been common in the newly industrializing and less-developed countries. Even where it has ended, as in many countries of Latin America, the military often remains a powerful actor in politics.

Forging Social Identities

In the aftermath of colonialism, many less-developed and newly industrializing countries have struggled with the challenge of forging a single nation out of highly diverse societies. Initially, where centralized political authority did not exist prior to imperialism, societies were not homogenized. Their diversity became problematic when imperial powers began categorizing societal groups and establishing political boundaries and economic and social hierarchies. Migration within empires further complicated these relations. Upon independence, several problems rose to the surface.

First, group divisions often have economic implications, just as they did under colonial rule. Some ethnic or religious groups favored under colonialism continue to monopolize wealth in the postindependence society. For example, in Malaysia and Indonesia, ethnic Chinese continue to hold a disproportionate share of national wealth, generating resentment among non-Chinese groups. Similarly, in Kenya, Uganda, and Fiji, the Indian population, originally brought in by the British as indentured labor, came to control a large portion of the business sector. The resulting outbursts of violence appear on the surface to be ethnic in nature, but in fact their origins are economic. In 1972, the Ugandan government under the notorious dictator Idi Amin expelled all Indians from the country, seizing their lands and businesses. Indigenous populations are among the poorest across Latin America, a situation that sparked the Chiapas uprising in southern Mexico in 1995 and antigovernment protests in Bolivia in 2005. Many civil conflicts in the less-developed and newly industrializing countries are driven in large part by economic concerns overlaid onto ethnic or religious differences.

Second, ethnic and religious divisions can similarly complicate politics. In countries where populations are heterogeneous, the battle for political power often falls along ethnic or religious lines, with each side seeking to gain control over the state in order to serve its own group's particular ends. Each ethnic or religious group competes for its share of public goods or other benefits from the state. This struggle may foster authoritarian rule, for a group that gains control over the state may be unwilling to relinquish or share it, and no one group can be confident that it could successfully dominate politics simply through the democratic process. As a result, where ethnic or religious divisions are strong, we often see the state dominated by one group while others are effectively frozen out of the political process.[6] In some countries, a majority or plurality may dominate politics, as people of European origin do in Mexico, while the minority indigenous population has little political power. In still other cases, a minority may dominate a much larger minority; in Iraq, where the majority population is of the Shia sect of Islam, the ruling Ba'ath Party was dominated by members of the minority Sunni sect. With the overthrow of Saddam Hussein, conflict has emerged not just with the occupying forces, but between Sunni and Shia over the future control of the country.

The economic and political difficulties that arise from such social divisions make the creation of a single national identity difficult. Amid such ethnic and religious diversity, many populations are much less inclined to see the postcolonial state as a true representation of their group's wishes, and states themselves have little beyond the initial struggle for independence on which to build a shared political identity for their people. At an extreme level, these ethnic and religious conflicts may take on the goal of secessionism, as disaffected groups seek to create their own autonomous or wholly independent territories. This is true of the minority Kurds in Iraq, many of whom seek an independent Kurdistan.

Gender is another important social issue in less-developed and newly industrializing countries. Gender roles imposed or reinforced by colonial rule persisted in many societies following independence, reinforced by rapid urbanization and the commercialization of agriculture, which tended to favor male labor and property rights. Because males are privileged in this way, society tends to view males as a more valuable addition to a family than females, an attitude that can limit women's access to important resources such as education and, consequently, greater economic advancement. At an extreme level, this favoritism can be deadly, taking the form of female infanticide. Estimates indicate that in India and

IN FOCUS

**Challenges to Building a
Unified Nation-State**

- Arbitrary political boundaries imposed by imperial powers.
- Ethnic and religious divisions among different groups in heterogeneous societies (often exacerbated by economic inequality).

INSTITUTIONS IN

ACTION

IMPERIALISM, ISLAM, AND MODERNITY

Given the current focus on the Middle East, it can be instructive to look at the development of politics and faith in the region in light of our discussion of imperialism and its impact on social, political, and economic institutions. We cannot do justice to such a long and complex history in such a short space, but we can draw out a few important elements. Islam was founded in what is present-day Saudi Arabia in 610 c.e. by the prophet Muhammad and quickly spread as part of an Islamic empire. Within a century, this empire had spread across the Middle East and North Africa into central Asia and southern Europe. From the fourteenth century onward, the Ottomans, Turkish rulers who gained control over the lands of Islam, extended their empire further into Asia and Europe. During its 600-year rule, the Ottoman Empire was one of the largest and most technically sophisticated empires in the world—a reminder that imperial power did not always flow from Europe outward.

Eventually however, the Ottoman Empire began to decline in power, for reasons that are varied and contested. These include corruption, the decline of effective leadership, and the absence of a strong middle class or property rights. It has also been suggested that the consolidation of Islam under the Ottomans stunted religious and intellectual diversity, limiting outside ideas or challenges. Others suggest that it was not Ottoman authoritarianism, but rather the empire's later decline, that led to this intellectual orthodoxy. Interestingly, these arguments can be compared to similar processes in China around the same time. Whatever the reasons, by the eighteenth century, the Ottoman Empire retreated in the face of sustained European pressure, which was followed by internal revolts by its subject peoples in the following century. When the empire finally collapsed in the aftermath of World War I, the remaining Ottoman lands were divided into numerous new states in the Middle East, including Turkey, Iraq, Saudi Arabia, Syria, and Lebanon. Much of the former empire came under the direct or indirect control of Britain and France.

Many intellectuals in the Middle East questioned why their part of the world, once dominant in the region, had fallen behind the West, and what could be done about it. This debate resulted in a period of modernist reform, within which emerged the concept of *salafism* in the late nineteenth century. Salafism (based on the Arabic word *salaf,* meaning "predecessors") sought to revitalize the institutions of the Middle East by returning Islam to its original spirit and intent while selectively borrowing Western institutions, such as democracy and republicanism. This would create a modern faith and society where reason and religion would be reconciled. These views were not necessarily pro-Western, but rather a response to Western imperialism, a way in which imperialism could be resisted and Islamic beliefs restored to their original intent. After World War I, salafism grew more hostile toward the West as imperialism deepened and societies in the Middle East experienced a bewildering array of changes. These included direct European control or local dictatorships backed by the European powers, competing ideologies and emergent nationalism, rapid changes in economic practices, and shifts and disruptions in traditional identities. For many, these were sources of confusion, humiliation, and spiritual emptiness. Faith in Western institutions declined, and salafists came to reject them as contrary to Islam. In addition, salafist thought was influenced by a more conservative version of Islam that dominates Saudi Arabia, known as *Wahhabism*. Rather than adapt their societies to modernity, as was the original intent, these salafists viewed Western modernity as alien, corrupt, and a rejection of God's authority. Islam became a center of resistance to this encroachment.

Most salafists are thus bound by a desire to resist Western culture and society by returning to what they see as the original spirit of Islam. For these practitioners, the emphasis is overwhelmingly social, focused on encouraging proper behavior. However, by the 1930s, a more politically oriented offshoot of salafism emerged, which explicitly sought to place Islam as the center of regime and state—what we would think of as fundamentalism. The main group behind this movement, the Muslim Brotherhood in Egypt, captured this idea in their slogan "The Koran is our constitution." Further offshoots of this fundamentalism came in the work of Sayyid Qutb (1906–1966). Qutb argued not only that Western institutions such as nationalism and democracy denied the sovereignty of God, but that Muslim states and societies themselves had entered into a period of *jahiliyya,* or ignorance, akin to the time before the Prophet. This notion of jahiliyya mirrored Marx's idea of false consciousness: people had become blinded to the truth through the corrupt practices of the West. Qutb thus argued that such people or leaders were not "true" Muslims, having strayed from the path of Islam. Like Lenin, Qutb called for a vanguard to resist this ignorance, to wage war (jihad) and destroy the enemies of Islam.*

Qutb's ideas were far from mainstream salafism, and their radicalism would inspire unsuccessful armed resistance against Middle Eastern governments. Qutb himself was eventually executed by the Egyptian government, and Islamic fundamentalists in many countries came to repudiate his views. During the 1980s, with the war in Afghanistan, these ideas took another turn. Jihad against the "near enemy"—the governments of the Middle East—would be ineffective so long as they were propped up by the "far enemy"—the United States and its allies. Jihad must therefore be used beyond the Middle East to set the stage for revolution in the Muslim world. This became the logic of bin Laden and his followers for September 11. This *jihad* approach is a far cry from the original ideas a century earlier, and in this change can be seen the tension of imperialism and its aftermath.

*See Sayyid Qutb, *Milestones* (Indianapolis: American Trust Publishers, 1990).

China, thousands of baby girls are killed each year, and an unknown number of female fetuses are aborted once their sex has been determined by ultra-sound examination. This has led to a gender imbalance in both countries. It has been argued that this imbalance has dangerous implications, creating a surplus of unmarried men that will foster more violence, authoritarianism, and perhaps international conflict.[7]

We might conclude that sexist institutions in these countries are a result of imperialism. But the situation is more complicated than that. Imperialism also brought with it many liberal notions of female autonomy, which these countries have since sought to reconcile with more traditional cultural values. For example, the rise of Islamic fundamentalism in countries such as Iran has been strongly supported by some women who view feminism as another example of foreign values being imposed on them by the advanced democracies. For other women, however, such fundamentalism can deny them their basic freedoms—education, careers, individual autonomy. For men, too, industrialization and urbanization have often meant a loss of traditional roles, while new opportunities are circumscribed by a lack of educational or economic opportunities. This can lead to marginalization and humiliation, the tinder of domestic and international conflict.

Generating Economic Growth

It is economic growth that attracts the most focus among those who study the less-developed and newly industrializing countries. Indeed, when we think of development, typically it is economic progress that comes to mind. Because of imperialism, rather than undergoing economic modernization on their own terms, these countries experienced rapid changes directed by the colonial powers: their economic development was geared to suit European needs and tailored to provide specific goods to specific external markets. Their experience is a far cry from those of Europe or North America, where economic development spurred by internal needs took place over the course of several centuries.

As a result, upon independence, many of these countries found themselves in a continued state of economic dependency on the former colonial powers. Language ties, infrastructure, and production all favored the continuation of these relationships. But such dependent relationships did not bode well for long-term development, since they stressed the production of agricultural and other basic commodities in return for finished products. The production of basic commodities does not require high-skilled labor, nor does it promise large profits in return; if anything, this form of economic production is much more unstable, subject to uncontrollable factors such as the weather or unexpected changes in the global market. For many less-developed countries, this unequal relationship was simply a new, indirect form of imperialism, or what has been called **neocolonialism**. Breaking this cycle of dependent development was thus the greatest concern for the less-developed countries following independence.

This resulted in two distinct economic policies that were applied throughout the less-developed world.[8] The first, known as **import substitution**, is a mercantilist idea that uses the state to create more positive conditions for the development of local industry. The logic behind import substitution is straightforward. Countries restrict imports, with tariff or nontariff barriers. This in turn helps spur demand for local alternatives. New businesses to fill this demand could be built with state funds by creating subsidized or parastatal (partially state-owned) industries. Patents and intellectual property rights could also be weakly enforced to tap into foreign innovations. Eventually, these firms would develop the productive capacity to compete domestically and internationally, and trade barriers could be lifted. Following World War II, import substitution was commonly used across Latin America and was also taken up in Africa and parts of Asia. For example, in Brazil in the 1970s, the government attempted to foster the creation of a domestic computer industry by erecting tariff barriers and supporting the development of local producers.

How successful was import substitution? Most observers have since concluded that it did not produce the benefits expected and may have set back economic development in these countries. Some have described import substitution as creating a kind of "hothouse economy." Insulated from the global economy, these firms could dominate the local market, but lacking competition, they were much less innovative or efficient than their international competitors, and they tended to draw money from the state rather than generate profits. The idea that these economies would eventually be opened up to the outside world became hard to envision; the harsh climate of the international market would quickly kill off these less competitive firms. This was true, for example, of the Brazilian computer industry.

Import substitution thus resulted in economies with large industries reliant on the state for economic support and unable to compete in the international market. These firms became a drain on state treasuries, compounding the problem of international debt in these countries, for states had to borrow internationally to build and subsidize their industries. Uncompetitiveness was compounded by debt, leading to economic stagnation (Table 9.3).

Not all less-developed countries pursued import substitution. Over the past several decades, the world has witnessed the rise of "Asian tigers"—Hong Kong, South Korea, Taiwan, and Singapore, with Thailand, Malaysia, and Indonesia often touted as the next wave—countries that achieved astounding levels of growth within a generation. Many observers have attributed their

Table 9.3 Import Substitution versus Export-Oriented Industrialization

Country	Economic System	GDP Per Capita (PPP, U.S. $) 1960	2002	Per Capita Annual Growth Rate, 1975-2002 (percent)
Ghana	Import substitution	1,049	2,130	0.3
Brazil	Import substitution	1,404	7,770	0.8
Argentina	Import substitution	3,381	10,880	0.4
South Korea	Export-oriented	690	16,950	6.1
Thailand	Export-oriented	985	7,010	5.2
Malaysia	Export-oriented	1,783	9,120	4.0

Source: *Human Development Report* 2004.

success to cultural factors, claiming the superiority of a Confucian work ethic, but others have asserted that the credit goes to their states, which pursued very different economic policies than those found in Africa or Latin America.

Among the Asian tigers, import substitution was discarded in favor of what has been termed **export-oriented industrialization**, which seeks to directly integrate into the global economy by concentrating on economic production that can find a niche in international markets. Like import substitution, export-oriented industrialization is mercantilist in the strong role played by the state in promoting domestic growth.

In Asia, countries that pursued an export-oriented strategy sought out technologies and developed industries that were focused specifically on export, capitalizing on what is known as the "product life cycle." Initially, the innovator of a good produces it for the domestic market and exports it to the rest of the world. As this product spreads, other countries find ways to make the same good more cheaply or more efficiently, eventually exporting their own version back to the country that originated the product. By this time, the originator country has moved on to a new innovation. Export-oriented growth seeks to capitalize on the product life cycle by seeking out these advantages, embracing technological advances in order to create new exports. Thus, in South Korea, initial exports focused on basic technologies such as textiles and shoes, but eventually moved into more complex areas such as automobiles and computers. This policy was not without its own problems; countries that pursued export-oriented industrialization also faced high levels of government subsidies and tariff barriers. Yet overall, this strategy of development has led to much higher levels of economic development. Some export-oriented countries, such as South Korea and Thailand, in 1960 had per capita GDPs far below those of many Latin American and even some African countries; but by the mid-1990s, they had come to far surpass many of their import-substituting rivals.

Why did some countries choose import substitution while others opted for export-oriented industrialization? One important factor was geopolitical. In Latin America, import substitution was influenced by the region's economic domination by the United States. During the Great Depression, Latin America's market for raw materials and agricultural exports to the United States dried up, devastating many of its economies; later, during World War II, although markets for some exports improved, finished goods became scarce as the United States directed its industrial production toward the war effort. As a result of these dislocations, Latin American scholars and leaders concluded that import substitution would be a means to insulate their countries from this unpredictable and, in their eyes, neocolonial relationship. And in other parts of the world, import substitution was seen as a way to resist Western domination and ensure greater equality among the citizens by giving the state an important role in directing the economy and redistributing income. India became well known for its so-called "license Raj," or bureaucratic control over the economy, while in Iran, the 1979 revolution led to widespread nationalization and state control over the economy.

In East Asia, however, development strategies were directly influenced by the Cold War and the role of the United States in this struggle. Backed by extensive American financial and technical support, many East Asian states specifically developed export-oriented industries; they were encouraged to tap into the American market as a way to industrialize their economies while protecting their own markets. The United States tolerated these more mercantilist policies as the price to pay for drawing these countries closer to the United States and preventing the spread of communism in the region. In short, the specific regional and geopolitical contexts of Latin America and Asia—and their countries' relationships with the United States in particular—influenced the paths of development they took.[9]

In recent years, both import substitution and export-oriented industrialization have been challenged. Although import substitution has long been criticized by liberals as inefficient and prone to corruption, the downturn of many Asian economies in the 1990s also led to critiques of export-oriented industrialization. In the wake of these economic difficulties, many less-developed and newly industrializing countries have adopted more liberal economic policies, often at the behest of the advanced democracies or international agencies. These policies of liberalization (often known as **structural adjustment programs**) have typically required privatizing state-run firms, ending subsidies, reducing tariff barriers, shrinking the size of the state, and welcoming

IN FOCUS

Three Paths to Economic Growth

Import substitution	Based on mercantilism.
	State plays a strong role in the economy.
	Tariffs or nontariff barriers are used to restrict imports.
	State actively promotes domestic production, sometimes creating state-owned businesses in developing industries.
	Criticized for creating "hothouse economies," with large industries reliant on the state for support and unable to compete in the international market.
Export-oriented industrialization	Based on mercantilism.
	State plays a strong role in the economy.
	Tariff barriers are used to protect domestic industries.
	Economic production is focused on industries that have a niche in the international market.
	Seeks to integrate directly into the global economy.
	Has generally led to a higher level of economic development than import substitution.
Structural adjustment	Based on liberalism.
	State involvement is reduced as the economy is opened up.
	Foreign investment is encouraged.
	Often follows import substitution.
	Criticized as a tool of neocolonialism and for its failure in most cases to bring substantial economic development.

foreign investment. These reforms are controversial for both scholars and those who experience the reforms, and their benefits have been mixed. We will discuss this in greater detail when we consider future directions for economic prosperity in the poorer countries.

Prospects for Democracy and Development

It is unclear where the less-developed and newly industrializing countries are heading in the new millennium. Some of these countries have managed to develop a mix of institutions that are providing greater prosperity and/or democracy for their citizens. Many others have failed to generate much freedom or equality. In these cases, institutions are weak and in turmoil, and people often feel marginalized, humiliated, and powerless. This can be the source of domestic conflict—civil war, military coups, genocide. It can also spill over into terrorism, both domestic and international. If we want to avert such disasters and help to foster some mix of freedom and equality that will generate prosperity, how can these goals be realized? There are no certainties, but scholars point to several possible paths.

Rebuilding State Power

State capacity, as noted earlier in this chapter, is one vital area that shapes both freedom and equality. In the past, international organizations and the governments of less-developed and newly industrializing countries often did not concern themselves with the idea of an efficient and efficacious state; instead, states that were wasteful, corrupt, and mismanaged were tolerated or even promoted. These states in turn created a risky environment for entrepreneurialism, fostered kleptocratic policies and political instability, and led to large (if weak) states that crowded out the private sector, civil society, and other organizations that promoted the public good. Aid and loans tended to provide little lasting benefit under these conditions.

As a result, over the last twenty years, liberal structural adjustment policies promoted by the West have favored "rolling back" these states by privatizing industry and reducing the size of the bureaucracy. Expectations were that a smaller state would mean a more vibrant market and society. But in recent years, it has become clear that simply rolling back state power does not in and of itself generate stability—indeed, the opposite is often the case. Effective development and participation that reach the majority of society require the rule of law as a basic foundation, and the rule of law requires a state that can generate and enforce those institutions. Thus, states need to be reformed not just in terms of strength, but also in terms of *scope*—that is, the kinds of things they take responsibility for. In certain areas, the scope of the state may need to be reduced, as in regard to permitting and licensing; in other areas, it may need to be increased and improved, as in regard to education and health care. Such reforms may require not an overall reduction in state strength, but rather its increase and redirection toward different goals. It is thus not the mere improvement of capacity that is important, but toward what end that capacity is directed.[10]

Identifying the need for and nature of state reform does not tell us how to achieve it. How does one make good government, weed out corruption, make certain that laws are enforced and enforced fairly, and create a state bureaucracy that has the expertise and independence to enact and enforce policy? Unfortunately, policy makers are less certain in this area.

One important suggestion has been to directly involve local actors in the reform process. This may seem obvious, but in recent decades, state reform in less-developed or newly industrialized countries tended to be dictated from the outside, with plans and experts brought in from the West to design and implement change. However, these changes were often drafted as "one size fits all" programs, created and implemented by consultants with little knowledge of local conditions, cultures, histories, or elites. When this is the case, even well-intentioned reforms tend to be quickly sloughed off or subverted by conditions on the ground—consistent with our understanding of institutions, which tend to be resistant to change. In a telling example, in the aftermath of the Iraq war, members of the U.S. military decided that the Iraqi traffic code needed to be reformed. One officer put in charge of this task provided the traffic code from his home state of Maryland, which he believed could simply be transplanted without Iraqi input or consideration of the local conditions. As one might imagine, this was not a success.[11] State capacity can also be improved by increasing oversight and participation by the citizenry in policy formulation and implementation, often through some form of devolution.[12] Both of these policies, however, require a state with a modicum of capacity and autonomy; where such elements are lacking, such as in failed states, there are no institutions left to reform.

Supporting Civil Society

Administration may be the foundation of economic and political development, but, as already indicated, of equal importance is the role of the public. In this regard, scholars often speak of **civil society**, which we defined in Chapter 6 as organized life outside of the state. Civil society binds people together, creating a web of interests that cut across class, religion, ethnicity, and other divisions; forms a bulwark through activism and organization against the expansion of state power that might threaten democracy; and inculcates a sense of democratic politics based on interaction, negotiation, consensus, and compromise. Within most less-developed and newly industrializing countries, civil society is weak. Individuals tend to be divided by ethnic, religious, economic, or social boundaries; what sporadic or spontaneous public activity exists does not help generate lasting community institutions. The state is also hampered by this lack of civil society, without which it can become enmeshed in clientelist relationships that prevent the formation of policies that serve society as a whole.

As in the case of administrative reform, building civil society has become a focal point for scholars and political actors involved in development. No longer is the state seen as the sole instrument for democracy and development; public activity is now viewed as a vital part of the equation. A first step in the development of civil society is civic education, in which communities learn their democratic rights and how to use those rights to shape government policy. Beyond education, organizational skills must also be strengthened so that the public is able to mobilize effectively and make its voice heard. These efforts need to go hand in hand with state reform. As mentioned earlier, state changes require participation not just from local political elites, but from the public as well. Moreover, where civil society is built in the absence of a state that can process their desires and demands, the result can be frustration and greater instability.

Central in this effort are **nongovernmental organizations (NGOs)**, which are national and international groups, independent of any state, that pursue policy objectives and foster public participation. Although many of the most prominent NGOs, such as Doctors without Borders or Amnesty International, originated in the advanced democracies, a vast array of local organizations have been created and staffed by citizens of the poorer countries themselves. In less-developed and newly industrializing countries, women are particularly active in the NGO movement. NGOs not only create the opportunity for the development of civil society, but also enable underrepresented segments of society to organize and expand their rights.

In recent years, NGOs have played a powerful role in many less-developed and newly industrializing countries, tackling a range of issues, including human rights, the environment, gender, health, minority rights, and poverty. Their work has been supported in part by foreign aid that was traditionally directed primarily at states. The efforts of NGOs to link up with other NGOs in other less-developed, postcommunist, or advanced democratic countries have given birth to a network of citizen initiatives. Some go so far as to view the spread of NGOs as a sign of an emergent global civil society that functions beyond the limits of any one state, something we will discuss in the next chapter.

Others, however, are critical of such policies. Some see in them a kind of neocolonial domination of the less-developed countries by Western NGOs that bring with them particular agendas of social, political, and economic change. It has also been argued that Western NGO promotion tends to support a few high-profile organizations to the neglect of many other groups that may be less formalized but no less important. As with state reform, civil society needs to be owned and sustained locally.[13]

Promoting Economic Prosperity

Economic prosperity is the third crucial need within the less-developed world. Above all, the diverse countries that fall into this category are defined by their lack of economic development and the pressing problems of poverty and inequality. Over the past half century, state-driven policies sought to promote growth; though some were successful, many others resulted in further debt and economic stagnation. Are there alternatives to these traditional models?

As in the case of states and society, solutions may be found by concentrating on people, providing policies that can build from existing institutions to empower individuals economically. In all of these cases, the starting point is the **informal economy**, a segment of the economy that is not regulated or taxed by the state. Typically, the informal economy is dominated by the self-employed or by small enterprises, such as an individual street vendor or a family that makes or repairs goods out of its home. In some cases, the informal economy may contribute up to 60 percent of a country's GDP, though by its very nature an informal economy is hard to measure. Women often play a large role in this economy: according to some research studies, in many less-developed countries up to 90 percent of women working outside the agricultural sector are part of the informal economy. The informal economy can exist for many reasons. Corrupt and highly bureaucratic state controls over the economy can deter individuals from starting formal businesses; in addition, certain social institutions, such as the role of women in the workplace, may discourage employment outside of the home. This is true, for example, of many Muslim women in Nigeria, who rely on home businesses to support their families.

Although the informal economy represents an important source of employment in less-developed countries, it has its limitations. First, by existing outside of the authority of the state, it does not generate tax revenues that could be spent on infrastructure or social welfare. Second, without regulation, informal workers are not subject to labor laws or state employment benefits. Third, and perhaps most important, informal economic activity is so small that it often suffers from financial problems, such as a lack of the capital necessary to expand. For example, many self-employed individuals must rely on loans to purchase the supplies or tools necessary for their business; yet given the small amount of funds needed and the absence of any collateral to secure such loans, banks are usually unwilling to extend credit to such entrepreneurs. Individuals are thus forced to turn to loan sharks, who charge extremely high rates of interest, eating up virtually all the profits that the individual then makes. Businesses operating in the informal economy are thus unable to grow into larger businesses and thereby to enter the formal economy.

There have been two important approaches to breaking this cycle. The first, pioneered by Peruvian economist Hernando De Soto, emphasizes the need to develop stronger property rights in the less-developed world. In all informal economies, De Soto argues, there is a vast amount of "dead capital"—land, homes, businesses—that lack basic property rights such as clear title to ownership. Codifying existing informal institutions and ensuring effective state protection of them would allow people to more easily tap into these resources. Formal property rights would allow for the development of credit, as well as allow states to tax and regulate the economy. Here again we see a need for state power to change more in terms of scope than strength.[14]

What of those who lack any capital? A second way to break this cycle is through **microcredit** (also known as **microfinance**), a system that involves not an individual lender and borrower, but borrowing groups made up of several individuals. Loans at reasonable interest rates are first provided to some of the group's members; once these borrowers (the majority of them women) begin to make loan repayments, funds become available to make loans to the next set of participants. Groups thus serve as a means of support and collateral, a combination of business and civil society. Microcredit systems were first developed in Bangladesh by the Grameen Bank, which has since become world-famous for its innovative strategy. These loans are quite small: in Bangladesh, Grameen Bank loans can be as small as $1; the average loan is only around $100. The system of group lending and support produces extremely high rates of repayment, in turn generating new sources of revenue that can be loaned out to new groups. Since its creation in the 1980s, microcredit has spread throughout less-developed, newly industrializing, and even advanced democratic countries, reaching over 80 million people. In recent years and in response to criticisms of more traditional lending practices, international aid has been channeled more toward microcredit as part of the greater emphasis on civil society.[15]

In Sum: The Challenges of Development

The material we have studied in this chapter can be applied across politically, economically, and socially diverse parts of the world. Although newly industrializing and less-developed countries differ in their levels of development, almost all share the legacies of imperial rule. The fusion of local institutions with those of the imperial power created challenges as these countries sought to chart their own independent courses. Weak states; conflicts over ethnicity, nation, religion, and gender; and incomplete and distorted forms of industrialization all contributed to instability, authoritarianism, economic stagnation, and overall low levels of freedom and equality. The newly industrializing countries seem to have overcome many of these obstacles, but it is unclear whether their strategies and experiences provide lessons that can be easily applied elsewhere in the world.

In the past, most prescriptions for these countries assumed that such solutions must come from the state, for only a centralized institution, it was believed, could amass the power necessary to ensure freedom and equality. Yet in many ways the state in this part of the world became more the problem than the solution, absorbing wealth, functioning in an arbitrary and often ineffective manner, and serving as a source of violent contention between rivals who sought to steal its resources. Thus, some now suggest that solutions should come from the bottom up, through decentralized and locally reformed government, civil society, and financial institutions. Rather than relying on "top-down" efforts to remake institutions, more flexible and modest solutions may be possible. Such plans are much less grandiose, as they rely on no huge projects close to the hearts of politicians and donors. It may also be much harder to evaluate: the impact of a $1 loan is much less easily seen than financial support for a large factory or a rural electrification scheme. Yet its effects may be no less powerful. Even though much of the world remains mired in poverty, instability, and violence, new ways of thinking offer hope for eradicating these problems by helping to forge the policy tools that will enable the citizens of these countries to take control over their own destinies.

NOTES

1. For two excellent studies of imperialism in practice, see L. H. Gann and Peter Duignan, eds., *Imperialism in Africa, 1870–1960* (Cambridge: Cambridge University Press, 1969–75); and Nicolas Tarling, ed., *The Cambridge History of Southeast Asia* (Cambridge: Cambridge University Press, 1992).
2. A general discussion of the impact of colonialism can be found in Paul Cammack, David Pool, and William Tordoff, *Third World Politics: An Introduction* (Baltimore: Johns Hopkins University Press, 1993). See also Philip D. Curtin, *The World and the West: The European Challenge and the Overseas Response in the Age of Empire* (Cambridge: Cambridge University Press, 2000).
3. Georgina Waylen, *Gender in Third World Politics* (Boulder: Lynne Rienner, 1996).
4. For a Marxist analysis of dependent development as it applies to Latin America, see Eduardo H. Galeano, *Open Veins of Latin America: Five Centuries of the Pillage of a Continent*, trans. Cedric Belfrage (New York: Monthly Review Press, 1998).
5. See Joel S. Migdal, *Strong Societies and Weak States: State-Society Relations and State Capabilities in the Third World* (Princeton: Princeton University Press, 1988).
6. For a discussion of these issues, see Dennis L. Thompson and Dov Ronen, eds., *Ethnicity, Politics, and Development* (Boulder: Lynne Rienner, 1986).
7. Valerie M. Hudson and Andrea M. Den Boer, *Bare Branches: The Security Implications of Asia's Surplus Male Population* (Cambridge, MA: MIT Press, 2005).
8. For a discussion of different paths of industrialization, see Stephan Haggard, *Pathways from the Periphery: The Politics of Growth in Newly Industrializing Countries* (Ithaca, NY: Cornell University Press, 1990).
9. Peter Evans, "Class, State, and Dependence in East Asia: Lessons for Latin Americanists," in Frederic C. Deyo, ed., *The Political Economy of the New Asian Industrialism* (Ithaca, NY: Cornell University Press, 1987), 203–226.

10. Francis Fukuyama, *State Building: Governance and World Order in the 21st Century* (Ithaca, NY: Cornell University Press, 2004).

11. William Langewiesche, "Welcome to the Green Zone," *The Atlantic Monthly* 294, no. 4 (November 2004): 60–88.

12. See the Columbia University Center for Earth Science Network's "Online Sourcebook on Decentralization and Local Government" at www.ciesin.org/decentralization/.

13. Marina Ottaway and Theresa Chung, "Toward a New Paradigm," *Journal of Democracy* 10, no. 4 (1999): 99–113.

14. Hernando De Soto, *The Mystery of Capital: Why Capitalism Triumphs in the West and Fails Everywhere Else* (New York: Basic Books, 2000).

15. See the Microcredit Summit Campaign at www.microcreditsummit.org, as well as the website of the Grameen Bank at www.grameen-info.org.

10 GLOBALIZATION

The central theme of this textbook has been the struggle to balance freedom and equality. Market forces can generate tension in this relationship; when societies clash over how to reconcile these two values, states must confront these problems using their capacity to generate and enforce policy. Democratic institutions presume that freedom and equality are best reconciled through public participation, whereas authoritarian and totalitarian systems withhold such rights. The variety of institutional tools available has led to a diverse political world, where freedom and equality are combined and balanced in many different ways. Here, in essence, is the core of comparative politics: the study of how freedom and equality are reconciled around the world.

But over the past few years, this study has taken on a new dimension, one more international in scope. Of course, domestic politics has always been shaped by international forces, such as war and trade, empires and colonies, migration and the spread of ideas. But to some observers, this interconnection between countries is changing in its scope, depth, and speed. Linkages between states, societies, and economies are intensifying, and at an increasingly rapid pace, challenging long-standing institutions, assumptions, and norms. This process, still ill defined and unclear, is commonly known as **globalization**, a term that fills some with a sense of optimism and others with anxiety and dread. Although the extent of globalization and its long-term impact remains unclear, behind it lies the sense that the battle over freedom and equality is becoming internationalized, no longer a concern to be solved by each country in its own way. What does this mean for comparative politics?

In this chapter, we will look at the concept of globalization and its potential impact on comparative politics and the ongoing struggle over freedom and equality. We will begin by defining globalization, sorting out what this term means and how we might measure it. Next, we will consider some of the possible effects of globalization and how it may change political, economic, and societal institutions at the domestic level. We will also ask some questions about the progress of globalization—whether it is in fact something fundamentally new, profound, and inevitable. We will then conclude with a discussion of how the old dilemma of freedom and equality may change in a globalized world.

What Is Globalization?

We could argue that we have lived in a globalized world for many thousands of years. Even as early humans dispersed around the world tens of thousands of years ago, they maintained and developed long-distance connections between one another through migration and trade. Such contacts helped spur development through the dissemination of knowledge and innovations; for example, it is speculated that the technology of written language was created independently only three or four times in human history: in the Americas, in Asia, and in the Middle East. All other written languages were essentially modeled after these innovations as the idea of writing things down spread to other communities.[1] Trade routes, too, forged connections between people who were only dimly aware of each other's existence. For example, in the first century C.E., the Romans treasured silk imported from distant China, although they did not fully understand how it was made or where it came from. Were these, then, "globalized" societies?

When we speak about globalization, we don't simply mean international contacts and interaction, which have existed for tens of thousands of years. According to political scientists Robert Keohane and Joseph Nye, one important distinction between globalization and these age-old ties is the fact that many of these longtime relationships were relatively "thin," involving a small number of individuals. Although such connections may have been extensive across a vast region, the connections were not intensive in their volume or personal impact. In contrast, globalization can be viewed as a process by which this web of global connections becomes increasingly "thick," creating an extensive and intensive web of relationships between many people across vast distances. In the twenty-first century, people are not distantly connected by overland routes plied by traders, diplomats, and missionaries; they are directly participating in a vast and complex international network through travel, communication, business, and education. Globalization is a system in which human beings are no longer part of isolated communities that are themselves linked through narrow channels of diplomatic relations or trade (Figure 10.1). Entire societies are now directly "plugged in" to global affairs. Thus, globalization represents a change in human organization and interconnection, but these are a function of those technological changes that make it possible.[2]

Globalization presents a number of potential implications for comparative politics. First, because of the thickening of connections between people

Figure 10.1 **MEASURING GLOBALIZATION: THE GLOBAL TOP 20, 2005**

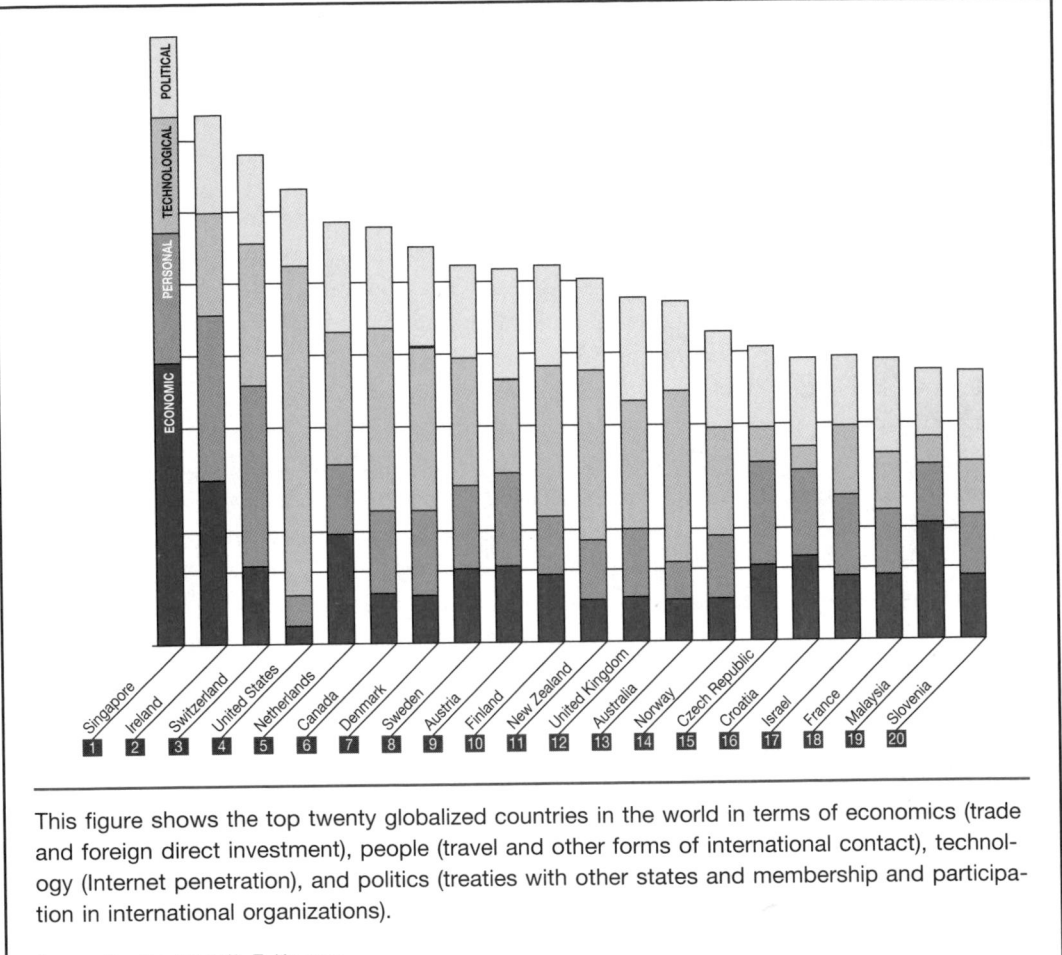

This figure shows the top twenty globalized countries in the world in terms of economics (trade and foreign direct investment), people (travel and other forms of international contact), technology (Internet penetration), and politics (treaties with other states and membership and participation in international organizations).

Source: Foreign Policy/A. T. Kearney.

across countries, globalization breaks down the distinction between international relations and domestic politics, making many aspects of domestic politics subject to global forces. Debates over environmental policy become linked to global warming; struggles over employment are framed by concerns about trade, outsourcing, and immigration; health care is influenced by pandemics like AIDS. As a result, political isolation becomes difficult or even impossible, and the line between domestic and foreign policy is blurred.

Second, globalization can also amplify politics in the other direction, essentially "internationalizing" domestic issues and events. Given that globalization deepens and widens international connections, local events, even small ones, can have ripple effects throughout the world. Computer viruses released in the Philippines can bring down systems in New York City; a panicky stock market in Russia can trigger an economic downturn in Brazil. These interconnections across space are further amplified by the speed of today's world. Whereas technological change once took years or centuries to spread from region to region, today a new software upgrade can be downloaded worldwide simultaneously. The Internet allows the rapid dissemination of news and ideas from every corner of the globe, no matter how remote. The world lives increasingly in the same moment—what happens in one place affects others around the world soon after.

In short, globalization is a process that creates intensive and extensive international connections, which in the process change traditional relationships of time and space. Will globalization overturn or transform the very foundations of politics? Would such a change make the world a better place—more prosperous, stable, and democratic—or just the opposite? And finally, is any of this inevitable? These are big questions of profound significance with little consensus. Let us first consider how we can think about the nature of institutions in a globalizing world.

Institutions and Globalization

We have spoken of globalization as a process, one that creates more extensive and intensive connections across the globe. These changes can in turn change the institutions of economics, politics, and societies. At the start of this textbook, we spoke of institutions as being a key reference point for modern life. Institutions are organizations or patterns of activity that are self-perpetuating and valued for their own sake. The modern world is a world codified by institutions. Institutions such as states, culture, property, and markets establish borders, set boundaries for activity and behavior, and allocate authority, norms, rights, and responsibilities. Moreover, by doing so, they establish local identity and control—a particular state, religion, or set of cultural values holds sway over this land and people, but not over there. Space and time are thus understood and measured through institutions.

The question we now ask is whether this will still be true in the future. It may be that before long, domestic institutions will no longer be the most important actors in people's lives. Long-standing institutions like states, cultures, or political economic systems now face a range of international forces and organizations that transform, challenge, or threaten their traditional roles. Let's look at some of the reasons why this might be the case.

To begin with, globalization is associated with the growing power of a host of nonstate or suprastate entities. Most can be grouped in three categories that we have already touched on in previous chapters: **Multinational corporations (MNCs)**, **nongovernmental organizations (NGOs)**, and **intergovernmental organizations (IGOs)**. While all three organizational forms are decades if not centuries old, the argument is that their role and impact are rapidly expanding as they benefit from and contribute to globalization. MNCs are firms that produce, distribute, and market in more than one country. MNCs, such as Microsoft, wield assets and profits far larger than the gross domestic products (GDPs) of most countries in the world and are able to influence politics, economic developments, and social relations through the goods and services they produce and the wealth at their disposal. NGOs, as we discussed in the last chapter, are national and international groups, independent of any state, that pursue policy objectives and foster public participation. NGOs such as Greenpeace and Amnesty International also wield influence in their ability to shape domestic and international politics by mobilizing public support across the globe. IGOs, groups created by states to serve particular policy ends, include the United Nations, the World Trade Organization, the European Union, and the Organization of American States. IGOs vary widely in their objectives, membership, and powers, but they tend to exert some form of authority over their member states.

In addition to these entities, there are organizations that are largely technological in nature. This is not new; all earlier waves of human interconnection were themselves dependent on technological changes, such as the domestication of plants and animals, the creation of the wheel, seafaring, and the

IN FOCUS

Nonstate Organizations and Globalization

Organization	Definition	Example
Multinational corporations (MNCs)	Firms that produce, distribute, and market their goods or services in more than one country	Microsoft, General Electric
Intergovernmental organizations (IGOs)	Groups created by states to serve particular policy ends	United Nations, European Union
Nongovernmental organizations (NGOs)	National and international groups, independent of any state, that pursue policy objectives and foster public participation	Greenpeace, Red Cross

telegraph. Most recently, globalization has been profoundly influenced by the Internet. Originally created by the U.S. government as a way to decentralize communications in the event of a nuclear war, the Internet has grown far past this initial limited objective to become a means through which people exchange goods and information, much of it beyond the control of any one state or regulatory authority. Unlike MNCs, NGOs, or IGOs, the Internet has little centralization to speak of, and so discussions of authority, sovereignty, and control become problematic. But as technological change facilitates non-state or suprastate actors, these actors in turn tend to foster further techno-logical change.

Are these organizations, whether the UN or the Internet, institutions? This is an important question, for as we have noted, institutionalization carries with it authority and legitimacy. Many would argue that yes, these organiza-tions do have a life of their own. Many MNCs, IGOs, and NGOs are legitimate and highly valued, such that they have become a seemingly indispensable part of the global system. The same could be said of the Internet or other forms of technology, such as satellite television or global positioning systems (GPS). As institutions, then, they carry and can call on a degree of influence and power. This may augment and improve the workings of domestic institutions; it may also conflict with or undermine them. Let us consider this idea fur-ther through the familiar categories of states, economies, and societies.

Political Globalization

In Chapter 2, we noted that in historical terms, the state is relatively new, a form of political organization that emerged only in the past few centuries. Because of their unique organization, states were able to quickly spread across the globe, supplanting all other forms of political organization. Yet we also noted that if states have not always been with us, it then stands to reason that there may come a time when states are no longer the dominant political actor on the face of the earth. States may at some time cease to exist. Some see globalization as the very force that will bring about this dramatic political change, but whether such a change is to be welcomed or feared is uncertain.

At the core of this debate is the fact that globalization and globalized insti-tutions complicate the ability of states to maintain sovereignty. In some cases, this loss of sovereignty is intentional, as states may give up authority to IGOs to gain some benefit or alleviate some existing problem. The European Union is an excellent example of this, though as we have seen, even under these con-ditions sovereignty is often given up reluctantly. In other cases, the loss of sov-ereignty may be unintentional and wholly unwanted. The growth of the Internet, for example, has had important implications for states regarding legal authority in many traditional areas, given the fact that the Internet does not acknowledge domestic boundaries or rules. Thus, software may be easily copied and shared, in spite of property rights or national security restrictions. Similarly, legal restrictions on certain forms of speech can be circumvented in a way in which traditional newspapers or television cannot, through e-mail, websites, or web logs. Future developments, such as electronic currency, may further erode the powers of states by undercutting their ability to print money, levy taxes, or regulate financial transactions—all critical elements of sovereignty.

What do these changes mean for state autonomy and capacity? One possible scenario is that the state will become bound to numerous international institutions that will take on many of the tasks that states normally conduct. In this scenario, a web of organizations, public and private, domestic and international, would shape politics and policy, set standards, and enforce rules on a wide range of issues where states lack effective authority. The rule of law would become less a preserve of individual states than a set of global institutions created for and enforced by a variety of actors.

Under this diffusion of responsibility, sovereignty would decline. States would no longer be able to act independently within their own territory and would be constrained within the international system by their reliance on the globalized world. Even the final preserve of states—the monopoly of violence—may lose its efficacy in a globalized world. Some argue that many of the vital issues that modern-day people face—environmental degradation, drugs, trade, technological innovation—cannot be dealt with through force. One cannot arrest computer viruses or enact sanctions against the hole in the ozone layer, and despite the U.S. call for a "war on drugs" and "war on terror," one cannot declare war in the conventional sense. For globalized states, then, war will become less viable, largely ineffective, and likely to undermine vital international connections. This narrowing of state sovereignty as a result of globalization is what *New York Times* columnist Thomas Friedman has referred to as a "golden straitjacket."[3] In this view, political globalization may bring about a more peaceful world order, constraining the tendencies toward violent conflict by dispersing sovereignty among numerous actors while constraining the capacity and autonomy of states.

It has also been argued that globalization will not only change the utility of force, but also the nature of public participation and democracy. The increasing interconnection between domestic and international institutions makes it more difficult for sovereign actors to function without oversight from other organizations and to hide their actions from others. The development of the International Criminal Court could be seen as an example here, where the enforcement of international laws and judicial authority opens the door to hold states and their leaders accountable for such things as human rights violations. NGOs can play a similarly powerful watchdog role, as such groups as Amnesty International and Transparency International already do. Globalization will thus make politics less opaque and more open to scrutiny to domestic and international communities.

In contrast to these optimistic views, others see political globalization not as a pathway to peace and participation, but as a source of dangerous fragmentation and weakened democracy. First, violence will not lose its utility in the international system as optimists hope; it will simply change form, much as it did when states themselves first appeared. According to this argument, globalization is fostering not only new organizations that may foster cooperation, but also violent international actors that in many ways are the exact opposite of the modern state. These groups are decentralized and flexible, hold no territory and exercise no sovereignty, and are able to draw financial and other support from across the globe. In many ways, then, they are not unlike other nonstate actors. Yet unlike NGOs or MNCs, these groups seek to achieve their objectives through the acquisition and use of force, applying it in ways that may be difficult for states or other international actors to counter. Globalized criminal organizations or terrorist groups are perfect examples of this new threat.[4]

For example, in the case of the Islamic fundamentalist terrorist network Al Qaeda, we see a group that is highly decentralized, in which individuals such as Osama bin Laden provide resources and guidance but allow a great deal of individual initiative and responsibility among individual operators. Such decentralization makes it very difficult for state intelligence agencies to gather information on or destroy such networks. The death of a leader, although a potential setback, will not destroy the group itself, since it does not depend on a hierarchical structure of command and control. This decentralization is further aided by globalized technology, such as cell phones, encrypted e-mail, websites, and satellite television, which allows terrorists to communicate, disseminate propaganda, access money, and recruit new followers. Indeed, such groups look more like the Internet itself than any formal nonstate actor. Although states may at times be able to use conventional force against such groups where they have a physical presence, as in the case of the U.S. attacks on Al Qaeda bases in Afghanistan, there is no central location to attack nor any easy way to keep such individuals from simply dispersing and regrouping elsewhere. States, the military capacity of which is geared toward fighting other states, may be ill equipped to battle small groups that can take advantage of globalization to attack and undermine existing institutions.

Second, many question how a more globalized political system can be more democratic. Although increased connections may increase transparency, this does not necessarily lay out a mechanism for individuals to act on that information. As we noted in Chapter 6, modern liberal democracy is based on republicanism, the ability to choose one's representatives through a competitive process. But who votes for international organizations? These bodies may be indirectly elected or appointed from the member states—or they may not be directly accountable to anyone at all. Thus, while one may laud the work of Greenpeace or the World Wildlife Fund, it is instructive to note that these organizations are not subject to popular democratic control nor necessarily more transparent than states themselves. This raises the concern of a "democratic deficit," an idea first raised with regard to the EU. If power moves to global institutions, representation and democratic control may grow weaker as citizens lack the ability to control these bodies and these institutions grow distant from the citizenry and their preferences. At an extreme, this could lead to a new form of global illiberalism, such as we discussed in Chapter 5, where representative institutions exist but have been "hollowed out" by the loss of sovereignty and by the power of global technocratic institutions and elites.[5]

These are two starkly different visions of politics in a globalized world. In both scenarios, states and state functions become more diffused as power shifts to the global level. For optimists, international cooperation follows, with these developments undermining the logic of war and increasing transparency. For pessimists, deepening international connections facilitate new violent organizations as well as weaken democratic ties between the people and their representatives. Some combination of both scenarios is also possible.

Economic Globalization

Politics is not the only realm in which globalization may be taking place; in fact, when many people think about globalization, economics is what typically comes to mind, and it is this area that generates the most controversy and debate. Over the past few decades, the world has seen a rapidly developing system of international trade and economic relations, fostered by technological change and dramatic shifts in world politics, such as the collapse of communism and the spread of liberalism. To give one example, between 1996 and 2005, world exports in goods and services nearly doubled in size from $6.6 trillion to nearly $12 trillion.[6]

Increased trade is just part of the picture. Technological change and the liberalization of markets in recent decades have also helped foster a growing internationalization of investment, as firms and funds move into markets overseas in pursuit of greater profits (Figure 10.2). **Foreign direct investment**, or the purchase of assets in a country by a foreign firm, represented just under 7 percent of world GDP in 1980. By 2003, it had grown to 23 percent.[7] As mentioned earlier, globalization is also associated with the emergence of a number of MNCs that dominate global markets. Assisted by more open mar-

Figure 10.2 **FOREIGN DIRECT INVESTMENT, 1980–2003**

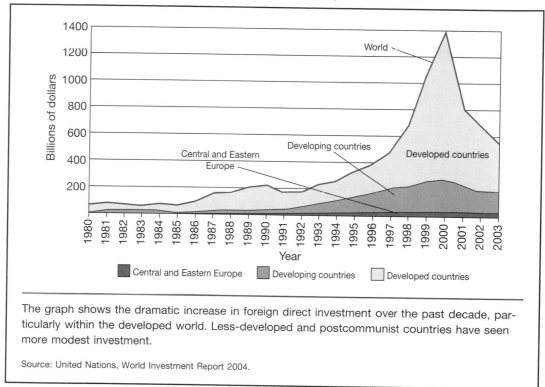

The graph shows the dramatic increase in foreign direct investment over the past decade, particularly within the developed world. Less-developed and postcommunist countries have seen more modest investment.

Source: United Nations, World Investment Report 2004.

kets and reduced costs for transportation, large firms such as IBM, Honda, McDonald's, and Johnson & Johnson control assets and make profits in the billions of dollars, often rivaling the GDPs of many countries in which they do business. For example, General Electric's annual profits in 2004 were approximately $12 billion, which is roughly equal to Nicaragua's entire GDP at purchasing-power parity.

These economic developments are compounded by expanding global communications. Recent recessions notwithstanding, the development of electronic commerce, with its ability to link far-flung businesses globally, is transforming the way in which markets, firms, and individuals interact. Technological innovations have reduced many of the traditional barriers to trade. Firms and people are able to buy goods and services from around the world using fewer or no intermediaries. As a result, markets are more open and firms face greater competition. A business in China or Chile, for example, can market its goods and services directly to other firms or individuals anywhere in the world. In the area of investment, too, online banking and investment allow people to move their money internationally with a few mouse clicks.

Many people liken the significance of the development of the Internet to that of the creation of railroads and the telegraph in the nineteenth century, which helped transform the way in which goods could be produced, marketed, and delivered.

Finally, economic globalization also applies not just to trade, firms, or finances, but also to labor. Globalization may shift not only where things are made, but also where labor is located. As noted in Chapter 7, the globe is currently experiencing a huge wave of migration, both between countries and within them, as people move from countryside to city (Figure 10.3). For example, in China, it is estimated that the country's "floating population"—individuals migrating, often illegally, from countryside to city and interior to the coast—is around 140 million, or nearly half the population of the United States.

Optimists see in these dramatic changes the mechanism for future global prosperity. Recalling our discussion of political-economic systems in Chapter 4, consider that globalization looks very much like the internationalization of a liberal economic system, with its emphasis on open markets and competition for goods and labor. Through the expansion of international economic connections, goods and services, labor, and other resources can be allocated more effectively through a broader market, unfettered by tariff barriers and other obstacles that states might erect. Countries are able to export what they produce best, encouraging innovation, specialization, and lower costs. Jobs are also

Figure 10.3 **WORLD MIGRATION TRENDS**

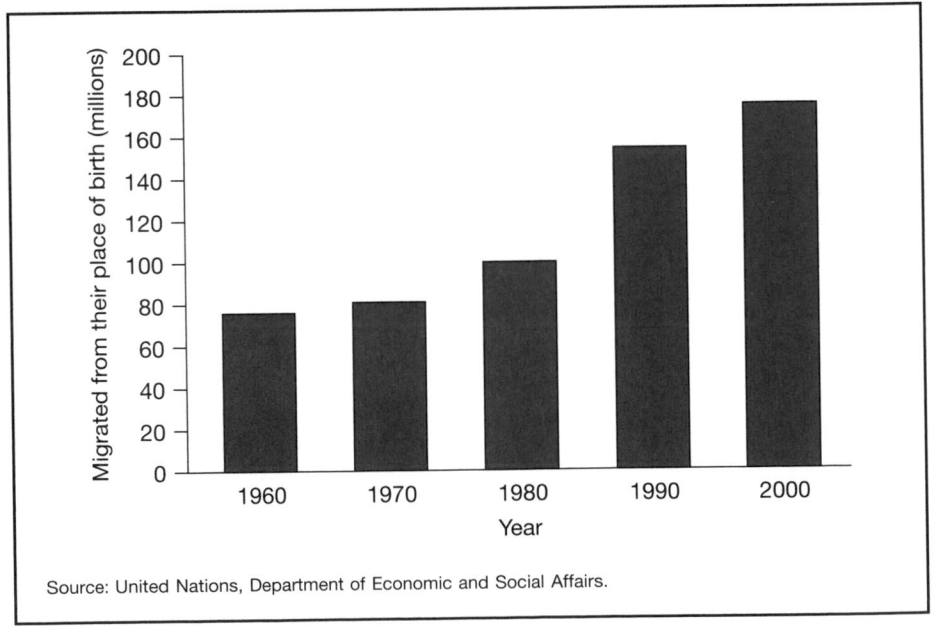

Source: United Nations, Department of Economic and Social Affairs.

created as capital flows and transnational corporations take advantage of new markets and new opportunities. People, too, can move to where there is work, whether domestically or internationally. In the end, wealth is diffused more effectively through open markets for goods, labor, and capital, increasing standards of living worldwide. Globalization is thus viewed as a positive trend, the means to lift billions out of poverty and generate greater prosperity by allowing more people to be a part of the global marketplace for goods and labor.[8]

Others view economic globalization with more suspicion, particularly those who are less enamored of a liberal political economy. Some equate increased trade with increased dependence, arguing that trade creates conditions whereby some countries will gain monopoly control over particular goods vital in the international economy, such as software, energy, biotechnology, or pharmaceutical products. The resulting unequal relationships in the international system will allow countries in control of crucial resources to dominate countries whose goods are less critical to the world economy. The globalization of investment and labor markets is also criticized as a system in which firms invest in countries with cheap labor and weak labor regulations in order to increase profits; these moves eliminate manufacturing jobs in the advanced democracies. This "offshoring" of jobs hurts workers around the globe as countries engage in a "race to the bottom," lowering standards and weakening regulations in order to keep or attract businesses. For societies with developed social democratic systems in particular, globalization is seen as a huge threat, demanding fewer social expenditures in the name of increased competitiveness. More generally, the emergence of large, far-flung corporations raises the fear that globalized businesses are increasingly able to avoid government oversight and public accountability. As economic globalization weakens state capacity and autonomy, it is replaced not with a global rule of law, but rather with a small cartel of powerful corporations that lack any national or democratic control.[9] Freedom and equality are thus compromised.

Does economic globalization support or obstruct global prosperity? The answer depends on how we compare the data as well as define prosperity. In the case of offshoring, there has been much discussion regarding the movement of industries overseas, especially those in the service sector, where technology can overcome problems of time and space. Call centers, data processing, and software programming are commonly cited examples, but others include medical diagnosis (such as reading X-rays or CAT scans) and film animation.[10] In 2002, offshoring amounted to about $1.3 billion, with estimates that by 2007 the number will rise to around $24 billion. How many jobs this will impact is unclear. Estimates for the number of jobs that could be affected in the advanced democracies (from which such offshoring tends to flow) range from 1 to 10 percent, or tens of millions of jobs.[11] But the issue is more complex than that. First, there is the question of whether the cost savings from

offshoring could translate into increased economic growth and new job opportunities to replace those lost. A second issue is the potential increase in employment in the less-developed and newly industrializing countries, which could
in turn reduce poverty there. A third consideration is whether outsourcing
will make it difficult for low-skilled workers to find new forms of employment, or at least ones that pay well. There is already evidence that offshoring

Figure 10.4 **GLOBALIZATION AND LIFE EXPECTANCY**

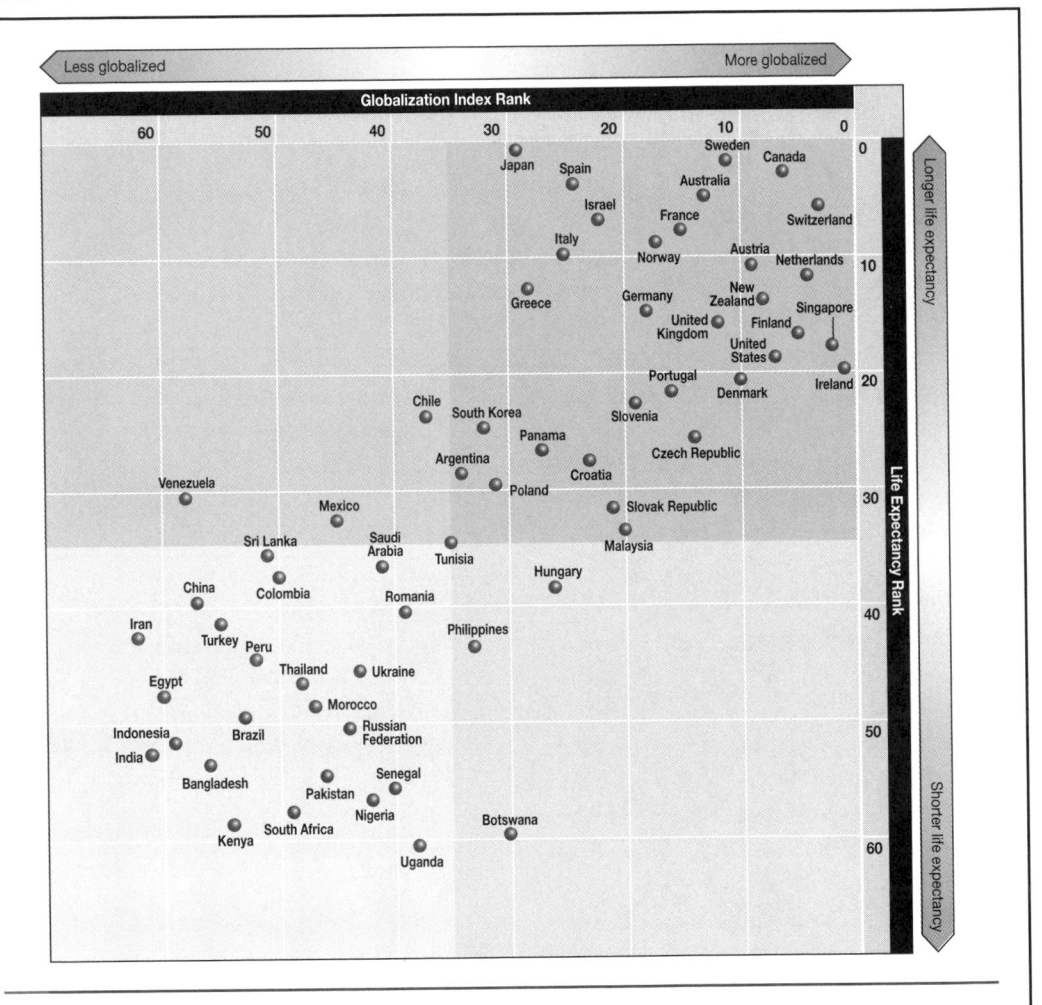

Studies indicate that the most globalized countries are also those with the highest life
expectancy. This is true not only of advanced democracies, but less-developed and newly
industrializing countries as well.

Source: Foreign Policy/A. T. Kearney.

has led to the decline in wages for low-skilled labor in the United States, which harkens back to our discussion of postindustrialism in Chapter 7.[12]

The picture is thus murky. As globalization has increased over the past quarter century, the percentage of the world's population that lives in poverty has declined and people's life expectancy has risen, particularly in parts of the world that are more globalized (China, India) compared with those that are not (Africa). This is a powerful piece of evidence in favor of globalization. But there is also evidence of a growing gap between rich and poor—if not between countries, then within them, as in China, India, and the United States.[13]

If the economic benefits or the dangers of globalization remain unclear and open to debate, is there any consensus on how globalization is changing economic institutions around the world? One assertion about which many supporters and opponents of globalization do agree is that, as a result of the deepening interconnections between economies around the world, there is a greater chance that local crises and problems may become global ones. The growing linkages of finance, trade, and markets now increase the likelihood that local events will ripple throughout the system. Frequently cited in this regard is the Asian financial crisis of 1997, in which growing concerns about future economic growth led to a sudden withdrawal of capital from the region, wiping out stock markets, throwing economies into recession, and increasing unemployment. This fear soon turned to panic as international investors began to withdraw their funds from less-developed and newly industrializing countries such as Brazil that were otherwise not connected to the Asian crisis. Terrorist attacks may have a similar effect, affecting markets worldwide. Greater economic linkages may create new opportunities for growth, but with these opportunities may come greater uncertainty, instability, and risk.

Societal Globalization

Whether globalization and the political and economic transformations it brings becomes an instrument of greater cooperation and prosperity or one of conflict and hardship may depend on how societies themselves are transformed by globalization.

We have explored how political globalization may challenge state sovereignty and power and how economic globalization binds markets for goods, labor, and capital. Societal globalization is a similar process, in which traditional societal institutions are weakened, creating new identities that do not belong to any one community or nation. As we know from previous chapters, in the premodern world, people's identities were rather limited and narrow, focused on such things as family, tribe, village, and religion. Only with the rise of the state did national identities begin to emerge, such that individuals began to see themselves tied to a much larger community of millions, strangers bound together by complex myths and symbols—flags, legends, symbols, anthems, culture. This transformation coincided with the development of sovereignty, whereby borders and citizenship reinforced the notion of national identity—one people, one state.

Some argue that as globalization proceeds, these central aspects of individual and collective identity are giving way. Just as the state and domestic economic institutions are being challenged, so, too, are the traditional identities of the past. New technologies, waves of migration, trade, and communication link people across vast distances, forging relationships between people on the basis of common interests and ideas rather than shared national symbols. Many find the Internet particularly powerful in this regard, in its ability to spread information, ideas, and cultural products to billions of individuals around the globe (Table 10.1). As the Internet continues to grow by leaps and bounds, people find ways to connect to one another across time and space, building and deepening connections to one another. E-mail and websites have been ways of doing this, but recently a new development has been the proliferation of web logs, or "blogs." Blogs range in interest, participation, prominence, and content, with readers and writers coming together from across the globe to create what some call the "blogosphere." Such virtual interconnections are, for many, stronger than the physical ones on which they have traditionally relied.

How might this process shape societal institutions and identities? There are two directions we can point to. The first is that societal globalization may engender a kind of global multiculturalism. The deepening of international connections between people and the exchange of ideas between them will transfer the dynamics of multiculturalism from the national level to the international one, with different cultures connecting and combining more through connections that are not bound by traditional barriers of time and space. Thus, the engines of multiculturalism will not be found where different cultures physically meet, as in the past. As a result, even those societies not traditionally associated with multiculturalism (such as ethnically homogenous countries) will themselves be a part of a globalized multiculturalism that they can contribute to and draw from. This means not only that a globalized society will draw from many sources, but also that the interconnection of such institutions at the global level will create new values and identities. This is important to note, because the argument about societal globalization is more than simply saying that people will be more interconnected, with national institutions having an international reach. It is also to say that new identities will form that emerge at the global level first, penetrating and transforming national institutions. One result of this outcome could be a global *cosmopolitanism*—a term that comes from the Greek *kosmos*, or universe, and *polis*, or state.

Table 10.1 Percentage of Population That Uses the Internet, 2000 and 2005			
	2000	**2005**	**Growth in Percent**
Sweden	44.9	73.6	164.4
United States	61.2	68.5	112.8
South Korea	40.0	63.3	166.0
United Kingdom	44.5	58.7	128.4
Japan	36.9	52.8	143.8
France	21.5	41.2	192.3
Malaysia	22.9	35.9	157.1
Czech Republic	13.6	34.5	253.0
Kuwait	8.1	22.4	278.0
Peru	19.9	16.3	82.8
Russia	2.5	15.5	619.4
Mexico	3.2	14.3	449.4
Brazil	3.6	12.3	346.4
South Africa	10.0	9.9	99.2
China	2.3	7.3	317.8
Iran	0.4	7.0	1820.0
India	0.5	3.6	684.0
Nigeria	0.2	0.5	275.0
Worldwide	*9.1*	*14.6*	*160.0*

Source: www.internetworldstats.com

Cosmopolitanism is thus a universal, global, or "worldly" political order that draws its identity and values from everywhere. Historically the cosmopolis was that physical space where such ideas usually came together, notably the city. In a globalized world, however, there is the potential for an international cosmopolitanism that binds people together irrespective of where they are.[14]

Parallel to a global cosmopolitanism is the idea of global democracy. We have already spoken of how globalization might shape political institutions at the domestic and international levels, though we focused largely on the development of nonstate and suprastate organizations as rivals to the state itself. When we focus on societal globalization and its effects on democracy, however, we return to our notion of civil society. The argument here is that growing international connections at the societal level would generate not only a form of cosmopolitanism, but a civic identity that stretches beyond traditional barriers and borders. This global civil society—organized life not simply beyond the state but above it—can take shape in such formal organizations as NGOs but also in such informal manifestations as social movements or more basic grassroots connections between people drawn by shared interests and values. This global civil society could in turn shape politics by creating new opportunities for concerted public action and new ways of thinking about politics and participation at the domestic and international levels.[15] Finally, this development of global cosmopolitanism and civil society has the potential to eliminate international conflict, though for reasons quite different from those outlined in the discussion of political globalization. Whereas political globalization imagines a "golden straightjacket" that makes war too costly for states to pursue, societal globalization would undercut national, patriotic, and other identities that states call on to justify war. Political globalization may make war unbeneficial, but societal globalization would make it unthinkable.[16]

In short, societal globalization may change the definition of who is "us" and who is "them." Identities become more diverse and capacious, more worldly, and with new avenues for democracy and peace.

As you might expect, there are critics of such views, skeptical of the notion that increased globalization will be beneficial to social progress. These criticisms are twofold. First, some critics contend that the onslaught of globalization will not generate global cosmopolitanism and multiculturalism but instead will overwhelm people with innumerable choices, values, ideas, and information that they are unable to understand, evaluate, or escape. They predict not a more globally enlightened public but rather confusion, alienation, and a public backlash as people seek to hold on to their traditional identities in the face of these changes. Nationalism and fundamentalism in many parts of the world, for example, may be a reaction to a globalized society that people find alien and hostile to their own way of life. This countervailing trend against globalization has been described by political theorist Benjamin Barber as "jihad," the impulse across many societies (Islamic or otherwise) to violently resist these alien ideas and values.[17] The September 11 attacks can be viewed in this light—as a strike against the values (and perceived source) of globalization rather than on the United States itself. As societal globalization increases in speed and impact, conflicts over ideas and values are likely to intensify, not decline.

A second criticism of societal globalization is that resistance against globalization is unlikely to win in the long run, but what of the end result? Rather than a global multiculturalism, cosmopolitanism, and civil society, societal globalization will result in assimilation and homogenization driven by a cultural and intellectual race to the bottom. Societies will trade their own cultures, institutions, and ideas for a common global society shaped not by values or worldliness but by materialism and consumption. Those things that make each society unique—languages, food, music, history, customs, values, and norms—will be absorbed, rationalized, and packaged for mass consumption everywhere. This outcome has been described by Barber as "McWorld," where what is most attractive in each society is sterilized, repackaged, and sold to the rest of the planet and where those things that lack mass appeal are thrown away or driven out, replaced by what satisfies the widest public and the lowest common denominator. What is distinct and cannot be globalized is lost, while that which is globalized are those things that have been stripped of any distinctiveness or identity. One scholar calls this "the globalization of nothing."[18]

Finally, although the emergence of a homogenized world may promise greater prosperity and even cooperation, it may also come at the cost of foundations of democratic society. When there are no longer any meaningful differences in ideas, and when choices are limited to the realm of consumption rather than that of values, participation and debate lose their meaning. Both freedom and equality become, in essence, meaningless concepts, since they are not goods or services that can be marketed, bought, or sold.

Globalization: Myths and Realities

Clearly, these heated debates over globalization show that it remains a highly controversial issue. Some believe that it will destroy old institutions, creating a world more unequal and less democratic—at worst, chaotic and violent; at best, bland and uninspiring. Others see within it new sources of prosperity, participation, and progress and predict that humans will look and act beyond the local context to see themselves as part of a single community with a shared commitment to freedom and equality. Yet what both of these views share is the belief that globalization is a major turning point in history. But is globalization really all that? Some argue that globalization, whether for good or ill, is overstated in many ways. First, globalization is not quantitatively or qualitatively different from past waves of global interconnection. Second, its effects are not as profound as many think. Third, it is not an unstoppable force or inevitable process. These arguments are each separate though related and so should be considered in turn.

Is Globalization New?

Many question the assumption that globalization is a fundamentally new development in human history, a change in institutions that is without prece-

MCDONALD'S AND GLOBALIZATION

As discussions and debates about globalization have progressed over the past decade, McDonald's has time and again become a reference point for scholars, activists, and pundits. Both advocates and opponents of globalization have used McDonald's as a proxy for globalization, a metric of how far globalization has progressed, given its spread of franchises in over one hundred countries. Those who favor globalization see in McDonald's the spread of fast and convenient food to societies where such things cannot be taken for granted, evidence of the power of globalization to improve people's lives and promote shared values. Opponents use the company to speak of homogenizing processes that strip out local culture, making McDonald's the frequent target of verbal or even physical attacks by various groups protesting globalization or American policies. Given its symbolic power, McDonald's seems to be an institution in its own right; few international protesters decry Subway sandwiches, even though it, too, can be found in over eighty countries.

Is McDonald's a good representation of globalization? In the 1990s, globalization optimist Thomas Friedman observed that no two countries with McDonald's had ever gone to war against each other, showing this as evidence that globalization brought with it peace. His optimistic argument was dashed, however, when NATO forces bombed Serbia in 1999 over ethnic conflict in Kosovo: Serbia's McDonald's was one of the first in a communist country, opened in 1988. The idea that the presence of globalized institutions like McDonald's undercut nationalism and other sources of war seems questionable. On the other end, critics of "McDonaldization" tend to ignore the degree to which McDonald's differs from place to place. It is not only that the menu changes—in India, for example, the restaurant sells no beef or pork, which may be hard to imagine for a restaurant that built its fame on hamburgers—but that the very role of McDonald's in a given society is very different from place to place. In one study of McDonald's in Asia, scholars noted that the franchise did have distinct effects on local perceptions of such things as restaurant hygiene and service. But local cultures also changed the meaning of the restaurant by making it a hub of social activity, such as birthdays or study groups—quite the opposite of what is normally associated with "fast food." In the Middle East, too, it has been observed that young people can embrace both McDonald's and Bin Laden without seeing any contradiction between the two.* In short, McDonald's may be a good proxy for globalization, not as a unifying or homogenizing force, but rather for the complicated ways in which domestic and international institutions are transformed through their interaction.

*James L. Watson, ed., *Golden Arches East: McDonald's in East Asia* (Stanford: Stanford University Press, 1997); Yaroslav Trofimov, *Faith at War: A Journey on the Frontlines of Islam, from Baghdad to Timbuktu* (New York: Henry Holt, 2005).

dent. At the turn of the last century, many countries experienced a surge of economic and other international connections not unlike those we have seen in the past few decades. Consider the development of modern imperialism. The spread of European power into Latin America, Africa, the Middle East, and Asia profoundly reshaped domestic and international relations as Western political, economic, and social systems were transplanted into these parts of the world. Within Europe, too, imperialism and the declining costs of transportation helped facilitate the migration of millions of people to North and South America and parts of Africa and Asia. By comparison, the current world of passports, visas, and immigration in some ways constrains human mobility far more than just a century ago. It was during the late nineteenth century that we begin to see the rise of the first nongovernmental and intergovernmental organizations, such as the International Telegraph Union (ITU), founded in 1865, and the Red Cross, in 1863. And those who marvel at the advent of Internet communication forget that the first transatlantic cable connected Europe and North America by telegraph in 1866, spurring a global system of rapid communications and trade.[19] In his famous work *The Economic Consequences of the Peace*, economist John Maynard Keynes wrote of the dramatic impact of such changes:

> The inhabitant of London could order by telephone, sipping his morning tea in bed, the various products of the whole earth, in such quantity as he might see fit, and reasonably expect their early delivery upon his doorstep; he could at the same moment and by the same means adventure his wealth in the natural resources and new enterprises of any quarter of the world, and share, without exertion or even trouble, in their prospective fruits and advantages; or he could decide to couple the security of his fortunes with the good faith of the townspeople of any substantial municipality in any continent that fancy or information might recommend.[20]

Sound like the new global economy? The time period Keynes wrote about was that prior to World War I. Indeed, the rise of Internet commerce, often heralded as a central piece of globalization, would not be possible without the previous establishment of such institutions as the telephone, national postal services, passable roads, ports, and commercial shipping—all things that far predate globalization.

For many, this period of international change would lead to the abolition of war and the spread of international law and world government. For others, however, these rapid changes also brought with it concerns and dangers not unlike those discussed today. Migration and trade brought fears of cultural destruction and violent resistance in response, including nationalism and eventually fascist ideas. Marxist and anarchist ideas also attracted followers around the world, some of whom sought revolution and engaged in terrorism. In these confusing and often violent developments, some saw an imminent collapse of Western society.

Such periods of intense international connection are not isolated to the nineteenth or early twentieth century; the conquest of the Americas, the Roman and Ottoman empires—all are examples of powerful international networks that dramatically reshaped large portions of humanity within a relatively short period of time, remaking institutions and changing the way people saw themselves and their relationship to one another. These examples suggest that it may be shortsighted of us to think that today's global interconnections are more dramatic than any before or that they portend changes that are beyond our power to control. History may help us better understand the present; we should not assume that what is occurring now is so unique that the past has nothing to teach us.

Is Globalization Exaggerated?

Another question to consider is whether globalization is as powerful and wide-ranging as we think. Although we have already pointed to some data that indicate some of the changes associated with globalization, on closer examination we could argue that much of what is pointed to is fuzzy and anecdotal. It is one thing to speak about "McWorld" or the power of NGOs, but how do we actually measure such things? Are we simply taking globalization at face value?

Some scholars have in fact argued that the scope of globalization is much less profound than we often assume. The area of economic globalization would seem to be the most unassailable, given the growing levels of international trade and investment. However, some economists have noted that in spite of these impressive increases, the total levels of international trade remain modest and far less than they would expect in a globalized world. U.S. exports represent only 10 percent of GDP, a number that has stayed the same since 1990. For the world as a whole, the increase has only been 5 percent.[21] In addition, international economic relations remain less "virtual" than we might think. For example, international trade drops to near zero at a distance of over 4,000 miles (7,000 kilometers). Foreign direct investment (FDI), too, is hardly globalized to the degree we might imagine. In spite of our image of FDI riding a wave of globalization to penetrate every corner of the globe, approximately 60 percent of such investments stay within the advanced democracies (see Figure 10.2). State boundaries, economic barriers, and cultural linkages still appear to have a powerful impact that limits the extent of global economic integration, with some speculating that economic globalization may be reaching its feasible limit.[22] Similarly, while some scholars and pundits link globalization

Figure 10.5 **GLOBALIZATION AND INEQUALITY**

Gap between Rich and Poor

| | Gotten Worse % |
| | Blame Globalization % |

Country	Blame Globalization %	Gotten Worse %
Canada	22	77
U.S.	14	67
France	25	82
G. Britain	18	68
Russia	24	92
Brazil	17	83
Mexico	14	63
India	22	71
Japan	13	56
Nigeria	20	77
S. Africa	22	73

A survey of over forty countries in 2003, showing that large majorities think that the gap between rich and poor has gotten worse. However, few place the blame on globalization.

Source: Pew Center for the People and the Press.

with inequality, publics appear not to. There is a global consensus that the gap between rich and poor is growing, but people do not believe that globalization is the major culprit (Figure 10.5). Domestic institutions and policies remain at the forefront of people's economic concerns.

In contrast to economic globalization, political globalization is much harder to measure. This makes the claims and counterclaims much more difficult to compare. At the core of political globalization is the idea that states are losing sovereignty to a web of international connections and actors, leading either to greater cooperation or to conflict. But it is difficult to measure the loss of sovereignty. If we go back to our core definition as the monopoly of violence, we can assert that in spite of new rivals like Al Qaeda, states remain the only real actor in the international system with such "hard power" as military might. After September 11, critics have rejected the assertion that the ability to wield

force is increasingly irrelevant and note that the threat of international terrorism can only be met through the kind of firepower that states enjoy. This
kind of power is itself dependent on financial resources: states must raise revenue and manage their economies. Here, too, in spite of expectations of a
decentralized globalized market, states remain able to levy taxes (even against
electronic commerce), defend property rights, and regulate business.

Perhaps the most telling example in this regard relates to the Internet. In
the 1990s, scholars and pundits alike saw the Internet as nothing short of revolutionary, a phenomenon that would upend domestic and international institutions, including the state. State sovereignty was no match for this powerful
decentralized force. But over time, states have learned how to manage the Internet in varying ways, forcing it to conform to domestic regimes and policies.
Electronic commerce has come under increasing domestic control, with countries levying taxes and compelling Internet auction sites like eBay to ban "offen-
sive materials" such as racist publications. Authoritarian regimes have taken
this control much higher. Contrary to expectations, states are able to censor
significant portions of the Internet and other forms of electronic communication, filtering out information and ideas that they wish to keep from their public. Perhaps one of the best examples of this is currently China. Even as China
pursues rapid modernization and integration with the global economy, the government also maintains a strong control over Internet access, blocking websites like that of Amnesty International. The government also has restricted
online chat rooms and discussion boards, monitoring and deleting content as
well as blocking the use of certain words. Such filtering even extends to text
messaging on cell phones. Similar forms of control can be found in many other
authoritarian countries, such as Cuba, Saudi Arabia, Iran, and Singapore.[23]

What of societal globalization? Here, too, we confront the limitations of
our data. Both supporters and opponents of societal globalization agree with
the proposition that national and local identities are giving way in the face of
a broader global identity. Whether this will be a peaceful process and whether
this is a positive outcome are the basis of their disagreement. But again we
must ask: Are these processes actually taking place? The picture is mixed. A
global survey of over forty countries indicated that while many people feel
that globalization has increased, in less than a third of those countries did a
majority say they had become more connected to others outside of their own
country.[24] Similarly, national identity continues to remain strong in the face
of globalization. The 2001 World Values Survey of over eighty countries similarly indicated that on average, around 10 percent of individuals see their primary identification with their continent or the world as a whole, over town,
region, or country. This figure has not moved significantly in the past twenty-
five years. Nor do countries with greater trade, foreign direct investment, or
Internet use, such as the majority of countries depicted in Table 10.2, show

Table 10.2 Globalization and Societal Identities

	1981	1990	2001
Strong national or local identity	75%	73%	77%
Weak supranational identity	14%	15%	12%
Strong supranational identity	11%	12%	11%

World Values Survey Question: "To which of these geographical groups do you belong to first of all?" (Compilation of answers given in United Kingdom, France, West Germany, Italy, Spain, Belgium, Netherlands, Denmark, Sweden, Iceland, Ireland, Finland, United States, Canada, Mexico, Argentina, South Africa, and Japan between 1981 and 2001.

any higher degree or faster growth of supranational identity.[25] Such data seem to undercut the proposition of a more interconnected and postnational world.

If the global cosmopolitanism hypothesis is disputable, what about the idea of a more homogenized world? This is perhaps the hardest thing to measure. On the surface, we can point to evidence of the spread of certain cultural products, such as American movies, and their penetration of global markets. But this also ignores the ways in which culture flows in different directions. The McWorld thesis tends to argue that cultural homogenization is all one way, from the advanced democracies outward. Yet this ignores the way in which cultural interaction and fusion flows in many directions, creating unique local connections. Hong Kong action films shape American movies; Brazilian soap operas become a hit in Russia; reggae influences European punk rock. Finally, even though certain cultural institutions do appear to have spread worldwide, does this mean that they actually mean the same thing in every country and culture? Some research concludes that in contrast to the "McDonaldization" hypothesis, institutions that on the surface appear identical can mean very different things in different places (see box on page 268). The medium is *not* the message.

Is Globalization Inevitable?

Let us, just for the sake of argument, reject all of the qualifiers raised above and assume that globalization is fundamentally different and profound in its effects. Accepting this, it often follows that globalization is a juggernaut that people, groups, societies, and states cannot control or resist. Even in the McWorld scenario, the idea of resistance is seen as a last-ditch effort, one that will inevitably fail.

Is globalization so unstoppable? We should be careful not to assume that what is under way now is somehow an inexorable process that cannot be stopped. To illustrate this point, let us again return to history, and to Keynes. After noting the profound changes that occurred before World War I, he remarked that above all, the average individual

> regarded this state of affairs as normal, certain, and permanent, except in the direction of further improvement, and any deviation from it as aberrant, scandalous, and avoidable.[26]

Yet this was not to be the case. The onset of World War I disrupted international trade; its effects were further compounded by a subsequent world depression. History suggests, then, that globalization is not unstoppable.

Globalization could be limited or reversed in a number of ways. One is economic crisis. The heady period of economic development a hundred years ago was finally undermined by financial collapse in the 1930s. In its immediate aftermath, trade, investment, and migration declined, often as a result of new national barriers that reflected increased isolationism, protectionism, and nationalism. Many of these barriers persist to this day, in spite of recent liberalization. For example, between 1901 and 1910, the United States accepted nearly 9 million immigrants, but it would not again reach even half that level until the 1970s. A major global recession could create pressure to roll back many of the elements of globalization that have developed over the past decade.

A second factor could be the return of the state. The political crisis brought on by September 11, the subsequent wars in Iraq and Afghanistan, and ongoing terrorism around the globe have called into question the wisdom of a borderless world. States are reasserting control in many areas in an effort to increase security, whether through tighter borders, greater surveillance, or stronger police and military. In addition, disagreements about how to deal with terrorism have increased tension between many countries, limiting cooperation. The long-term result of September 11 may be the construction of new obstacles to globalization and an increased emphasis on centralized state power. Institutions, we recall, are not so easily dislodged.

Third, further globalization may be stymied by public opposition. Many people's concerns about how globalization might affect such things as the environment, labor standards, and democratic practices around the world are being translated into antiglobalization activism—aided, ironically, by new technology such as the Internet. The protests against the World Trade Organization (WTO) in Seattle in 1999 are perhaps the most notable example of such activism: there, for the first time in the WTO's history, members were unable to begin negotiations on a new round of trade liberalization measures. Although this failure was not simply, or even primarily, due to public protests, widespread opposition in the street by activists from around the world certainly helped to complicate matters.[27] Similar protests against the EU helped scuttle the proposed constitution in 2005 (see Chapter 7). Such opposition can be found on both sides of the political spectrum, which may lead to antiglobalization coalitions with broader appeal.

These concerns all echo the past. Historian Niall Ferguson has suggested several causes for the collapse of globalization a century ago, among them the overstretch of one dominant power, unstable alliances and rivalry, rogue states, and the spread of revolutionary ideologies opposed to capitalism. In one form or another, Ferguson argues, all of these factors are again at work.[28]

Throughout human history, societies have gone through periods of international connection and isolation. Some of these contacts have been relatively thin, involving relatively few people, but in other cases, many millions became directly connected to and a part of a larger world. Although today's globalization may look qualitatively different from waves of globalization in the past, what we are experiencing now may not be an unprecedented or irreversible force. Globalization may fail through its own flaws or through concerted action against it. Nothing is set in stone.

In Sum: Freedom and Equality in a Globalized World

Our world may now be undergoing a profound shift in the face of globalization, though this is subject to debate. If our world does in fact become truly globalized, the struggle over freedom and equality may shift from the domestic to the international arena. Both values will be measured not just within states, but between them: Does one country's freedom or equality come at the expense of another's? How can freedom or equality be balanced globally in the absence of any single sovereign power or dominant regime? Under these conditions, the very meanings of freedom and equality may evolve as new ways of thinking about individual choice and collective aspirations emerge. These changes could lead to greater stability, peace, and prosperity. They may also lead to greater conflict and chaos. The latter possibility takes us to our next and final chapter, where we consider the sources, forms, and objectives of political violence.

NOTES

1. Jared Diamond, *Guns, Germs and Steel: The Fate of Human Societies* (New York: W. W. Norton, 1997).
2. See Robert O. Keohane and Joseph S. Nye, Jr., "Introduction," in Joseph S. Nye, Jr., and John D. Donahue, eds., *Governance in a Globalizing World* (Washington: Brookings Institution Press, 2000), 1–41.

3. Thomas Friedman, *The Lexus and the Olive Tree* (New York: Farrar, Straus, and Giroux, 2000).

4. John Arquilla and David Ronfeldt, eds., *Networks and Netwars: The Future of Terror, Crime, and Militancy* (Washington: Rand, 2001), www.rand.org.

5. John Fonte, "Democracy's Trojan Horse," *National Interest* 76 (Summer 2004: 117–127.

6. International Monetary Fund, *World Economic Outlook 2004* (Washington, DC: International Monetary Fund, 2004), 228.

7. *World Investment Report 2004* (New York: United Nations Conference on Trade and Development, 2004), 399.

8. John Micklethwait and Adrian Wooldridge, *A Future Perfect: The Challenge and Hidden Promise of Globalization* (New York: Random House, 2000).

9. William Grieder, *One World, Ready or Not: The Manic Logic of Global Capitalism* (New York: Simon & Schuster, 1997).

10. Julia Nielson and Daria Taglioni, "Services Trade Liberalization: Identifying Opportunites & Gains," OECD Trade Policy Working Paper 1 (2004).

11. *World Investment Report 2004*, 154.

12. Robert C. Feenstra and Gordon H. Hanson, "Globalization, Outsourcing, and Wage Inequality," NBER Working Paper 5424 (1996), www.nber.org.

13. See Robert Wade, "Winners and Losers," *The Economist*, April 26, 2001; "Convergence, Period," *The Economist*, July 18, 2002.

14. David Held, *Democracy and the Global Order* (Cambridge: Polity Press, 1995).

15. Mary Griffiths, "e-Citizens: Blogging as Democratic Practice," *Electronic Journal of e-Government* 2, no. 3 (December 2004), www.ejeg.com.

16. Mary Kaldor, *Global Civil Society: An Answer to War* (Cambridge: Polity, 2003).

17. Benjamin Barber, *Jihad versus McWorld: How Globalism and Tribalism Are Reshaping the World* (New York: Random House, 1995).

18. George Ritzer, *The Globalization of Nothing* (Thousand Oaks, CA: Pine Forge Press, 2003).

19. Tom Standage, *The Victorian Internet: The Remarkable Story of the Telegraph and the Nineteenth Century's On-Line Pioneers* (New York: Berkely, 1998).

20. John Maynard Keynes, *The Economic Consequences of the Peace* (New York: Harcourt, Brace and Howe, 1920), 11–12.

21. World Bank, *World Development Indicators 2005*, www.worldbank.org.

22. Paul Hirst and Grahame Thompson, "The Future of Globalization," *Cooperation and Conflict* 37, no. 3 (2002): 247–266.

23. "Internet Under Surveillence 2004," *Reporters Without Borders*, www.rsf.org/.

24. Pew Center for the People and the Press, "Views of a Changing World 2003," http://people-press.org.

25. Ronald F. Inglehart, Miguel Basanez, Jaime Diez-Medrano, Loek Halman, and Ruud Luijkx, "Human Beliefs and Values: A Cross-Cultural Sourcebook based on the 1999–2002 Value Surveys," (Mexico City, Siglo XXI, 2004); Jai Kwan Jung, "Globalization and Global Identities: Over-Time and Cross-National Comparisons from The World Values Surveys in 1981–2001" (unpublished paper, Cornell University, 2005).

26. Keynes, *The Economic Consequences of the Peace*, 12.

27. Jeffrey J. Schott, "The WTO after Seattle," in Jeffrey J. Schott, ed., *The WTO after Seattle* (Washington: Institute for International Economics, 2000), 5.

28. Niall Ferguson, "Sinking Globalization," *Foreign Affairs* 84, no. 2 (March/April 2005): 64–77.

11 POLITICAL VIOLENCE

The turn of the century marked a new global threat. This danger was not surprising; for decades, loosely affiliated radicals had been staging attacks worldwide, killing civilians, government officials, and heads of state. These attacks drew from local grievances while bound by a common ideology that sought the destruction of states and regimes these radicals viewed as tyrannical and corrupt. Globalization helped facilitate the spread of these ideas and their followers, who moved from country to country, eluding detection and capture. The attacks in New York and Washington, D.C., directed at key symbols of America's national and global power, were another chapter in what had already been a long battle.

In response to these attacks, Americans asked themselves to what extent freedom should be sacrificed for national security. Foreigners and those viewed as possible accomplices or sympathizers became subject to public scrutiny, deportation, and sometimes questionable prosecution. Around the world, governments stepped up similar controls, limiting civil liberties in democratic countries and increasing repression in authoritarian ones. Another concern was whether greater economic integration and immigration had made the United States and other countries more vulnerable to such attacks.

The time we are speaking of is not today, and the danger is not that of violent religious extremists. It took place over a century ago, and the danger then was anarchism and communism. In 1881, anarchists killed Russian czar Alexander II; in 1889, Empress Elizabeth of Austria; in 1894, French president Carnot; and in 1901, U.S. President William McKinley. In 1917, the Russian Revolution swept away the czarist regime, and short-lived revolutionary regimes followed in Hungary and Bavaria. In 1919, a series of mail bombs were sent to political and economic elites across the United States, and shortly thereafter there were explosions in seven American cities, including Washington, D.C., where the home of the attorney general was severely damaged. In 1920, a wagon carrying several hundred pounds of explosives and shrapnel was planted in front of Wall Street in New York City, killing over thirty people. The government's response to this "Red Scare" was the Palmer Raids, in which thousands were arrested and many held without charge for long periods or deported.[1]

The questions surrounding the communist and anarchist attacks one hundred years ago are the ones we ask about political violence today: Why would anyone want to kill in a seemingly indiscriminate manner? What are their motivations? Are there some "root causes" for such violence? How should a government respond? How can future attacks be prevented? Is our very way of life at stake? Such questions do not have easy answers, nor do they have answers that provide much consensus. People have been trying to make sense of political violence for as long as it has existed; and it has existed, in different forms, for as long as there has been politics. Simple answers are attractive because they help bring clarity to such a confusing and disturbing topic. But the reality, as is often the case, is much more complex.

It is the goal of this chapter to try to bring some order to this complexity, providing some ways to think about political violence and its implications. We will begin by defining our terms: What do we mean by political violence, and how does this relate to the political institutions we have already covered, such as the state? Next, we will look at some of the motivations of political violence, examining the differing (and often conflicting) explanations for why such violence occurs. From there we will concentrate on two important forms of political violence: revolution and terrorism. Each is an important phenomenon that can put governments, regimes, and states under threat. They are also highly loaded political terms that stir emotional responses, complicating analysis. We will look at some of the different ways revolution and terrorism can be defined and understood. In addition, we will explore the extent to which the two are related—how terrorism is often a tool to achieve revolution. Once we have these concepts and arguments before us, we will put them into some context by looking at contemporary forms of political violence motivated by religion. Finally, we will conclude with a discussion of how states and societies prevent or manage political violence and what this means for freedom and equality.

What is Political Violence?

This textbook began with a focus on the state. This institution is the cornerstone of modern politics, one that we defined in its most basic terms as the monopoly of violence or force over a territory. Across human history, centralized political authority has been a part of this monopoly, whereby states vanquish their domestic rivals, defend themselves from external threats, and establish order and security at home. This has been described as the shift from "private war" to "public war," meaning that individuals lose the freedom to use violence against one another, turning that right over to the state. This right is exchanged for a greater sense of security for all.

Of course, the state's monopoly of violence is never perfect or complete. Other states always represent a potential threat, given their own capacity for violence. Even at the domestic level, violence persists in such forms as murder and armed robbery. In many countries, such problems, though persistent, are manageable and do not threaten the stability and security of the state, society, or economy. But under certain conditions, this may not be true. Public violence may grow so pervasive or destructive that the state loses its control in this area. Governments, regimes, even states are subject to attack, and sovereignty is weakened or lost.

It is this kind of violence, what we call **political violence**—that is, violence outside of state control that is politically motivated—that is the focus of this chapter. This is not to say that other forms of violence are not important in their own right. Endemic crime, for example, can threaten political stability, and many forms of violence at the domestic level may have political roots. Warfare, too, is clearly a violent and political act. But in the case of political violence, we are speaking of a phenomenon that operates beyond state sovereignty, neither war nor crime, and that seeks to achieve some political objective through the use of force. Such definitions are always cleaner in theory than in reality, of course. For example, the Irish Republican Army, in its quest for British withdrawal from Northern Ireland, has carried out attacks against state and civilian targets in the United Kingdom, conducted bank robberies and engaged in various criminal activity, and simultaneously served in elected government positions through its political wing, Sinn Fein. The lines between domestic and international and between war, crime, and politics are often quite blurry.

Why Political Violence?

Although defining political violence presents some challenges, a more controversial issue is why political violence occurs. What leads to civilians taking up arms against a state or its citizens toward some political aim? The reasons given by scholars are diverse and have changed over time, but we can group them into three basic categories: institutional, ideational (based on ideas), and individual. These three explanations overlap to some degree, such that where one explanation ends and the other begins is not always clear. At the same time, such explanations are often in contention, with scholars or policy makers tending to favor one explanation over others. We will examine each of these before we look at how these explanations are used more specifically in studies of revolution and terrorism.

Institutional Explanations

As we have covered institutions at length, what we mean by this term should be relatively clear; we are referring to those self-perpetuating organizations or patterns of activity that are valued for their own sake. Institutions define and shape human activity, and institutional explanations argue that their specific qualities or combination are essential to political violence. The emphasis can be on political institutions, such as states or regimes; economic institutions, such as capitalism; or societal institutions, such as culture or religion. Moreover, this explanation can be based on either a constraining or an enabling argument. It may be that institutions contain certain values or norms that implicitly or explicitly encourage such violence or that certain institutions constrain human activity, thus provoking political violence as a backlash. To give one example discussed in Chapter 6, it has been suggested that presidentialism is more prone to political violence than parliamentary models, possibly because the concentration of executive authority in one individual's hands reduces power sharing and compromise and increases political polarization. Institutional explanations can be seen as a quest for a "root source" for violence, a necessary condition for such actions to take place.

Ideational Explanations

If institutional explanations emphasize the impact of fixed organizations and patterns in fostering political violence, ideational explanations focus more on the rationale behind that violence. By **ideational** we simply mean having to do with ideas. Ideas may be institutionalized—concepts rooted in some institution such as a political organization or a religion—but just as often are uninstitutionalized, with no real organizational base. The argument here is that ideas play an important role in political violence in the way they set out a worldview, diagnose a set of problems, provide a resolution, and describe the means of getting there. Any or all of these elements can be bound up with a justification of violence. For example, scholars of suicide terrorism have focused on the ways in which groups use particular ideas, such as self-sacrifice and glory, to motivate individuals, binding them to a greater cause. These ideas can draw on religious beliefs, as in the case of violent Islamic fundamentalists linked to Al Qaeda. Or they may draw on secular ideas such as nationalism, as with the Tamil Tigers in Sri Lanka, who have used large numbers of suicide attackers in their quest for national independence.

These ideational factors take us back to our discussion of political attitudes in Chapter 3. As we noted there, political violence is more likely to be associated with attitudes that are radical or reactionary, since each attitude views the current institutional order as bankrupt and beyond reform. This

IN FOCUS

Explanations for Political Violence

Explanation	Reasoning	Example
Institutional	Existing institutions may encourage violence or constrain human action, creating a violent backlash.	Presidentialism
Ideational	Ideas may justify or promote the use of violence.	Some forms of religious fundamentalism; nationalism
Individual	Psychological or strategic factors may lead people to carry out violence.	Humiliation

reminds us that it is not only the content of the ideas that matters, but the place of those ideas relative to the domestic political status quo. Ideas seen as conservative in one context may become a source of radicalism, and thus violence, elsewhere.

Individual Explanations

Finally, individual explanations center on those who carry out the violence themselves. Here the scholarship emphasizes the personal motivations that allow people to contemplate and carry out violence toward political ends. Scholars who study individual explanations to political violence usually follow one of two paths. One emphasizes psychological factors, conditions that lead individuals toward violence. Such factors can be a function of individual experiences or they may be shaped by broader conditions in society, such as standard of living, level of human development, or gender roles. Such an approach tends to concentrate on how people may be driven to violence as an expression of desperation or aberrant behavior. For example, some scholars of religious violence emphasize the role of humiliation as a motivating force, a sense that one's own beliefs are actively marginalized and denigrated by society. Revolutionaries or terrorists, in this view, act out of despair. A contrary approach, however, rejects this view, seeing political violence as a rational act, carried out by those who believe it to be an effective political tool. Strategy, rather than despair, drives these actions. Political violence is in this view not an expression of deviancy, but carefully wielded by those who understand its costs and potential benefits.

One important element of comparison across these three explanations is how they approach free will—that is, to what extent people are the primary actors in political violence. Institutional explanations often are quite deterministic, seeing people shaped and directed by larger structures that they do not control. An individual's recourse to violence is simply the final step in a much larger process. In contrast, individual explanations place their focus squarely on people as the primary makers of violence who choose to do so. Ideational explanations lie somewhere in between. Ideas are influenced by institutions, but are also actively taken up and molded by individuals to justify political violence.

A second element of comparison concerns universal versus particularistic explanations. Institutional explanations tend to be more particularistic, stressing the unique combination and role of institutions in a given case that are not easily generalized elsewhere. Individual explanations tend to center on those personal or psychological attributes common to all humans that can lead to violence. Ideational explanations, again, lie somewhere in the middle, generalizing the importance of ideas while noting the very different lessons that different ideas impart.

Which explanation is most convincing: institutional, ideational, or individual? These explanations are often placed in competition with each other, but it may be that they actually work in conjunction. Institutional factors provide a context in which particular preconditions, problems, and conflicts may emerge. Ideational factors help describe and define those problems, ascribe blame, and provide solutions by calling for the transformation of the status quo. These ideas in turn influence and are shaped by individuals and groups who may already be prone to violent activity. In the case of the Basque independence group Euskadi Ta Askatasuna (ETA), in Spain, institutional factors include a long period of repression under authoritarian rule and its effects on the region; ideational factors include a belief among ETA members and supporters that the Basque people face cultural extermination at the hands of the Spanish; and individual factors include the role and motivations of many Basque youth in conducting "kale borroka" (urban struggle) in their quest for an independent, revolutionary Basque state. This example helps illustrate the interconnection of these three factors and why political violence is relatively unpredictable and has emerged in a variety of contexts. We will consider these various explanations next as we look specifically at revolution and terrorism.

Forms of Political Violence

So far, we have spoken of political violence in fairly general terms, defining it as violence outside of state control that is politically motivated. Even under this definition, political violence can manifest itself in many different forms:

assassinations, riots, rebellions, military coups, civil war, and ethnic conflict, to name a few. We will concentrate on two forms of political violence: revolution and terrorism. Revolution is important to study because of its profound effects. Revolutions have ushered in sweeping changes in modern politics, overturning old institutions and dramatically transforming domestic and international relations. Terrorism, while less sweeping, holds our attention as a similar challenge to modern political institutions whose impact on domestic and international politics has spiked in recent years. Both are forces that seek dramatic change. Yet in many ways, revolution and terrorism are the opposite of one another. Revolution conjures up the image of a spontaneous uprising of the masses, who take to the streets, seize control of the state, and depose the old regime. In contrast, terrorism is much more secret and hidden, a conspiratorial action carried out by a small group. But there are similarities in their sources and goals. As we analyze and compare the dynamics of revolution and terrorism, we will draw out some of these elements, as well as show how these seemingly disparate forms of political violence can be linked.

Revolution

The term *revolution* has many connotations. Although we speak of revolution as a form of political violence, the word is also used in a much more indiscriminate manner. Any kind of change that is dramatic is often described as revolutionary, whether the change is political or a trend in clothing. Related to this, the term *revolution* has a generally positive connotation, one that speaks of progress. People speak of dramatic change as positive, and "counterrevolution" is seen as an attempt to turn back the clock to a darker time. This should not be surprising; across much of the world, significant political change has been a result of revolution, and in these countries, revolution is often associated with independence, sovereignty, and development. This is true even in countries where the legacy of revolution is more contested, as in contemporary Russia. Thus, *revolution* is a loaded term, albeit with positive connotations.

For our purposes, we shall speak of revolution in a more limited manner. **Revolution** can be defined as a public seizure of the state in order to overturn the existing government and regime. There are several factors at work here. First, revolutions involve some element of public participation. To be certain, there are typically leaders, organizers, and instigators of revolution who play a key role. But unlike a coup d'état, where elites overthrow the government, in revolutions the public does play an important role in seizing power. Russia is an interesting example. While we typically speak of communism's triumph in 1917 as a revolution, some scholars call it a coup, with

Lenin and a handful of followers seizing control of the state rather than some mass action. Second, revolutions seize control of the state. This distinguishes such actions from such violence as ethnic conflicts, where groups may gain local control or even seek independence but do not or cannot take over the entire state. Finally, the objective of revolution is not simply the removal of those in power, but the removal of the entire regime itself. Protests or uprisings to pressure a leader to leave office are not necessarily revolutionary. At their core, revolutions seek to fundamentally remake the institutions of politics, and often economic and societal institutions as well. As a result, scholars sometimes speak of "social revolutions" to indicate that they are referring to events that completely reshape society.

Must revolutions be violent? This is a tricky question. Given the dramatic goals of revolution, violence is often difficult to avoid. Governments will resist overthrow, and such conflict can often lead to the fragmentation of the monopoly of violence, with parts of the state (such as elements of the military) often siding with revolutionaries. The immediate aftermath of revolutions can also be very bloody, as the losers are killed or carry out a counterrevolutionary struggle against the new regime.

However, not all revolutions are violent. In 1989, communist regimes in Eastern Europe collapsed in the face of public pressure, sweeping away institutions that many thought immovable. In most cases, violence was limited; Romania is the only country that experienced a violent struggle between the communist regime and revolutionaries that led to numerous deaths and destruction. Because of this absence of violence, many scholars would resist calling the collapse of communism in Eastern Europe revolutionary, preferring instead to speak of these changes as *political transitions*. Yet in most important ways, these events did fulfill our definition of revolution. South Africa, too, is a case where we see a change in regime from apartheid to multiracial democracy, but the elite-driven, largely nonviolent, and slow negotiated process makes most scholars uncomfortable with calling this a revolution.

What causes revolution? There is no agreement on this question, and the consensus has changed over time, with scholars grouping studies of revolution into three phases. In the first phase prior to World War II, scholars tended to describe, rather than explain, revolution. When causes were ascribed, explanations were often unsystematic, blaming bad government policies or leaders. With the behavioral revolution of the 1950s and 1960s (see Chapter 1), social scientists sought more generalized explanations. This new research took on varied forms and areas of emphasis, but shared in common a view that dramatic economic and social change or disruption, such as modernization, was central in sparking revolutionary events. These views tended to focus on the role of individuals as potential revolutionaries, seeking to understand what motivated them. For example, one of the main arguments that emerged out of this work was a psychological approach known as the **relative depriva-tion model**. According to this model, revolutions are less a function of specific conditions than the gap between actual conditions and public expec-tations. Improving economic or political conditions might still lead to revo-lution if, for example, such change leads to increased public demands that are eventually unmet, fostering discontent. It has sometimes been suggested that the 1979 Iranian Revolution is an example of relative deprivation at work. As Iran experienced rapid modernization in the decades prior to the revolu-tion, this only increased expectations for greater freedom and equality, espe-cially among young adults. This is what is meant by relative deprivation: it is not the absolute conditions that influence revolution, but rather how the pub-lic perceives them.

By the 1970s, these studies of revolution began to lose favor. Critics argued that theories of revolution predicated on sudden change could not explain why some countries could undergo dramatic change without revolution (as in Japan during the early twentieth century) or what levels of change would be enough to trigger revolution. In the specific case of the relative depriva-tion model, there was little evidence that past revolutions were in fact pre-ceded by rising expectations or discontent. Similarly, there were many cases where both expectations and discontent rose but revolution did not result. New studies of revolution took a more institutional approach, moving away from a focus on public reactions to a focus on the target of revolutions: the state.

Most influential in this regard has been the work of Theda Skocpol and her landmark book *States and Social Revolutions*. Focusing on France, China, and Russia, Skocpol argued that social revolutions required a very specific set of conditions. First is competition between rival states as they vie for military and economic power in the international system through such things as trade and war. Such competition is costly and often betrays the weakness of those states that cannot match their rivals. Second, as a result of this competition, weaker states often seek reform in order to increase their autonomy and capac-ity, hoping to change domestic institutions in order to boost their interna-tional power. This can include greater state centralization and changes in agriculture, industry, education, and taxation. Such changes, however, can threaten the status quo, undermining the power of entrenched elites, sowing discord among the public, and creating resistance as a result. The result is discontent, political paralysis, and an opening for revolution. In this view, it is not change *per se* that is central to revolution, but the power and actions of the state. Other actors are of relatively little importance.

The institutional approach to revolution became the dominant view dur-ing the 1980s, paralleling a wider interest in institutions and the power of the state. Yet institutional approaches themselves became subject to questions

IN FOCUS

Shifting Views of Revolution

Phase	Approach	Criticisms
First: pre–World War II	Studies of revolutionary events	Unsystematic and descriptive
Second: post–World War II; behavioral revolution	Studies of disruptive change, such as modernization, as driving revolutionary action	Not clear why change or rising discontent leads to revolution in some cases and not others
Third: 1970s–present	Studies of domestic and international state power as providing the opening for revolution	Too focused on institutions, to the neglect of ideas and individual actors

and criticism. Some argued that an overemphasis on institutions ignored the role played by leadership or ideas in helping to catalyze and direct revolutionary action. In addition, if earlier approaches did not seem to fit with the historical record, institutional approaches were themselves hard to disprove, essentially asserting that if there were a revolution, the state must have been weak and under international pressure.

These concerns were underscored by the revolutions in Eastern Europe in 1989. There can be no doubt that changes in the international system, specifically the Cold War and the Soviet Union's loosening of control over Eastern Europe, led to conflict and paralysis within these states. At the same time, however, public action was mobilized and shaped by opposition leaders who were strongly influenced by the ideas of liberalism, human rights, and nonviolent protest. In addition, mass protest appeared influenced by strategic calculation: successful public opposition in one country changed the calculations of actors elsewhere, increasing their mobilization and demands. Drawing on these events, some scholars have moved back toward more individual and ideational approaches. While state actions do matter, so do the motivations of opposition leaders and the public as a whole, their views regarding political change, and the ability to bring it about. Small shifts in ideas and perceptions may have a cascading effect, bringing people into the streets when no one would have predicted it the day before—including the revolutionaries themselves.[2]

As important as the cause of revolution is its impact. If a revolution does manage to sweep away the old regime and install a new one, the effects can be profound, but also with surprising continuities from the past. The first major impact is that revolutionary regimes often institutionalize new forms of politics, transforming the existing regime. Revolutions help pave the way for new ideas and ideologies: republicanism, secularism, democracy, liberalism, and communism were all marginal ideas until revolutions helped place them at the center of political life. Revolutions have served to destroy well-entrenched regimes and legitimize new and radical alternatives. They have also been responsible for dramatic economic and societal changes, such as the end of feudalism and the development of capitalism. This is why we tend to think of revolutions as positive events: from hindsight their effects are often seen as progressive. If ideational factors are often underplayed as a *source* of revolution, it is certainly true that these factors are central in the creation of revolutionary *regimes*.

This is not to say, however, that such changes could not have taken place without revolution. For example, many states have made rather dramatic transitions from one regime to another through more evolutionary change. India and its struggle for independence from the United Kingdom is a good example where nonviolent protest, rather than revolution, led to independence and the creation of the world's largest democracy. South Africa, too, is a country that most observers in the 1980s expected would fall to bloody revolution. Yet here, too, a peaceful transition was possible. In both cases, charismatic leaders (Gandhi, Mandela) played a key role in averting revolution and bringing about change.

Though revolutions may be instruments of progress, it is important to note what they do not achieve. In spite of the call for greater freedom or equality that is a hallmark of revolution, the reverse is often the case. Revolutionary leaders who once condemned the state quickly come to see it as a necessary tool to consolidate their victory, with the result being that power is often centralized to an even greater extent than before. This is not necessarily bad if this centralization of power can facilitate the creation of a modern state with a necessary degree of autonomy and capacity. Revolutions are often the foundation of a modern state. However, revolutionary leaders may seek a high degree of state power as part of the construction of an authoritarian or totalitarian regime, rejecting democracy as incompatible with the sweeping goals of the revolution. Cuba, China, Russia, France, and Iran are all cases where public demands for more rights ended with yet another dictatorship with uncanny echoes of the previous authoritarian order. Mexico is another good example. The 1910 revolution swept away the previous corrupt dictatorship, but was soon replaced by a one-party regime, itself corrupt and dictatorial, that held power until 2000.

A second impact is that revolutionary change, or the lack of it, often comes at a high cost. Revolutions are often destructive and bloody. The events that

INSTITUTIONS IN

ACTION

THERMIDOR: THE INSTITUTIONALIZATION OF REVOLUTION

Our discussion of revolutions has emphasized the degree to which these events are driven by a desire to sweep away old institutions and create some new, often utopian order. Great creative as well as destructive energies are unleashed by such revolutions in this quest for radical change. In spite of this, revolutionary zeal inevitably exhausts itself, as people grow disenchanted with perpetual turmoil, insecurity, the reappearance of mundane problems, and politics. Inevitably, **thermidor** sets in, or a period of conservatism and the loss of revolutionary idealism and zeal. This word refers to the eleventh month in the French Revolutionary calendar, when the French Reign of Terror came to an end in 1794 and a more conservative regime came to power. Across all revolutions one finds this tension between those who would seek to keep the spirit of the revolution alive, no matter what the cost, and those who would rather consolidate the revolution through new and old institutions. The former are accused of zealotry, while the latter are accused of betraying the revolution. Revolutions often devour themselves because of this tension. For example, in China in the 1960s, Mao unleashed the Cultural Revolution against the Communist Party itself, which he saw as having lost sight of its original revolutionary goals. Similar conflicts can be seen in the early years of the Russian and Mexican revolutions, and such battles continue to deeply influence contemporary Iranian politics. The end result can be a deep sense of disappointment, disengagement, and cynicism among the population, who feel that they have been betrayed. This can play into the hands of authoritarian leaders, who rely on such disengagement as a way to maintain control. Revolutions by their very nature seek to escape the oppressive weight of existing institutions, but in the end they find they are unable to escape them, as their radicalism becomes the new conservative status quo.

bring revolutionaries to power may themselves not claim many lives, but in the immediate aftermath, revolutionary leaders and their followers often feel a need to use violence against their perceived enemies to prevent counterrevolution and pave the way for a new order. The Mexican Revolution led to the death of a million and a half people; the Russian Revolution and subsequent civil war may have claimed well over 5 million. This violence can become an end in itself, as in the case of France's Reign of Terror after 1789. Enemies, supporters, and bystanders alike may all be consumed by an indiscriminate use of violence. In addition, it has been suggested that revolutionary states are also more likely to engage in interstate war, whether to promote their revolutionary ideology or because other countries feel threatened and/or see an opportunity to strike during this period of turmoil.[3] The long war between Iran and Iraq (1980–1988) can be cited here. Iraq attacked Iran in part because it hoped to take advantage of Iran's revolutionary turmoil and because Saddam Hussein feared that Iran would export its revolution to Iraq. Given the fragmentation of state power and the loss of the monopoly of force associated with revolution, greater violence is not surprising.

Terrorism

The word *terrorism* is, like *revolution*, loaded with meaning and used rather indiscriminately. However, these conceptual difficulties stem from issues that are opposite of those surrounding revolution. While revolution's conceptual fuzziness comes in part from its inherently positive connotation (leading people to associate the term with all sorts of things), the word *terrorism* is highly stigmatized, a term no one willingly embraces. As a result, terrorism has become confused with a variety of other names, many of which are misleading, while others use the term indiscriminately to describe any kind of political force or policy they oppose. This has led some to conclude that it is effectively impossible to define terrorism, falling back on an old cliché: "One man's terrorist is another man's freedom fighter." Such a conclusion runs against the whole purpose of political science, which is to define our terms in an objective manner. We should therefore seek out a definition as precise as possible and use it to distinguish terrorism from other forms of political violence with which it might be confused. Certainly, one thing we should note is that terrorism has claimed far fewer lives than revolution, in spite of its recent increase (Figure 11.1 and Table 11.1). It is not so much the scale of the violence that holds our attention, but rather whom that violence is directed toward.

Terrorism can be defined as the use of violence by nonstate actors against civilians in order to achieve a political goal. As with revolution, there are several components at work in this definition, and we should take a moment to clarify each. First, there is the question of nonstate actors. Why should the term not be applied to states as well? Do they not also terrorize people? Indeed, as we shall discuss later, the very concept of terrorism originally referred to state actions, not those of nonstate actors. Over time, the term came to be associated with nonstate actors who used terrorism in part because conventional military force was not available to them. This, however, does not mean that states cannot terrorize. Rather, other terms have come to stand in for such acts. When states use violence against civilian populations, we speak of war crimes or human rights violations, depending on the context. Both can include such acts as genocide and torture. Finally, there is **state-sponsored terrorism.** States do sometimes sponsor nonstate terrorist groups as a means

Figure 11.1
DEATHS FROM TERRORISM WORLDWIDE, 1998–2005

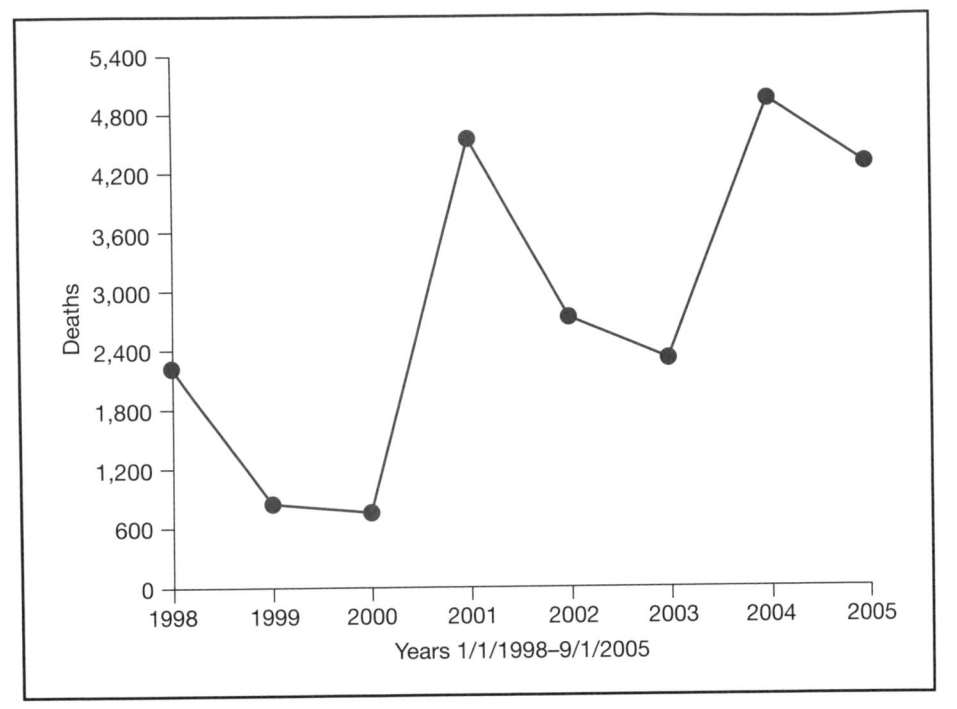

Source: National Memorial Institute for the Prevention of Terrorism.

to extend their power by proxy, using terrorism as an instrument of foreign policy. For example, India has long faced terrorist groups fighting for control over Kashmir, a state with a majority Muslim population (unlike the rest of India, which is majority Hindu). These terrorists are widely thought to be trained and armed by Pakistan, whose state leaders contend that Kashmir should be joined to their country. In short, we speak of terrorism as a non-state action not because states are somehow above such violence, but rather because other terminology exists to describe these actions (Figure 11.2).

Second, our definition of terrorism emphasizes that the targets of violence are civilians. Here the issue of intentionality is important. In violent conflicts, there are often civilian casualties. But terrorists specifically target civilians, believing that such targets are a more effective way to achieve their political ends than by attacking the state. As a result, we can make a distinction between terrorism and **guerilla war**. In contrast to terrorism, guerilla war involves nonstate combatants who largely accept traditional rules of war and target the state rather than civilians. Often the line between these two can be blurry: Is killing a policeman a terrorist act or a guerilla act? Still, the central distinction remains, not only to observers but also to those carrying out the violence. We will speak more of this in a moment.

Finally, there is the issue of the political goal. It is important to recognize that terrorism has a political objective; as such, it is not simply crime or a violent act without a larger goal. Here, too, the lines can be less than clear: terrorists may engage in crime as a way to support their activities, while criminal gangs may engage in terrorism if they are under pressure from the state. But in general, terrorism and other forms of violence can be sorted out by the primacy of political intent.

In short, while one man's terrorist may be another man's freedom fighter, such an observation is little more than an assertion that people judge terrorism in different ways, condemning or excusing such activity, depending on the context. Our task instead must be to define terrorism in objective terms and apply the term where it fits.

What are the causes of terrorism? As with revolution, there are varied and conflicting hypotheses, and these have changed over time as the nature of terrorism has shifted. In addition, because terrorism is so amorphous and shadowy, we find few comprehensive theories as we do in studies of revolution. Rather, scholars and policy makers have considered several competing explanations.

It is often argued that economic inequality or marginalization is central to terrorism. This may be a function of unequal economic relations within

Table 11.1 Terrorist Incidents by Region, 1/1/1998–9/1/2005

Region	Incidents	Fatalities
Middle East/Persian Gulf	5,640	8,152
South Asia	3,203	4,787
Western Europe	2,808	396
Latin America and the Caribbean	1,497	1,381
Eastern Europe	1,101	1,819
Southeast Asia and Oceania	463	966
Africa	331	2,187
North America	104	2,994
East and central Asia	88	138
TOTALS	15,235	22,820

Source: National Memorial Institute for the Prevention of Terrorism.

countries or between them. The level of education is often asserted to play an important role as well, with the less educated more susceptible to terrorist organizing and rationalizations for violence. Political institutions, too, are a common explanation, though the arguments are less clear. It is frequently argued that terrorism emerges where individuals feel shut out of the political process, but there is also the view that democracies' open societies provide ideal conditions for terrorists to form and operate.

In recent years, scholars have been attempting to flesh out some of the most common explanations to see whether they hold up to empirical scrutiny. Educational explanations do not appear to be a strong explanation for terrorism; research indicates that increased education does not reduce support for terrorism. On the contrary, terrorists tend to come from more educated backgrounds compared with the population as a whole, and universities have frequently been centers of terrorist organization and recruitment. One distinction here may be between the "foot soldiers" who actually execute the terrorist acts and the more educated terrorist leadership. But there are also many examples where terrorist groups were composed almost entirely of highly educated indi-

Figure 11.2 **FORMS OF STATE AND POLITICAL VIOLENCE**

TARGET \ ACTOR	State	Nonstate
State	War	Guerilla war
Civilians	Human rights violations (domestic) State-sponsored terrorism War crimes (international)	Terrorism

This chart distinguishes between forms of political violence, depending on who carries out the violence and who is the target of that violence. This includes both state and nonstate actors.

viduals, such as the Marxist European terrorists of the 1970s or the religious organization Aum Shinrikyo in Japan in the 1990s (discussed shortly).

Economic explanations are equally problematic. We know that terrorists are not necessarily impoverished; Osama bin Laden's personal wealth is estimated to be in the millions of dollars. Although it may seem reasonable that poverty would be a motivation for terrorism, research on this topic finds instead that poverty tends to foster apolitical views and a detachment from political action. Here, too, research indicates that terrorists tend to come from economically advantaged backgrounds and that terrorist activity is not clearly correlated with low or deteriorating economic conditions, just as we saw in the case of revolution.[4]

Explanations regarding the role of political institutions may be on firmer ground. Research in this area has found that while economic and educational factors may not be central in fostering terrorism, there does appear to be a correlation between regime type and the emergence of terrorist groups. Some have concluded that highly authoritarian regimes are the primary source of domestic and international terrorism. This appears logical. For example, most of the September 11 hijackers, as well as the majority of non-Iraqi fighters captured or killed in Iraq, are from Saudi Arabia, one of the least democratic countries in the Middle East. Other researchers, however, have noted that when one looks across the range of domestic and international terrorism around the world, transitional regimes (those having recently moved from authoritarianism) and illiberal regimes are the most frequent targets of terrorism. Why? It would appear that such regimes create both opportunity and motivation for terrorism to develop, through such things as weak state capacity and legitimacy, political instability, and poorly institutionalized mechanisms for public participation and resolving conflict.[5] Authoritarian regimes appear much more effective at stifling terrorist threats, while democratic states' participatory institutions also help undercut terrorists' legitimacy. There is one caveat to this observation. In a more globalized world, terrorism that is repressed in one country may seek to redirect its efforts elsewhere, and more open democratic states make tempting targets. Thus, while democracies are good at limiting domestic terrorism, they may become subject to international terrorism that has its origins in more repressive regimes.

Ideational explanations are similarly useful and problematic. It has been commonplace to explain terrorism by blaming some ideology, religion, or set of values. However, given the way in which terrorism has shifted and morphed over time, these explanations often cannot explain cause and effect particularly well. This having been said, ideas are important in that they can provide justification for terrorist acts; such violence needs to have a political goal to motivate its members.

Some have asserted that irrespective of the particular set of ideas, what is crucial is their connection to nihilist or apocalyptic views. By **nihilism**, we

IN FOCUS

Regime Type and Terrorism

Regime Type	Effect on Terrorism	Result	Risk of Terrorism
Authoritarian	Authoritarianism may foster terrorism, but the state can repress domestic terrorists; the state is unhindered by civil liberties.	Limited terrorism, but may be redirected outside of the country toward more vulnerable targets	Lower
Democratic	Participatory institutions and civil liberties are likely to undercut public support for terrorism.	Domestic terrorism less likely, but may be a target of international terrorism generated in authoritarian regimes	Moderate
Illiberal/transitional	Weak state capacity, instability, and limited democratic institutions may generate both opportunities and motivations for terrorism.	Terrorism more likely, with domestic and/or international support	Higher

mean a belief that all institutions and values are essentially meaningless and that the only redeeming value one can embrace is that of violence. In this view, violence is desirable for its own sake. Nihilism can also be combined with utopian and apocalyptic views, whereby violence can destroy and thus purify a corrupted world, ushering in a new order.

Finally, individual explanations for terrorism have been a consistent source of focus, with researchers seeking to understand the personal motivations of terrorists. As mentioned earlier, one common explanation centers on feelings of injustice coupled with humiliation—that an individual or community's self-worth has been denigrated by others. Such feelings can generate frustration, anger, and, most importantly, a desire for vengeance. In addition, terrorist groups can play a role in providing a sense of identity and solidarity for otherwise alienated or humiliated individuals. Political violence can be a source of meaning, giving one a sense of greater purpose. In fact, it has been argued that terrorist groups resemble religious cults, with an emphasis on community, the purity of the cause, faith in the rectitude of the group's own beliefs and actions, and the belief that retribution paves the way toward some utopian outcome.[6]

The effects of terrorism are harder to discern than the effects of revolutions. The first question to ask is whether terrorists are able to achieve their goals. In the case of revolution, the political violence is by definition successful—we study cases where regimes have been successfully overthrown. In the case of terrorism, however, we are looking at the acts and actors, rather than the events or outcomes.

One general observation we can make is that terrorists are mostly unsuccessful in achieving their stated long-term outcomes. Terrorists often seek some dramatic change in the existing domestic and/or international order, and their actions usually do not achieve this particular objective. However, this is not to say that terrorism has no impact. Economically, terrorism can be highly successful in depressing tourism, foreign direct investment, stock markets, and other sectors of the economy. Society can be similarly affected, not just from the effects of a weakened economy, but by increasing anxiety and insecurity, undermining people's sense of well-being.

Terrorism can also have a distinct effect on politics. Countering terrorism can be a costly and frustrating process with little to show for it, diverting national resources while failing to address public concerns. An eroded sense of confidence in the state can be the result. In the quest for greater security, governments and their citizens may also favor increasing state power and curtailing civil liberties in the hope that such steps will limit terrorists' scope for action. However, this can lead to a weakening of democratic institutions and civil rights. The result can be less trust in government and less public control over it. At an extreme, terrorism can help bring down a democratic regime. In 1992, Peruvian president Alberto Fujimori dissolved the legislature and suspended the constitution, which he justified in part as necessary to battle two separate terrorist groups that had destabilized the country. Much of the public supported this action, seeing it as the only way to reestablish order. Terrorism in Russia by Chechen separatists similarly helped pave the way for Vladimir Putin to win the presidency in 2000, and subsequent attacks have been used as a justification for removing democratic institutions and limiting civil liberties.

This destruction of democracy, of course, is precisely what terrorism seeks—justification for their violence and another step toward destabilizing existing institutions. Terrorism uses violence against civilians as a way to disrupt the institutional fabric of state, society, and economy, calling into question all those things we take for granted, including stability, security, and predictability. By disrupting these most basic elements of modern life and instilling fear, terrorists believe that this will help pave the way for their political objectives. We will turn to these considerations at the end of the chapter, when we discuss how to counter political violence.

Terrorism and Revolution: Means and Ends

The question of what terrorists want leads us to consider terrorism and revolution as related forms of political violence. While we might think of these two as quite separate, it was not always this way. In modern politics, the concepts of terrorism and revolution were initially bound together as part of a single process, having their origins in the French Revolution. For revolutionary leaders like Maximilien Robespierre, terror was an essential part of revolution. Robespierre argued that "terror is nothing other than justice, prompt, severe, inflexible; it is therefore an emanation of virtue" in the service of revolutionary change.[7] Thus, terror was not only a positive act, but a tool in the service of the revolutionary state.

Over time, this concept of terrorism and revolution began to shift. Revolutionaries who embraced the lessons of Robespierre concluded that terror need not be a tool to consolidate revolution once a regime has been overthrown, but could in fact be the means toward that revolutionary end. A small group could speak for and lead the masses, instigating violence as a way to spark revolution. These revolutionaries thus openly embraced the name "terrorist" as an expression of their desire to use violence to achieve their political goals. Although the terrorist label has become stigmatized over time, this relationship between terrorism and revolution remains in place.

Terrorism can therefore be understood not simply in terms of who is directing political violence and at whom. In terms of its political goals, terrorism is often revolutionary in nature. Terrorists rarely seek limited goals, such as political or economic reform, since the entire system is seen as illegitimate. Rather, they believe that through their seemingly indiscriminate use of violence, all the dominant institutions can be shattered, overthrown, and remade. Consider, for example, this passage from an early manifesto of the Peruvian terrorist group Shining Path:

> The people rise up, arm themselves and rebel, putting nooses on the necks of imperialism and reaction. The people take them by the throat, threaten their lives and will strangle them out of necessity. The reactionary meat will be trimmed of fat, they will be torn to tatters and rags, the scraps sunk into mire, and the remainders burned. The ashes will be thrown to the winds of the world so that only the sinister reminder of what must never return will remain.[8]

This link between terrorism and revolution also helps to distinguish between terrorism and guerilla war. We mentioned earlier that the line between these two forms of political violence is blurry, but that we can distinguish between the two in terms of their targets. (Guerilla war seeks to abide by traditional rules of war, avoiding the targeting of civilians.) This decision is driven by political goals. Guerillas typically accept that their opponents are legitimate actors, and they themselves seek to be regarded as legitimate by their opponents and the international community. Demands, while sometimes extensive (such as greater civil rights or independence for an ethnic group) do not deny the legitimacy of the other side, as is normally the case with terrorism. These distinctions matter, in that such differences in means and ends will affect the degree to which states can negotiate with such groups to bring an end to conflict.

For example, during the civil conflict in Algeria in the 1990s, there operated two nonstate groups: the Islamic Salvation Front (FIS) and the Armed Islamic Group (GIA). Both opposed the Algerian regime, which suppressed Islamic fundamentalist groups, but took very different forms of opposition. The FIS created an armed wing that targeted specific parts of the state seen as directly supporting the regime. The FIS, which began as a nonviolent political movement, simultaneously declared that they could come to a compromise with the regime if certain demands were met, such as democratic elections. In contrast, the GIA rejected the entire regime and political process as un-Islamic and argued that anyone they viewed as having cooperated with the state in any manner, such as voting, deserved to be killed. The GIA's killing was thus much more indiscriminate and widespread, directed at state, society, and the FIS. Jihad, they argued, was the *only* means to an Islamic state.[9] While the FIS declared an end to their struggle after negotiations with the Algerian government, the GIA continued its battle until its leadership was killed, only to be replaced by a similarly uncompromising group that continues into the present.

In short, revolution and terrorism have close connections. Terrorists often have revolution as their ultimate goal and use violence more widely in the belief that this will help set the stage for revolution. More limited use of force, as in guerilla war, reflects a desire to participate in or work with existing institutions, rather than overthrow them. The issue, then, for nonstate wielders of violence is whether they desire a seat at the political table or seek to knock the table over.

Political Violence in Context: Faith, Terrorism, and Revolution

Now that we have considered different ways to approach political violence, particularly revolution and terrorism, let us apply these ideas to the most pressing example in contemporary domestic and international politics: religious violence. As we discussed in Chapter 3, in recent decades we have seen the rise of movements that view religion as absolute and without error and that seek to make faith the sovereign authority over states and people. This religious fundamentalism is a major challenge to traditional ideologies in part because it is modeled after ideology itself. But while such fundamentalism may be uncompromising (as with many ideologies), it is not necessarily violent. Fundamentalists may believe that reestablishing God's sovereignty can be done through democratic or peaceful engagement in politics or by withdrawing from these corrupt practices altogether. But within this strain of thought there is also a violent approach.

What are the conditions under which religion becomes a source of political violence? The factors here echo much of our earlier discussion, including institutional, ideational, and individual factors. First, one common factor is hostility to modernity. In this view, modern institutions, driven by states and nations, capitalism, ideology, secularism, individualism, and material prosperity, have stripped the world of greater meaning and driven people to alienation and despair. This is not to say that those who adopt this view have not been able to share in the fruits of modernity. Political violence is often embraced by those who initially embraced and enjoyed modernity but at some point turned away from its "corrupt" lifestyle. These antimodernist views have emerged in many different contexts—societies with varying levels of development as well as different regime types. They do, however, seem to be most powerful in societies where modern institutions are adopted from the outside and only poorly grafted onto traditional structures and values. It is at this border between traditional and modern institutions that the contradictions can be sharpest. This may explain why adherents of an antimodern mind-set are often urban and well-educated individuals: such persons are often most deeply immersed in modernity and may feel its limitations most sharply (see, for example, the discussion of salafism and jihadism in Chapter 9). This clash between traditional and modern institutions seems to provide much of the friction that fosters hostility.

A second factor is what sociologist Mark Jeurgensmeyer calls "cosmic war."[10] In this view, the world around us can be described in stark terms of good and evil, light and dark. This is often called a **Manichean** approach, a term drawn from a long-extinct faith that viewed the world in such terms. In this Manichean view of cosmic war, the modern world not only actively marginalizes, humiliates, and denigrates the views of the believers, but seeks their outright extermination. Those who hold this view see themselves as soldiers in a struggle between the righteousness of faith and its enemies (modernity), a war that transcends space and time. This is often bound up in conspiracy theories that point to shadowy forces in league to exterminate the good. With these views, violence against civilians can be rationalized because the conflict is viewed not in terms of civilians versus combatants, but in terms of the guilty versus the innocent: those who do not stand on the side of righteousness are by definition on the side of evil. Scholars note that this dehumanization of the enemy is an important component in justifying violence against civilians, as social or religious taboos against murder must be overcome.

Third, religion as a source of political violence is often connected to messianic, apocalyptic, and utopian beliefs. Although the forces of darkness (modernity) have gained the upper hand, its opponents believe that this sacrilege will eventually be utterly destroyed through a violent apocalypse. The role of the righteous is to help bring this Armageddon about, triggering events that will lead to the destruction of the modern world. Evil will be destroyed by divine retribution and justice will be served. These views of violent apocalypse are often tied to some messianic belief that a savior will trigger the apocalypse or that by triggering an apocalypse, a savior will appear. Following the apocalypse, a new utopian order will be established, re-creating the sovereignty of God and reuniting humanity with the true faith.

With these beliefs, violence not only is acceptable and necessary but becomes a form of ritual sacrifice, whether in the form of self-sacrifice (martyrdom) or the sacrifice of others. There is a departure from holy texts and religious leaders and institutions in that individuals take unto themselves the decision of who is righteous or evil, who should be sacrificed, and why. When these factors are present, violence is much more likely.

Such groups or movements are an extreme form of fundamentalism, since their path to violence requires a dramatic reinterpretation of the faith in a way that dramatically divorces it from its mainstream foundations. These groups thus tend to break away from the mainstream faith and other fundamentalists, who they accuse of having lost their way, presenting their radical alternatives as a restoration of religious truth. Muslim, Christian, or other fundamentalists would thus find many of these views as horrific and far removed from their view of faith. To reiterate, it is a mistake to confuse fundamentalism with violence.

Now that we have outlined some of the most significant factors involved in religiously motivatived political violence, let us consider some specific examples to see these factors at work.

Within Al Qaeda and similar jihadist groups, individuals like Osama bin Laden or Muhammed Atta (one of the leaders of the September 11 attacks) were steeped in modernity before turning to religion and religious violence. This violence is understood as part of a global struggle against infidels that goes back centuries. Hence, when Bin Laden refers to the West as "Crusaders" in his 1996 manifesto, he is reaching back to the battles between the Islamic and Christian worlds in the Middle Ages. In the modern world, Bin Laden argues, this crusade against Islam and its followers continues, though the

West's conspiracies are often cloaked by international organizations like the United Nations or multinational corporations.

In the September 11 attacks, we can see how the logic of cosmic war also fits into apocalyptic beliefs. Al Qaeda carried out these attacks not simply to weaken the United States, but to provoke a backlash that they believed would intensify the conflict between the Islamic and non-Islamic worlds, which would in turn lead to the overthrow of "un-Islamic" regimes in the Middle East and the eventual collapse of the West.

In these circumstances, not only are civilians fair targets, but Muslim civilians as well, whether in the United States, Europe, or the Middle East. This is justified by the fact that their "collaboration" with the forces of evil means by definition that they are not true Muslims and therefore can be killed, sacrificed to the cause. Recalling our discussion of the GIA in Algeria, its leader justified their widespread violence against the public by stating that "all the killing and slaughter . . . are an offering to God."[11]

Such views have strong parallels to certain violent strains drawn from Christianity. In the United States, racist groups assert that Western Christianity has been corrupted and weakened by a global Jewish conspiracy and seek to rebuild Western society on the basis of a purified white race. One particularly important figure in this ideology was William Pierce, who died in 2002. Pierce, who held a Ph.D. in physics and was at one time a university professor, formed the National Alliance in 1974. Pierce departed from Christianity altogether as a faith tainted by its association with Judaism, offering instead a "cosmotheist" faith that viewed whites as a form of superior evolution on the road to unity with God. In his manifesto *The Turner Diaries*, written in novel form, Pierce described the creation of a dedicated underground that would attack symbols of American authority, seize territory, and eventually launch a nuclear attack against the country itself. This apocalypse destroys the state, allowing the revolutionaries to exterminate all nonwhites and those who do not accept the new order. This genocide is eventually extended worldwide.[12]

Timothy McVeigh's bombing of the federal courthouse in Oklahoma City in 1995, which killed 167 people, was directly inspired by *The Turner Diaries* and Pierce's argument that terrorism could trigger revolution. Pierce, while disassociating himself from McVeigh's act, nevertheless stated that McVeigh was

> a soldier, and what he did was based on principle. . . . He was at war against a government that is at war against his people. . . . In this war the rule is: Whatever is good for our people is good, and whatever harms our people is evil. That is the morality of survival.[13]

Pierce's views and those of related movements continue to attract follow-ers throughout North America and Europe; it is estimated that as many as 200,000 copies of *The Turner Diaries* have been sold, and the book has been translated into several European languages.

This violence extends outside the monotheistic religions of the West. In the 1980s, Japan saw the emergence of a new religion, Aum Shinrikyo ("Supreme Truth"). Aum was headed by Shoko Asahara, a partially blind mys-tic who claimed that he had reconnected with the true values of Buddhism that had been lost in the modern world. Asahara claimed that the world had gone through a series of thousand-year stages since the time of Buddha, with each one moving further away from his teachings. The current period was one of total degeneration, based on materialism and worldly desires. Aum attracted thousands of members in Japan, as well as in Russia following the collapse of communism. Aum's followers, who were overwhelmingly well edu-cated and included scientists and doctors, felt alienated by a materialistic soci-ety and were in search of spiritual meaning.

Asahara initially believed that the group should try to engage Japanese politics and fielded candidates for parliamentary elections in 1990. When all these candidates were defeated, however, Aum took on a more apocalyptic tone. Asahara claimed that a global war triggered by the United States would destroy the planet by the end of the decade, although those who followed Aum would survive. Aum began actively to investigate how to construct weapons of mass destruction in the apparent belief that such tools could be used to sow discord and help bring this apocalypse about. Aum followers worked on developing chemical, biological, and radiological weapons before settling on the deadly poison sarin. The use of violence against civilians was justified with the argument that those who had not embraced Aum had already experienced a "karmic death," making violence more akin to a mercy killing.[14]

In 1995, members of Aum placed bags of sarin in the Tokyo subway, killing twelve and injuring several thousand. Had the poison been more refined, the casualties would have been much higher. The Japanese government quickly cracked down on Aum and arrested Asahara and several of his followers, though a fragment of his original organization, having renounced terrorism, continues to this day.

In these three cases we see important similarities. First, these groups rad-ically reinterpret an existing faith by arguing that it has departed from the true path. These actions come not from traditional religious leaders, but from radicalized individuals who have condemned modernity. Osama bin Laden, William Pierce, and Shoko Asahara each claimed for themselves the ability to reinterpret traditional faith in a new, overtly ideological manner. Second, through this interpretation, they recast the world in terms of an ultimate show-down between good and evil, purity versus corruption. Third, as the defenders of truth, they placed themselves in the role of warriors in the service of faith, able to mete out justice against all those who are seen as the enemy, whether state or society. Fourth, this violence was described not as an unfortunate necessity, but as a sacrifice to the cause that would purify humanity and bring forth utopia.

Interestingly, religiously motivated political violence has many parallels with similar acts carried out by nonreligious groups. Secular and even antireligious revolutions and terrorism have often been driven by very similar motives, consistent with our earlier observation that politically violent groups often resemble religious cults. The failures and humiliations of modernity, the creation of a group of "true believers" who see the world in stark terms of good versus evil, the idea of a global apocalypse that will destroy the old order and usher in a utopia can all be ascribed to many forms of political violence where religion is not a factor. Our earlier quote from the Shining Path, a Peruvian group that rigidly adhered to a Maoist version of communist ideology, could just as easily have come from a religiously motivated group. A wide range of ideas, secular or religious, can be radically reinterpreted and put in the service of political violence.

Do such conclusions give us any better understanding of future manifestations of political violence? In this regard there has been a sharp debate among scholars whether environmental and animal rights groups might become more violent in the future. Some assert that these are inherently peaceful movements that would never tolerate such activity, while others point to arson and other property damage already committed by groups such as the Animal Liberation Front. In fact, many of the elements we have considered—hostility to modernity, a struggle in which the fate of the planet hangs in the balance, and the belief in apocalypse and utopia—can be found in the writings of more radical environmentalists.[15] Again we can see the similarities between ideology and religion and the similar ways in which both can be used to justify violence.

Countering Political Violence

Our discussion indicates that political violence is a varied and constantly shifting force in the modern world. So long as states monopolize force, there will be actors who seek to wrest this power back into their own hands to pursue their own political objectives. Violence can be motivated by institutional, ideational, and individual factors—most likely some combination of the three. Religious violence is currently at the forefront of comparative politics, though we see that in many ways these acts are highly politicized and ideological, just as ideologically motivated violence often takes on religious qualities.

Given the amorphous nature of political violence, what can states do to manage or prevent it? This is difficult to answer, since the response partly depends on the nature of the political violence itself. Although violence differs across time and from place to place, we can nevertheless make a few tentative observations, understanding that these are not ironclad answers.

One finding that we draw from our discussion of revolution and terrorism is that the nature of the existing regime does appear to make a difference. Recall the findings that terrorism is less likely to emerge from democratic societies. We can also observe that revolutions, too, do not occur in democracies. Why would this be the case? The simplest answer is that democracies allow for a significant degree of participation among a wide enough number of citizens to make them feel that they have a stake in the system. While democracies produce their own share of cynicism and public unrest, including political violence, they also appear to co-opt and diffuse the motivations necessary for serious organized or mass violence against the state and civilians. Again, this is not to say that democracies are impervious to political violence; Timothy McVeigh and Shoko Asahara have recently proved otherwise. Our observation is merely that democracies appear to be more effective at containing and limiting such groups.

This explanation based on regime type may help explain why, for example, religiously motivated political violence in the West has had a much smaller impact than in the Middle East, where authoritarian states are the norm. Of course, as we noted earlier, one of the dangers is that in an interconnected world, terrorism and revolution sparked by one kind of regime can easily spill beyond its borders. While democracy may be an important factor in preventing domestic violence, this will not necessarily prevent the development of political violence elsewhere. Indeed, the paradox here is that open democratic societies may limit domestic conflict but make for a much more tempting target for political violence that is internationalized.

One might conclude that if regime type is an important factor, then regime change should be a central goal for reducing political violence. Perhaps. However, such a policy is fraught with problems. First, research indicates that the successful institutionalization of democracy is predicated on how that regime change takes place. Regime changes that are top down (elite directed or through external intervention) or involving societal violence are less likely to produce a democratic outcome in the long run (Figure 11.3).[16]

The result instead is more likely to be an illiberal regime where democracy is weakly institutionalized. And as we noted earlier, such a regime, with

Figure 11.3 **REGIME CHANGE AND FREEDOM**

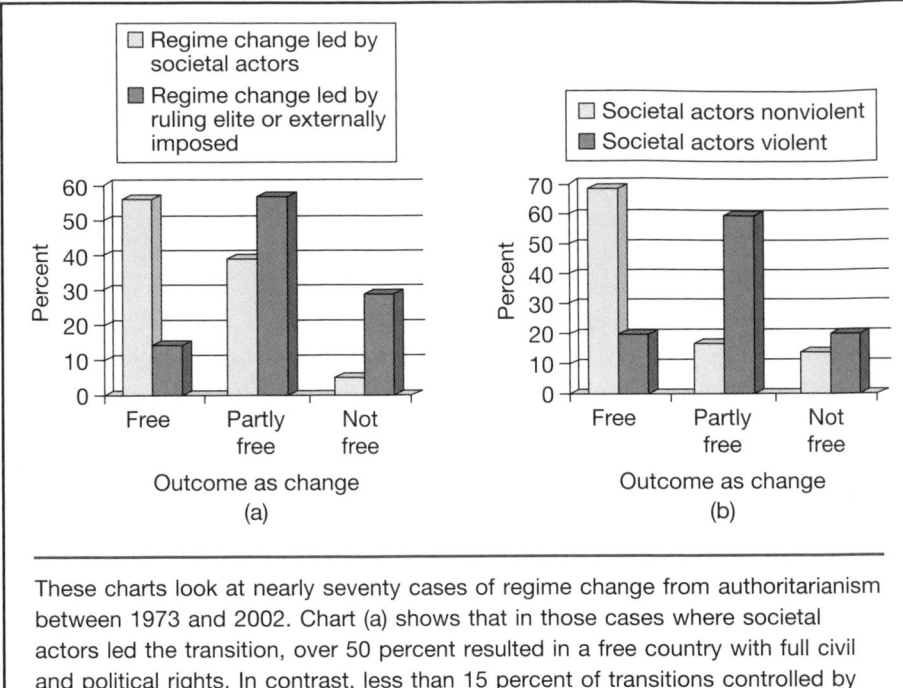

These charts look at nearly seventy cases of regime change from authoritarianism between 1973 and 2002. Chart (a) shows that in those cases where societal actors led the transition, over 50 percent resulted in a free country with full civil and political rights. In contrast, less than 15 percent of transitions controlled by those in power or imposed by other states led to a free political regime. Chart (b) indicates that in those cases where societal actors refrained from violence, nearly 70 percent resulted in a free country with full civil and political rights. In contrast, only 20 percent of transitions with societal violence resulted in a free political regime.

Source: Freedom House.

its combination of truncated and unstable freedoms, can provide both the motivation and opportunity for political violence to emerge. In short, regime change can in fact increase, not reduce, the number of regimes that foster political violence. Iraq would appear to be sad evidence of this, a case of an externally imposed regime change that led to a disintegration of the state and widespread political violence, including terrorism. In contrast, countries with strong civil societies are more likely to experience peaceful transitions to democracy that develop from the grass roots.

What about states that are already liberal democracies and yet face political violence from domestic or international actors? In this case, the classic dilemma of freedom versus security raises its head. In the face of threats, democratic states and their citizens will often favor limiting certain civil liberties and increasing state autonomy and capacity in order to bring an end to political violence. Such an approach may be effective by giving the state greater leeway against actors who cannot be fought with traditional criminal approaches. In the United States, the 2001 Patriot Act is an example of such counterterrorism, with its increased powers to conduct public surveillance. In India, the 2002 Prevention of Terrorism Act allows for the detention of suspects for up to six months without charging them with a crime. Both countries have recently experienced serious terrorism, so support for such legislation is not surprising. Yet even Canada, with no similar threat, shows strong public support for restrictions on civil liberties (Figure 11.4).

There are several dangers here. First, an excessive focus on security over freedom may be dangerous to democracy. By placing too much power in the hands of the state to observe and control the public, there is the threat that individual rights will be seriously eroded, and with it democracy. Second, such actions can in fact contribute to political violence, since they confirm the idea that the state is conspiring to destroy its opponents, thus justifying violent resistance. Third, the increase of state control typically means greater centralization of power, which may not increase security and may create new targets for political violence. An example will help elucidate these arguments.

In recent years, the United States and many other countries have proposed a national identification card that would be linked to a central national (perhaps international) database. Such a card could be used widely to track the public and regulate access into secure areas, such as buildings, planes, or nuclear power plants. However, such a move raises several concerns. ID cards created to counter terrorism can be used to track a variety of actions, many unrelated to national security. This has already been an issue with closed circuit television (CCTV) cameras, which are widely used in public spaces. In the United Kingdom, estimates are that several million CCTV cameras are already in use. Anonymity, privacy, and individual rights could be lost through an incremental and even voluntary process, weakening democracy and even playing into the logic of political violence as necessitating resistance against an oppressive state. Moreover, there is the risk that a system such as a national ID card could become a target in itself. A centralized database used to control access to secured areas across a country could be hacked, providing unauthorized access, or the entire network could be intentionally targeted and crashed, essentially paralyzing all transactions that relied on this system.[17]

Such concerns may lead us to conclude that alternative methods may be more flexible and encroach less on civil liberties—for example, better trained security at potential targets instead of national ID cards. However, such actions do not provide the public a demonstration that something obvious is being done to alleviate the insecurity that comes from political violence. People often seek dramatic and visible solutions because such solutions provide

Figure 11.4 VIEWS ON COUNTERING TERRORISM: CANADA AND THE UNITED STATES

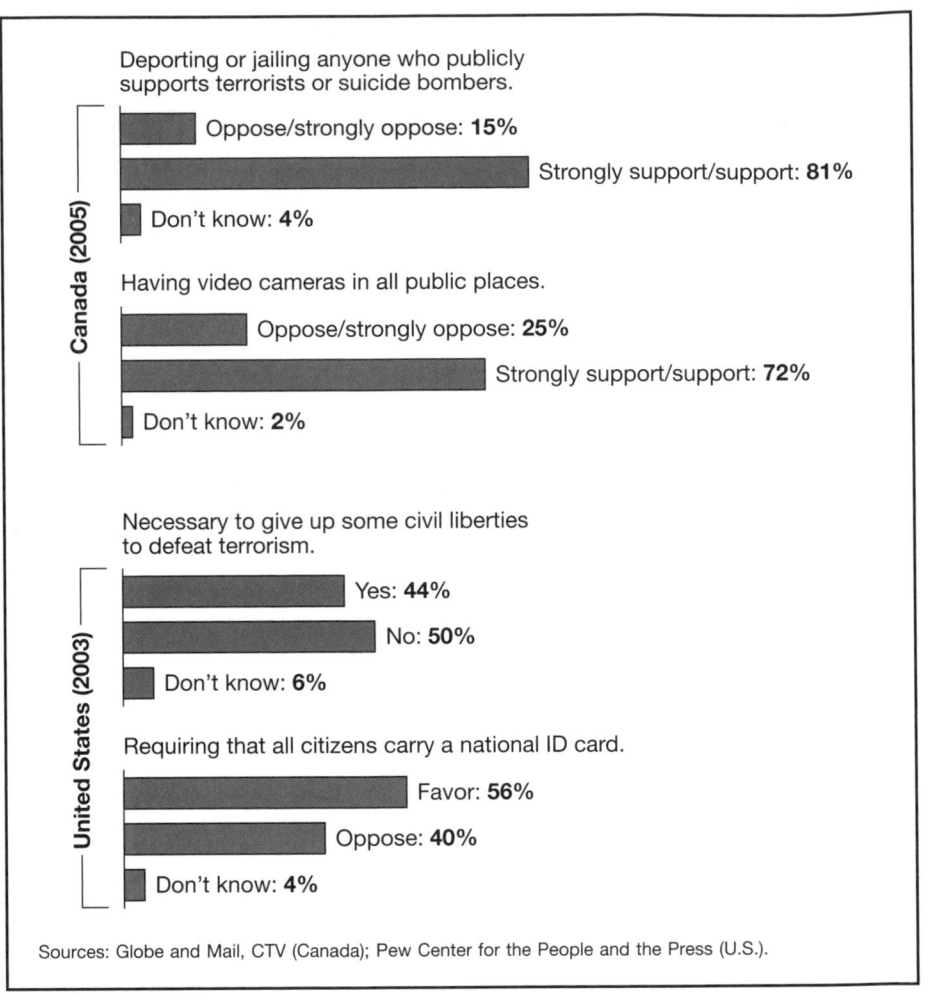

Sources: Globe and Mail, CTV (Canada); Pew Center for the People and the Press (U.S.).

a sense of security, although in reality they may have limited or even counterproductive effects. The old adage attributed to Benjamin Franklin is worth recalling: "Those who would give up essential liberty to purchase a little temporary safety deserve neither liberty nor safety."[18]

In Sum: Meeting the Challenge of Political Violence

Political violence is a complex issue for scholars, states, and societies. Often its objectives are cast in idealistic terms as a part of necessary historical change. At the same time, this violence often comes at a tremendous cost of human life, with violence often becoming an end in itself. Because political violence is a response to existing institutions, it is difficult to pin down exactly how it emerges, what motivates it, and how states should respond. Like a virus, it may suddenly emerge in unexpected places, ravaging the population before disappearing again. Or it may lie dormant for many years, only to break out when a certain set of conditions come together.

There is clearly no one way to stop or prevent political violence. Each case is different and requires its own approach. However, we have noted that in general, democracies have been most effective at limiting political violence. If we accept the analogy of political violence as a virus, it suggests that one means of response to political violence is immunization. Countries may be able to immunize themselves by maintaining and strengthening civil societies that help reduce the appeal or societal impact of political violence.[19] While such actions will never eradicate the danger, they may be able to limit its spread and damage by undercutting the motivations behind it. To think of political violence as a public health issue may provide new ways of countering this danger in the future.

With these ideas at hand, we can conclude with some thoughts on the dilemma of freedom and equality. The goal of this textbook has been to study the way in which politics unfolds around the world, shaped by the various institutions that help define economies, societies, and states. The struggle for individual freedom and collective equality is fought at several levels. Within states, this battle takes shape as power is centralized and policies made; within societies, as ideas are created and identities given form; within economies, as resources are allocated and wealth distributed. The interaction of these institutions and conflicts is the fuel of comparative politics, generating different forms of representation and community, values and violence.

These changes before us are at once uncertain and potentially profound. We may stand at the end of one era in comparative politics and at the rise of a new one, whose possible changes may be for good or ill and whose outcome we cannot foresee. By understanding these forces, we arm ourselves with the ability to shape the future and define the course of human progress.

NOTES

1. M. J. Heale, *American Anticommunism: Battling the Enemy Within, 1830–1970* (Baltimore: Johns Hopkins University Press, 1990).
2. Timur Kuran, "Now Out of Never: The Element of Surprise in the East European Revolution of 1989," *World Politics* 44, no. 1 (October 1991): 7–48.
3. Stephen M. Walt, *Revolution and War* (Ithaca: Cornell University Press, 1996).

4. Alan B. Krueger and Jikta Malečková, "Education, Poverty and Terrorism: Is There a Causal Connection?" *Journal of Economic Perspectives* 17, no. 4 (Fall 2003): 119–144.

5. Alberto Abadie, "Poverty, Political Freedom, and the Roots of Terrorism," October 2004, NBER Working Paper No. W10859, http://papers.ssrn.com.

6. Randy Borum, *Psychology of Terrorism* (Tampa: University of South Florida, 2004).

7. Maximilien Robespierre, *On Political Morality*, 1794.

8. *We Are the Initiators*, Shining Path Manifesto, Shining Path Central Committee, 1980.

9. Mohammed M. Hafez, "Armed Islamist Movements and Political Violence in Algeria," *Middle East Journal* 54, no. 4 (Autumn 2000): 572–591.

10. Mark Juergensmeyer, *Terror in the Mind of God: The Global Rise of Religious Violence* (Berkeley, CA: University of California Press, 2003).

11. Quoted in Hafez, "Armed Islamist Movements," 590.

12. Brad Whitsel, "The Turner Diaries and Cosmotheism: William Pierce's Theology," *Nova Religio* 1, no. 2 (April 1998): 183–197.

13. William Pierce, "The Morality of Survival," May 2001, www.natvan.com.

14. Daniel A. Metraux, "Religious Terrorism in Japan: The Fatal Appeal of Aum Shinrikyo," *Asian Survey* 35, no. 12 (December 1995): 1140–1154.

15. Gary Ackerman, "Beyond Arson? A Threat Assessment of the Earth Liberation Front," *Terrorism and Political Violence* 15, no. 4 (Winter 2003): 143–170.

16. "How Freedom Is Won: From Civic Resistance to Durable Democracy," Freedom House Special Report, 2005, www.freedomhouse.org.

17. Stephen T. Kent and Lynette I. Millett, eds., *IDs—Not That Easy: Questions About Nationwide Identity Systems* (Washington, DC: National Academy Press, 2002).

18. Anonymous, *An Historical Review of the Constitution and Government of Pennsylvania* (London, 1759), i.

19. Ami Pedazhur, "Struggling with the Challenges of Right Wing Extremism and Terrorism within Democratic Boundaries: A Comparative Analysis," *Studies in Conflict and Terrorism* 24 (2001): 339–359.

GLOSSARY

abstract review   Judicial review that allows the constitutional court to rule on questions that do not arise from actual legal disputes.

advanced democracy   A country with institutionalized democracy and a high level of economic development.

anarchism   A political ideology that stresses the elimination of the state and private property as a way to achieve both freedom and equality for all.

authoritarianism   A political system in which a small group of individuals exercises power over the state without being constitutionally responsible to the public.

autonomy   The ability of the state to wield its power independently of the public.

behavioralism   A movement within political science during the 1950s and 1960s to develop general theories about individual political behavior that could be applied across all countries.

bicameral system   A political system in which the legislature comprises two houses.

bureaucratic authoritarianism   A system in which the state bureaucracy and the military share a belief that a technocratic leadership, focused on rational, objective, and technical expertise, can solve the problems of the country without public participation.

capacity   The ability of the state to wield power to carry out basic tasks, such as defending territory, making and enforcing rules, collecting taxes, and managing the economy.

capitalism   A system of production based on private property and free markets.

cartel   A small number of producers that, although each individually is unable to dominate a market, collaborate to do so together.

central bank   The state institution that controls how much money is flowing through the economy, as well as how much it costs to borrow money in that economy.

Central Committee   The legislature-like body of a communist party.

central planning   A communist economic system in which the state explicitly allocates resources by planning what should be produced and in what amounts, the final prices of goods, and where they should be sold.

charismatic legitimacy   Legitimacy built on the force of ideas embodied by an individual leader.

citizenship   An individual's relationship to the state, wherein citizens swear allegiance to that state and the state in return is obligated to provide rights to those citizens.

civil rights   Individual rights regarding equality that are created by the constitution and the political regime.

civil liberties   Individual rights regarding freedom that are created by the constitution and the political regime.

civil society   Organizations outside of the state that help people define and advance their own interests.

clientelism   A process whereby the state co-opts members of the public by providing specific benefits or favors to a single person or a small group in return for public support.

coercion   Compelling behavior by threatening harm.

colonialism   An imperialist system of physically occupying a foreign territory using military force, businesses, or settlers.

communism   (1) A political-economic system in which all wealth and property are shared so as to eliminate exploitation, oppression, and, ultimately, the need for political institutions such as the state. (2) A political ideology that advocates such a system.

comparative advantage   The ability of one country to produce a particular good or service more efficiently relative to other countries' efficiency in producing the same good or service.

comparative method   The means by which social scientists make comparisons across cases.

comparative politics   The study and comparison of domestic politics across countries.

concrete review   Judicial review that allows the constitutional court to rule on the basis of actual legal disputes brought before it.

conservatism   A political attitude that is skeptical of change and supports the current order.

Constituency   A geographical area that an elected official represents.

constitutional court   The highest judicial body in a political system that decides whether laws and policies violate the constitution.

co-optation   The process by which individuals are brought into a beneficial relationship with the state, making them dependent on the state for certain rewards.

corporatism   A method of co-optation whereby authoritarian systems create or sanction a limited number of organizations to represent the interests of the public and restrict those not set up or approved by the state.

country   Term used to refer to state, government, regime, and the people who live within that political system.

coup d'état   A move in which military forces take control of the government by force.

culture   Basic institutions that define a society.

democracy   A political system in which political power is exercised either directly or indirectly by the people.

devolution   A process in which political power is "sent down" to lower levels of state and government.

direct democracy   Democracy that allows the public to participate directly in government decision making.

economic liberalization   Changes consistent with liberalism that aim to limit the power of the state and increase the power of the market and private property in an economy.

electoral system   A set of rules that decide how votes are cast, counted, and translated into seats in a legislature.

empire   A single political authority that has under its sovereignty a large number of external regions or territories and different peoples.

equality   A shared material standard of individuals within a community, society, or country.

ethnic conflict   A conflict in which different ethnic groups struggle to achieve certain political or economic goals at each other's expense.

ethnicity (ethnic identity)   Specific attributes and societal institutions that make one group of people culturally different from others.

executive   The branch of government that carries out the laws and policies of a state.

export-oriented industrialization   A mercantilist strategy for economic growth in which a country seeks out technologies and develops industries focused specifically on the export market.

failed state   A state so weak that its political structures collapse, leading to anarchy and violence.

fascism   A political ideology that asserts the superiority and inferiority of different groups of people and stresses a low degree of both freedom and equality in order to achieve a powerful state.

federalism   A system in which significant state powers, such as taxation, lawmaking, and security, are devolved to regional or local bodies.

first past the post   An electoral system in which individual candidates compete in single-member districts; voters choose between candidates, and the candidate with the largest share of the vote wins the seat.

foreign direct investment   The purchase of assets in a country by a foreign firm.

freedom   The ability of an individual to act independently, without fear of restriction or punishment by the state or other individuals or groups in society.

fundamentalism   A view of religion as absolute and inerrant that should be legally enforced by making faith the sovereign authority.

Gini index   A statistical formula that measures the amount of inequality in a society; its scale ranges from 0 to 100, where 0 corresponds to perfect equality and 100 to perfect inequality.

glasnost   Literally, openness. The policy of political liberalization implemented in the Soviet Union in the late 1980s.

globalization   The process of expanding and intensifying linkages between states, societies, and economies.

government   The leadership or elite in charge of running the state.

gross domestic product (GDP)   The total market value of all goods and services produced by a country over a period of one year.

gross national product (GNP)   The total market value of all goods and services produced by the residents of a country, including income from abroad.

guerilla war   A conflict whereby nonstate combatants who largely abide by the rules of war target the state.

head of government   The executive role that deals with the everyday tasks of running the state, such as formulating and executing policy.

head of state   The executive role that symbolizes and represents the people both nationally and internationally.

human development index (HDI)   A statistical tool that attempts to evaluate the overall wealth, health, and knowledge of a country's people.

hyperinflation   Inflation of more than 50 percent a month for more than two months in a row.

ideational   Having to do with ideas.

illiberal regime   Rule by an elected leadership through procedures of questionable democratic legitimacy.

imperialism   A system in which a state extends its power to directly control territory, resources, and people beyond its borders.

import substitution   A mercantilist strategy for economic growth in which a country restricts imports in order to spur demand for locally produced goods.

indirect democracy   Democracy in which representatives of the public are responsible for government decision making.

inflation   An outstripping of supply by demand, resulting in an increase in the general price level of goods and services and the resulting loss of value in a country's currency.

informal economy   A segment of the economy that is not regulated or taxed by the state.

initiative   A national vote called by members of the public to address a specific proposal.

institution   An organization or activity that is self-perpetuating and valued for its own sake.

integration   A process by which states pool their sovereignty, surrendering some individual powers in order to gain shared political, economic, or societal benefits.

intergovernmental organization (IGO)   Group created by states to serve certain policy ends.

intergovernmental system   A system in which two or more countries cooperate on issues.

judicial review   The mechanism by which courts can review the actions of government and overturn those that violate the constitution.

laissez-faire   The principle that the economy should be "allowed to do" what it wishes; a liberal system of minimal state interference in the economy.

legislature   The branch of government charged with making laws.

legitimacy   A value whereby an institution is accepted by the public as right and proper, thus giving it authority and power.

less-developed country (LDC)   A country that lacks significant economic development or political institutionalization or both.

liberal democracy   A political system that promotes participation, competition, and liberty and emphasizes individual freedom and civil rights.

liberalism   (1) A political attitude that favors evolutionary transformation; (2) An ideology and political system that favors a limited state role in society and the economy, and places a high priority on individual political and economic freedom.

manichean   Referring to a view of the world that divides it into stark terms of good and evil.

market   The interaction between the forces of supply and demand that allocates resources.

marketization   The creation of the market forces of supply and demand in a country.

mercantilism   A political-economic system in which national economic power is paramount and the domestic economy is viewed as an instrument that exists primarily to serve the needs of the state.

microcredit   A system in which small loans are channeled to the poor through borrowing groups whose members jointly take responsibility for repayment.

military rule   Rule by one or more military officials, often brought to power through a coup d'état.

mixed electoral system   An electoral system that uses a combination of single-member districts and proportional representation.

modern   Characterized as secular, rational, materialistic, technological, and bureaucratic, and placing a greater emphasis on individual freedom than in the past.

modernization theory   A theory asserting that as societies developed, they would take on a set of common characteristics, including democracy and capitalism.

monopoly   A single producer that is able to dominate the market for a good or service without effective competition.

multimember district (MMD)   An electoral district with more than one seat.

multinational corporation (MNC)   Firm that produces, distributes, and markets its goods or services in more than one country.

nation   A group of people bound together by a common set of political aspirations, the most important of which is self-government.

national conflict   A conflict in which one or more groups within a country develop clear aspirations for political independence, clashing with others as a result.

national identity   A sense of belonging to a nation and a belief in its political aspirations.

nationalism   Pride in one's people and the belief that they have a unique political destiny.

nation-state   A state encompassing one dominant nation that it claims to embody and represent.

neocolonialism   An indirect form of imperialism in which powerful countries overly influence the economies of less-developed countries.

neocorporatism   A system of social democratic policy making in which a limited number of organizations representing business and labor work with the state to set economic policy.

newly industrializing country (NIC)   A historically less-developed country that has experienced significant economic growth and democratization.

nihilism   A belief that all institutions and values are essentially meaningless and that the only redeeming value is violence.

nomenklatura   Politically sensitive or influential jobs in the state, society, or economy that were staffed by people chosen or approved by the Communist Party.

nongovernmental organization (NGO)   A national or international group, independent of any state, that pursues policy objectives and fosters public participation.

nontariff barriers   Policies and regulations used to limit imports through methods other than taxation.

one-party rule   Rule by one political party, with other parties banned or excluded from power.

parastatal   Industry partially owned by the state.

party-state   A political system in which power flows directly from the ruling political party (usually a communist party) to the state, bypassing government structures.

patrimonialism   An arrangement whereby a ruler depends on a collection of supporters within the state who gain direct benefits in return for enforcing the ruler's will.

patriotism   Pride in one's state.

perestroika   Literally, restructuring. The policy of political and economic liberalization implemented in the Soviet Union in the late 1980s.

personal rule   Rule by a single leader, with no clear regime or rules constraining that leadership.

personality cult   Promotion of the image of an authoritarian leader not merely as a political figure but as someone who embodies the spirit of the nation and possesses endowments of wisdom and strength far beyond those of the average individual and is thus portrayed in a quasi-religious manner.

plebiscite   A nonbinding vote called by a government in which the voters express an opinion for or against a proposal.

Politburo   The top policy-making and executive body of a communist party.

political attitude   Description of one's views regarding the speed and methods with which political changes should take place in a given society.

political culture   The basic norms for political activity in a society.

political economy   The study of the interaction between states and markets.

political ideology   The basic values held by an individual about the fundamental goals of politics or the ideal balance of freedom and equality.

political-economic system   The relationship between political and economic institutions in a particular country and the policies and outcomes they create.

politics   The struggle in any group for power that will give one or more persons the ability to make decisions for the larger group.

political violence   Violence outside of state control that is politically motivated.

postindustrialism   The shift during the last half century from an economy based primarily on industry and manufacturing to one in which the majority of people are employed in the service sector, which produces the bulk of profits.

postmodern   Characterized by a set of values that center on "quality of life" considerations and give less attention to material gain.

presidential system   A political system in which the roles of head of state and head of government are combined in one executive offices.

parliamentary system   A political system in which the roles of head of state and head of government are assigned to separate executive offices.

privatization   The transfer of state-owned property to private ownership.

property   Goods or services that are owned by an individual or group, privately or publicly.

proportional representation (PR)   An electoral system in which political parties compete in multimember districts; voters choose between parties, and the seats in the district are awarded proportionally according to the results of the vote.

public goods   Goods, provided or secured by the state, available to society and which no private person or organization can own.

purchasing-power parity (PPP) A statistical tool that attempts to estimate the buying power of income across different countries by using prices in the United States as a benchmark.

qualitative method Study through an in-depth investigation of a limited number of cases.

quantitative method Study through statistical data from many cases.

quota A nontariff barrier that limits the quantity of a good that may be imported into a country.

radicalism A political attitude that favors dramatic, often revolutionary change.

rational-legal legitimacy Legitimacy based on a system of laws and procedures that are highly institutionalized.

reactionary Someone who seeks to restore the institutions of a real or imagined earlier order.

referendum A national vote called by a government to address a specific proposal, often a change to the constitution.

regime The fundamental rules and norms of politics, embodying long-term goals regarding individual freedom and collective equality, where power should reside, and the use of that power.

regulation A rule or order that sets the boundaries of a given procedure.

relative deprivation model Model that predicts revolution when public expectations outpace the rate of domestic change.

rent seeking A process in which political leaders essentially rent out parts of the state to their patrons, who as a result control public goods that would otherwise be distributed in a nonpolitical manner.

republicanism Indirect democracy that emphasizes the separation of powers within a state and the representation of the public through elected officials.

revolution Public seizure of the state in order to overturn the existing government and regime.

rule of law A system in which all individuals and groups, including those in government, are subject to the law, irrespective of their power or authority.

semipresidential system An executive system that divides power between two strong executives, a president and a prime minister.

separation of powers The clear division of power between different branches of government and the provision that specific branches may check the power of other branches.

service sector Work that does not involve creating tangible goods.

shock therapy A process of rapid marketization.

single-member district (SMD) An electoral district with one seat.

social democracy (socialism) (1) A political-economic system in which freedom and equality are balanced through the state's management of the economy and the provision of social expenditures. (2) A political ideology that advocates such a system.

social expenditures State provision of public benefits, such as education, health care, and transportation.

society Complex human organization, a collection of people bound by shared institutions that define how human relations should be conducted.

sovereignty The ability of a state to carry out actions or policies within a territory independently from external actors or internal rivals.

state (1) The organization that maintains a monopoly of force over a given territory. (2) A set of political institutions to generate and execute policy regarding freedom and equality.

statecraft The study of how to govern.

state-sponsored terrorism Terrorism supported directly by a state as an instrument of foreign policy.

strong state A state that is able to fulfill basic tasks, such as defending territory, making and enforcing rules, collecting taxes, and managing the economy.

structural adjustment program A policy of economic liberalization adopted in exchange for financial support from liberal international organizations; typically includes privatizing state-run firms, ending subsidies, reducing tariff barriers, shrinking the size of the state, and welcoming foreign investment.

suffrage The right to vote.

supranational system An intergovernmental system with its own sovereign powers over member states.

tariff A tax on imported goods.

terrorism The use of violence by nonstate actors against civilians in order to achieve a political goal.

theocracy A nondemocratic form of rule where religion is the foundation for the regime.

thermidor A period of conservatism and declining zeal or idealism following a revolution.

totalitarianism A nondemocratic regime that is highly centralized, possessing some form of strong ideology that seeks to transform and absorb fundamental aspects of state, society, and the economy, using a wide array of institutions.

traditional legitimacy Legitimacy that accepts aspects of politics because they have been institutionalized over a long period of time.

unicameral system A political system in which the legislature comprises one house.

unitary state A state in which most political power exists at the national level, with limited local authority.

weak state A state that has difficulty fulfilling basic tasks, such as defending territory, making and enforcing rules, collecting taxes, and managing the economy.

INDEX

Page numbers in *italics* refer to figures and tables.